FREEDOM
FIGHTERS

FREEDOM
FIGHTERS

by
ANNE WILLIAMS
and
VIVIAN HEAD

Futura

A *Futura* Book

First published by Futura in 2007

ISBN 13: 978-0-7088-0780-4

Produced by Omnipress, Eastbourne

Printed in the EU

Futura
An imprint of Little, Brown Book Group
Brettenham House
Lancaster Place
London WC2E 7EN

Photo credits: Getty Images

The views expressed in this publication are those of the
author. The information and the interpretation of that
information are presented in good faith. Readers are
advised that where ethical issues are involved, and often
highly controversial ethical issues at that, they have a
personal responsibility for making their own assessments
and their own ethical judgements.

CONTENTS

PART THREE:
EARLY MODERN FREEDOM FIGHTERS

PART FOUR:
18TH AND 19TH CENTURY
FREEDOM FIGHTERS

PART FIVE:
MODERN FREEDOM FIGHTERS

INTRODUCTION

One man's terrorist is another man's freedom fighter

The subject of freedom fighters will always be a controversial one, as the saying above points out. Freedom fighters are generally the leaders of revolutions, which can be social, political – or both. However, there is a fine line between what one person considers a freedom fighter and the other a terrorist.

The term 'freedom fighter' is commonly understood to imply the 'good guy' or 'hero', while the word 'terrorist' conjures up the image of the 'bad guy' or 'villain'. Whichever label we put on these revolutionaries they are still both 'fighting' for their cause in what they feel is the best possible way. The best way to differentiate between the freedom fighter and the terrorist is that the terrorist uses terror tactics, killing indiscriminately, to gain the maximum impact. The freedom fighter, on the other hand, is a person who fights for liberty and freedom from oppression. Of course, that is not to say that the freedom fighter will never use terror tactics if they feel that is the best way to gain liberty for his or her people and country.

One definition of a freedom fighter given by an English dictionary is 'a person who takes part in an armed rebellion against the constituted authority (especially in the hope of improving conditions)'. This book aims to give details of people who fought for their beliefs and country and to provide an understanding of the struggles of people such as Nelson Mandela, Martin Luther King, Gandhi, Che Guevara and many many others.

As the Commander-in-Chief of the Continental Army, the achievements of George Washington must give him a place in history as one of the famous freedom fighters. He fought hard and long to free American colonists from British oppression and exploitation. With the aid of his ill-trained troops, Washington embarked upon a war that was to last six, tough years. It was his faith in the cause and his devotion to the ideals it typified that made him the symbol of the United States – the spirit of the Revolution.

Freedom prospers when religion is vibrant and the rule of law under God is acknowledged.

The above is a quote that many people would agree with, and one man who would certainly have the same opinion is Osama bin Laden. However, these are not the words of Osama bin Laden. They were spoken by Ronald Reagan, president of the United States of America from 1981–1989. Reagan was a man who felt strongly that anyone opposing the Soviets were 'freedom fighters'. It is widely acknowledged that he authorized the CIA to covertly support the Mujahideen (including bin Laden) in the jihad against the 'unholy empire', in other words the U.S.S.R. It is well known that the Contras received financial and military support clandestinely from the United States when Ronald Reagan's administration was in charge. It was determined to overthrow the Sandinista National Liberation Front in Nicaragua because of its Marxist views.

Mohandas Gandhi (1869–1948) was a major political and spiritual leader of India and the Indian independence movement. He believed strongly in the *ahimsa* (total nonviolence), which eventually led to India's independence. He said:

Nonviolence is the law of the human race and is infinitely greater than and superior to brute force.

Gandhi was also the inspiration for civil rights and freedom across much of the world. Martin Luther King, Jr was another well-known Civil Rights leader who was famous for practising Gandhi's views on nonviolence. He believed that the black community should unite with the white community and live in harmony, a difficult dream to fulfil when African Americans were being persecuted on a daily basis.

Many people have fought for freedom from slavery and these freedom fighters have struck blow after blow against the institution, rallying for Black unity, freedom, rights and power. John Brown fought hard for his beliefs, and yet he remains one of history's most controversial and perhaps misunderstood figures. In the 1850s he instigated a righteous crusade against slavery that was based on his religious beliefs, but it was all carried out with appalling violence. In the end Brown was hanged as a terrorist, an execution that started a chain of events culminating in the Civil War. In contrast, the epic poem written by Stephen Vincent portrays a far more heroic figure, as the first line shows:

John Brown's body lies a-mouldering in the grave, but his soul goes marching on. Glory, glory, halleluiah.

Nelson Mandela is another true freedom fighter. He fought hard and long in his struggle against apartheid. For his beliefs, Mandela was imprisoned for 27 years, and yet in less than five years after his release he was awarded the Nobel Peace Prize. He will be long remembered for his self-sacrifice in his effort to free South Africa from the evils of apartheid.

These are just a few examples of infamous freedom fighters who fought hard for their cause, but somewhere along the way were branded terrorists.

PART ONE

ANCIENT FREEDOM FIGHTERS

MOSES

The story of Moses and Exodus is possibly one of the most important events in the history of the Jews and has become an important symbol for freedom fighters throughout the world. He was a great prophet, leader, teacher and freedom fighter in the true sense of the word. The Bible clearly sees Moses as the founder of the Jewish nation and the leader who freed them from slavery in Egypt. Moses also shielded the Jews from the wrath of God and mediated with God on their behalf.

Moses was probably born in the late 14th century BC to the slaves Amram and his wife, Jochebed. He was born in the Nile Delta in Egypt where, even under heartless slavery, the Israelites had grown to a great multitude. His birth was during a time of great unrest, when the current Egyptian pharaoh had ordered the drowning of all male children born to the Hebrew slaves. The Egyptians were nervous due to the rapid increase in the Jewish population and, afraid that they may take over the country, the pharaoh announced:

There are too many of them, what if they rise up against us.

He immediately ordered that all Hebrew baby boys be killed at birth as he was frightened that they would grow up hating the Egyptians and try to take over the country.

At first Moses' parents tried to keep his birth a secret, but aware that their baby was in danger, they came up with a plan that they hoped would save his life. Making a basket watertight, they placed the baby Moses inside, and left it to float on the side of the River Nile. Moses' sister, Miriam, stood guard to make sure no harm came to her brother. One day the pharaoh's daughter came down to the river to bathe, and she discovered the baby floating in the basket. Taking advantage of the situation, Miriam approached her and said if she would like to take the baby home she knew a lady who could act as a nursemaid. Of course she was referring to her own mother, Jochebed. The pharaoh's daughter decided not only to take the baby home, but also to take the woman as a nursemaid for her adopted son, who she named Moses. The name is of Hebrew origin, and its meaning is 'saviour'. It is also similar in sound to a word meaning 'drawn out of the water'. The child Moses was, therefore, raised as an Egyptian prince in the house of the pharaoh.

Little is known of Moses' childhood, but his mother made sure that he never forgot his Hebrew routes. The first record of unrest in the Egyptian household was when Moses, now in his fortieth year, lost his temper with an Egyptian who had beaten a Hebrew slave to death. Moses had great compassion for his people and was so outraged by the attack that he turned and killed the Egyptian. This is when Moses shows his first deep commitment to fighting injustice. However, his actions were condemned not only by the pharaoh but also by his fellow Hebrews and led to him being forced to flee from Egypt.

Moses ended up in the desert wilderness of Midian on the Sinai peninsular, and it was his time here that provided him with the training that he would later need while leading the Israelites in the desert. Moses lived with the priest of Midian, Hobab (Jethro) and his daughter Tzipporah, who Moses later married. Moses became a shepherd tending his father-in-law's flock of sheep and Zipporah bore him a son, Gershom. Moses showed a lot of compassion towards his flock and it is thought that he was chosen to lead the Israelites because he had showed himself to be such a worthy shepherd.

One day while Moses was tending his sheep on Mount Horeb, he saw a burning bush, but he was puzzled when he was unable to put out the flames. As he started to turn away from the bush, Moses heard a voice claiming to be that of God. He told Moses that he must return to Egypt and free the Hebrews from slavery.

I have indeed seen the misery of my people in Egypt. I have heard them crying out because of their slave drivers, and I am concerned about their suffering. So I have come down to rescue them from the hand of the Egyptians and to bring them up out of that land into a good and spacious land, a land flowing with milk and honey . . . And now the cry of the Israelites

*has reached me, and I have seen the way the
Egyptians are oppressing them. So now, go. I am
sending you to Pharaoh to bring my people the
Israelites out of Egypt.*

(Exodus 3:1-10)

Moses knew that he had to obey the voice of God,
but due to a speech impediment (a stutter) he felt
unworthy of delivering God's message. God told him
to go to his older brother Aaron and ask him to do the
talking on his behalf. Moses returned immediately to
Egypt where, on arrival, he was welcomed by Aaron,
who agreed to act as his spokesman. Their meeting
with the pharoah was not so successful and he refused
to release the Hebrew slaves.

Moses asked for God's help, and together they used
strong measures to convince the pharaoh to change
his mind. Dreadful events took place in Egypt as it was
ravaged by ten plagues:

1. The waters of the Nile turned to blood
2. Egypt had a plague of frogs
3. Egypt had a plague of mosquitoes
4. Egypt had a plague of flies
5. All the sheep and cattle belonging to the Egyptians
   died from an illness
6. The Egyptians suffered from a plague of boils
7. Egypt experienced the worst hailstorm in its
   history
8. Egypt suffered a plague of locusts, which destroyed
   all their crops

9. Egypt was plunged into darkness for three days
10. God struck down all the first-born children and
    domestic animals in Egypt

Before each of the plagues Moses warned the pharaoh of what was about to happen, but each time he failed to listen to the warnings. However, the last plague, which was the worst of them all, got the pharaoh's attention, as the eldest son in every Egyptian family, including the pharaoh's, were killed. (God warned Moses to make a mark on every door belonging to a Hebrew house, so that all the Hebrew children would be safe.) The pharaoh was distraught at losing his eldest son and ordered that all the Hebrew slaves be set free.

THE EXODUS

The Hebrews knew they had to leave quickly before the pharaoh changed his mind, and they hurriedly gathered together as much food as they could to last during the long journey. The men, women and children formed a long procession as it moved forward towards the Egyptian frontier. As they feared, the pharaoh had indeed changed his mind about freeing the slaves and sent his army to bring them back. The army caught up with the Hebrews on the banks of the Red Sea, and seeing no way out the slaves feared for their lives. Knowing they were trapped, Moses once more turned to God to ask for his advice, and he instructed Moses to lift up his rod. As he raised his arm the waters of the Red Sea parted, leaving before them a dry path. Immediately the Hebrews started running along the path surrounded either side by walls of turbulent water. When the last of the Hebrews was safely on the other side, Moses once again lifted his rod and the water of the sea closed in, trapping the pharaoh's army and drowning them.

The Hebrews were safe from the Egyptian army, but they still had the arduous task of crossing the desert and their supplies were running low. The journey was long and they were heading for Canaan, which God had promised them would be their new land of plenty. Six weeks after leaving Egypt, the Hebrews became restless as they started to feel the effect of the journey and the lack of food, and they started to blame Moses for taking them away from Egypt. They told him they would rather be well-fed slaves than free men who died from starvation. Moses told them that God would not allow them to starve, and when he prayed once more for guidance, God told Moses, 'I will give the people food'.

The next morning the sands of the desert were covered with a white food that tasted like honey. Moses named the food manna, and the Hebrews ate greedily. God also sent a flock of quails, which the Hebrews killed and ate. Strengthened in body and in spirit the Hebrews continued their journey.

A few days later they came to a place with no water and again the Hebrews abused Moses for putting them at risk of dying from thirst. God told Moses to hit a rock with his rod. As he did so water gushed out from a crack in the rock and the multitude had plenty to drink.

Moses felt that too much of his time was spent in settling the disputes that constantly arose, and so with the help of his father-in-law, Hobab, he chose a few good men to lead the Hebrews. For three months they travelled across the desert, and eventually Moses and the freed slaves arrived at the foot of Mount Sinai in the Sinai peninsula. God summoned Moses to meet him on the summit, and as he climbed thunder struck and lightning lit up the sky. He went alone to meet God and stayed on the mountain top for 40 days. During those 40 days God showed Moses the Ten Commandments which were carved on tablets of stone. These Commandments provided a set of moral and religious rules by which the Hebrews should live once they arrived at Canaan. God also gave Moses the exact measurements for the Arc of the Covenant, which was a portable, boxlike shrine that would eventually contain the tablets of stone.

And the glory of the Lord abode upon Mount Sinai, and the cloud covered it six days; and the seventh day God called unto Moses out of the midst of the cloud. And the appearance of the glory of the Lord was like devouring fire on the top of the mount in the eyes of the children of Israel. And Moses entered into the midst of the cloud, and went up into the mount; and Moses was in the mount forty days and forty nights. Exodus 24: 16-18

THE TEN COMMANDMENTS

The Ten Commandments appear in the Old Testament of the Christian Bible and are also present in the Jewish scriptures. Below is a list of the laws in modern language:

1. You shall have no other Gods but me.
2. You shall not make yourself any idol, nor bow down to it or worship it.
3. You shall not misuse the name of the Lord your God.
4. You shall remember the Sabbath day and keep it holy.
5. Respect your father and your mother.
6. You must not kill.
7. You must not commit adultery.
8. You must not steal.
9. You must not give false evidence against your neighbour.
10. You must not be envious of your neighbour's goods. You shall not be envious of his house or wife, nor anything that belongs to your neighbour.

While the Hebrews were waiting for Moses at the foot of the mountain, they were restless and became angry because they thought their leader had deserted them. They abandoned their faith and made a new god for themselves, a golden calf. When Moses returned and found his people dancing and worshipping the golden calf he was furious, but acting like a true parent to his adopted children Moses scorned them. He never turned against them, even when God threatened to blot out all the Jews and build Moses a new nation. Moses replied to God, 'Then blot me out too', and he broke the stone tablets and destroyed the image of the calf. God, seeing Moses' loyalty, forgave his people for their loss of faith and told Moses to cut a second set of stone tablets. Moses once again climbed the mountain carrying the tablets, and God gave him the Ten Commandments for a second time.

This time when Moses returned to his people, they listened as he told them what God had told him. God had made a covenant with the Hebrews at Sinai in which he agreed to look after them forever if they lived by the law of the Ten Commandments.

THE DEATH OF MOSES

Moses had led his people close to Canaan, the Promised Land, and he was keen to see this land of supposed milk and honey before he died. Moses was now an old man – in fact he was 120 years old, and for most of his life he had been the faithful leader of the Children of Israel. Not only had he freed them from slavery, but he had also prepared them for the Ten Commandments at Mount Sinai. But this was probably one of the saddest moments in the life of Moses when God denied him the pleasure of entering Canaan, although the real reason for this has never been documented. Moses had performed many miracles with God's help and possibly one of his actions had caused displeasure.

God asked Moses to climb Mount Nebo where, from the top, he could see the Promised Land. Moses looked on in wonder at the land that had been promised to the Hebrews, and he felt proud that he had led them there. It was a land rich with hills and valleys, springs and streams, wheat, vines and olives, a land of plenty.

When Moses had seen all he wanted, God spoke to him, 'Behold the time has come for you to die'. Moses died on the mountain with God looking over him and was buried in a secret grave. The freed slaves mourned for their leader for 30 days and wondered who would be their new leader. Joshua, who had helped Moses for many years, took over his role and eventually led them to their new land.

Moses was truly a freedom fighter who served his people and God right up until the end. He was undoubtedly a mighty leader, leading approximately two-and-a-half million people out of Egypt. He stood by them when they turned against God, and through his strength and courage the Israelites came to start a new life in the Land of Plenty.

SPARTACUS

In the first century BC, Roman economy was based on either agriculture or conflict, and for centuries citizens were both peasants and soldiers. However, this all started to change during the Second Punic war (218–202 BC) when Romans started to leave their shores and fight their battles overseas in places such as Greece and Macedonia. Many of these wars lasted for years and by the time the Roman soldiers returned to their land, they found their farms had gone into bankruptcy. Italian cities were growing rapidly and the farmers felt the best way out of their plight was to sell their farms and move out of the country. Gradually, what were once small farms became large plantations, and men who could not be used for military service were employed as slaves.

The slaves had many children and soon their numbers were reaching enormous proportions, unable to support themselves in any other way, worn down as they were by poverty. At the same time, the new landowners were becoming extremely rich, using either prisoners of war or simply buying men from slave traders as a cheap form of employment. Slaves were frequently punished by their powerful owners and were known to be routinely crucified if they were rebellious in any way.

GLADIATORS

The stronger of the slaves were often trained as gladiators to fight in the arena. Roman citizens loved the bloody spectacle of gladiatorial combat which, like many sporting events of that time, originated as a religious event. Slaves trained in gladiator schools fought with weapons and armour of their choice and could earn their freedom if they survived up to five years of combat. Even though a gladiator was only required to fight maybe two to three times a year, it was rare that they survived past the first couple of years because they were required to fight to the death. While successful gladiators were held in high esteem, in terms of social status they were little better than convicts and, in fact, several well-known gladiators were convicted criminals.

Spartacus was a gladiator who gained a high reputation through his skill as a fighter. He was born in Thrace (now Bulgaria) and, it is thought, went on to serve as an auxiliary in the Roman army. He deserted from the army but was captured and sold into slavery. He was a strong, bold slave and was soon chosen to train as a gladiator in the school of Batiatus in Capua. It was this gladiatorial school in Capua that became the scene of one of the most influential slave revolts in history.

SLAVE REBELLION

Although the reasons are unclear, it is certain that in 73 BC Spartacus, a Gallic slave Crixus and a Germanic slave Oenomaus led a revolt of the entire school of gladiators at Capua. In total 74 gladiators seized knives and tools from the kitchen and managed to break free. They killed several guards and stole weapons and armour from the Batiatus school store.

Their reputation spread quickly as they rampaged the country seizing whatever they could by looting. Farm labourers heard of the revolt and joined them from all over the region and, within a short space of time, Spartacus's army of slaves fled to the slopes of Mount Vesuvius, where they set up camp.

Their numbers quickly swelled and they overran the region, pillaging and looting and sharing the spoils among the men, despite the fact that Spartacus tried desperately to restrain them.

The Romans were slow to respond to the army led by Spartacus, because they thought they were dealing with nothing more than an unruly mob that could be easily overcome by force. Little did they realize that Spartacus had done a good job in training his men and they now numbered in their thousands.

The Roman Senate sent a praetor, Claudius Glaber, with an army of 3,000 ill-trained soldiers to quell the rebels. When they arrived at Mount Vesuvius, Claudius quickly realized that there was only one way up, and that was by a narrow path. The remainder of the mountain was both steep and slippery and did not afford them access to the rebel's camp. Despite his small and untrained army, Claudius came close to success. He managed to isolate the gladiators on a hilltop, which was covered with vines, and it looked as if they had run out of luck.

Spartacus and his men, however, were unhindered by the difficult conditions, and used to living on a mountain, they overcame the encroaching army by sliding down ropes made by the plentiful amount of vines growing there. They descended the mountain by night and managed to get behind the enemy lines. Instead of the Romans putting an end to the slave revolt, the slaves not only surprised the Roman army, causing them to flee in panic, but they also took all of their weapons.

Hearing of their success, more and more slaves joined the group of rebels, and soon Spartacus's army numbered more than 70,000 men. Spartacus, wishing to avoid further confrontation with the Romans, decided to lead his men across the Alps and out of Italy. Crixus, however, had other ideas, and encouraged by their victory, he wanted to stay and continue raiding the countryside. Consequently, the band of men broke up into two separate groups.

Spartacus spent the winter in Thurii, making weapons and armour to prepare for the next Roman army, which he knew would soon follow them. The Senate dispatched two Consular armies, consisting of four separate legions, against the slaves. One was led by Publicola and the other Clodianus. Crixus, now the leader of 3,000 men, was defeated and killed at Mount

Garganus and lost two-thirds of the slaves who had refused to travel with Spartacus. Spartacus and his men were intercepted by one of the consuls and prevented from escaping by the other, but his men were now so well armed and trained, they turned on the two consular armies and defeated them both separately.

In honour of his friend Crixus, the Gaulish leader, Spartacus held funeral games, which included gladiatorial type combat between the captured Roman soldiers.

With the Alps now clear for the rebels to cross, Spartacus started gathering his troups. However, once again the Gauls and the Germans refused to follow his lead and so Spartacus changed his plans and returned to southern Italy.

MARCUS LICINIUS CRASSUS

In 73 BC the slave revolt was at its height and was becoming somewhat of an embarrassment for the Roman Senate. The war had been going on now for approximately three years and in recent months no new generals had come forward to take on Spartacus and his army. That is until Marcus Licinius Crassus, famous for his family and wealth, undertook to assume the command against Spartacus. This was when things started to turn in favour of the Romans. Crassus placed himself and his six legions on the borders of Picenum, expecting that Spartacus would be heading that way. He sent his lieutenant, Mummius, with two of the legions to spy on Spartacus and report back on his movements, but on no account were they to take part in any armed conflict. However, Mummius ignored the general's orders and at the first opportunity he started firing at the slave army, but the Roman legions were easily overcome and a great many were killed.

Mummius was punished severely for not obeying orders and Crassus used the old Roman punishment of decimation. This was not a practice in common use as it was harsh, but Crassus wanted to make his point. By lot, he chose one in ten men for capital punishment and the surviving nine men were ordered to club the man to death.

Having reassembled and rearmed his men, Crassus led his men against a detached segment of Spartacus's army. They succeeded in wiping out around 10,000 of the rebel slaves and then moved on in pursuit of Spartacus, who by this time had retreated through Lucania towards the sea. He had hoped to retreat to Sicily, with the aid of some Cilician pirates. However, after the band of pirates had set up a deal with Spartacus, they deceived him and simply sailed away, leaving him and his men stranded.

Spartacus left the coast and set up his men in the peninsula of Rhegium. Crassus and his large army caught up with them and strategically built an exceptionally strong and high wall across the neck of the peninsula, trapping Spartacus and his men, who waited until their supplies started to run low. Taking advantage of a snowy, stormy night, Spartacus and his entourage managed to fill up part of the ditch with earth and tree branches. Spartacus managed to get around one-third of his army over the wall and headed for the port of Brandsium. The remainder of his men, around 12,000, were killed while trying to break free.

ROMAN VICTORY

Crassus, in the meantime, had written to the Senate to release Lucullus in Thrace and Pompey in Spain to help in the fight against Spartacus. However, Crassus was keen to win the victory for himself and not have to share it with his successful rival, so consequently he put on the pressure to defeat Spartacus. The Romans were closing in on Spartacus from all sides. Marcus Lucullus, fresh from a victory over Mithridates, landed at Brundisium, and Spartacus had no choice but to face his pursuers. In the ensuing battle between the slave army and the Romans, the rebels were struck down in huge numbers. This time the Romans were the dominant force, and by the end of the battle Spartacus himself was wounded by a spear thrust deep into his thigh. He continued to fight bravely on one knee, holding his shield up in defence, and fought off his attackers for as long as he was able. There is no record of how many slaves were actually killed in the final battle, nor indeed was the body of Spartacus ever identified.

Crassus not satisfied with the victory alone, scoured the countryside for survivors and prepared a grotesque punishment. Up to 6,000 slaves were lined up along the Appian Way, which led from Rome to Capua, where they were crucified and their bodies left to rot as a cruel reminder to any other slaves who considered starting a rebellion.

SPARTACUS REMEMBERED

Spartacus's determination to free the slaves and his drive to break the bonds of his oppressors is an intriguing story, and his memory lives on today. He should be admired for his courage and tenacity and also for his ability as a great Thracian warrior. Spartacus was a freedom fighter who was born into a different age, a time when honour and strength were greatly respected. The epic film Spartacus, made in 1960 with Kirk Douglas playing the lead role, has made sure that his name will never be forgotten.

JESUS

Over the years history has taught us that the price of human freedom is costly. The story of Lucifer, whose name became synonymous with evil, is a fine example. He is generally considered to have been a prominent archangel in heaven who rebelled against God and his doctrines. Through his sin of pride, Lucifer supposedly plunged his followers, both in heaven and on earth, into a lifetime of bondage.

God sent His Son, Jesus, to earth to bring freedom to mankind, and it can be said that the incarnate Son of God is the advocate of all freedom fighters. Jesus quite willingly and unselfishly took on the task of attempting to take away the sin of the world. Whether you believe that Jesus was in fact a man or a mere myth is, of course, personal choice, but his story is one that will never be forgotten.

HIS MISSION

Jesus was born into a poor family, who were strict Jews and observers of the Jewish law. Although he had humble beginnings, Jesus was raised at a time when Rome governed Palestine, which caused revolutionary passion. Jesus himself later became caught up in this fervour, due to his friend and disciple, John the Baptist. John was known to have strong political views aside from his religious beliefs, and he was leading a political movement when he became acquainted with Jesus.

At the time when Mary was pregnant with Jesus, Roman government, under Caesar Augustus, had declared a tax on all the peasants, which forced Mary and her husband Joseph to travel to Bethlehem. It is also a possibility that Joseph felt it would be better to take Mary away from Nazareth due to the shame of having conceived out of wedlock. It was in Bethlehem that Mary gave birth to Jesus in a lowly stable, a far from fitting place for one who would eventually become the people's Saviour.

The Herod family was the ruling dynasty in Israel at the time of Jesus' birth, and Herod the Great, who was born about 75 BC, was angered when he heard the news that a new leader had been born. Herod was certainly no stranger to political ruthlessness, and with the news of the birth of the 'King of the Jews', his natural reaction was to seek out and kill his potential rival. However, many innocent children were killed in the effort, as he ordered that all male children in Bethlehem who were two years old or under were to be slain. Joseph was forewarned by an angel that Herod was looking for their child and that they should to flee to Egypt.

Little is recorded of the early years of the life of Jesus, with the exception of an incident when he was just 12 years old. Jesus visited Jerusalem with his parents during the feast of the Passover, but at some stage Mary and Joseph lost sight of him and started to frantically search the streets. They eventually found him in the temple sitting in the midst of learned teachers, with whom, to their great astonishment, he was holding a serious conversation. The learned men were dumbfounded by his wisdom, and this was probably the first indication of the great prophet Jesus was to become.

Jesus was probably about 30 years old when he met John the Baptist, who had already started a religious movement to prepare for the coming of the Messiah. Jesus asked John the Baptist to baptize him in the Jordan river near Bethany so that he could begin his ministry.

Following his baptism, and before Jesus could start his ministry, there had to be one ultimate test. He was lead by the Holy Spirit into the wilderness, an unoccupied part of Palestine, to be tempted by the devil. His public ministry would be full of demands, temptations and possible misdirections, so God had to know for certain that Jesus would not fail in his task. He needed to understand the ways in which a human being could easily be distracted, particularly when evil masquerades in the form of something that seems of greater benefit. The Spirit of God tested Jesus to see if his character was strong enough to become a leader of men.

Jesus successfully avoided the temptations put in front of him and began his mission by making tours of the surrounding towns and villages. He performed various miracles to prove who he was, deeds described as raising the dead, casting out devils, healing the sick, calming the storms by command and many other awe-inspiring actions.

To aid him in his ministry, Jesus chose a selected group of 12 disciples, or followers who were called apostles. They were Simon (also known as Peter), James, John, Philip, Bartholomew, Thomas, Matthew, James, Thaddaeus, Simon, Judas Iscariot and Matthias (who was chosen to bring the number back up to 12 after Judas lost faith).

Some were already disciples of John the Baptist, but there does appear to have been quite a mixture of religious beliefs among the 12 apostles. However, they were acquainted with the Scripture and knew exactly what was expected of them. The Apostles were God-fearing people who had shown integrity and mercy towards others. Above all they were diligent, honest and pious people, and totally dedicated to the their leader. Although they were not men of high education, they were certainly not illiterate. Most of them spoke Aramaic and Greek, and they had all been educated in the knowledge of God.

Jesus' mission is thought to have lasted about three years, in which time his chosen disciples received special teaching and shared their leader's deepest religious experiences. However, Jesus was soon to realize that his teachings were arousing opposition, and worse still he knew that one of his own disciples was turning against him. Not everyone shared his beliefs, and knowing that he was about to face great danger, Jesus prepared for the end of his mission. The

Romans still considered Jesus to be a threat to their authority and plotted to have him removed from the streets.

THE LAST SUPPER

Jesus gathered all 12 of his apostles together for one final meal, which became known as 'The Last Supper'. He explained to them that it was necessary for him to die to form a strong covenant between man and God, and that it would be up to the 12 apostles to carry on his teachings. He then took bread and wine, blessed it and passed it around to his disciples, saying, 'This is my body . . . this is my blood'. This tradition is still carried out today when Christians receive Holy Communion.

Following the meal, Jesus led his disciples to the Mount of Olives, which was a hill on the east side of Jerusalem. He knelt down in prayer with his disciples but was interrupted when a group of chief priests and captains from the temple, led by Judas Iscariot, approached him. Judas went up to Jesus and gave him a kiss of betrayal, after which Jesus was bound and taken back to the house of the high priest. He was ridiculed by the officers of the temple, who spat in his face, punched him and left him blindfolded in the dark. He was given the death sentence, but the Jewish leaders could not carry this out until they received the blessing of the Roman governor, Pontius Pilate.

The next morning Jesus was brought before Pilate, saying that they had found the man who had been corrupting the Jewish nation. Pilate was more leniant than the persecutors, and said that he felt Jesus did not deserve punishment by death and ordered him to be beaten. But the officers cried out in defence, 'Get rid of this man. Crucify him, crucify him'. Pilate, not wishing to displease his people had Jesus brutally whipped and then turned him over to the Roman soldiers to be crucified. This was their normal way of dealing with dissent.

The soldiers continued to mock Jesus and made him wear a crown made out of woven thorns. They beat him with their fists and then made him walk through the streets carrying a heaven wooden cross on his back. They led him to a place called Calvary, and erected the cross between two criminals who were being executed. Jesus was nailed to the cross and left to die as a deterrent to any would-be followers who might wish to carry on with what they considered to be Jesus' rebellion. Jesus died about three hours later and his body was taken down by two of his loyal followers, Joseph and Nicodemus. His body was laid in a tomb and as ordered by the Jewish leaders, was sealed and guarded by Roman soldiers.

THE RESURRECTION

The Bible states that on the third day after Jesus' burial an angel of the Lord rolled back the stone guarding the tomb. The Roman soldiers ran in fright, but when Jesus' followers found the tomb empty, they were amazed and confused. There will always be suspicions regarding the Resurrection of Jesus Christ but for Christians this is a paramount part of his ministry. They will tell you that Jesus foretold his own death and resurrection, which happened exactly as he had predicted. Secondly, the resurrection is the only plausible explanation for his empty grave as it was closely guarded by Roman soldiers and sealed with an enormous boulder. There are many theories, but the favourite is that he rose from the dead bodily, showing himself to many of his followers to prove that he was still alive and that they should spread the word. He instructed his disciples to continue with his work and after 40 days Jesus was taken up to heaven, as they watched on in awe.

GREATEST FREEDOM FIGHTER?

Take a visit to any part of the world and talk to someone about religion, and you will soon find out that everyone, whatever their belief, has heard of Jesus Christ. Jesus is without doubt one of the most out-standing personalities of all time, who was a great leader, a great teacher and who sacrificed his life for the sake of others. The influence that Jesus has had on the lives of ordinary people has never been surpassed. Many men and women have dedicated their lives to spreading the Christian message and they themselves have risked torment, torture and even death. So Jesus could go down in history as the greatest freedom fighter, forsaking everything so that the human race could be free.

CARATACUS

Caratacus (also spelt Caractacus) was the king of the Catuvellauni and a freedom fighter against the Romans. Together with his brother, Togodomnus, they led the first British resistance against the Roman invasion, which was commanded by Aulus Plautius.

THE CATUVELLAUNI

The Catuvellauni tribe occupied the central part of England, which comprised London, Hertfordshire, Bedfordshire, Buckinghamshire, Cambridgeshire, Oxfordshire, parts of Essex and Northamptonshire. It is strange that nowhere in the writings of Julius Caesar is there a mention of the Catuvellauni, and yet they were definitely the most outstanding tribe in Britain at the time when Claudius invaded in AD 43.

The tribe were renowned for their well organized structure and effective fighting strategy, which was due to the strength of their leaders. The Catuvellauni were an inland tribe that fought to expand their territory to take advantage of the new found wealth that came from trading with Europe. They also wanted to dominate any neighbouring tribes that were a threat to their superiority, and finally they wanted to gain access to the nearby coastal regions of Britain, giving them better defence of their already expanding territory.

ANTI-ROMAN CAMPAIGN

Caratacus, Adminius and Togodumnus were thought to be sons of the British king, Cunobelinus. By AD 37, the old chieftain handed over his leadership to his three sons. The three brothers became leaders of an anti-Roman campaign, which lasted for almost nine years. Their armies were a force to be reckoned with and they defeated anyone who threatened their territories in the south-east of England. They managed to vanquish the Trinovantes, an opposing tribe, from their old tribal town of Camulodunum (Colchester), making it the new Catuvellauni capital. From this capital they extended their empire into Kent. There were only two tribes who had not been affected by the Catuvellauni tribe, the Regni – who had strong hill forts in the South Downs, and the Iceni in Norfolk and Suffolk.

Adminius, in complete contrast to his two brothers, was in full support of Rome. Caratacus and Togodumnus talked their father into exiling their brother and to drive him out of his base in Verulamium. Adminius immediately fled to Rome to ask Gaius Calligula for help in reasserting his position in Britain. This resulted in a completely abortive mission by Calligula, who took his army to the coast of France but failed to even make it across the Channel.

The news got back to the two brothers, which only fueled their hatred for Rome, and another period of tribal warfare broke out.

Cunobelinus died in AD 40, at which time Caratacus and Togodomnus assumed complete control over the Catuvellauni lands. Feeling secure in the strength of their armies, the brothers moved northwards up the Thames valley into the territory of the Dobunni, a warring tribe of the Severn valley and the Cotswolds. The Dobunni had a close association with the Atrebates who, because of their location in Britain, were one of the more successful tribes. For many years before the Romans arrived, the Atrebates had been trading with European tribes. The king of the Atrebates, Verica was distinctly pro-Roman, so the two brothers thought that he was a prime target. Trusting that Rome would not bother to come to his defence, Caratacus and Togodumnus attacked the Atrebate tribe, confiscated their land and sent their king Verica on his way to Rome.

Little did they realize that this action would force the Romans into intervening. Verica appealed to the emperor Claudius for assistance, which led to his invasion of Britain in AD 43. The command against the British was led by Aulus Plautius, and in the early battles at Medway and Thames, Caratacus and Togodomnus fought side by side. The Romans proved to be the dominant force and the British tribal casualties were high. Togodumnus was killed at the Battle of Medway. Plautius gained an advantage over the British when he ordered his men to stop on high ground opposite the main British force on the banks of the river. Plautius used a strategic plan to distract the attention of the Britons, while a small number of highly trained 'Batavians' swam across the river at the widest point. The Batavians were allies of the Romans and the bravest and most feared of all the German tribes. They were an elite force trained to such a high degree of fitness that they were able to swim in full armour. Once they reached the other side, they scattered the British horses which were used to drive their chariots. The British, who were completely taken by surprise, were hopelessly unorganized for battle, and the Romans soon made easy work of the tribal army.

THE FINAL DEFEAT

Caratacus met his final defeat at the hands of the Roman governor, Ostorious Scapula, in AD 51. Although there is little historical evidence, it is quite certain that the last battle fought by Caratacus was in the area we know today as Shropshire.

Caratacus had fought and won many battles for the British and was considered as a high-ranking general. He was prepared for battle against the Romans and gathered together the various tribal armies ready for action. He chose a hill fort that would not only allow them easy access to the Romans when they approached, but also offer them a place to retreat if things went badly. On the less steep parts of the hill Caratacus ordered his men to build ramparts out of stones and then got the British warriors to place themselves in front of the defences. The river, which was in front of them, also afforded them a certain amount of protection.

The tribal leaders encouraged their men, while Caratacus told his men that this battle would be the beginning of their freedom from slavery. He told them how his ancestors had fought back the forces of Julius Caesar and how, through their bravery, the British had been freed from the threat of being ruled by the Romans. His warriors cheered as he made his speech, and they all vowed allegiance to their leader.

When Scapula arrived with his troops they faced a daunting sight. Not only did they have to cross the river but they also had to break down the ramparts built by the British tribesmen. They were shocked by the numbers that covered the hillside, but Scapula's men told him that they were ready for battle. The Romans carefully surveyed the area and tried to work out the best way to attack the British. The Romans were ripe for battle and crossed the river with ease. When they reached the ramparts the British warriors threw their missiles, and at that stage in the battle the Romans received the most casualties.

However, the Romans were famous for their *testudo* (literally meaning 'tortoise'), which was one of the best known tactics used during warfare. The *testudo* was generally used when approaching fortifications and basically involved a number of men in a carefully arranged formation. Each man had a long rectangular shield, which he overlapped with neighbouring shields to form one continuous roof over the men's heads. All other shields were held to the front, left and right sides, which formed a protective barrier against anything that was thrown at them. Once the *testudo* was formed, only the heaviest of missiles was capable of penetrating the formidable wall.

Using this famous tactic, the Romans advanced once more up the hill and succeeded in tearing down the stone ramparts. Once exposed, the battle turned into an even hand-to-hand combat, and realizing they were being overpowered by the Romans, the British tried to retreat to the top of the hill. But the Romans were determined and the higher ground did not offer enough protection for the tribesmen, so the Roman soldiers rushed into attack. Having no breastplates or helmets to protect them, the Britons were soon broken. Not only were they killed by the swords and javelins of the legionaries, but they also had to face the auxiliaries to their rear who fought with sabres and spears.

It was a glorious victory for the Romans who not only captured Caratacus, but his wife, daughter and brother as well. Caratacus sought the protection of Cartimandua, who was the warrior queen of the Brigantes, the largest British tribe. Cartimandua had made a pact with the Romans, in exchange for which she was allowed to maintain control of her lands. When Caratacus asked for her help, she betrayed him to the Romans, and by so doing she deprived Celtic Britain of its most influential military leader.

Caratacus was placed in chains and sent to Rome. Everyone was keen to see the man who had managed to defeat the Romans for so many years. The people were summoned to watch Caratacus and his family in a triumphal parade. The original plan was to kill them after the spectacle, but Caratacus was permitted to speak to the Roman senate:

> . . . *My present loss is as glorious to you as it is degrading to myself. I had men and horses, arms and wealth. What wonder if I parted with them reluctantly? If you Romans choose to lord it over the world, does it follow that the world is to accept slavery? Were I to have been at once delivered up as a prisoner, neither my fall nor your triumph would have become famous. My punishment would be followed by oblivion, whereas, if you save my life, I shall be an everlasting memorial of your clemency.*
> FROM THE MANUSCRIPTS OF TACITUS

Possibly because Caratacus acted with such dignity he was spared the customary death of strangulation and received an official pardon. He was allowed to live in Rome with his family in peace.

HIS FIGHT FOR FREEDOM

The defeat of Caratacus effectively ended the large-scale organized resistance to the Roman Empire in Britain. The people of Britain were not prepared to just accept Roman rule and because of Caratacus, who led a bloody campaign against the Roman invaders for many years, Britons were spared from threatened slavery. Both Caratacus and his brother, Togodumnus, will always be remembered in history as leading lights of the British anti-Roman faction, both fighting for the freedom of their people.

BOUDICCA

Around 2,000 years ago much of Britain belonged to the Roman Empire, and the people who lived under their rule were known as Celts. Celtic Britain was divided up into many separate kingdoms that were ruled by overlords or kings. Boudicca (also known as Boadicea) was the queen of the Brythonic Celtic Iceni people. The Iceni were a tribe who lived in Norfolk and Suffolk in the eastern part of Britain. Although the Iceni prospered due to thriving trade with the Romans across the English Channel, trading also brought problems. The Romans were constantly trying to suppress the Celtic religious culture and also brought about considerable economic changes, which included heavy taxation and money lending.

The Romans used many ways of forming alliances with British tribes. One of these was the client-ruler system, where the British ruler or king was forced to comply to a series of treaties and taxes in return for protection provided by the Roman legions against other British tribes. When the 'client' died, the system was reviewed. The Iceni tribe worked under this client-ruler system.

BOUDICCA AND PRASUTAGUS

Boudicca is thought to have been of royal descent but little else is known of her early life. She has been described as a tall woman with flaming red hair, a harsh voice and a piercing stare. Boudicca became a member of the Iceni tribe when she married their king, Prasutagus.

Prasutagus was a brilliant warrior and a worthy king, but he was under constant strain from fighting with the Romans and neighbouring tribes. His role as king was to protect his kingdom, his people and most of all his family. Boudicca bore her husband two daughters who were little more than teenagers when their father died in AD 61. Boudicca was already anguished at the suffering of the Iceni from the high taxes and other indignities forced on them by the Romans. When the Roman emperor, Nero, learned of the death of Prasutagus, he moved in quickly to assess the extent of his property. Prastagus had left a will in which half of his property would go to Nero and the other half to his two daughters on his death. Boudicca, not knowing about the will, expected that her late husband's inheritance would be passed on to her, but this was not to be the case. Nero declared the will invalid and the Iceni lands and property were confiscated and nobles were treated no better than slaves.

Boudicca was incensed at the tactless way in which the Romans treated her people, and she declared herself as leader of the Iceni tribe. During his rule Prastagus had lived well on money borrowed from the

Romans, but on his death his subjects became liable for his debt. Nero's representative, Decanius Catus, decided to make an example of the Iceni people and called in the debt. But the funds were not available, Boudicca was flogged, her two daughters were raped and all the property belonging to the Iceni was forfeited to the Romans.

BOUDICCA'S UPRISING

The actions taken by the Romans was too much for the new queen of the Iceni, and she decided that she would take on Nero and his legions. Disgusted by the acts of violence they had witnessed, and fearing far worse, the Iceni stood by Boudicca and told her that they were prepared to fight for their lands. The Iceni were also joined by the Trinovantes, a neighbouring tribe, who were also tired of the high taxes and misappropriation of their land. Eventually, tribes that had spent many years feuding, came together and joined Boudicca when she called for war. Those who showed their allegiance to Rome were to eventually witness Boudicca's wrath.

Boudicca's first opportunity to rebel came when the Roman governor, Seutonius Paulinus, and his troops were stationed in Anglesey and North Wales, seeking out rebels who had fled there for safety. When Paulinus heard of Boudicca's uprising, he immediately marched his troops towards the rebels.

It is believed that Boudicca had amassed an army of around 10,000 people when she led her first attack at

Colonia Claudia Victricensis (now Colchester). In this Roman municipality lived a colony of retired Roman officers and their families. Boudicca and her army were intimidating and attacked the city without warning. Some of the veterans of Colonia managed to hide out in a temple for a couple of days, but the farmers were ill-equipped and no longer skilled in the art of defence, or indeed fit enough to take on the might of Boudicca's army. The city was totally ransacked, set ablaze, and all of its inhabitants killed.

The Roman Ninth Legion, headed by Petilius Cerialis, was sent to help Paulinus and were camped about 130 km (80 miles) north of Colonia. When he heard of the attack, Cerialis quickly marched his legion of around 5,000 men towards the city to offer some relief. However, Boudicca and her army, flushed with success, ambushed Cerialis and his men several kilometres outside the vanquished city. The Roman legion was virtually routed and every infantryman killed. Cerialis himself managed to escape and returned with a few of his cavalry to their base in the north.

Boudicca and her rebellious army moved on, heading this time for Londinium (London). Meanwhile, alarmed by the amount of carnage, the Roman procurator, Catus Decianus, fled from his headquarters in London. He took everything with him, including all his staff, which meant that it left Britain temporarily without any government.

Paulinus, who had marched his legion over some 400 km (250 miles), managed to reach London before

Boudicca. At the time of the revolt London was an area of approximately 135 hectares (330 acres) of farmland and was without any fortifications. It was occupied by around 30,000 people of both Roman and British descent. Paulinus had expected to find London ransacked by the time he reached the city, but finding it untouched decided to retreat as he knew without fortifications it would be a difficult place to defend. Paulinus felt it would be better to sacrifice this one city in an effort to bring an end to the rebellion. Despite the pleading of the inhabitants of London, nothing would change his mind and Paulinus left them to the fate of the British.

Boudicca's attack on London was savage where, according to the Roman historian Tactitus, she had all the women rounded up and murdered. She ordered her men to cut off one breast, stuff it into the victim's mouth and then have them impaled on large stakes. This action was possibly the result of the cruel treatment her daughters received at the hands of the Romans. London was burned to the ground, feeling the full force of the British vengeance.

The British marched away from London and headed northwest towards Verulamium (St Albans), a city made up entirely of British citizens who were sympathetic to the Roman rule. Verulamium was the third largest city in Roman Britain. It is estimated that around 70,000 died in the assaults on the three towns (Colonia Claudia Victricensis, Londinium and Verulamium).

THE LAST BATTLE

Seutonius Paulinus had managed to amass a force of around 10,000 Roman legionnaires and British supporters of Rome. They took up a prominent position at the edge of a forest near a narrow gorge. Paulinus placed his men at the top of a hill which was covered on one side by a thick forest, meaning that the Roman army would only have to face the rebels from one direction.

Somehow, the Verulamiums had received word of Boudicca's rebels, and when they entered the city they found it had already been evacuated. The majority of the citizens took all of their belongings with them. Undeterred they ransacked the city, rasing it to the ground and killing any residents who had refused to leave their homes.

Following their attack on Verulamium, the British army amassed at the foot of the hill where Paulinus and his legion were waiting to attack. The British army were joined by their families – mothers, fathers, grandparents, children, livestock and chariots – all prepared to fight for their right to be free. Apparently it was the custom of the Celts to go into battle with women and children as it was hoped that their screaming might unnerve the enemy.

The two forces were within reach of one another and they prepared for battle. Boudicca is said to have been both exhausted and injured, but she still appeared a formidable adversary clad in her tartan kilt. While Paulinus encouraged his men and convinced them that they could win this battle, Boudicca wound her troops into a frenzy and commanded them to charge.

Paulinus was definitely at the advantage, and he was able to determine the way in which the battle was fought. The British were hemmed in not only by the forest, but they were also restricted by the small opening that afforded access to the top troops on the hill. Their chariots only acted as a hindrance, as there was no way they could manoeuvre them through the narrow gorge or up the steep incline. The Romans stood prepared in a tight formation, using their shields to create a protective barrier against the British spears. When the British were within range, the Romans changed their formation into a wedge shape, and showered their opponents with a barrage of javelins. The javelins were quickly followed by large numbers of auxiliary infantry then line after line of Roman infantry.

The majority of the advancing British rebels were killed, and chaos soon mounted in the rear guard when they realized that they were completely trapped. As the last of the Roman infantry closed in on Boudicca and her forces, the British were pinned down not only by their dead but also by the families waiting at the base of the hill. The Romans were victorious and were ruthless, killing women and children alike, taking no prisoners.

Boudicca survived the battle, only to poison herself when she arrived back home, rather than end up in the hands of the Romans. There is no doubt that had she been taken captive, Nero would have made sure she was made a laughing stock and most probably would have subjected her to unspeakable torture.

The Roman senator, Cassius Dio, wrote that the British gave Boudicca a fitting funeral for a queen and a hero. There are many conflicting reports about her burial, but it has been suggested that her body was buried at Stonehenge on Salisbury Plain in southern England. It is dubious, though, that the stones set up by the Druids actually mark her tomb. Paulinus, who was glorious in his victory, set about destroying all the territories of any Celtic tribes who had rebelled or remained neutral.

THE AFTERMATH

Boudicca was a proud and strong warrior who fought for the freedom of her people from the constraints of Roman rule. However, her revolt actually caused an increase in the severity of their rule, making them more determined to quell the Celtic tribes who were not completely under their domination. Her legend did live on, however, and Celtic tribes who had little allegiance with Rome, remained determined to fight for their freedom.

As for the survivors of Boudicca's uprising, when they returned to their lands after what was possibly as long as a year of fighting, their lands were barren and many starved to death. The Romans continued to lay waste to Iceni farms, even resorting to building drainage channels to take all the water away from their soil. They deprived farmers of their weapons, stole their money and continued to make their lives miserable for many years.

Boudicca will always be remembered in British history for her courage in taking on the powers of Rome. In 1902 a large bronze statue of Boudicca riding in a chariot was placed next to the Houses of Parliament in, ironically, what was once the Roman capital, London. Even today, Boudicca remains one of the greatest heroines of Britain for her glorious, if bloody, revolt against the Romans.

BAR KOKHBA REVOLT

The Bar Kokhba revolt took place at a time when Rome was governed by Emperor Publius Aelius Hadrian, a distinguished commander and administrator. When he first became emperor in AD 118 it appeared that he was sympathetic to the Jews, allowing them to return to their homeland and also granting permission for the rebuilding of their city and Holy Temple, both of which were destroyed in the Great Revolt of AD 66–70. The Jews became more confident, and their expectations of a better life rose as they made plans to start rebuilding. However, the Jews were always treated with some suspicion by the Romans because of their different religious beliefs and way of life, and it wasn't long before Hadrian went back on his word.

The emperor decided to visit Jerusalem before he would allow the Jews to start any rebuilding. When he arrived, Hadrian was shocked to see what was once a thriving and proud city in ruins and immediately ordered its reconstruction. What the Jews didn't realize was that the rebuilding Hadrian had in mind was not to be a city for the Jews to start a new life in, but a pagan city that was to be sanctified to the pagan god Jupiter. Hadrian told the Jews that he would be appointed as the high priest and that the city was to be renamed Aelia Capitolina.

The Jews felt betrayed and prepared to rebel. Secretly they built hideouts in caves and starting preparing weapons. In AD 123, the Jews started surprise attacks on the Romans, but instead of improving the situation these attacks made life worse for the Jewish people.

Hadrian decided to reinforce his troops and sent an extra legion, the Sixth Ferrata, into Judea to try to put a stop to the attacks. Hadrian appointed Tinneius Rufus as governor, and he proved to be a harsh ruler known for his mistreatment of Jewish women. Rufus was not a supporter of Jewish beliefs and traditions and prohibited the custom of circumcision. The religious origin of Jewish circumcision is in the Torah, in which God told Abraham, 'every male among you shall be circumcised' as part of a covenant made between God and the Jewish people. The Jews felt that if the Romans banned what was one of their most important beliefs, they would lose their identity, as this was an important physical difference as well as a basic part of their religion. They knew it was time to revolt – a time to strike for their independence.

RABBI AKIVA AND SIMON BAR KOKHBA

Rabbi Akiva ben Yosef was not only one of Israel's great sages but also a revolutionary. Starting life as a shepherd, he went on to learn the Torah, which gave him enough knowledge to guide Jews and inspire an army. Akiva felt betrayed – he had believed Hadrian and his promises – and he told the Jews they should ignore the Roman prohibitions and take up arms against them. While Rabbi Akiva could act as the spiritual leader, he knew he needed a strong military commander if they were to lead a successful revolt. For this role he chose a man by the name of Simon Bar Kokhba, whose name meant 'son of a star'. Akiva had such faith in Bar Kokhba that he saw him as the Messiah, their saviour and liberator.

Together, Akiva and Bar Kokhba organized and trained thousands of soldiers to fight for the independence and welfare of the Jewish people. Bar Kokhba was a strong and powerful leader and was determined that his warriors would be the same. To make sure that his army only contained the strongest men he set them a strict test. He said that only men who would be prepared to bite a finger off their right hand would be worthy of being in his army – 20,000 men passed this test. Akiva was against this form of recruiting as he thought it was unwise to send out warriors with imperfections, so he devised an alternative test of strength. He suggested that anyone who could uproot a Cedar of Lebanon tree while riding past it on a horse would be deserving of joining their army. Another 20,000 passed this new test and soon Bar Kokhba had amassed an army of around 580,000 men. He trained a strong and ferocious group of followers and soon he felt ready to start their revenge on the Romans.

TO WAR

Little by little Bar Kokhba's army took over Palestine. They seized towns and built walls and underground passages as a form of fortification. Under the powerful leadership of Bar Kokhba, the Jewish army had seized about 50 Palestine strongholds and nearly 1,000 town and villages, including Jerusalem. The news spread fast of their success and before long Jews from other countries joined the crusade. At last the Jews were able to celebrate their independence from Roman dominance.

To celebrate their victory the Jews had coins minted bearing the words 'The freedom of Israel' written in Hebrew. The Pagan god in Jerusalem was replaced by an alter to the Jewish god, and the inhabitants starting to build a wall around the city.

Despite their current euphoria, Bar Kokhba knew it wouldn't be long before the Romans fought back, so he kept his army in top condition, ready to fight at any time. This was a wise move on his part as Hadrian had already dispatched one of his best generals, Publis Marcellus, to help Rufus. The Jewish army were ready and quickly overcame the Roman legion, who had heavy casualties. The turning point of the war for the Romans was when Hadrian sent one his best generals, Julius Severus, directly from Britain. In total Hadrian sent 12 army legions from Egypt, Britain and Syria to stop the Jewish rebels.

Severus made the tactical decision to reconquer Palestine little by little, just as the Jews had originally done. He realized that due to the exceptionally large number of Jewish rebels it would be hard to break them in an outright war. Slowly they managed to break down the Jewish strongholds. Where they couldn't overpower the Jews, the Romans made sure that they were unable to get new supplies so they eventually grew weak from lack of food. It wasn't until he knew he had the upper hand, and most of the strongholds had been recaptured, that Severus stepped up his attack to outright war.

THE FINAL BATTLE

The Roman army had forced Bar Kokhba to retreat to a fortified city in Jerusalem called Betar. It was a fairly large city located on a road between Bet Guvrin and Jerusalem and was, as the Jews thought, virtually impenetrable. Betar was a vital military stronghold due to its strategic position on a mountain ridge, and it was the place to which thousands of Jewish refugees had fled during the war.

Severus was unsure how to penetrate the stronghold at Betar, but it was in the height of summer and he felt as long as he could hold out the Jews would soon run low on supplies. What he didn't know at that time was that Betar was supplied by an underground passage.

One night a messenger returned to speak to Severus and told him that he would not be able to overpower Betar as long as Eleazor of Modin continued his vigilant prayers. Since the outset of the Jewish revolt this Rabbi had sat in sackcloth and ashes praying for God to keep their stronghold safe. One day a Roman managed to penetrate the city of Betar and pretended to whisper into the ear of Rabbi Eleazor. When the news got back to Bar Kokhba he questioned the elderly Rabbi, asking him what the man had said to him. When Eleazor replied that he didn't know what he was talking about, Bar Kokhba lost his temper and started to kick the Rabbi. Due to his weakened state and age he died instantly, and from this moment Bar Kokhba's followers started to lose their faith in him.

Severus, on hearing this news, was delighted that the Jews were starting to crack and, with the help of a Jewish traitor, he was shown the secret entrance into the fortress. The result was catastrophic and on the ninth of Av (July–August in the Gregorian calendar) Severus led his men in what was to be the total destruction of Betar. At the end of the siege around 500,000 Jews were dead. Those who were not killed were either sold as slaves, managed to hide out in caves or fled to other countries.

As for Bar Kokhba, his body was found on the battlefield, although apparently not killed by a human, but strangled by a huge serpent. His followers, who once believed him to be their Messiah, started to have their doubts and thought that it was the death of Rabbi Eleazor that was their downfall.

The life of Rabbi Akiva did not end peacefully, either. He chose to ignore the Roman prohibitions and was declared a criminal for his teachings of the Torah. He was eventually captured and tortured and died a martyr's death.

THE END OF THE REVOLT

After the battle of Betar, although there were still a few skirmishes, essentially the war was over and the Jews lost their independence. Jews were sold into slavery or transported to Egypt, and Hadrian finished building his pagan city of Aelia Capitolina, where Jews were now forbidden to live. The only time they were allowed to enter the city was on the 9th of Av, when they were allowed to mourn their dead on the anniversary of the battle of Betar.

Hadrian continued to discriminate against the Jews, forbidding any teaching of the Torah, the observance of the Sabbath, circumcision, Jewish courts, meeting in synagogues or any other ritual practice. Many great sages were martyred and this persecution was to last until after the death of Hadrian, when discussions started about a reconciliation.

Simon Bar Kokhba had fought hard and loyally for the freedom of the Jewish civilization and has become a symbol of valiant national resistance. The Zionist youth movement took the name 'Betar' from the site of the last Jewish stronghold, and Israel's first prime minister, David Ben-Gurion, took his name from one of Bar Kokhba's famous generals.

Even though the Jewish revolt against the Romans ended disastrously, with many deaths, there was no doubt that Bar Kokhba and his followers had no other alternative than to fight. He was trying his hardest to free his people, and he proved himself to be a great general with a magnificent army. Bar Kokhba gave hope to the Jews in times of great hardship, giving them a taste for independence and also letting them experience what it was like to fight for what they truly believed in.

ZENOBIA OF PALMYRA

Queen Zenobia has been described as being as brave as Diana, the Roman goddess of the hunt, and as beautiful as Venus, the Roman goddess of love and beauty. She was a brilliant warrior queen, who will be remembered for her ruthless ambition in leading her people to war against Rome. She fought to defend the eastern part of her empire in the name of her young son, Vaballathus, and her story is both compelling and fascinating.

PALMYRA

Palmyra, the 'place of palms', was a trading community near the borders of the Roman and Persian Empires. Palmyra was actually the Roman name for a city that the locals called Tadmor. It was situated right at the edge of the Syrian desert between Syria, which was occupied by the Romans and Babylonia, occupied by the Persians. The city was directly on the Silk Route and a stopping place for traders – Palmyra was the site of an oasis watered by the Efqa spring. The spring provided limitless supplies of water, which came from underground supplies at the base of the Jebel Muntar mountain. This strategic position in the desert meant that Palmyra prospered and became a vital trading link for silk from the Mediterranean to the Orient.

Around AD 114 Palmyra became part of the Roman Empire, and at the beginning of the third century Emperor Septimius Severus made the city into a colony. He treated the people well and encouraged new constructions of streets, arches, temples and statues, until eventually Palmyra became one of the greatest cities of the Roman Empire. The people of Palmyra were permitted to elect their own senate and became financially independent. The inhabitants of the city became wealthy and lived well, but this prosperous era was to come to an end in AD 227. The collapse of the Parthian Empire and the Sassanids taking over the throne of Persia meant that Palmyra was now at the centre of the conflict between Persia and Rome.

In c.AD 230 Septimius Odaenathus, a member of the ruling family of Palmyra, became a senator in Rome. He was advanced to consul in AD 258 and consolidated his power in Palmyra by taking the title 'Chief of Palmyra'.

Although Palmyra had a good relationship with Rome, the Roman Empire itself was in a state of crisis. The 'Crisis of the Third Century' (as it became known) was a name given to the crumbling and near collapse of the Roman Empire between AD 235 and 284 caused by the endless waves of external invasion, internal civil war and eventual economic collapse. When the conflict reached a crisis point, Rome went to the ruler of Palmyra for help. The western provinces of the empire had broken away from Rome, forming a rebel state known as the Gallic Empire. While in the east,

Roman frontiers were under pressure from the Sassanid Persians.

In AD 260 the Roman emperor Valerian led a legion of men into battle against the Sassanid forces, who were under the control of King Shapur I. Shapur had already penetrated deep into Roman terrority on several occasions, and he had taken control of Antiochia in Syria in an earlier battle. In an effort to stop any further encroachments on Roman territory, Valerian led his men eastward towards the Sassanid borders. At first he was successful in recapturing Syrian provinces, but he was eventually defeated at Edessa by King Shapur's army and was taken captive by the Persians.

This defeat meant trouble for Palmyra, because it left the eastern provinces vulnerable to Persian supremacy. At first, Odaenathus tried to placate King Shapur by offering him luxurious gifts, but when his offerings were contemptuously rejected, he decided to give Rome his total support. Gathering his forces, Odaenathus set out with his army and successfully fought against the Sassanid for several years. In honour of his outstanding success, Odaenathus was given the titles Dux Romanorum (leader of the Romans) and Imperator (commander) by the Roman emperor Gallienus. Gallienus had found a rare ally in Odaenathus, and he granted him control of the armies in the east. His successes meant that Roman rule was once more restored in the east and, still riding high on his earlier victories, Odaenathus took his army and headed for Cappadocia in Turkey to fight the the East Germanic tribe the Goths.

However, his new found glory was to be short-lived because Odaenathus and his elder son, Hairan, were both assassinated in AD 267. Most historical records put the blame of his nephew Maconius for the murders, but later records implicate Gallienus. Gallienus seemed to have reached the decision that it was time to put an end to the independent power of Palmyra and there have been suggestions that he was behind the plot that saw Odaenathus killed. It is at this point that Zenobia comes into the story.

SEPTIMIA ZENOBIA

Although there is a certain amount of uncertainty of the origins of Septimia Zenobia, it is believed that her father was either of Arab or Aramaean origin and her mother most probably an Egyptian. She was born in the early 240s AD and it appears she came from a long history of Syrian and Abyssinian queens, starting with the legendary Queen of Sheba. Zenobia, herself, claimed to be a descendent of Cleopatra VII.

Zenobia met and married Odaenathus while still in her early teens and took her role as the Queen of Palmyra seriously. She was Odaenathus's second wife and bore him one son, Vaballathus, although Hairan, his son by his first wife, was heir to the throne. She was intellectually well-equipped for the title and was fluent in many languages, including Greek, Latin, Egyptian and Amharic. She has been described as a rare beauty with pearly white teeth and dark hair and eyes, but above all she had an incredible strength of character.

She accompanied her husband on many of his campaigns and proved to be a worthy adversary. Possibly the greatest strength in Zenobia's character was her driving ambition, and on hearing about the death of her husband and his son, she soon realized that the power of Palmyra was now in her hands.

On the death of Odaenathus, Zenobia automatically took the title of Queen of Palmyra as regent for her infant son. The people of Palmyra were astonished by the way she took control, using her wide knowledge of politics and appointing many philosophers, scholars and theologians to rule in her courts. Fired by ambition, Zenobia was tired of Roman domination and decided she would take her own army and try to conquer all of Rome's territories.

Emperor Lucius Domitius Aurelian was now emperor of Rome, following the death of Gallienus, and with Rome now starting to crumble, Zenobia felt it was time to break the alliance. In AD 269, while the Roman armies were busy fighting in northern Italy, Zenobia took her armies into Egypt, defeated the defending army of 50,000 and consequently added Egypt to the tiny kingdom of Palmyra.

The Romans were furious at losing Egypt, and Emperor Claudius II Gothicus sent his army to fight against the Palmyrenes. It was a hard-fought battle, but the Romans were defeated and Zenobia retained hold on Egypt. Outraged by further losses and powerless to do anything about it, Rome grew weaker while Zenobia and her kingdom grew stronger.

Zenobia and her army went on to annex most of

Syria's small neighbouring lands and also took large chunks of Asia Minor to add to her ever expanding empire. What was once a small and weak kingdom, Palmyra now stretched from the Nile river in Egypt to the Bosphorus River in modern-day Turkey.

Zenobia's army, proud of their queen and warrior, gave her the title of 'The Most Illustrious and Pious Queen, and she certainly lived up to the title. She declared that Palmyra was now independent of Rome. She showed respect to the long-suffering Jews of Alexandria and she held frequent meetings with the bishops at Antioch.

Rome had taken a back seat until Zenobia took one step too far and decided to remove the image of the Roman emperor from the coins of Alexandria and have Palmyra's own currency minted. This really was the last straw and her greed for power was eventually to be her undoing.

THE DOWNFALL OF ZENOBIA

Across the water in Rome, Emperor Aurealin had kept a close eye on the movements of Zenobia and her people. Aurealin was a talented and skilled commander who had helped to rebuild the walls of Rome. In AD 272, the emperor decided enough was enough and he set out on his campaign to bring down Zenobia.

The Romans and the Palmyrenes met at the Orontes river in Antioch. When Aurealin caught sight of the heavily armoured Palmyrene army, with Zenobia proud and defiant shouting orders to her men, he realized that his men needed to outsmart them. He ordered his men not to engage in direct combat but to pretend to flee, therefore forcing the Palmyrene army to follow them. The tactic worked well and it wasn't long before Zenobia's cavalry exhausted themselves in the heat. Taking advantage of the Palmyrene's weakened state, the Roman army took the upper hand and attacked, completely outflanking the tired cavalry, which resulted in heavy losses.

Zenobia was distraught at losing the battle and retreated to Antioch. Not wanting to lose face with the people of the city, she took a man who resembled Aurelian, dressed him up as the emperor and presented him to the crowds. However, Aurelian's army were not far behind, and knowing that she did not have the men or strength to go into another battle, Zenobia left for the city of Emesa under the cover of night, riding 160 km (100 miles) across the desert. Shortly after, Zanobia got word that Aurealin had entered Antioch and was warmly greeted by its residents. It appeared that her once loyal allies were now supporting her enemy.

THE FINAL BATTLE

When Zenobia arrived at Palmyra she started to prepare to defend the city. All along the walls were machines and archers, hopefully making the walls impenetrable to the Romans. Aurelian arrived a few days later and immediately started to attack, but Zenobia had planned her defence well and the Romans could make no impression. Exhausted,

Aurelian sent a message to Zanobia, offering her lenient terms under which she could surrender.

For I bid you surrender, promising that your lives shall be spared, and with the condition that you, Zenobia, together with your children shall dwell wherever I, acting in accordance with the wish of the most noble senate, shall appoint a place. Your jewels, your gold, your silver, your silks, your horses, your camels, you shall hand over to the Roman treasury. As for the people of Palmyra, their rights shall be preserved.

Zenobia was far too proud to surrender to the Romans and refused Aurelian's terms. She knew that it would be difficult for the Roman army to penetrate the Palmyra defences, but she also knew that many of her previous allies had now shown allegiance to the Romans. Zenobia was all too aware that it wouldn't be long before their supplies ran low, forcing them to surrender. Downhearted and desperate, with her kingdom crumbling around her, Zenobia mounted on a camel and stole away at night from Palmyra. She headed towards the Euphrates in the hopes of begging her previous enemy, the Persians, to send help. Zanobia managed to reach the Euphrates river, but before she was able to cross the water, she was captured. Whether she was just tracked down or whether she had been betrayed, is not really known.

The year was now AD 272 and after Zenobia fled her precious city, Palmyra surrendered to the Romans.

The once-proud queen was brought before Emperor Aurelian, to whom she continued to defend herself vigorously. But Aurelian was not prepared to listen and there was nothing she could do to convince him to allow her to return to the empire that she had built up from virtually nothing.

Aurelian arranged a triumphant procession through the streets of Rome in celebration of reconquering all the lands that had been lost to Palmyra. Zenobia was paraded in front of the crowds as a victory trophy with her feet shackled with golden chains, but still she held her head high.

Zenobia's life was spared and there are discrepancies about how she lived the remainder of her life. One historian records that Aurelian gave her an estate on the Tiber where she appears to have married a Roman governor and built herself a new life.

A PLACE IN HISTORY

Even though Zenobia's fight for freedom failed, this need not undermine her accomplishments. Her conquests were many and she will certainly go down in history as the greatest woman to have ever challenged Rome. As for the city of Palmyra, without Zenobia it would have never received recognition and would probably have remained the small oasis in the middle of a big desert. As it is, a small city grew and stood against the forces of both Rome and Persia, all thanks to one brave, noble, beautiful and memorable woman. It is easy to understand why she became known as the

Queen of the East, when you consider that she was a brilliant military tactician, so tough that she would march for kilometres on foot at the head of her troops, and of course she was always at the front of the action, fighting for what she believed to be rightfully hers.

THE AN SHI AND HUANG CHAO REBELLIONS

The An Shi and the Huang Chao Rebellions took place during the Tang dynasty, which ruled in China from 618 to its downfall in 907. The Tang dynasty is considered to be an important period in Chinese history and has been regarded by historians as the strongest empire in the eighth century. At its height the Tang dynasty spread from what is now known as Manchuria in the north-east to the present-day Vietnam in the south-west. Its capital, Chang'an, was an important centre for trading along the Silk Route, taking goods such as paper, silk and spices to the west. Buddhism, which had originated in India more than 1,000 years before the Tang dynasty was formed, had now become a traditional and permanent part of Chinese culture.

Under Tang rule the government perfected a system of examinations that were based on Confucianism. The exams were used to test the knowledge of members of the civil service, in an effort to draw the most suitable people into government. This system gave people from all walks of life the opportunity to become officials on the strength of their talents.

Due to successful military actions of the Tang army, the Tang frontiers were secured and their boundaries expanded. Also under the Tang regime, agriculture made a gradual recovery and large areas of wasteland were cultivated and paddy fields started to thrive with a new system of irrigation.

The Tang Empire was founded by the Li family and, historically, it can be divided into two separate periods – the early period and the late period. The early period was a time of great prosperity, while the late was a period of rapid decline. The so-called golden age was to last until the reign of Emperor Xuanzong, when the actions of the An Shi rebellion greatly weakened the Tang dynasty.

EMPEROR XUANZONG

Tang Xuanzong, also named Li longji, was the grandson of the only female monarch in Chinese history, Empress Wu Zetian. At the start of his rule, the Tang dynasty was thriving and people lived in a time of peace with little or no crime. Trading was at its height and the Tang army had reoccupied many lost territories. However, this age of plenty was merely a facade that covered up a lot of depravity.

Over the years, Xuanzong became more and more extravagant, spending the majority of his time in search of pleasure. He became infatuated with a young concubine by the name of Yang Guifei, a love that was so exceptional that the emperor started to neglect his political duties. His government soon crumbled around him, which was not made any better by the fact that Yang had appointed dishonest and double-crossing people in high administrative positions. The government became more and more corrupt, and in 755 the famous An Shi Rebellion attempted to take it down.

AN LUSHAN

Yang Guifei had taken a young general named An Lushan under her wing, and it didn't take long before the young man started to accumulate power. Xuanzong appointed Lushan commander of three garrisons in the northern territory – Pinglu, Fanyang and Hedong – and this, in effect, gave him control over the entire northern area. An Lushan, didn't like what was happening to the government and decided he would try to end the corrupt rule of Xuanzong. An Lushan was a powerful commander with around 164,000 men and, taking advantage of the poor defence surrounding the palace, he decided to start a rebellion. To avoid any suspicion, Lushan feigned friendship with the emperor, even allowing himself to be called the adopted son of Yang Guifei. However, Xuanzong's chief minister, Yang Guozhong, did not approve of the young commander's power and position and, fearing that he was going to cause trouble for the government, the minister demanded Lushan's dismissal.

In 755, wanting to punish Guozhong, An Lushan started his revolt. He took his army and moved quickly along the Grand Canal in the modern Hebei province, and captured the city of Luoyang within the first year.

An Lushan declared himself Emperor of the Great Yan dynasty. However, the route to Chang'an, the capital, was blocked by troops that had remained loyal to Xuanzong and his minister. Guozhong, who had far inferior troops, ordered his men to attack Lushan's army on open ground. Lushan's far superior fighting force soon overpowered them, which left the road open to the capital. Realizing that the capital was now exposed to attack, Xuanzong decided to flee to Sichuan.

On his journey Xuanzong stopped at the Mawei Inn in Shaanxi, where his bodyguards demanded the death of the unpopular minister Yang Guozhong and his cousin, Lady Yang. With his army on the verge of mutiny, Xuanzong knew he had to agree and ordered their execution. While the emperor's father fled one way, his son, Suzong, fled towards Lingwu in the modern-day Ningxia province. On arriving at Sichuan, Xuanzong abdicated in favour of his son. Suzong was proclaimed emperor, and one of his first jobs was to appoint two new generals, Guo Ziyi and Li Guangbi, to try to put a stop to the rebellion.

The two generals, realizing that they needed to strengthen their troops, decided to borrow soldiers from the Huihe tribe, who were an offshoot of the Turkish Tujue Tribe. With the added numbers, the Tang forces managed to recapture the cities of Chang'an and Luoyang.

To add to their victory, the Tang forces were helped by unrest within the government established by the rebels. An Lushan was murdered by his own paranoid son, An Qingxu, who was subsequently killed by the subordinate Shi Siming, who had been an ally to Lushan throughout the rebellion. Siming had managed to regain occupation of the city of Luoyang, overpowering the Imperial army. The murder of An Qingxu had a roll-on effect and Shi Siming was also killed by his own son, Si Chaoyi. It was obvious now that the government was in a state of complete chaos, and Lushan's once loyal soldiers, started to defect to the Tang army. When Luoyang was captured by the Tang army in 763 for the second time, Si Chaoyi committed suicide, which brought an end to the rebellion that had lasted for almost eight years.

The rebellion cost the lives of an estimated 36 million people which was around two-thirds of the total tax-paying population. This was the highest death toll recorded for more than 1,200 years, until the death toll during World War II reached more than 62 million people.

The revolt also severely damaged the once thriving industries, destroyed many towns and cities, and peasants were uprooted from their homelands. Warlords soon started to take control of sections of the country, refusing to pay homage to the new, weakened Tang government. In fact, the Tang dynasty never did recover from the effects of the An Shi rebellion, and the government and its military gradually lost its power. An Lushan fought hard to free the Tang dynasty from the corruption that had infiltrated the government, and although it was not as successful as perhaps he had hoped, the An Lushan rebellion had a deep impact on the financial situation of the central government.

POWER OF THE EUNUCHS

Although the eunuchs did not play a significant role in the early part of the Tang dynasty, following the An Shi rebellion they became an important political power. In ancient China castration was both a traditional punishment and a means of gaining employment in the Imperial service. The value of such employment meant that certain eunuchs gained immense power, which may have superseded that of the ministers. The already shaky Tang government was now being threatened by the rise of the eunuchs. On two separate occasions state officials attempted to destroy the eunuchs' power, but their attempts failed and the eunuchs managed to maintain control until approximately 835.

HUANG CHAO REBELLION

Problems arose in the Tang dynasty when the administrative system set up for the peasants started to fail. The system originally allowed peasants equal land allotment on which they paid an annual tax to the government in the form of grain or cash. However, this system started to fall apart when the population growth increased rapidly, leaving them with much smaller plots of land but the same taxes. Unable to pay their taxes, the peasants started to abandon their land, which subsequently had a major effect on the economy. The corrupt government ministers were greedy and were determined to collect their taxes, which resulted in many skirmishes and the death of many farmers.

Around AD 875 Huang Chao and Wang Xianzhi started a peasants' uprising. Huang Chao attempted to enter politics by taking the civil service examination but, after failing to pass, he started to doubt the justice of the government. He, along with Xianzhi, joined the illegal salt dealing business. Many impoverished peasants and merchants, fed up with paying high taxes, along with big salt gangs, started to form an anti-government rebellion.

At the time much of northern and central China were suffering from severe drought and famine. Many of the peasants hit by starvation joined various criminal gangs and started to revolt against the Tang rule. The mobs started to gather more and more supporters and Huang Chao trained them in the art of guerilla warfare. Wang Xianzhi had the same idea and started to train his own fighting force.

When the Royal Court of Tang heard about the uprising they not only despatched troops but also started rumours to cause rivalry between the two gangs. The Tang government decided to reward Xianzhi with a formal office in the Imperial court and bribed the members of his gang who turned against Huang Chao.

Huang Chao, who had already led several successful missions with his band of peasants, managed to
convince Xianzhi to join them in their revolt against
the emperor. Xianzhi agreed and began to fight the
Tang forces, but it wasn't long before he was caught
and executed by the government. Large numbers of
Xianzhi's followers decided to join Huang Chao's
group, which meant that his army almost doubled in
size. Added to this Huang Chao managed to enlist
many more impoverished farmers, merchants and
anarchists, until he had around 600,000 men.

His formidable army plundered and burnt numerous
cities, including Luoyang, which at that time was the
largest city in China. Huang Cho took control of
Luoyang and Chang'an and then proclaimed himself
as first emperor of the short-lived Qi dynasty.

Although Huang Cho tried to convince Tang
officials to join his new court, it was mainly made up
of criminals and people who had no idea of how to
govern a country. The majority of the Tang court had
fled to Chengdu in the Sichuan province, and Emperor
Xizong started a counter-attack against the rebel
troops. The emperor gained the support of the Turkish
chieftain Li Keyong, and together they started to
harass Huang Chao's newly formed regime. Emperor
Xizong succeeded in forcing Huang Chao to surrender
Chang'an in 881, and the rebel fled the city. Many of
Huang Chao's once loyal supporters turned allegiance
and returned to the Tang dynasty.

In 882, Zhu Wen, who Huang Chao considered to
be one of his loyal supporters, deserted his former

leader and joined the Chinese regular army. They rewarded him with the rank of general, and he subsequently drove Huang Chao to his former home of Tai Shan. Feeling totally downhearted and deserted by the majority of his men, Huang Chao resorted to committing suicide in 884, which forced the end of the rebellion.

Although the Huang Chao rebellion was smaller than that of the An Shi rebellion, it was significant in that it did bring about the eventual downfall of the Tang dynasty. His rebellion was in protest of the anarchist and corrupt movement formed by the Tang government, and it was also the first rebellion of any importance that was carried out by peasants that had actually succeeded.

PART TWO

MEDIEVAL FREEDOM FIGHTERS

HEREWARD THE WAKE

An action hero of Anglo-Saxon descent, Hereward the Wake is best remembered for his revolt against William the Conqueror. Just 40 years after his death, his escapades were recorded in verse in *The Exploits of Hereward the Saxon*, which helps to give an insight into his life and achievements.

Hereward was the son of Leofric, Earl of Marcia, and Lady Godiva, and he was almost definitely born in the county of Lincolnshire. He probably inherited his brave spirit from his mother, who is remembered for having staged a protest on behalf of her own subjects who were forced to pay an oppressive tax called the Heregeld by her own husband, Leofric. Godiva pleaded endlessly with Leofric to lift the heavy taxes and he is alleged to have said, 'You will have to ride naked through Coventry before I will change my ways.' Certain that his modest wife would never do such a thing, he was completely taken aback when Godiva took him at his word.

She chose market day in Coventry, when the streets were at their busiest, and rode naked with only her long golden hair to cover her body. Leofric was so amazed at the spectacle he immediately stopped the town from having to pay the dreaded Heregeld. He also seemed to undergo some kind of religious conversion at around this time in his life. Together, Godiva and Leofric funded a Benedictine monastery in Coventry where they were both eventually buried.

As a youth Hereward was handsome with a large frame, and from an early age he proved himself to be extremely brave and strong. As he was born into a noble family, he received training in combat and learned how to ride a horse in heavy armour, becoming adept at using both a bow and arrow and a spear.

While Hereward was still a young boy his father was called to the courts of Edward the Confessor. Hereward did not fare so well here, as the king was a scholar and did not favour armed combat. It is reported that Hereward was often in trouble for either fighting with the local boys or for planning adventures that brought them all into disgrace. But the misadventure which made him an outlaw, was when he wrestled a young Norman page on the roof of one of the low Saxon houses. Hereward was angry and let the boy roll off the roof, which sent him running to the king with his sob story. Fed up with all his antics, Leofric and Edward decided to banish the young Hereward from court and send him away from England for an indefinite period in the hope that he would change his ways.

At the age of 19, after seeking advice from his godfather, Gilbert of Ghent, Hereward left England.

Little is recorded of the time that Hereward was abroad, but we do know what was happening back in England during his absence.

NORMAN INVASION

The Normans were descendants of Rollo and his Vikings, who had become a powerful force living in the north of France. England, at the time, did not have the forces to be able to defend itself, and the death of Edward the Confessor caused problems and saw the return of Hereward the Wake.

In 1066, Edward the Confessor, was an old and sick man who was not expected to survive the year. Edward had no children and no surviving siblings and consequently there was no direct heir to the throne on Edward's death. When he died on January 5, 1066, there were four claimants to his throne – William of Normandy, Harold, Edgar Etheling and Harold of Wessex.

The King's council chose Harold Earl of Wessex, as the next king of England. Harold was at that time the most powerful man in England but he knew that as soon as William, Duke of Normandy, heard the news, he would invade England. William's claim to the English throne was based on his assertion that, in 1051, Edward the Confessor (who was his distant cousin) had promised him the throne, which meant that he believed Harold was a usurper. William knew he would not be able to take over the rule of England peacefully, so he decided he would have to take it by means of war.

Hereward was in Flanders when he heard the news that William the Conqueror was in England. He had been told how the Normans were oppressing his people, taking their land and turning them out as if they were beggars. On his arrival in England he found that the Normans had not only taken his family's estate, but they had also murdered his father and brother and left his brother's head nailed to the door of their house. His mother had been raped and his beloved England was now in the hands of a band of foreigners.

Hereward was incensed and went to his old friends and former playmates and asked them to join him in avenging the Normans. They were only too pleased to join their old friend, and they headed off towards the Hereward estate. On arrival they found the Normans wining and dining in the hall and, surprising them with the fierceness of their attack, Hereward and his band of men slaughtered them all. The next day 14 Norman heads were nailed above the door of his home, to replace that of his brother's.

Knowing that his life would now be in danger, Hereford fled to the Isle of Ely with his band of loyal men. Ely, which was situated on the Fens, offered them a perfect defensive location with its maze of waterways, which divided the great swampy marshes. Hereward set up camp and it wasn't long before they were joined by hundreds of Saxons who had been driven from their homes by the Normans. Hereward soon won the respect of his band of freedom fighters and was appointed their leader.

Hereward started to attack the Norman strongholds one by one, usually leaving Ely by night and returning before the light of day.

PETERBOROUGH ABBEY

One of the most famous of Hereward's attacks was the ransacking of Peterborough Abbey. Hereward heard that the Abbot of Peterborough Abbey, which lay about 39 km (24 miles) from Ely, had died, and there was a rumour that William planned to replace him with a Norman by the name of Turold. Turold had a reputation of being a stern and strong man with military leanings and Hereward decided they would storm the abbey and plunder all of its riches. Peterborough itself was a land full of riches and had earned the name 'Golden Borough'.

Hereward and his men arrived by ship early in the morning, but the monks had received warning and they stood in their path. Using their great numbers, Hereward's men forced their way into the city and burned the monk's houses and entered the great abbey. Here they discovered an enormous amount of treasure in the forms of gold and silver shrines, money, large crucifixes, books and other raiments. They took everything and returned to Ely, to the shelter of the Fens, with the fruits of their plunder. Hereward defended their action by saying that they were simply protecting the English religious artefacts from the godless Normans.

WILLIAM THE CONQUEROR

William the Conqueror was trying his hardest to rule England, but there was much unrest among his people and his own court. The Saxons were not happy being ruled by a foreign king, and more and more Saxon earls and lords escaped to Hereward's camp in Ely. William had heard about Hereward's attacks on various parts of the country, and he knew that he had to try to stop the rebel army.

William moved his court to the Castle of Cambridge, which was just a few kilometres from the camp at Ely. He sent ships to fight from the sea and also brought an army to fight the Saxon rebels on land. The Fens were practically impassable, and three times William was foiled in his attempt to build a causeway to the Isle of Ely. William tried his hardest to starve the rebels into coming out, but Hereward in his wisdom had built up supplies of wheat and grain, and there was always a good supply of fish and fowl to be caught, so this plan had no effect.

On William's third attempt to build a causeway, Hereward even managed to enter his court in disguise. Hereward was riding to the court on his horse when he met with a potter selling his goods. He bargained with him to exchange clothes and lend him his pots and under this guise he entered the court and managed to overhear William's plans. Hereward was nearly caught when he was taken to the kitchens where a cook wanted to buy his dishes. He was recognized by one of the soldiers and had it not been for the speed of his horse, Swallow, he would not have escaped with his life.

William eventually succeeded in building a causeway, which was 3 km (2 miles) long and made of felled trees, stones and earth. He had planned long and hard how to defeat Hereward, and his army blocked all the outlets to the sea with boats. This meant that Hereward and his men now had no way of escape, but still they sat tight in their fortified camp at Ely.

William moved his men along the causeway towards Ely, but Hereward had his men hiding in the reeds and the Saxon archers fired a stream of arrows at the Normans. In the chaos, the causeway started to shake and eventually collapsed into the bog. The majority of the Norman knights, hampered by their heavy armour, were unable to swim and drowned.

Embarrassed by his failure, William ordered for a stronger causeway to be built with a tower. As he launched his second attack, William had a witch taken to the top of the wooden tower where she screamed her dark spells onto the occupants of Ely. Hereward was once again prepared for the attack, and this time, instead of using arrows, they defended themselves with fire. Making sure that the wind was at their backs, the Saxons set fire to the vegetation on the fens. The fire spread quickly, burning the tower, the witch, the causeway and many Norman knights.

The second attack was an even greater failure than the first, and William knew he had to use a different tactic if he was ever going to drive Hereward out of Ely. Hereward was eventually let down by one of the monks from the Abbey of Ely, who had grown tired of the constant fighting. He stole out of the camp and went to William, telling him of a secret way through the marshes that would lead William and his men to Hereward. This made it possible for William to surprise the Saxons, and his army killed a good many of Hereward's men.

Hereward himself managed to escape with a handful of his men. A fisherman hid Hereward in his boat, which he had kept secreted for just such an occasion, and there he lay under a pile of straw. When a party of Normans came to buy some fish from the fisherman, Hereward leapt from his hiding place, seized one of the Norman's horses and rode away to safety.

TIRED OF FIGHTING

With the remainder of his followers, Hereward set up camp deep in the forests of his own estate. Here they lived in relative safety with plenty of food, and it is from this point in his life that the information becomes rather sketchy. There are stories that he continued to strike at William from secret bases with small bands of men, but eventually Hereward grew tired of the fruitless fighting and sent word that he wished to make peace.

William the Conqueror had gone from strength to strength and Hereward realized that it was now useless to resist him. William, showed compassion to Hereward, who he admired for his strength and courage over the years. He offered to restore Hereward's castle and estate and said he could live there in peace if he would promise to cease any further conflict. Hereward remained true to his promise and eventually married an Anglo-Saxon woman of noble background.

Hereward lived into old age, but he was allegedly killed by a Norman knight whose brother had been killed by Hereward or one of his men. Hereward was caught completely unawares in his house and, although he managed to slay many of his attackers, was eventually killed.

HIS LEGEND

Hereward the Wake goes down in history as a resistance fighter who tried to stop the might of the Normans taking over Saxon England. His success, you might say, was not in defeating the Normans but in making them see that they could not make the Saxons live by their rules, and in making the Saxons accept that the Normans were there to stay. Due to his endeavours the two nations came to live side by side. Hereward was seen as a hero, and his story has captured the imagination through songs that were sung about his exploits hundreds of years after his death. Even into the 13th century people visited an old, ruined, wooden castle in the fens, which became known over the years as Hereward's Castle.

ROBIN HOOD

Robin Hood is probably the world's best loved 'outlaw', who is famous for his gallantry, stealing from the rich to feed the poor in his fight for injustice. The stories of Robin Hood and his 'Merry Men' and their various adventures have been portrayed for nearly 700 years, and he is possibly one of the most romanticized figures in English literature. His story has been told through the songs of wandering minstrels, who used both fact and fiction to capture the imagination of their public.

Although the question of Robin Hood's existence may never be completely answered, his legend has definitely taken on a life of its own. This legend is of a man who fought against evil men who misused their authority, such as the Sheriff of Nottingham and Guy of Gisborne.

SHERWOOD FOREST

As stated in the story of Hereward the Wake (see page 84), two nations had learned to live side by side, the Normans and the Saxons, and for many years this was the case. When Robin Hood was a young man

England was ruled by Richard Coeur de Lion (the Lion Heart). He was a fair and brave ruler, who hated mean and cruel acts and was always on the side of the underdog. He influenced the Normans, teaching them that their strength lay in kindness to those who were less fortunate and not in fighting and cruelty.

However, Richard was called overseas to fight in Palestine, where the Christian people had fallen into the hands of the heathens. During his absence, Richard left England in the control of two bishops. He asked them to treat his people well and promised he would reward them well on his return.

However, Richard had a brother, Prince John, who was a completely different character in every way. He was angry that Richard had not chosen him to rule while he was away. He approached the bishops and said he would take the responsibility for England. The bishops, believing him to be a fair man, agreed, but little did they know that he was going to do everything in his power to take over the throne from his brother permanently.

Under John's rule the Saxons started to suffer. John favoured the Normans, believing them to be the more powerful force, and in an effort to gain their support he started to give them land. Unfortunately, he did not have any land of his own and so he stole from the Saxons, making them homeless and improverished. It was a time of great unrest and the nation soon fell under civil war as greedy nobles fought among themselves.

Robert of Huntingdon was one Saxon noble who

remained untouched by the greed of Prince John. He had one son, Robert, who became better known as Robin. He was tall, strong, handsome and a wonderful archer – and he was brave, fearless and hated what was happening to his beloved England and people. Robin's father had one serious enemy, Prince John, who was determined to kill the earl and take all his goods and land. One day, Robert was taken by surprise and John's soldiers attacked, burning his house to the ground, taking everything that belonged to him, and eventually killing him. Robin, being such a brilliant archer, managed to defend himself and fled to the great forest of Sherwood. It was here that he made the oath:

I swear to God and the King,
To help the weak and fight the strong,
To take from the rich and give to the poor,
So God will help me with His power.

HIS BAND OF MERRY MEN

Robin soon realized that he was not the only one to take refuge in Sherwood forest. Others, who had been driven from their homes by the evil John had gone to live there, and before long Robin started to make plans to get his revenge on those people that had caused such injustice. The people listened and supported Robin, and soon they formed a band of people who became known as the 'Merry Men'. The most remembered of his band of men were Friar Tuck, Will

Scarlet, Maid Marian, Much and Richard at the Lee. Robin was no longer known as Robin of Huntingdon, his followers called him Robin of Sherwood. It is believed that he obtained the surname 'Hood' by the green hooded cloaks that he and his men wore.

His group of followers soon forgot that Robin was a noble earl and treated him as an equal. One of his greatest friends was a man who was to become known as Little John (because of his great height), but ironically when they first met they fought each other.

Winter had been a boring time for Robin and his band of men. Nothing much had happened and apart from a few people passing their camp on horseback they saw no one. They lived in caves and spent most of their time making bows and arrows, boots and other items of clothing. One sunny, bright morning, Robin became restless and wandered off into the forest in search of an adventure. As he got deeper into the forest he came to a wide river that was swollen from the winter rains. The only way across was by a narrow, rickety bridge, which would only allow one person to cross at a time. As Robin started to cross the bridge, he noticed an exceptionally tall man crossing from the other side. Robin called to the stranger and told him to wait until he had got to the other side before crossing, but the stranger replied that he had as much right as the other did to use the bridge. This made Robin angry and he drew an arrow out of his quiver and said that he would shoot if the man did not get off the bridge. The stranger did not move and told Robin that if he dared to shoot, he would beat him until he was black and blue. He called Robin a coward as it was unfair to shoot a man who was only armed with a stick. Robin, who hated to be called a coward, stepped off the bridge, threw his bow and arrows onto the bank and cut himself a thick stick of oak.

Robin, who always loved a good fight, got back on the bridge and approached his opponent. It was difficult to fight on the ramshackle old bridge because it swayed from side to side and with every strike they made, the bridge threatened to crumble into the water below. They continued to hit each other, the blows coming fast and furious, until the stranger could stand it no more and hit Robin with one almighty blow, sending him backwards into the river. Robin disappeared under the water and for a moment the stranger was tempted to dive in after him as he thought he had drowned his opponent. The stranger called after Robin to see if he was alright and to his surprise he saw him climbing out further down the river. The current was very strong and Robin had to grab hold of an overhanging branch to haul himself out. The stranger was impressed by his bravery and said he had not met anyone for a long time who was so adept at fighting with a stick. The couple introduced themselves and ended up shaking hands.

Next, Robin put a bugle to his mouth and blew so that the sound resonated through the forest. Before long Robin and the stranger were surrounded by a band of men, dressed in green, all carrying bows and arrows. At first Robin's men were angry with the stranger who had dared to fight with their leader. But soon the men were all laughing when Little John, as he was to become known, found out that he had actually fought with the famous Robin Hood of Sherwood Forest. They asked if he would like to join their band for dinner.

Back at the camp, Robin soon learned that Little John was not only a fine fighter, but he was also quick-witted and wise. Robin asked him if he would like to become a permanent member of his 'Merry Men'. John was delighted and from that day he always stayed with Robin and the two men became great friends.

ALLAN-A-DALE

Robin was out as usual looking for an adventure when he came across a jovial knight. He was dressed in scarlet satin, wore a hat with feathers and was happily humming a tune. Robin wondered who the knight could be but on that occasion didn't stop to speak to him as he was on more important business.

The following day Little John and Much met the same knight. It was difficult to believe that it was the same man as on this occasion as he was dressed in grey and walked slowly with his head hung low. So intent was the knight at looking at the ground, that he didn't notice Little John and Much until the last minute and was unable to draw his bow and arrow. The two men grabbed the knight by the arms and led him, struggling, back to Robin Hood, who was sitting beneath a large oak tree.

Robin, who was always polite, bowed and asked the

knight if he had any money to spare for his band of men. But the knight looked at Robin with solemn eyes and told him that he was poor apart from the wedding band that he had kept for seven years. Robin felt sorry for him and asked him why he was so sad. The knight replied that his name was Allan-a-Dale. He told Robin that he had fallen in love with a beautiful woman seven years ago. She loved him dearly but her father was angry when he learned they wanted to marry. He told them that they were both too young and anyway they had no money. He said that if they were prepared to wait seven years and a day then he would allow them to become betrothed.

The knight continued his story and explained that yesterday should have been their wedding day, but when he went to claim his bride her father told him that he was not fit to marry his daughter. The father also told the knight that his daughter was to be married the next day to an old knight and, although he was ugly, he had a large amount of wealth. Robin was angry that the girl's father should go back on a promise and said that he was prepared to help the knight.

And what wilt thou give to me, said Robin Hood,
In ready gold or fee,
To help thee to thy true love again,
Abnd deliver her unto thee?

Once again the knight looked forlorn, as he told Robin that he had nothing to give. He had no money, he was untrained in the art of the bow and arrow and all he could offer was to sing and play the harp. Robin laughed, patted the young knight on the back and told him that tomorrow would be his wedding day. Robin asked the knight how far it was to the church where the wedding was to take place, and he replied at it was at Dale Abbey, which was only about 8 km (5 miles) away.

Robin rose early the next morning and dressing himself as an old harp player, told Little John to follow a little later with 24 of their men, who were to be all dressed in green. They were to bring with them Friar Tuck and Allan-a-Dale.

When Robin arrived at the door of the abbey, the first person he met was the Bishop of Hereford dressed in his finest robes, ready to perform the marriage ceremony of Lady Christabel and the old knight. When the bishop asked Robin what he was doing there, Robin replied that he had heard there was to be a wedding and he would like to sing a song, but he would first like to meet the happy couple.

Robin wait in the abbey and sat behind a large pillar, not far from the altar. Soon the wedding guests started to arrive in all their regalia, and he could hear their whisperings saying that it was so sad that such a young and pretty girl had to marry an old and ugly knight. One said that apparently she was in love with another man and they couldn't understand why he didn't just come and carry her off. Robin was pleased to hear this because it meant that the people felt sorry for Christabel and did not agree with what her father was making her do. A hush fell over the abbey as the bridegroom arrived. He certainly was as old and ugly as Allan-a-Dale had described him, and nothing could be heard except the noise of his cane hitting the stone floor as he hobbled up the aisle.

There were gasps of admiration as everyone turned to look at the stunning bride. She was very beautiful and walked with slow, heavy paces on the arm of her father. She was dressed in a beautiful, white satin dress but her face was sad and pale. She was followed up the aisle by choir boys singing the sweetest wedding song.

As the bishop opened his book to start the wedding vows, Robin sprang from behind the pillar and stood beside the bride. He told the bishop that he must stop the wedding for it was not right that the beautiful young Christabel should be forced to marry someone she did not love. The bishop asked who he was and what authority he had to order the wedding not to take place.

Robin threw off his disguise and cried 'I am Robin Hood,' and put his bugle to his mouth. Everyone tried to move forward to get a look at the man about whom they had heard so much.

Then there was a great commotion as 24 men, all dressed in green, came running into the abbey. The first man to reach Christabel was Allan-a-Dale himself. Robin said to the congregation that it was a pity not to have a wedding as everyone was dressed in their finery and turned to Christabel and asked her to choose a bridegroom out of his band of men.

Her face, which was once so pale, immediately lit up and colour returned to her cheeks. She slowly raised her eyes and looked at Allan-a-Dale, slipping her hand daintily inside his. Everyone was delighted and Robin ordered that the bishop continue with the wedding vows.

But the bishop declined to marry the couple, as he said it was the law that everyone must be asked in church three times before they are allowed to be married. 'In that case,' said Robin, 'we must get someone else to marry them.' Friar Tuck came forward and asked if he could borrow the bishop's fine robes. It took the congregation quite a while to stop laughing as the sight of the fat, jolly friar who stepped up to take over the ceremony.

The wedding was talked about for many years and the people attended said that it was the happiest bride they had ever seen.

ROBIN HOOD AND THE BUTCHER

One of Robin Hood's greatest enemies was the Sheriff of Nottingham, who would have done anything to have Robin killed. The sheriff was a wicked man who treated the Saxons with contempt, taking away their lands, stealing their money and leaving them with nothing. He would even resort to cutting off their fingers or ears as a form of punishment. Those who had been mistreated by the sheriff generally ran into Sherwood Forest in search of Robin, who would readily give them shelter and food. Sometimes they would return home, but more often than not they would stay in the forest and join Robin's band of men.

The sheriff was aware that Robin helped these people, which made him dislike him even more and he was always overjoyed if he managed to catch one of Robin's men. However, no matter how hard he tried, he could not catch Robin, even though he dared to go into Nottingham on many occasions. The sheriff was far too much of a coward to go into the forest himself, realizing that his men were no match to Robin's band of rebels. Robin's men fought hard because they loved their leader, unlike the sheriff's men who only fought because they were scared of what he might do to them.

On one occasion Robin met a butcher who was riding through the forest towards Nottingham market. He carried his meat in two panniers on either side of his sturdy grey pony. The roads were nothing more than rough tracks and everything had to be carried on horseback, as the wheels of a cart would simply have stuck in the mud.

Robin stepped out from behind a tree and stood in front of the butcher's pony. He asked the man what he was carrying in his panniers, to which the butcher replied, 'Fine prime beef and mutton for Nottingham market. Do you want to buy some?'

Robin told him that he would like to buy all the meat and the pony as well, as he would like to see what sort of butcher he would make if he went to the market. The butcher agreed, and after exchanging clothes, Robin mounted the pony and headed off to sell his meat. The butcher was proud to be seen in Robin Hood's suit of Lincoln green and felt grand.

When Robin arrived in Nottingham the town was busy with market stalls and people bustling about everywhere. He found it difficult to ride his pony through the crowds, but he managed to get to the corner where the butchers had their stalls. Robin laid out his meat and starting calling to the crowds to come and buy, announcing that his was the cheapest meat on the market. Not knowing anything about the price of meat, Robin was selling his prime beef at only tuppence a pound, while it generally went for around tenpence. As soon as the crowds heard that someone was selling their meat so cheaply, they gathered around his stall eager to buy as much as they could. All the other butchers stood idle until Robin had no more meat to sell, talking angrily about the stranger who had invaded their pitch. They knew it was no good to just stand their moaning, so they went over to the new butcher and asked him if he would like to join them for a meal with the Sheriff of Nottingham at the town hall.

Robin readily agreed, and as he walked along with the other traders they started to ask him questions to see if they could find out who he was. Robin, however, managed to avoid answering their questions directly, and by the time they had arrived at the town hall they really were none the wiser.

The Sheriff of Nottingham had a house in close proximity to the town hall, and as their meal was not quite ready, the butchers went to greet the sheriff's wife. She talked happily with the traders and showed a lot of interest in the new man who was able to sell his meat at such an inexpensive price. Robin was handsome and polite and the sheriff's wife was quite disappointed when the butchers were called away for their meal. She said she hoped she would see him again soon, and Robin bowed low and thanked her for her kindness.

Round the dinner table the sheriff sat at one end, while Robin, as the newest member, had the place of honour on his right-hand side. The dinner turned out to be rather boring because, other than Robin, the remainder of the butchers were quiet and sulky as they had done no trade that morning. Robin smiled to himself, because if the sheriff knew that it was Robin Hood who he had made his guest of honour he would have had him clapped into chains and thrown into the darkest dungeon he could find.

Robin's joviality eventually rubbed off on the party of butchers and before long they were all laughing merrily and joining in. Only the sheriff of Nottingham remained grumpy, as he tried to work out how he could buy the meat of this ignorant butcher and make a lot of money for himself.

He asked Robin if he had any cattle for sale, and nearly jumped for joy when Robin told him he had a large amount of fertile farmland and good fat stock. The sheriff was an exceptionally greedy man and started to rub his hands together in glee when he realized how easy it would be to fool this butcher.

Robin told the sheriff that he would be starting for home in the morning and that he would be more than happy for him to accompany him back to his land. The sheriff said he would be delighted and made Robin promise that he wouldn't sell his stock to any other traders. Robin laughed and said that he would not go back on his word.

When the sheriff arrived home that night he took gold from his from counting house and placed 300 pounds in a money bag, which he put under his pillow. He tried to sleep that night but he was far too excited at the prospect of making so much money.

The sun shone brightly the next morning and Robin and the sheriff rode out of the city chatting quite happily. Before long the sheriff realized that they were on the road that headed into Sherwood Forest and he started to feel edgy. The sheriff told Robin of a band of rebels that lived in the forest that might jump out and rob them and that they were led by a man named Robin Hood. Robin laughed, and told the sheriff not to worry as he doubted very much that they would be bothered by the band of rebels.

By chance Robin spotted a large herd of good fat deer deep in the forest and pointed them out to the sheriff. He asked him what he thought of his horned beasts, to which the sheriff replied in a shaky voice that he thought he should return to Nottingham.

Robin, who feigned surprise, asked if he wanted to leave without buying his fine herd of deer, especially as he had come this far and had the money ready. When Robin mentioned the word money, the sheriff turned pale and told him that he had no money in his saddle bag, only pebbles. Robin laughed and put his horn to his mouth and gave three blasts. Within minutes Little

John and his band of merry men arrived on the path in front of them.

'Good morning, Little John,' said Robin.

'Good morning, Master Robin,' he replied, 'What orders have you for today?'

Robin said he hoped that they had something nice for dinner as he had bought an honoured guest to dine with them. Little John replied that the cooks were busy but they would never have expected such a distinguished guest as the Sheriff of Nottingham. Little John bowed in front of the sheriff and said that he hoped he intended to pay honestly for his meal.

The sheriff was visibly shaking when he realized he had been fooled by the infamous Robin Hood. If only he had known the day before he would have had him arrested and by now he would be safe behind bars.

The men escorted the sheriff into their camp and they all sat down to an exceptionally fine dinner. The sheriff gradually started to relax thinking that perhaps they would not treat him too badly after all.

When the meal was over Robin told the sheriff that he now had to pay for his meal. The sheriff started to panic at the thought of losing his precious money, and he pleaded that he had no money with him and he was little better than a pauper. Little John asked him what he had in his saddle bags, to which the sheriff replied, 'Only pebbles, nothing but pebbles, I told you before.' By now the sheriff was really frightened and Robin told Little John to search the saddle bags. Little John did as he was told and emptied the contents onto the ground, counting out 300 pounds in gold coins.

Robin turned and spoke sternly to the sheriff. He told him that he would keep all of the money and divide it out among his men, as it was not half as much as he had already stolen from his people. He said that the sheriff had done so many evil things that he ought to be hanged, but as his wife had been so kind to him yesterday, Robin said he was prepared to let him go. He warned the sheriff that if he didn't start to change his ways, he wouldn't be so lenient the next time they met.

Robin laughed as he watched the ashen sheriff climb on board his dapple grey pony, slapping the sheriff's mount on the rump as it trotted off towards home.

ROBIN HOOD AND THE MONK

It was Whitsuntide and Sherwood Forest was quiet and bright on a May morning. Robin was sullen as he had not been to church for more than a fortnight. He told his men that he needed to go into Nottingham city to make peace with God. Little John agreed to accompany him, but neither heeded the warning of the other men saying that they should take some backup if they were going into the city.

On the way Robin and Little John started a shooting contest in which they bet each other for pennies. Unfortunately, it ended in a squabble and Little John turned round and let Robin go on alone.

Robin entered the church of St Mary not even bothering to put on any form of disguise. In full view of the congregation, he was instantly recognized and a buzz went round the church. A treacherous monk sent word to the sheriff that the famous Robin Hood was in town and called for the gates of the city to be closed.

Gathering a large number of soldiers around him, the sheriff headed for the church. Robin, who was in prayer and sorry for having argued with his closest friend, was taken by surprise. A fight broke out in which Robin killed 12 of the sheriff's men and wounded many more, until he broke his sword over the sheriff's head. Robin was taken captive and thrown into Nottingham jail.

News of Robin's incarceration quickly spread to his men back in Sherwood Forest. They were deeply concerned that the sheriff would have their leader hanged, but Little John told them to keep their faith and headed off towards the city in the company of Much, the Miller's son. On their way they came across the monk who had betrayed Robin, riding along with his page on the road to London.

The monk was on his way to London to tell the king that the sheriff had managed to capture Robin Hood. Little John and Much managed to trick the pair and, after killing them both, went on the mission to London themselves. The king was delighted with the news and gave the pair a generous award. He also issued them with a warrant and sent them back to Nottingham to collect Robin Hood and bring him back to London unharmed.

When Little John and Much arrived in Nottingham they found the city gates were locked and the whole place was swarming with guards who had been ordered to protect the sheriff's special prisoner. When Little John produced the warrant they were granted immediate entrance into the city.

The pair went straight to the Sheriff of Nottingham and showed him the warrant containing the king's seal. The sheriff was overwhelmed that the king was so pleased with him and drank himself into a deep sleep. With the sheriff asleep, Little John and Much were able to gain access to the cells without any hindrance and tricked the guard into opening the door. Robin was delighted to see his two friends. He was armed with a new sword, and they managed to fight their way out of the sheriff's quarters and fled back into the shelter of the forest.

When the sheriff woke the next morning and found the jailer and several of his men dead, he ordered an immediate search of the streets, ordering his men to leave no stone unturned until the fugitives were caught. But it was far too late – Robin, Little John and Much were already safely back in Sherwood Forest.

The king, realizing that Little John had made fools of them all, did not punish the Sheriff of Nottingham. Meanwhile, back in the forest Robin and Little John made up their differences and waited, in anticipation, for their next adventure.

ROBIN HOOD AND MAID MARIAN

Before Robin came to live in Sherwood Forest he often used to go hunting, shooting wild animals. The only animal that was forbidden was the deer, which belonged to the king, and no one was allowed to hunt or kill the sacred animal.

On one of his hunting expeditions Robin met a beautiful lady who was dressed completely in green velvet. Robin was dumbstruck, he had never seen anyone so lovely. She was graceful, with shiny, black hair and beautiful skin, and at her side hung a quiver of arrows. Robin stood for ages watching the lady shooting and felt that he had fallen in love with her right from the first moment he saw her.

Unable to get her out of his thoughts, Robin started to ask questions and found out that her name was Marian. He also found out that she was the daughter of the Earl of Fitzwalter, and that the family had recently come to live in a castle not far from where Robin himself lived.

The next time Robin met Marian in the forest he started to talk to her and the pair became good friends. They met frequently and hunted together all the time. Robin soon asked Marian if she would marry him so that they never need to be parted again. Marian was overjoyed at the prospect of having Robin as her husband and went home to tell her father.

Unfortunately, misfortune befell the couple because while they were in the middle of making their wedding plans, Robin's father was killed and Robin was left with nothing. He wrote her a sad letter saying that he had nothing to offer her now, and that he couldn't expect a beautiful lady like herself to come and live in a cave in Sherwood forest. He told her he would love her always but it would be better if they did not meet again.

Marian cried all day when she read the letter and thought that her heart might break in two. She was sad and lonely and to her it seemed as though the sun had forgotten to shine. At last she could bear it no longer, and she decided to go into Sherwood Forest and search for Robin, hoping that it would take the pain away if she saw him again.

Marian knew that it would not be safe for a woman to travel through the forest on her own, so she decided to disguise herself as a knight and dressed herself in full armour. She wore a steel helmet with a white feather crest and covered her face with a visor.

Robin, who also loved to wear disguises, had gone out in search of adventure dressed as a Norman knight. Needless to say, despite the size of the forest, the two 'knights' met and Robin stopped Marian and in a deep and scary voice said, 'Stop, Sir knight of the white feather. No one passes through the forest without leave from me.'

Marian, not recognizing his voice and unable to see his face through the visor, was scared and tried hard to stop her legs from shaking. Thinking he was a Norman knight, Marian drew her sword and stood prepared to fight.

Robin stood his ground and said that the knight's mission must be one of evil if he wasn't prepared to speak, and the fight began. Marian was adept at using a sword and the fight lasted for more than an hour. Robin wounded her in the arm, but was surprised how well the slender knight fought. Marian started to grow tired and weak and Robin felt rather sorry for the brave young knight. Robin, who forgot he was posing as a bold Norman knight, spoke in his normal voice. When Marian heard his voice, she dropped her sword with a cry of delight and ran towards him. Lifting her visor he saw that it was the woman he loved and regretted deeply that he had hurt her. They both laughed, cried and would not let go for fear of losing one another once again.

Robin eventually led Marian to a clean brook where he bathed her wounds and she explained to him how sad she had been since he went away. He told her how he didn't know how to live in the forest without her and eventually they agreed that she would stay and become one of his merry band of men.

As they walked along arm in arm, Robin and Marian met Little John who was shocked to see his leader merrily chatting with a strange, young knight. He told Little John that this was his Maid Marian who he thought he had lost forever.

Taking Marian back to the camp, Robin sent her to one of the caves where they had a store of fine dresses. Then he blew his horn and summoned all his men under the Trysting Tree. It was here that Robin pronounced Marian as his queen and all the men knelt and kissed her hand, vowing to serve her as a queen as they served Robin, their appointed 'king'.

THE SILVER ARROW

Time and time again the Sheriff of Nottingham tried to set traps to catch Robin Hood, but each time he failed.

With every failure he grew more and more angry until eventually his need for vengeance took over his life. The sheriff decided that he would go to the king and ask him for more soldiers so that he could kill Robin and his band of thieves.

Taking many soldiers and servants, the sheriff headed off on the arduous journey to London. He was exhausted when they completed their journey and, after resting for a while, the sheriff dressed in his finest clothes and set off for the palace.

The king listened intently while the sheriff told of how Robin and his rebels stole from the rich Norman nobles, helped the impoverished Saxons and, most importantly, hunted the king's deer. The king was angry and chastised the sheriff for not making his people uphold the law. He told him to return to Nottingham and that, when the king next visited the city, if he found that law and order had not been restored, he would have the sheriff replaced.

The sheriff was downhearted all the way home and kept trying to devise a plan in which he might be able to get Robin under his power. At last a thought came into his head that he felt certain would work. He decided he would have a magnificent silver arrow made with a golden head and offer it as a prize to the man who could shoot the best.

Robin Hood was reportedly the best archer in the whole of England. He could shoot further and straighter than any other and the sheriff felt sure that he would be unable to resist the challenge. He knew that Robin and his men would hear about the contest and that they would try to win the valuable prize. He planned to have all his soldiers ready so that when they arrived, Robin and his men would all be seized. Everything was set, the arrow was made, the date was set and the soldiers were all in their positions.

Back in Sherwood Forest there was a brave new member of the 'Merry Men' by the name of David of Doncaster. His sister lived in Nottingham and worked as a servant at the sheriff's house. David often used to go in disguise to visit his sister, but on one occasion she rushed out to meet him and told him of the sheriff's plan to kill Robin and his men.

David hastily returned to the forest to warn Robin of the sheriff's plan. However, when he got back to the camp he found out that the news had already reached Robin of the shooting competion. The men were gathered together and talking excitedly about the prize, already preparing their bows and arrows for their trip to Nottingham.

David told Robin about what the sheriff had planned and that it was all a trap. But Robin, who rarely listened to any warnings, told David that he was a coward and that if he wasn't brave enough to enter the competition, then he should stay at home with the women. David was hurt and turned away. Robin realized that he had been harsh on his latest recruit and called him back and apologized. He then asked David to tell him everything that he knew as it would never do if they all walked straight into the sheriff's trap.

They discussed what would be their best plan of action as none of the men wished to miss their chance of claiming the silver arrow. In the end they decided that they would go to Nottingham but they would all be dressed in different coloured disguises.

They spent the next few hours deciding what to wear, and realizing that it would not be safe to all travel together, they worked out who would travel with who. Robin invited David to travel with him and so early on the Tuesday morning in groups of twos and threes, Robin and his band of merry men set off for Nottingham. They all travelled by different routes so as not to cause suspicion and when they arrived at the city it was easy to get lost among the large crowds that had gathered. The sheriff had announced that the day of the competition would be a holiday, so everyone was there regardless of age or position. The sheriff kept a close watch from a window in his house for the famous Lincoln green, but he was bitterly disappointed when he didn't spot one of Robin's men.

The man in charge of the competition was called the Master of the Lists, and he announced to the crowd that it was time for the competition to begin. The sheriff looked down the list of 800 competitors and noticed that neither Robin Hood's name, nor indeed any of his men's, were written down. He told the Master of the Lists to wait a little longer as he felt sure they would not be able to resist the competition. The crowd started to grow restless and soon the Master of the Lists said they could wait no longer.

The match took place on a large open plain, at the end of which were set up 50 targets. The targets were all painted with different coloured circles, the centre white, then a red, then a black and finally a yellow. The archers stood at the opposite end of the plain, from where they had to shoot an arrow as close as possible to the centre of the target.

It was all exciting and the tension mounted as more and more archers started to hit the centre target. Anyone who missed the target altogether was eliminated from the competition and Robin and his men shot superbly. Each time Robin fired his arrow it went straight into the centre of the white circle.

Just after Robin had fired an arrow he found he was standing close to the sheriff and his wife. He overheard them talking and felt angry to think that the sheriff believed that he and his men were frightened to come into Nottingham. He longed to tell the sheriff then and there exactly who he was, but he knew that it would be foolish and made him even more determined to win the silver arrow prize.

The competition came to end and the man dressed all in red was the outright winner – of course it was Robin Hood. The sheriff's wife presented him with the prize and Robin thanked her politely, just as he always did when he was around a lady.

Robin and his men returned to Sherwood Forest just the way they had come, in small parties and all by different roads. No one had suspected who they were and least of all the Sheriff of Nottingham.

Back at home, however, the sheriff's wife was commenting on the handsome young man who had won the competition, and how he looked like the young butcher with whom they had once dined. The sheriff looked aghast, but did not dare tell his wife that the young butcher was in fact the famous Robin Hood.

Back in Sherwood Forest, Robin and his men celebrated in fine form and all sat down to a fine supper. As they passed the magnificent silver arrow around, Robin said it was a shame that he couldn't tell the sheriff that not only had they attended his competition but that Robin himself had won the prize.

Little John suggested that Robin write a letter to the Sheriff of Nottingham telling him that he had won the coveted silver arrow. So Robin wrote an arrogant letter to the sheriff and gave it to Little John, who rode to the outskirts of Nottingham and shot it into the city on the end of an arrow.

ROBIN HOOD AND KING RICHARD

When Richard the Lionheart returned to England from Palestine he was dismayed to find England in such a sorry state. His brother, John, had treated the Saxons badly and had committed many cruel and unjust acts, so the people were extremely happy when the king returned. He started trying to put right all the wrongdoings of his brother and on hearing about Robin Hood decided to ride to Nottingham himself to learn the truth about the man living in Sherwood Forest.

Nottingham greeted their king with open arms and there were many balls and parties held in his honour. Richard would often go into Sherwood Forest to hunt but he never met the one person he had heard so much about. He heard stories of how Robin Hood and his men would always stop abbots and knights and make them pay a toll for passing through the forest, but however hard he tried, King Richard was never stopped. Little did he know that Robin saw the king on many occasions, but he made his men hide because he thought he would be angry with them for killing his deer. He didn't think that the king would approve of them stealing from the Norman nobles and priests and so for that reason they made sure they stayed out of his way.

Robin and his men thought highly of King Richard and would never dream of stopping him or indeed of asking him for money. Robin told his men that they should follow the king, and that if he went to any dangerous parts of the forest they should stay close by in case he got into any trouble.

One day the Bishop of Hereford heard King Richard complaining that he had never met Robin Hood. The bishop told the king that if he were a bishop, he would probably meet Robin more often than he cared to. The king laughed but said nothing. However, the next day he, and 12 of his nobles, disguised themselves as monks and rode once more into the forest.

It wasn't long before they met Robin leading a group of his men ready to attack any rich knight or bishop who passed their way. Robin mistook the tall, handsome king as an abbot, and knowing that abbots usually had more money, Robin took the king's horse by the head and demanded money. The king replied that they were messengers from the king and that he had demanded to see Robin, and as proof he was wearing a ring bearing the king's seal.

Robin looked closely at the ring and recognizing it as the king's knew that he was certainly a messenger from the king himself. Robin immediately took off his hat and bowed before the messenger and said, 'God bless the King.'

The king replied that he was a traitor as he was quite prepared to rob them of their money. Robin in his defence told him that he only robbed the rich monks and abbots because they stole from the poor. He said they should show a good example to the Saxons, but instead they lived wicked lives and he thought they ought to be punished. He added that if they had acted correctly and ruled England well while King Richard was away, then there would not be so many people living as paupers in the forest. Robin added, that as messengers to the king they were welcome to everything they owned and that they must come and dine with them tonight.

Cautious as to what kind of meal they could possibly receive that had been cooked in the forest, at first the king hesitated. However, he was determined to find out more about this legendary man and accepted the offer. Robin led the king and his men back to their encampment in the trees.

The group arrived at a big open space and the king noticed that a table had been laid for a large number of people. It resembled an enormous picnic with everything laid out on the grass. Robin and his men tied up their horses and told the men where to sit. Several page boys ran up to the king and his men with bowls of clean water so that they might wash their hands.

The king was shocked to find how civilized it was and how comfortable their life in the forest really was.

The king was even more astonished when every one of Robin's men bowed in front of him in reverence and he thought to himself that these men honour their leader as if he were a king.

Then they all sat down and Friar Tuck said grace before they all tucked into a fine banquet. The king swore he had never eaten better as he tucked into venison, fowl and fish straight out of the river.

When he had finished eating the king turned to Robin and asked why he hunted the king's deer if he was such a loyal supporter. Robin replied that he could not allow his fine men to starve and that if the king were here right now he would probably agree with him. The king laughed and said that it was a bold thing to do and although he had to agree that it was a resplendent feast, he doubted if the king would agree with him killing his deer.

Robin stood up and raised his cup full of ale and asked each one of his men to fill their cups and drink to the health of the king. As entertainment Robin and his men gave a brilliant display of archery.

The king then took Robin to one side and asked if the king pardoned him, would he be willing to leave the woods and serve as his subject. Robin didn't hesitate and said that he would be willing to serve King Richard of England with all of his heart. Robin's men all agreed, and the king said, 'Richard has need of good men and true such as you.'

Robin asked if the messengers would be prepared to

return to the king and ask for his forgiveness, at which the king felt he could no longer keep his secret. He flung off the monk's hood and revealed his face to Robin and his men.

At once Robin and his men bowed but the king ordered that they stand up again. 'I give you your pardon gladly. Stand up, my friend, I doubt if in all England I have more faithful followers than you and your men.'

There was much excitement in the camp as the men prepared to leave for the city. They arrived in Nottingham shouting and singing, and everyone came out of their houses to see what was going on. At first people shouted saying that Robin Hood had killed the king. Then they saw that it was the king himself who was in fact leading the throng of merry men through the town of Nottingham.

The only person who was sorry to see Robin Hood and his men arrive with the king was the sheriff. He couldn't believe that the person he hated most in the world had now been pardoned by the king himself.

Robin approached the sheriff and asked if they could be friends and even paid him back the 300 pounds that he had forced him to pay for his dinner in the forest. The sheriff, being a greedy man, was so delighted to get his money back that he almost forgave Robin for all the tricks he had played on him over the years.

The next day Robin and his men headed off for London for their new life with King Richard. However this spell wasn't to last for too long, because Richard was killed in a minor siege at the castle of Châlus-

Charbrol in Limousin, France, on March 26, 1199. The siege was an example of the uncontrollable rebellions of Aquitaine that Richard had contended with all his life. His death was bad news for Robin Hood because Richard was succeeded by his evil brother, John.

There was no love lost between John and Robin and so once again, Robin and his band of merry men had to flee back to the forests of Nottingham.

THE DEATH OF ROBIN HOOD

Robin Hood survived into old age and although his hair had greyed, his body remained upright and he remained as strong and brave as ever. Little John and Robin were hardly ever apart and loved each other dearly. Slowly Robin started to grow weaker and one day he sadly said to his friend Little John that he was no longer able to fire an arrow. Robin suggested that John took him to see his cousin, the Prioress of Kirkley Abbey, to see if she could cure him.

Together they set off to the abbey and, being in the height of winter, the roads were thick with snow. On the journey Robin became sick and was unable to stay upright on his horse, so Little John carried him on the last part of the road in his arms trudging through the deep snow.

It was Christmas Eve when they arrived at the abbey and the prioress greeted them both warmly. She was shocked to see how pale and frail Robin had grown and said that she must bleed him immediately. The ancient art of bloodletting was used to cure all ailments, whereby they made a small cut in the patient's arm and allowed the blood to flow for a few minutes into a cup.

Little John hadn't noticed the evil look on the face of the prioress as she bent over her cousin. Had he seen it, he would most certainly have taken Robin away again. As it was he left him quite happily in what he thought was the caring hands of his cousin. She asked Little John to carry Robin to a room on the south side of the abbey that overlooked Sherwood Forest. Little John gently carried Robin through cool passages until they reached a small room. The prioress said it would be nice and quiet here away from the other members of her household. Little John wanted to stay while she treated his friend, but she told him she needed perfect quiet and that he must wait in another room. Unhappily, John walked away from his friend and went out into the abbey garden. Despite the freezing cold he sat down under a tree where he could watch the window of the room where Robin was being treated.

Little did John realize that the prioress was an evil woman who had always hated her cousin. Despite the fact that Robin had always treated her well, she had always prayed that something horrible would happen to him. At last Robin was weak and she had him under her power. Her intentions were not to cure him but to kill him, and as soon as the prioress was alone with Robin she made a cut in his arm and allowed his blood to flow. When it was time to stop the flow of blood, instead of bandaging it tightly, she left it loose so that the blood continued to flow freely. Then she turned the key to his room and left Robin to die.

Robin was so tired from his long journey that he soon fell asleep. He slept for many hours and all the time his faithful friend sat patiently under the tree just watching the window and waiting.

When Robin eventually woke he found he was so weak he was unable to move any part of his body. He saw that the blood was still flowing from his arm and that if he didn't do something quickly he knew he would die. He tried to raise himself up to the height of the window but he did not have the strength in his arms. Then he realized he still had his bugle horn and he managed to raise it to his mouth and blow three very faint blasts.

On hearing the sound of the horn Little John jumped to his feet and ran as quickly as he could to the room where he was lying. Finding the door locked he put all his weight against it and managed to force his way into the room. Finding his friend and master close to death, Little John quickly bound his arm. Full of sadness and anger over the treatment he had received from the prioress, Little John asked one favour from Robin. He begged Robin to allow him to bring all of his men from Sherwood Forest to the abbey, kill the wicked prioress and to burn the abbey to the ground.

Robin said he could not grant his friend that wish as he had never hurt a woman in his life, and so Little John had to promise that he would not punish her for what she had done. Robin died in the arms of his loyal friend after shooting his final arrow out of the window of the abbey. At the time of his death the convent bells rang out for the Christmas Eve service.

The nation mourned when they learned of the death of the valiant Robin Hood. Little John and the band of merry men came together for the last time and buried their leader exactly where his last arrow fell, in the garden of Kirkley Abbey in Yorkshire.

They placed a stone over the top of the grave with the following inscription:

Here, underneath this stone,
Lies Robert, Earl of Huntingdon;
No archer ever was so good,
The people called him Robin Hood.
Such outlaws as he and his men
Will England never see again.

THE LEGEND LIVES ON

The adventures of Robin Hood have captivated by writers for centuries, dating back to the 14th century ballads. The most famous early writing is a 15th-century ballad series called A Gest of Robyn Hode. Since then many books, films and television series have elevated the lovable outlaw to a mythical status.

A number of prominent authors wrote about Robin Hood in the 18th and 19th centuries, including Sir Walter Scott and John Keats. The legend of Robin Hood became a popular inspiration for children's tales during the Victorian era, including a successful collection called *Robin Hood and Little John*; or, The

Merry Men of Sherwood Forest (1840) by Pierce Egan. The 20th century saw several movies, but perhaps the two most famous were *Robin Hood* (1922), a silent film starring Douglas Fairbanks, Sr, and T*he Adventures of Robin Hood* (1938), an action-adventure with Errol Flynn. More recently, Kevin Costner played the leading man in *Robin Hood: Prince of Thieves* (1991).

WILLIAM TELL

The national hero of Switzerland, William Tell, has become a symbol of political freedom and independence. He is viewed as a freedom fighter in the noblest of traditions.

William Tell was born in medieval Switzerland when tax rebellions led to the creation of the Everlasting League (1291–1315) and the eventual defeat of an empire. After the Swiss Empire fell, the country was divided by conflict, and powerful local dynasties such as the Zahringen, Kyburg and Habsburg started to fight over territory and taxes. The Habsburgs, who lived in a canton in the valley of the Rhine eventually became the most powerful leaders as they gained more and more wealth. They appointed themselves dukes of Austria and some were even elected to the position of emperor. Gradually the Habsburg family acquired the territories of Schwyz, Uri, Unterwalden and Lucerne, and on the death of the Habsburg ruler Count Rudolf II in 1232, these territories were divided between his two sons, Albert IV and Rudolf III.

The regions of Schwyz, Uri and Unterwalden had largely been unaffected by the new tax laws. However, in 1273 Albert IV's son, Rudolf, was elected German king and Holy Roman emperor, and he immediately used his new position to enforce a tax on Trans-Alpine trade. Rudolf had already been in control of most of the route from the Rhine to Schwyz and Unterwalden, but the opening of the St Gotthard Pass greatly increased the value of these areas. In an effort to take complete control of the tax of the three regions, particularly Uri, which was not yet under his regime, Rudolf appointed a new bailiff by the name of Hermann Gessler to enforce feudal and imperial authority over the Swiss people.

The proud mountain folk of Uri joined with their neighbours from Schwyz and Unterwalden in an effort to resist the Austrians' cruel oppression. Unprepared to bow to Gessler's authority, and when the new bailiff took his laws one step too far, the citizens knew it was time to rebel.

HAT ON A POLE

Gessler decided to raise a pole in centre of the square at Altdorf and, using his hat decorated with peacock feathers as a symbol of imperial power, he placed it on top of the pole. He ordered the citizens of Altdorf to bow before the hat every time they passed to show their respect for the government.

William Tell was a mountaineer who lived in a nearby village called Bürglen in the region of Uri. William was married to Hedwig, and they had two sons, William and Walter, who was the youngest. Tell was an expert archer and was determined to resist the domination by the Austrians. He arranged secret meetings of the local villagers, who had all sworn to stand by each other and fight for their freedom. Most were simple shepherds who didn't even own a bow and arrow, let alone know how to fight. Gradually, without trying to bring any attention to themselves, they built up a store of spears, swords, battle-axes and bows and arrows. They taught themselves how to fight, and eventually everything was ready – all they needed now was the signal to rebel.

William Tell and his youngest son Walter went into the village of Altorf one day to visit his father-in-law. Whether or not he had heard of Gessler's command to bow to the hat, or whether he chose to ignore the order is not really known, but Tell walked past the pole without bowing. Gessler was furious when he heard about it and, fearing that others would follow his lead, ordered that William Tell be arrested. On hearing that the man was an accomplished marksman Gessler decided to set Tell a challenge.

THE CHALLENGE

Gessler ordered Tell to shoot an apple off the top of his son's head. If he was successful they would both be freed, if he failed, both he and his son would be killed. Tell begged with Gessler not to make him do this as he was frightened that the boy might move, or his hand might tremble, and he would kill his son.

'Say no more,' Gessler replied. 'You must hit the

apple with your one arrow. If you fail, my soldiers shall kill the boy before your eyes.'

Two soldiers seized Walter and tied him to the trunk of a tree. The young Walter showed no fear and stood straight and quiet, trusting his father. Gessler rode up to the boy and bending down out of his saddle placed an apple on top of his head.

A crowd of people had gathered by this time, wondering what all the commotion was about. When they were told what Tell had to do, they grew quiet as they saw the look of horror on his face.

Gessler ordered that his soldiers clear a path and they pushed people aside, scattering them to left and right. The soldiers measured 100 paces and marked the spot. Gessler ordered Tell to stand on the mark, as it was from there that he had to shoot the apple.

Trying to keep a steady hand, Tell withdrew an arrow from his quiver and studied it carefully. Instead of placing the arrow in his bow he put it in his belt and then chose another. Again he examined it carefully and after a few minutes placed it in the bow.

The crowd gasped as William Tell took a step forward and raised his bow. His arm started to tremble, tears came into his eyes and the bow dropped from his hold. He knew he was unable to fire the arrow for fear of harming his son, all his courage and strength seemed to have deserted him.

The crowd stood silent, but a small voice spoke from beneath the large tree, 'Shoot, father, I am not afraid. You cannot miss.'

Once more Tell raised his bow as the crowd

watched and waited with heavy hearts. Tell released the arrow and it flew straight through the frosty air. One second later the silence was broken when the crowd started cheering. The apple lay on the floor cleanly pierced right through the middle.

Tell was unable to move as one man untied his son and another took the apple to Gessler. Gessler was furious and not at all impressed that he had managed to hit the apple without killing his son. Young Walter rushed up to his father crying that he knew he could do it, and pressed his head into his father's chest. Just as Tell was starting to realize that it was all over, the first arrow fell from his belt. Gessler, still on his horse, had been watching them carefully and he rode up to Tell asking him what was the meaning of the second arrow.

Tell told him that it was an archer's custom to always have a second arrow ready, but Gessler didn't believe his story. Tell did not answer and Gessler told him that if he told the truth he would spare his life.

Looking straight into Gessler's eyes, Tell replied that since he had promised him his life, he would tell him the truth. 'If that first arrow had struck my child, the second one was meant for you, and be sure I had not missed my mark a second time.'

Gessler was furious and his face grew red with rage. He told him that his bow and arrow would have little use where he was going and ordered his soldiers to arrest Tell once more. Gessler told Tell that he was sentencing him to life imprisonment in the dungeons of his castle at Küssnacht.

Tell's father-in-law, William Fürst, was in the crowd and boldly stepped out in front of Gessler. He told the bailiff that it was a law among the Swiss people that they could not be imprisoned outside of their own canton. He said that if he was taken outside of Uri, Gessler would be going against their ancient rights of freedom.

Gessler shouted at Fürst that they were here to obey his law not teach him theirs, and ordered his soldiers to take Tell to the boat waiting for them at a place called Fluelen.

Walter clung desperately to his father, sobbing uncontrollably. Tell was unable to hold his son as his hands had been tethered behind his back, so he told him gently not to cry and to go with his grandfather and tell his mother what had happened.

THE ESCAPE

The crowd followed behind as William Tell was led down to the boat. The soldiers pushed Tell roughly into Gessler's boat, where he was told to sit in the middle of several guards. His bow and arrows, which had been taken from him, were thrown on a bench next to the steersman. Gessler himself climbed on board and soon the boat was making its way across the blue waters of the lake.

The crowds stood watching for ages, realizing that the leader they loved and trusted had been taken away from them forever. What they didn't notice when the boat left the shore was just how dark the sky overhead had become. The Swiss were well aware just how fierce and quickly a storm could build up over the lakes. However, the Austrians were unaware just how dangerous the storms could be, and the wind got stronger and stronger. Soon the small boat was being tossed about wildly by the great waves, and the oarsmen, despite rowing with all their might, made no headway. The waves broke right over the top of the boat, filling it with water, and the risk of sinking was evermore present. The captain stood at the helm, pale with fear, helpless as he watched his boat start to break up.

Gessler, aware of the dangers, sat still and quiet wrapped in his mantle. One of Gessler's servants pleaded with him to untie William Tell, as he was the one person who understood the Swiss storms and could help get them out of trouble. Gessler was frightened that they might all lose their lives, so he agreed that his prisoner could be cut free. He told Tell that this did not mean he was a free man, and once they reached the shore he was still to be taken to the dungeons.

The rope which bound Tell's hands was cut and he took his place at the helm of the boat. Although the boat was still being tossed about by the force of the storm, Tell held the wheel steady while the oarsmen rowed with all their might, more confident in the hands of an experienced sailor.

Tell headed towards a part of the shore that he knew would afford him a place to escape. He cunningly manoeuvered the boat closer and closer and, quickly glancing around, he grabbed his bow and arrows, which lay beside him, and jumped for freedom.

As he leapt he managed to give the boat a backward push with his foot, sending it with its captors back out into the stormy waters. Tell landed on a flat area of rock and then ran off into the surrounding forest.

It had all happened so quickly that it took the men on the boat a couple of minutes to realize that Tell had actually managed to escape. As his prisoner vanished into the trees, Gessler stood up and shouted in anger. However, the little boat was being tossed about so badly by the storm, the oarsmen did not go near the shore again for fear of being broken to pieces on the rocks. As it was each one of the occupants of the boat expected to drown at any minute. Luck was on their side, however, and before long the storm died down and they were able to row safely to the shore of Schwytz.

REVENGE

As soon as they were on dry ground again, Gessler resumed his old confidence and demanded his horse. He rode off towards his castle with his heart full of hatred and swearing revenge on the man who had tricked him.

However, Gessler was not the only one who wanted revenge. William Tell hurried through the woods he knew so well determined to catch up with Gessler. The once peace-loving man, Tell was filled with anger for the man who had risked his son's life. He knew that there was only one thing he could do was to kill Guessler, not only for his own personal revenge but also to give his people a better life. Tell was certain that

Gessler would make his way back to his castle at Küssnacht, and there was only one road which led from the lake. Without stopping for either food or drink, Tell made his way through the woods until he arrived at a place called Hollow Way, where the road became narrow and the banks rose steeply to either side. It was here that he intended to wait for his arch enemy and free his people of this evil tyrant.

As he sat and waited many people passed along the road. One of them was a woman who stopped and spoke with Tell, explaining how Gessler had put her husband in jail, leaving her to wander about begging with her children. This story made Tell even more angry, and he knew in his heart that the deed he was about to carry out was fair and just.

Tell sat for many hours before he heard the distant sound of marching feet on the road. As the sound grew nearer he realized it couldn't possibly be Gessler and his soldiers, for there was a lot of laughter and music. It turned out to be a wedding party, which temporarily took Tell's mind of what he was intending to do.

As the sun was starting to set, Tell heard the sound of horses' hooves and a page dashed down the road shouting to everyone to make room for the governor. Tell soon heard the angry voice of Gessler as he spoke to his guards, 'I have been far too mild a ruler over these people. They grow too proud. But I will break their pride. Let them prate of freedom indeed. I will crush . . .' But he never finished his sentence because an arrow sped through the air and, with a groan, Gessler dropped dead. Wiliam Tell smiled and thought at least my second arrow found its mark!

Gessler's soldiers fell into immediate confusion and rushed to his aid, but it was too late because the arrow had gone straight through his heart. They wondered who would have dared shoot the bailiff, but their questions were soon answered when they heard a voice. They all turned round and saw William Tell standing boldly on the banks at the side of the road.

'Seize him,' one of the soldiers yelled and several of them scrambled up the bank after him. Tell, was too wise and knew the area well, and he sped off through the bushes and was nowhere to be found. The soldiers gave up the search as night fell, and returned to the road to take Gessler's body back to his castle at Küssnacht.

No one really grieved for Gessler because he had been a hard ruler and, wherever the Swiss heard the news, there was much rejoicing.

William Tell returned to his men in Uri and began to organize the uprising against the imperial control. After putting up with the encroachments and restrictions of the Habsburg emperor for so long, the men of Schwyz, Uri and Unterwalden were ready to fight back. and they formed the Everlasting League in August 1291.

THE REPUBLIC OF SWITZERLAND

On the death of Rudolf I in 1291, the three forest districts of Shwyz, Uri and Unterwalden started to campaign against the election of his Habsburg successor, Albert. The Everlasting League was formed in order to check any further encroachments and to do whatever they could to support anti-Habsburg candidates for the German crown.

On November 15, 1315, after many years of fighting, the Everlasting League experienced its first great military victory over the Habsburgs. Although the Habsburg forces outnumbered those of the three districts, Duke Leopold I's troops had to negotiate two mountain passes to get to the heart of Switzerland. Aware of the Duke's movements, the Swiss were able to block the Morgarten pass. The Swiss army, composed of only peasant infantry, hid on the slopes of the pass above the Imperial army. As soon as the Duke's men arrived in the pass the Swiss hurled rocks and tree trunks down upon them, and the majority of the Imperial troops were either killed or wounded. Duke Leopold himself was one of the few that managed to escape from the disastrous battle.

The impact of the battle was enormous. It was the first time that the Imperial army had been beaten by peasant troops, and it forced Duke Leopold to recognize the independence of the Forest Cantons. It marked the end of the supremacy of the feudal cavalry and it led to the beginning of the Republic of Switzerland.

THE WILLIAM TELL OVERTURE

The first written version of the legend of William Tell was in a 15th-century ballad. It later served as the basis for the famous Friedrich Schiller's *Wilhelm Tell* (1803), which was based on chronicles of the Swiss liberation movement. This became the inspiration for *Guillaume Tell* (William Tell), an opera by Gioacchino Rossini. The opera is in four acts and lasted approximately six hours. It was first performed at the Paris Opéra on August 3, 1829. Today, the opera itself is rarely performed, but it will always be remembered for its famous overture, which was used as the theme for the *Lone Ranger* television series.

There was a German-made film made in 1935 called *Legend of William Tell* in which Hans Marr plays the leading role. In 1958, Conrad Phillips played William Tell in a television series entitled *The Adventures of William Tell*, directed by Terry Bishop and Quentin Lawrence. In 1998, Kieren Hutchison played the part in another television series entitled *The Legend of William Tell* directed by Declan Eames and Geoff Husson. In 2006, a film called *The Legend of William Tell*, directed by Fred Olen Ray, outlined a story about a boy who must prove himself by defeating bullies and winning an archery contest.

Possibly the most well-known book about William Tell is *William Tell Told Again* by P. G. Wodehouse, which was first published in 1904. No matter how you remember William Tell, he will always live on as a real hero and a powerful freedom fighter.

THE PEASANTS' REVOLT

The Peasants' Revolt, which took place in 1381 in England, was a major event in the history of freedom fighters. The familiar names that are associated with the Peasants' Revolt, or Tyler's Rebellion as it is sometimes called, are Wat Tyler and John Ball, who was a Lollard priest. They both took prominent parts in the revolt, but little is known about their backgrounds.

The seeds of the revolt went a long way back in history, watered by the continuous oppression of the poor in both the towns and the countryside. Although the peasants were theoretically 'free' men, they were bound by feudal obligations or serfdom and were sick of the injustices they had had to endure for so many years. They were bound by law to work the land on which they lived to provide services and goods for the owners of the land. Under the feudal system they could not receive cash for their services, nor could they pay rent instead of working. If they were treated unfairly by their landlords, the law did not permit them to speak up against them in court, and if they left the land of their own free will, the law permitted that they could be hunted and imprisoned, as it was considered a crime. Seeing no way out of this form of bondage, the peasants knew that as they were unable to change the law they would need to revolt.

Over the centuries the conditions for the peasants became worse, while the nobles not only thrived but blatantly displayed their riches for all to see. The Hundred Years War, which was initiated by King Edward III, drained England of its wealth and its manpower, and as a result it was the lower classes who suffered the most. Added to this, the Black Death plagued England in 1348, and killed millions, which greatly reduced the labour force and led to unstable economic conditions. This led the English government to restrict wages in an attempt to control the rising costs that were being demanded by the remaining skilled labourers. To solve the situation the government introduced the Statute of Labourers, which was a vain attempt to set a maximum wage. It stated:

- No peasants could be paid more than the wages paid in 1346
- No lord or master should offer more wages than paid in 1346
- No peasants could leave the village to which they belonged

It imposed harsh penalties on those who remained idle, but the statute was poorly enforced and unsuccessful. Even though some peasants decided to ignore the statute, they knew that disobedience would lead to severe punishment.

Suffering from servitude, controlled wages and unfair taxes, the peasants found it harder and harder to get themselves out of the deep hole that was being dug for them by the corrupt government.

To make matters worse, when King Edward III died his crown was taken over by his young grandson, Richard. Not mature enough to take control of the country, Richard appointed John of Gaunt to be his spokesman. Things went from bad to worse when it was obvious that Gaunt was not in the least bit interested in the welfare of the workers. His aim was to fight and expand the empire. He needed money for his constant expeditions abroad, and this money was raised by harsher and more injurious taxes.

Society at that time was divided into three main segments – warriors, priests and peasants. The warrior class consisted of royalty, nobles and knights, who were wealthy enough to own their own horses and the weapons needed to go to war. The priests were divided into two classes, the officials and the lower clergy, who were roughly equivalent to the noble classes and the peasantry. The archbishop, bishops and abbots were equal to barons with great temporal power, while the poor parish priest was little better off than his peasant parishioners. The peasants were mostly bound by feudal law to their landlord. The merchant class and the urban industrial workers were midway between the nobles and the peasants and, although they were free, they were often at the mercy of their landlords, the abbots. So gradually, serfs, labourers and parish priests started to question what was happening to them.

POLL TAX

The revolt finally erupted when John of Gaunt imposed a new tax, the Poll (or head) Tax, the funds from which would be used to cover the expense of war. Unlike the normal taxes, this one would be paid by both peasants and landowners, and although it was only intended to be a one-off event, it was so successful it was repeated three times.

The first Poll Tax collected 4 pence from every adult over 14 years old. Then it was stayed at 4 pence per adult but was raised for the rich, and finally in 1380 was raised to 12 pence per adult.

The barons were in favour of the new tax system, especially if they were the tax collectors, as they were able to line their own pockets with some of the funds. It was hard on the peasants, however, especially as they were forced to pay in cash rather than goods, which they could not afford. By 1380 many of the peasants were hiding from the collectors to avoid payment, and soon the amount collected start to drop away.

JOHN BALL THE PRIEST

The Church was in a weak position following the Black Death, with many of its clergy now poorly educated, which lost them a great deal of respect. The Church was also the major landowner, and abbots and bishops alike sided with the barons against the peasants. The peasants felt betrayed, feeling that the Church should be an organization that should be there to help them rather than exploit them. John Ball was a rebellious priest who started to preach against the Church and the barons. He expounded the doctrines of a man named John Wycliffe (1320–84) who was a theologian and early proponent of reform in the Roman Catholic Church. Ball's preaching on equality and freedom landed him in prison on more than one occasion.

THE UPRISING

When John of Gaunt examined the Poll Tax returns for 1380, he was not happy about the amount of money that had been collection. The tax collectors were sent out once again with instructions this time to collect the full amount owing.

On May 30, 1381, one of these tax collectors, a man named Thomas Bampton, went to Fobbing in Essex and ordered the villagers of Fobbing, Stanford and Corningham to come and see him. The law-abiding citizens who turned up for the meeting were aghast when they learned that they would have to pay the hateful Poll Tax for a second time. On top of that the villagers were told that they would have to pay the taxes of the people who had failed to turn up. The peasants were up in arms and, not surprisingly, a riot ensued in which Bampton and his men were beaten and driven from Fobbing.

The government sent the Chief of Justice, Sir Robert Belknap, to try to calm down the situation, but he suffered the same fate as the others. Word soon spread throughout the county, and soon peasants from all over Essex banded together and started to turn on their landowners. They headed towards the manor houses, which they razed to the ground, subsequently destroying any records of taxes, duties and debts. They broke open prisons and castle dungeons, gathering more and more supporters everywhere they went.

By June 7 the revolt was widespread. The peasants living in the counties of Kent, Suffolk, Hertfordshire and Norfolk all joined together in attacking manor and religious houses alike.

At this point Wat Tyler appears to have been appointed as the leader of the revolt. Little is known of his past, but he possibly served as a soldier in France and showed remarkable skills in controlling the mobs of rebels.

On June 10 the Kent branch of the rebels, led by Tyler, marched on Canterbury and burst in during a High Mass service in the church. They demanded that the monks chose a new archbishop from one of their members, calling the current archbishop a traitor. They moved from the church and ransacked the castle and the archbishop's palace, until the mob had taken over total control of the city. Corrupt members of the government were attacked and landlords were forced to sign papers giving freedom and leases to their former serfs.

MARCH ON LONDON

John Ball and several other leaders urged the peasants to go to London to see the king to plea their case. It was the groups of rebels from Essex and Kent who decided to go to London, and by June 12 the Essex men were camped in some fields at Mile End which was just outside Aldgate. The next day the members from Kent caught up with them and arrived at Blackheath. Unaware that the rebels were coming, neither the city of London nor the king himself were prepared. Workers from London rose in support of the peasants and their demands, and they set about attacking political targets in the city. The king, who was only 14 at the time, was moved from Windsor to the Tower of London to offer him some protection. The mob burned down the Savoy Palace, which was the home of John of Gaunt, and set fire to the Treasury's Highbury Manor, destroying many legal records. They broke open Fleet Prison, killed many lawyers and foreign merchants, but they did little damage to the city of London itself on the orders of Wat Tyler.

Realizing that the mob were taking control, King Richard agreed to meet them the next day at Mile End. The rebels waited patiently and true to his word on June 14, King Richard, with a handful of lords and knights, met the Essex peasants at Mile End. The peasants pledged their allegiance to their king and handed him a petition demanding:

- that Poll Tax was abolished
- free pardons for all rebels
- charters would be given to the peasants laying down their rights and privileges
- all 'traitors' would be put to death

Richard agreed to the demands, but said that it

would have to be up to a royal court to decide whether a person was a traitor or not. Hoping this would appease the peasants and that they might now leave London, the king arranged for a group of clerks to start writing out the agreed charters.

However, the king was unaware that he had been outwitted by Wat Tyler, because while they had their meeting another band of peasants had entered the Tower of London. In the Tower they found three of the people they despised the most – the archbishop of Canterbury, Simon Sudbury, Sir Robert Hailes, the King's treasurer, and John Legge (the creator of the Poll Tax). They dragged the three men out onto Tower Hill and executed them. The group of rebels considered these men traitors and held them responsible for many of the injustices they had suffered for the past decade or so.

Having received their charters, many of the peasants at Mile End started to leave, believing that their demands had been met and that from now on life would be a lot easier. However, Wat Tyler and a hard core of the peasant rebels stayed behind. Tyler demanded another meeting with the king, saying that he had further demands. Once again the king agreed to meet them, this time at Smithfield, which was an open area within the city walls.

This time the rebels demanded:

- an end to all lordship beyond that of the king
- all the Church's estates be confiscated and divided up among the wider populace

• there were to be only bishops throughout the whole kingdom

As before the King Richard agreed to all the demands put before him.

THE DEATH OF WAT TYLER

The king, having done everything the peasants had asked, ordered the rebels to return to their homes. Tyler, who still refused to take orders from anyone of higher rank, sent for a jug of water to rinse out his mouth. This was considered to be an insolent act in front of a king, which angered the mayor of London. To exacerbate the situation, the king heard one of his valets, who was from Kent, say aloud that 'Wat Tyler was the greatest thief and robber in Kent.'

Wat Tyler did not take kindly to the insult and ordered one of his followers to behead the valet. The valet replied that whoever struck him, would be struck in return, and Tyler got ready to strike him with his dagger. William of Walworth, the Mayor of London, attempted to arrest Tyler, but Tyler was too quick for him and stabbed the mayor. Luckily, the major was wearing armour, so the dagger simply skidded off the surface. The mayor retaliated and gave Tyler a deep cut in the neck, followed by a severe blow to the head. During the scuffle a member of the king's household drew a sword and ran towards Tyler. He plunged his sword two or three times through the body of Tyler, and left him lying for dead on the ground.

The peasants, who had not seen what had happened, prepared their bows and arrows to attack the king and his men. The king managed to convince them that it had been an accident, and he asked them to ride with him to the field of St John of Clerkenwell.

In the meantime the mayor had ridden hastily back to London and commanded everyone in charge to come to the aid of the king, who was in trouble. Then he returned to Smithfield to make sure that Wat Tyler was dead, but when he arrived his body was nowhere to be seen. He asked what had become of the traitor and was told that he had been carried by a group of his followers to a hospital for the poor near St Bartholomews. The mayor rode to the hospital and had the severely injured Tyler taken back to Smithfield, where he cut off his head. He placed Tyler's head on the top of a pole and carried it with him to meet the king at Clerkenwell.

When the king arrived at Clerkenwell he was joined by a group of armed men, and they managed to keep the peasants confined. When the peasants saw the mayor riding up with their leader's head impaled on a stake, they realized that they had been led into a trap, and pleaded to the king for pardon.

The king sat proud on his horse and proclaimed that all the previous promises he had made were now null and void and said, 'Serfs you have been and are, you shall remain in bondage, not such as you have hitherto been subjected to, but comparable viler.'

He told them to return home peacefully, and in effect the London revolt was over. Although there were pockets of continued resistance in places, the renewed strength of the nobles proved to be too strong. Many of the leaders of the revolt, including John Ball, were executed, but significantly there were no mass reprisals.

AFTERMATH OF THE REVOLT

On the surface, the rebellion appeared to have been a failure and for a while the position of the serfs and labourers was made worse. But on the positive side the 1381 Peasants' Revolt did make people more aware of their value and importance to the community. The actual abolition of serfdom eventually came about through the growth of towns, commerce and industry, and even if the rebels did not initially win their fight for freedom, they certainly didn't lose.

Landowners had certainly been unsettled by the scale of the revolt and started to rethink the conditions in which they expected their people to work. Eventually the parliament gave up trying to control the wages the landowners paid to their peasants. The much hated Poll Tax was never raised again and the lords started to treat their peasants with much more respect. All these things marked the breakdown of the feudal system, which was by this time becoming extremely outdated.

JOHN WYCLIFFE

John Wycliffe is probably best remembered for translating the Bible from Latin into English, making it accessible to people who would previously have not been able to understand the words of God. However, he was also a famous English theologian and reformer known as *The Morning Star of the Reformation*. Considered to be a man ahead of his time, Wycliffe strongly criticized the false teachings carried out in the Catholic Church. He formed a heretical group, known as the Lollards in the latter part of the 14th century, but intense persecution wiped out both his followers and his teachings. Hundreds of years later, the reforms, of which Wycliffe only dreamed, were resurrected by Martin Luther.

HIS EARLY LIFE

John Wycliffe was born c.1324 in Hipswell, Yorkshire, at a time when England was becoming recognized as an important nation. The English language had grown out of a mixture of old Saxon and Norman French and, by the time of Wycliffe's birth, the two races had merged into one and spoke one language.

The 14th century was a time when the papacy had a lot of power, and there were no real true preachings of the word of God. Most commoners had never even seen a Bible and possibly wouldn't have been capable of reading it anyway. Although portions of the Bible had been translated into English, most of it was in Latin, and the majority of the nobility possessed a copy that was written in French.

Many English people felt as though they were enslaved by the Church and that by giving donations they would be pardoned for their sins. For example, if a man died without leaving something to the Church, the Church automatically took over the person's estate. The Vatican itself was becoming exceptionally wealthy through enforced taxation, which grieved the English because they felt the money was going to armies with whom they were possibly at war.

Oxford University was becoming well established as an important academic centre and was considered by many as the leading University in Europe. Academic qualifications were thought very highly of and Wycliffe was respected for his tremendous ability to learn.

Wycliffe is believed to have attended Oxford University when he was around 13, and became a student at Merton College. At the time when Wycliffe started his studies, a professor by the name of Thomas Bradwardine was coming to the end of his career. The professor was a great believer in the true word of God and felt that others should follow his path. Bradwardine taught that it was God and only God that could save men from their sins, and through him the people of England and Europe started to question their beliefs. Wycliffe was greatly influenced by other famous Oxford scholars, for example, Roger Bacon, Robert Grosseteste, Richard Fitzralph and in particular William of Occam.

In 1348, England was struck by the plague, a terrible time in history known as the Black Death. It started in Asia and spread rapidly across Europe, causing the loss of approximately one half of the population. Wycliffe was deeply disturbed by the plague and felt sure that it was a sign from God that this was leading to judgement day. In an effort to take refuge from these thoughts, Wycliffe started studying the word of God.

At Oxford, Wycliffe proved himself to be an out-standing scholar and was highly respected by his fellow students and lecturers. His studies covered a wide range of subjects, including the law of optics, chemical analysis, physiological genesis of sleep, geometrical and arithmetrical rules and national economics, but his great love was the study of theology and ecclesiastical law.

Wycliffe was offered the post of head of Balliol College in 1360, when its founder, John de Balliol, died. However, Wycliffe was forced to give up this post the following year when he was presented with the parish of Fylingham in Lincolnshire, although he continued to reside at Oxford.

After obtaining a bachelors degree in theology, Wycliffe pursued an avid interest in the study of the Bible. His skill at understanding the scriptures caught the eye of the archbishop of Canterbury, Simon Islip, and in 1365 he placed Wycliffe at the head of Canterbury Hall, where 12 young men were preparing to become priests. It was here that the seeds of resentment of the Catholic Church were planted. When Simon Islip died, the new bishop of Canterbury, Simon Langhman, fired Wycliffe and appointed a monk to the head of Canterbury Hall. Angered, Wycliffe appealed to the Roman Catholic Church, but to no avail as he was only a secular priest and the position had to be filled by a monk.

By 1372 Wycliffe had become a doctor of theology, which entitled him to teach at Oxford University, where he became known not only as a brilliant scholastic theologian but also the most respected debater of his time. Throughout his career he took advantage of his title of doctor of theology.

ECCLESIASTICAL POLITICS

John Wycliffe did not really gain his place in history for his teachings but from his activities in ecclesiastical politics. His reformatory work started around the mid-1370s and came to prominence due to an ongoing dispute between Edward III and the Court of Rome over papal levies. The pope had demanded an annual payment of 1,000 marks, which was meant to acknowledge that the sovereignty of England was under the control of the Catholic Church. For several years the king refused to pay and Wycliffe wrote several documents that refuted the pope's claims and upheld the right of parliament to limit the power of the

Church. Because of his views, Edward III appointed Wycliffe as one of the English delegates at a peace congress in Bruges in 1374. Although the conference itself failed, it did win Wycliffe the patronage of John of Gaunt, who was the fourth son of Edward and the leader of an anti-papal faction. Wycliffe returned to England after two years even more convinced of the immense corruption of the Church in Rome.

Since King John had been on the throne, England had been trying to gain its freedom from the restrictions of the Catholic Church in Rome. This constant struggle gave Wycliffe a wonderful opportunity to express his views about the papacy and also enabled him to greatly undermine the influence it had on the people of England.

Wycliffe was awarded the position of Rector of Lutterworth for his efforts in Bruges, a title that he retained until his death in 1384. Wycliffe's influence was now widespread, not only with his colleagues at Oxford but also with influential members of parliament. The pope himself was furious at Wycliffe's heresy and tried several ways to have him imprisoned, but he was unsuccessful. Wycliffe wrote many articles and pamphlets against the practices and doctrines of Romanism. His followers readily accepted his works and started to come to him for training. His flock became so large, Wycliffe started to send them out to preach the gospel of Christ, for which they received the nickname 'Poor Preachers', or the Lollards.

The monks, who realized that Wycliffe was becoming quite a threat, accused him of heresy. In 1377, the bishop of London, Courtenay, summoned Wycliffe to St Pauls for a meeting, in which Wycliffe had to answer for his heresies. John of Gaunt and Lord Percy (Earl Marshal of England) both accompanied Wycliffe to act as moral support. News of their visit had reached London and a large crowd had gathered outside St Pauls. The meeting was to be held in the chapel, and when Courtenay saw that Wycliffe had bought backup he lost his temper. A ruckus broke out between Courtenay and John of Gaunt, which became so heated that the trial had to be abandoned and the three friends returned home.

In 1377, both Edward III and the Black Prince died, leaving 11-year-old Richard II to take the throne. Luckily for Wycliffe, the new king and his mother were supportive of his views and not afraid to make these observations known. Parliament constantly sought the advice of Wycliffe, but it appears in 1378 his popularity started to go into decline in matters of a political nature.

Competition against Wycliffe's heretical teachings were steadily mounting, and in April 1378 he was called before the papal bulls at Lambeth. As before, a large crowd gathered, which made the bishops nervous, realizing what considerable support Wycliffe had achieved. During the proceedings a mandate arrived from the queen mother, which forbade them taking any action against Wycliffe, and reluctantly having to obey her demands, he was dismissed with the simple command to refrain from teaching.

Wycliffe, of course, did not adhere to this request and made his views clear in a lengthy paper pointing out the considerable errors within the papacy. He also made clear that a number of reforms should be carried out if the Church was to be true to the words of Christ. This was a brave act on his part considering the power of the Catholic Church at the time, but Wycliffe felt that he always had God on his side.

TRANSLATION OF THE BIBLE

The major achievement in Wycliffe's life, and no doubt the influence behind the papal power in England being overthrown, was his translation of the Bible from Latin into English. This translation, which was finished in the year 1382, is supposed to have occupied him for many years, with the main aim of making the word of God available to every man who was able to read. Today we take it for granted that we can read God's words in English, but until Wycliffe's translation the only version available was Jerome's Latin Vulgate. His work in making the scriptures available to the ordinary person was much opposed by the clergy, but Wycliffe believed that it was absolutely essential.

It was a mammoth task in which every word had to be hand written. Today, more than 600 years later, there are still about 170 hand-written copies available. This gives an idea of just how many people were involved in the task, and it has been estimated that it would have cost a man as much as six months' wages to buy a copy of the New Testament.

Wycliffe, apart from his translation work, continued to train and send out his Lollards, and soon their teachings spread throughout England. They attracted a lot criticism and their enemies tried everything in their power to stop them. They were easily recognizable because they went bare-footed, wearing long dark red gowns and carrying staffs and a copy of Wycliffe's Bible – or at least part of it – and preached where anyone would listen.

THE LEGACY

Wycliffe gradually grew weaker and weaker following a stroke in 1382. In December 1384, Wycliffe experienced numbness and collapsed while he was saying mass. He had suffered a second stroke and, although he regained consciousness, he was left paralyzed and unable to speak.

Word that John Wycliffe was dying spread rapidly across England, and on his last day many clerics, including his enemies, crowded into his room at Lutterworth. He finally died at the age of 64 on December 30, 1384, from the results of the stroke.

The name of John Wycliffe will always be synonymous with the Bible and for his bold preachings against the hierarchy of the Roman Church. Wycliffe was buried in Lutterworth, but even after his death his enemies could not leave him in peace. In 1416, the ecumenical Council of Constance, whose chief aim was the repression of heresy, condemned Wycliffe as a dangerous heretic on 267 different counts. In 1428, under Bishop Robert Fleming of Lincoln, Wycliffe's writings were burned, he was excommunicated, and his bones were exhumed from consecrated ground, burned and cast into the river.

The legacy of Wycliffe's teachings could not be destroyed like his body, as he not only had an effect on the history of England but also many other protestant countries. He openly supported reform to reduce the amount of corruption of the Catholic Church, in which priests squandered charity money for their own personal use. Wycliffe was also against transubstantiation, which claimed that the bread and wine used during Eucharist were the actual body and blood of Christ. Wycliffe's teachings claimed that these were merely symbols. Wycliffe spent the majority of his life fighting against the overwhelming power of the Catholic Church in England with considerable boldness and perseverence. His name should definitely be high up on the list of honoured freedom fighters.

JOAN OF ARC

Mention the words 'freedom fighter' and the name Joan of Arc springs to mind. She was an inspired, young patriotic girl, who rose from peasantry, leading her people gloriously into battle. Almost single-handedly, she rallied the French to defend themselves against the unbelievably strong forces of the English army. Her guidance and support on the battlefield led to victory in all her battles and helped to unite French citizens everywhere. Joan of Arc became a national heroine of France and also a saint of the Roman Catholic Church. She was the inspiration of many people to come.

THE EARLY YEARS

Jeanne d'Arc (Joan of Arc) was born on January 6, 1412, to Jacques and Isabelle d'Arc in the small village of Domrémy on the borders of eastern France. Her father was a peasant farmer who found it hard to make ends meet, having a large family to support. Joan was the youngest of a family of five and spent much of her childhood playing in the fields and forests of the Meuse river valley. Although Joan was not taught to read and write, she became quite skilled in the art of sewing and spinning and many said she was old beyond her years. Even as a young child she could often be found kneeling in the local church deep in prayer.

At the time of her birth, France was going through a turbulent period. The fourth king of the Valois dynasty, Charles VI, was on the throne and, as a young man he experienced fits of madness that would recur for the rest of his life. These fits, which would probably now be recognized as schizophrenia, rendered him incapable of making any decisions. His uncle, Philip II, Duke of Burgundy, assumed the regency on the spot, immediately dismissing Charles's advisers. This was to be the start of a major feud that would divide the kings of France and the dukes of Burgundy for the next 85 years. The two warring factions became known as the Armagnacs and the Burgundians, and in May 1413, while Joan while still a baby, the conflict resulted in the Cabochien Revolt in Paris.

The English king, Henry V, took advantage of the turmoil in the French regency and invaded France. He won a dramatic victory in 1415 at Agincourt and then went on to control other towns in the north of France. The English returned in 1417, conquering a large section of northern France, and two years later they gained the support of the new Burgundian duke, Philip the Good. He agreed to recognize Henry V as the legal heir to the French throne, rejecting the rightful heir, Charles VI, who was the last heir of the Valois dynasty. The English right to the throne of France had been granted as part of a treaty in an effort to put an end to the raging Hundred Years' War.

War darkened the majority of Joan of Arc's childhood and was obviously a considerable influence in her later life. When the English invaded northern France, Joan would have witnessed the frightened farmers abandoning their land, and on one occasion the village where she lived was burned. The farms became overgrown with scrub and trees and the plight of the peasants almost led to them taking up arms and trying to drive the English out of their country themselves.

THE VISIONS

Joan of Arc was about 13 when she heard 'the voice' for the first time. It was around midday in the height of summer, and Joan was sitting in her father's garden enjoying the sunshine. She became aware of a gentle voice that seemed to be talking to her, but there was no one in sight. At first she was frightened and unsure of the message the voice was trying to portray. It was telling Joan that she had to go the aid of France before it was too late. Joan tried to ignore the voice, hoping that it had just been her imagination.

After this first occasion, Joan heard the voice many more times; usually accompanied by a bright light. Joan soon realized that this was nothing to be frightened of and that the voice came from God through a messenger, Saint Michael the Archangel. Saint Michael is identified in the Bible as one of the principal angels, and his name was the war cry of the good angels in the battle fought in heaven against Satan and his followers. The voice would occasionally be accompanied by two other angels, St Catherine and St Margaret. For a long time Joan told no one about the voices, afraid that people would consider her mad. The voices were always soft and low, and as the years passed, their commands became more and more pressing. St Catherine and St Margaret told Joan that she had been chosen by God to help Charles VII drive the English out of France. It was then that Joan told her parents about her visions, but her father, unsure of her sanity, refused to allow her to go to the king.

In 1428, the situation in France had become criticial, as the English prepared to attack the city of Orléans. Joan's voices continued and became more pressing, urging her to help Charles. In May of that year, Joan's friends (who believed in her divine visions) obtained a horse and some boys' clothing for her. Dressing as a boy not only afforded her better protection but also acted as a disguise in case the group was captured. It was also possible that Joan could have been raped if her true identity had been discovered. Joan's friends accompanied her to the military commander at Vaucouleurs, Robert de Baudricourt. Baudricourt was not prepared to take the rantings of a 16-year-old peasant girl seriously, and Joan was forced to return home.

Shortly after her return, the villagers of her home village, Domrémy, were forced to take refuge in the nearby city of Neufchâteau, when they found themselves in the path of a Burgundian army led by Lord Jean de Vergy. His army attacked Vaucouleurs and forced Baudricourt to pledge his neutrality, which in effect took him out of the war.

On October 12, 1428, the English army, under the lead of the Earl of Salisbury, besieged Orléans. Charles found himself in a hopeless situation, whereby the last major city defending the heart of his now dwindling territory was in the hands of the English.

When Baudricourt heard of the siege of Orléans, he sent for Joan, realizing that her original predictions to him had come true. In January 1429, Joan arrived again in Vaucouleurs where, this time, she was able to gain the confidence of Baudricourt. He arranged for an armed escort to take Joan, once again dressed as a boy in a tightly laced tunic and pants, through enemy territory to Chinon. She left Vaucouleurs on February 13 and arrived 11 days later in Chinon. After waiting a couple of days, Joan was taken to see Charles.

It took a long time for Joan to convince Charles that she was telling the truth, but because of the desperate position he was in, after many days of questioning, he was willing to listen to her. However, before he would allow her to go to Orléans, Charles made Joan visit his religious advisers in Poitiers. She was questioned for six weeks by a group of theologians, before they gave their approval for Charles to grant her command of an army.

JOAN'S ARMY

Charles VII had a white suit of army made for Joan and a banner, which he told her she had to carry into battle. The banner bore a figure of the Virgin carrying a shield and two angels supporting the arms of France on one side. On the front were the words 'Jesus Maria' and a figure of God seated on clouds and holding a globe.

Joan was taken to her army who were stationed at Blois, about 56km (35 miles) outside of Orléans. Finding the men in a disorderly state, Joan set about knocking them up into an army she would be proud to take into battle. She began to reform her men by banning any prostitutes from the camp, prohibiting swearing and asking them to go to church on a regular basis. Her presence seemed to have a good effect on the army, who were originally unwilling to fight for what they felt was a lost cause. Soon they started to volunteer for the new campaign, and word went round that the army in Blois had a saint as their leader.

BREAKING THE SIEGE

Joan and her army arrived at the siege of Orléans on April 29, 1429. A small force came out to meet them at Chécy, a few kilometres upriver from Orléans. The approach to Orléans by land was difficult as all the roads were blocked by the English army. At each of the three gates, the English had a camp that was fortified by a moat and a rampart.

Joan's plan was to arrive in Orléans by the River Loire, which flowed right by the walls of the city. Boarding in a secluded place, and first loading the barges with grain, Joan took advantage of the swift current. Getting her men to row quickly, Joan and her army arrived at Orléans, taking the English by surprise. Armed English troops immediately took to the water in small boats in an effort to prevent the French from landing. However, their efforts were in vain and they were forced to retreat with many of their men wounded.

As Joan entered the city she was greeted with rejoicing, for not only had she bought fresh hope, she had also bought much-needed supplies for a near-starving population.

At dawn the following day, with Joan riding proud on her spirited mount, she led her troops to attack the English camps. She soon had the English in a state of confusion as her army captured their fortifications, filling the moats and setting fire to the towers, which the French had erected. They soon overpowered the camps at the other two gates, and as the English were stationed in different positions around the city walls, they were unable to come to each other's aid. Soon the siege of Orléans was totally broken and there were hardly any English soldiers left to tell the story of the heroic leader of the French army.

The English commander, John Talbot (later Earl of Shrewsbury), was humiliated by the defeat at the hands of a woman and, with a group of specially picked 4,000 horsemen, he marched against Orléans. Talbot was doubtful that the Maid, as she had become known, would dare to meet his army. His plan was to either take her captive or kill her as the French troops entered the gates of the city. Talbot totally under-estimated the character of Joan of Arc, and once again the English were taken by surprise when they were greeted with shouts as Joan's men charged the French cavalry. Panic seized the British soldiers, fearing that they were fighting a force strengthened by angels, and they dropped their swords and abandoned the fight. Talbot's shouts of encouragement went unheeded as his men turned and took flight.

The French army had no opposition, and soon most had either been captured or killed, with the exception of Talbot, who made a rapid escape on his horse.

JOAN OF ARC IN REIMS

The breaking of the siege at Orléans led to the support of several prominent figures. Duke Jean V of Brittany, who rejected his former allegiance with the English, promised to send troops to Charles's aid. The Archbishop of Embrun advised Charles to consult Joan on any future matters concerning war, as he believed her to be divinely blessed.

Joan's strengths lay in her ability to get her soldiers to listen to her and follow her lead. She achieved this through her self-confidence, her determination and her outstanding courage. When she met up with Charles again at Loches, she convinced him to take an army north to Reims (also spelt Rheims), where he was to be officially crowned king. This, however, was not a simple assignment, as Reims lay deep within enemy territory. To clear a path to Reims the French would first have to defeat the remaining English positions in the Loire Valley. Under the command of the Duke of Alencon, the army advanced to Jargeau, 16km (10 miles) to the south-east of Orléans. The Duke of Alençon, having been impressed with Joan's performance at Orléans, agreed to all of her decisions regarding military tactics.

As Joan led her men into battle, proudly carrying her banner aloft, she was hit in the helmet with a stone and fell from her horse. She immediately remounted and encouraged her men to storm the ramparts. Soon the English were taken and driven back across Jargeau's bridge; losses to the French were minimal. Joan proceeded to lead her army in an astounding series of victories, which soon left the route into Reims clear.

The coronation of Charles VII finally took place on 17 July, 1429. Joan of Arc stood close to Charles, holding her banner, proud to be near the sovereign as he received the crown that had been denied him years earlier.

On the day of the coronation Joan wrote a letter to the Duke of Burgundy, asking him why he had not been present at the coronation of Charles VII. She suggested that they should put their differences aside and form a peace treaty. Although the duke never arrived in Reims he did send his emissaries, but the 15-day truce that was declared, was not exactly the solution that Joan had been looking for. In fact such a short truce would hardly give the English and the Burgundian troops time to regroup. Charles, in the meantime, taking advantage of the treaty, took his army on a tour of the Ile-de-France, accepting his patrons' hospitality wherever he stopped. Joan, believing that the principal aim of her mission had been achieved, was looking forward to returning to her family.

This was not to be the case, because the army of the Duke of Bedford was close. Bedford had sent a challenge to Charles to meet him for a showdown.

THE SIEGE OF PARIS

The two armies met at the village of Montpilloy, a few kilometres outside Crépy, on August 14. Joan led her men in a charge against the English to try and draw them out of their strongholds. Only minor confrontations took place and both armies withdrew on the night of August 15.

The French army went north-west to Compiègne and sat it out while negotiations with the Burgundians were being discussed. On August 21 a treaty was signed offering a four-month truce, which was designed to prevent Charles's army from continuing its offensive. A peace conference was arranged for the following spring, although there is evidence that the English were preparing to attack once more.

While Charles stayed in Compiège, Joan and the Duke of Alençon left of their own accord, arriving at St-Denis on August 25. They succeeded in taking over St-Denis with no opposition, but their siege on Paris was not so successful. Joan was riding out in front of her troops, as usual, when she was hit in the thigh with a crossbow dart. Although she continued to urge her men to fill in the moats surrounding the fortifications, on this occasion they disobeyed her orders and carried her back against her will. The Duke of Alençon forcibly had her removed from the battlefield and ordered the assault to be abandoned. Their armies returned to St-Denis where Charles was now located.

When Charles learned that his two commanders were considering returning to Paris over a bridge that Alençon had built, the king ordered that the bridge was to be destroyed. Joan of Arc, to her dismay, had no choice and was forced to lay down her arms in the church of St-Denis.

JOAN OF ARC'S LETTERS

The period of inactivity that followed left Joan with a restless feeling. Despite being able to see her beloved family again, the voices were still telling her that her mission was not over. Joan did not take part in any military action until November 4, when there was a small skirmish at Saint-Pierre-le-Moutier.

The next siege at the town of La-Charité-sur-Loire was a dismal failure. Due to the terms of the treaty Joan and Alençon had no backing from the royal court; receiving no supplies or money with which to sustain their armies. After a month the French armies withdrew, abandoning their artillery.

Joan spent the remainder of the winter at various royal courts, while the English and the Burgundians started to regroup their men for further battles. Joan filled her time by writing letters, which she dictated to the scribes in her army. She had become famous for the letters that she wrote during her time as a warrior. There were 23 in total, 11 of which survive today – five originals and six as copies.

Two of her final letters were thought to have been dictated from the town of Sully-sur-Loire. On March 16, 1430, she dictated a letter to the citizens of Reims, saying that she would come to their aid in the event of a siege. On March 23, 1430, a letter was sent to the Hussites, addressed as 'the heretics of Bohemia', in which she threatened to lead a crusade against them unless they return to orthodox Catholicism.

The final letter she ever wrote was dictated on March 28, 1430, once again to the citizens of Reims. The document laid out details of the latest events and encouraged the people of Reims to sit tight until help came. The original of this letter is held in the archives of the Maleissye family, descendants of Joan of Arc.

Below is the English translation of that final letter:

Very dear friends and good friends, may it please you to know that I have received your letters which mention how word had been brought to the king that there were a multitude of traitors in the city of Rheims. Please know that it was certainly true that he had been told there were many who belonged to a conspiracy and who would have betrayed the city and brought in the Burgundians. But thereafter the king learned otherwise because you had sent him assurances, for which he is well pleased with you. And know that you are in his favour, and if you will have to fight, he will aid you in the event of a siege. And he well knows that you have much suffering to endure from the hardships which these treasonous Burgundian enemies inflict on you; so he

*will deliver you, if it pleases God, very soon – that is
to say, as soon as is feasible. So I beg and request,
very dear friends, that you defend the city for the
king and that you keep good watch. You will soon
hear my good news in greater detail. I will not write
any more for the present except that all of Brittany
is [now] French and the Duke must send three
thousand soldiers to the king, paid for two months.
I commend you to God, may He watch over you.
Written at Sully on the 28th of March.*

[signed] 'Jehanne' ('Joan')

The signature at the end of the letter was written in a
different hand to the body text. With each letter the
signature improved, indicating that Joan spent time
practising how to write her own name.

CAPTURE

After a period of inactivity, Joan took to the field again
accompanied by a small band of men – among them
her brother, Pierre; her confessor, Friar Jean Pasquerel;
her bodyguard, Jean d'Aulon and a mercenary unit of
around 200 men led by Bartolomew Baretta. They
headed for Lagny-sur-Marne, where French troops
were in conflict with the English.

On April 22, 1430, when Joan and her men were
stationed at Melun, she received a message from her
voices, warning her that she would be captured before
June 24 (St John's day). Being captured or betrayed
had always been her greatest fear and yet, despite the

warning, Joan returned to Campiègne. When she arrived, Joan was surprised to find the city under siege by the Duke of Burgundy's captain, John of Luxembourg. He had a reputation as an accomplished leader and Joan new she was up against a formidable opponent.

Joan managed to gain access to the city by sneaking past John's guards and subsequently led several brave attempts to try to overcome the Burgundian army. However, being totally outnumbered, Joan failed to stop the city of Compiègne from falling into the hands of John of Luxembourg. Joan succeeded in holding off the Burgundian soldiers for long enough to allow the citizens of the city to escape, but in the process she found that her own army's escape route had been cut off by the British army. The British had lain in waiting, and as the French made a final attempt to get out of the city, Joan was pulled to the ground by a French archer.

John of Luxembourg was delighted with his prize, which he considered to be a far greater asset than the winning of the city of Compiègne. Joan told her captors that there was nothing they could do that would make her betray King Charles VII and that she would remain loyal to him even if it cost her her life.

News quickly reached Charles VII that his favourite captain had been captured. One of his clergymen, Archbishop Renaud, started spreading a rumour that it was Joan's own fault that she had been captured and that she had ignored her king's orders. Charles had been considering the surrender of Compiègne to the Duke of Burgundy in the hope that it would appease the situation, but the people of the city had refused to give up, not wishing to be ruled by Burgundy. Joan had simply gone to the aid of a city that was under siege out of loyalty to her king and her people, which undermined the rumours spread by the archbishop.

Charles tried to bargain with the French to return Joan in exchange for a ransom. Joan, however, was a special case, and the Duke of Burgundy was not prepared to give her up that easily. Joan hoped she would die quickly, because she greatly feared torture and imprisonment, especially a long imprisonment.

THE TRIAL

Joan was held prisoner in the fortress of Beaurevoir in Rouen and after four months was sold to the English for the sum of 10,000 francs. On July 14, 1430, The bishop of Beauvais, Pierre Cauchon, was given the job of procuring Joan and arranging her trial. Cauchon was a long-time supporter of the Anglo-Burgundian faction and, claiming episcopal jurisdiction over Joan, held her as a suspect of witchcraft and invocation of the devil.

Although female prisoners were generally held in a Church-run prison under the guard of nuns, Joan was not offered this privilege. She was imprisoned in the castle of Rouen which was a secular millitary prison which was watched over by English soldiers. For fear of being raped, Joan clung to her famous uniform of the tightly laced tunic and pants as she knew that a dress would offer her no protection.

Joan of Arc's trial included several hearings, which lasted from February 21 to the end of March 1931, in front of a small hand-picked court. During the trial Joan was forced to stand in a specially built iron cage – which was barely large enough for her to remain upright – and chains bound her hands and feet.

After three weeks of cross-examination, Cauchon started to worry that he did not have enough evidence against Joan. Her honest and high-minded answers were creating a favourable impression, as was the testimony of several women who had been appointed by the Duchess of Bedford. After hearing that Joan was a virgin – and therefore by implication could not be a witch – Cabouchon realized that he would need a few tricks up his sleeve to achieve his ultimate goal of having her burnt at the stake.

Pierre Cabouchon gradually started to repress the favourable evidence and, with the aid of his helpers, came up with 12 separate charges against her. Cabouchon claimed that the charges were based on answers that Joan had given during the cross-examination. Joan was unable to read and write, so when she was asked to sign a confession she was at a disadvantage as she had no idea what it said. Joan, who was still only 19 years old, was tired and ill, but even the threat of torture did not make her crack.

She was taken to a torture chamber in the castle of Rouen, where her captors showed her the terrible instruments of pain and described exactly what they were going to do to her. Still she wouldn't break her code of loyalty, and on May 23 she was taken to the cemetery at the abbey, where she listened to a sermon by Guillaume Erard. In the distance she could see the stake and executioner in place and she prepared herself for the fate to come. However, this was just another ploy to frighten Joan into signing a confession. At the end of the sermon Cabouchon stood up and read a short version of the confession to Joan. He told her that her life would be spared if she agreed to never carry arms, wear soldiers' clothes or cut her hair short, but Joan simply remained silent.

After reading the confession, Cabouchon announced the sentence of the court – death by burning at the stake. With the threat of death hanging over her, Joan finally relented and signed what she thought was the short eight-lined confession. After a trial in which Joan had shown exceptional intellect, Cabouchon finally tricked her by taking advantage of her inability to read. He had substituted the short confession, which he had read out, with one that was far more damaging. Had Joan been able to read what was on the paper, there is no doubt she would never have agreed to sign the substituted confession.

Cabouchon showed clemency on Joan after she put her mark on the false confession and told her that she would have to spend the rest of her life in prison, rather than be burned at the stake. At least, this is what he led her to believe.

THE FINAL DECEIT

Joan captor's did not stick to their promises of allowing her to attend Church or confession. She was also not handed over to the Church as they had sworn, but left to the mercy of the English jailors, who continually taunted her with threats of rape. As agreed with Cabouchon, since signing the confession, she had only worn women's clothes. Little did she know that Cabouchon had another trick up his sleeve.

On waking one morning, she looked around her cell, but was unable to find the clothes she had taken off the night before. The only garments on the floor were her 'forbidden' pants and laced tunic. Joan pleaded with her guards to return her dress as she had to relieve herself, but the guards refused to allow her to leave her cell until she was dressed. She put on the forbidden clothes, which was exactly what Cabouchon wanted. In the 15th century it was a sin for a woman to wear men's clothes, and the fact that Joan had already renounced never to wear them again, left her in a dangerous position. At the time Joan may not have realized what the outcome of this action would be, but Cabouchon took advantage of the situation and moved quickly.

Joan was charged and convicted with being a relapsed heretic. Not wishing to be responsible for her death, Cabouchon and his ecclesiastical officers handed Joan over to the state authorities. Her punishment – death by burning at the stake in the marketplace of Rouen.

Her once loyal supporter, Charles VII, did nothing to help her, knowing that the English still had powerful allies in France. The English were only too happy to see Joan put to death as they didn't want her courage to be emulated by others.

Joan had always been terrified of death and she

turned to her confessor, Brother Martin l'Advenu, to comfort her. She asked him to bring her a crucifix so that she could hold it as she suffered. As she stood tethered to the stake, she asked that Brother Martin stand away so that he was untouched by the flames.

As the fire was lit beneath her, the crowd was noisy, but as the first flame touched Joan of Arc, the crowd fell silent, and all that could be heard were her last words:

Jesus, Jesus, Jesus!

Court officials were worried that Joan would be seen as a martyr and because heretics could not be buried in cemeteries, they ordered for her ashes to be scattered on the waters of the Seine.

HER NAME IS CLEARED

As the corrupt circumstances of her trial and subsequent execution came to the public knowledge, anyone who was involved tried to exonerate themselves. Charles VII, who had done nothing to stop the execution, petitioned to have the verdict overturned. But it wasn't until 1455 that anything was done, when Joan's family applied to Pope Callistus III to reconsider the charges against their daughter.

Luckily for them, one of the clerk's at the original trial, Guillaume Manchon, was still alive and was prepared to testify about the injudicious manner in which the trial was carried out. On June 7, 1456, the judges overturned the verdict that had condemned Joan to death.

Joan of Arc's status in the Church was restored and the new verdict was read out in the Rouen market-place where Joan had died 25 years earlier.

HER PLACE IN HISTORY

Joan of Arc was beatified in 1909 by Pope Pius X and on May 16, 1920, she was declared a saint by Pope Benedict XV. On June of that year, the French parliament announced that there would be an annual festival in her honour, which would take place on the second Sunday in May.

Joan of Arc is the patron saint of France and most probably their greatest heroine. It was her inspiration that played an important part in the liberation of France. Her accomplishment as a freedom fighter seems all the more honourable because she achieved so much despite of her gender. She distinguished herself as a warrior with her courage and morals, rising, not from a noble background, but from that of a simple peasant. Not once did Joan of Arc waver from her religious beliefs, and she continues to be a symbol of all that is best in a human being. She believed in herself, she believed in God, she believed in her people and, because of this, she changed the course of French history.

JACK CADE

Jack Cade is rather an enigma as even his real name is an uncertainty. There certainly were Cades around the Kent area in the 15th century and possibly this was his true name. However, he was also known as John Mortimer and sometimes John Aylmere, and many of his supporters claimed he was a cousin of Richard, Duke of York. Some reference books claim he was of Irish origin but was raised in Kent, where he allegedly murdered a woman in 1449. Cade fled to France, but he returned to live in Kent under an assumed name.

Whatever his true identity, Cade earned his reputation as a freedom fighter when he led a rebellion in 1450 against the harsh policies of Henry VI. From the competent way in which Cade handled his men, it is possible that he received some military training during his spell in France. He showed a high degree of military prowess and proved to be a formidable leader. His personality was strong and dominating with a high level of intellect, but without some form of military training it is doubtful that he would have gained so many loyal followers. Although the majority of his followers were peasants and small landowners, they also included a number of squires and knights.

CAUSE OF THE TROUBLE

The rebellion itself came about due to the disorderly state of England in 1450. The constant struggle with France in the Hundred Years War (1336–1565) had left England financially unstable. Henry VI, who was already an unpopular king, started to impose crippling taxes that made life exceptionally hard for the peasants, who, prior to the new restrictions, had struggled to make a living. On top of this was the greed of certain royal officials who, through misappropriation of the tax funds, starting to line their own pockets.

In 1450, matters concerning Henry VI's corrupt government started to boil over into serious political unrest. In January, Adam Moleyns, Lord Privy Seal and Bishop of Chichester, was murdered by a mutinous group of seamen after an argument over their wages. Also in January the chief councillor of the king, William de la Pole, 1st Duke of Suffolk, was held responsible for England's loss of possessions in northern France. He was arrested and imprisoned in the Tower of London. He was banished for five years, but in May 1450, en route to France, his ship was intercepted and he was executed. The person or persons behind his murder remains a mystery.

The commoners demanded that the king take back many of the grants of land and money he had given to his favourite court members. The chronic condition of the royal finances, private feuds and escalating lawlessness, all fuelled the growing resentment against the power, wealth and influence of the king and his parliament. Added to this was the conflict between Henry VI and Richard, Duke of York, who had a strong claim to the throne, but was living in virtual exile in Ireland at the time of the rebellion.

THE START OF THE REBELLION

Jack Cade is thought to have assumed the name John Mortimer, cousin to Richard, Duke of York, and thereby identifying himself with the York family. Taking advantage of the chaotic state of the government following the death of William de la Pole, Cade issued a manifesto to Henry VI demanding the removal of several of the king's chief ministers and demanding the return of Richard from Ireland.

A large number of people flocked to join Cade from both Kent and East Sussex, but it was certainly more than a mere peasants' revolt. Because wealthy landlowners and prominent clergy had also been affected by the taxes and corrupt laws, Cade was joined by many people of standing. Using military precision Cade assembled an army that was prepared to take on the king's men.

Henry VI and Queen Margaret were in Leicester on government business when they learned of the death of William de la Pole and received the omnious news of Jack Cade's rebellion. Cade had formed his army quickly and by the second week in June, 1450, he had set up camp in Blackheath with his newly formed army.

The king ordered Thomas, Lord Scales, to rally

some troops together and to meet the rebels to find out exactly what their grievances were.

Cade had already presented to the embassy 15 Articles of Complaint, listing their true complaints against the king and his government.

Both the king and his queen were defiant when they received the articles, stating that the rebels' demands were impossible. What agrieved them the most, was the suggestion that Richard, Duke of York, should be brought back to head the government. Henry IV was furious that a band of insurgents should make such outrageous demands on him and his men.

Lord Scales, with his newly formed troops, rode through the city of London in mid-June, ready to take on the rebels assembled at Blackheath. However, Cade had been forewarned of their imminent arrival and had managed to slip away with his men into the forests of the Weald of Kent. The royal army went in pursuit but were lured into an ambush. Cade and his men quickly overpowered Scales and his men, killing many of them, including two royal commanders, Sir William Stafford of Grafton and Sir William Stafford of Somerset. Happy with their success in battle, Cade and his men returned to their camp at Blackheath.

Back in the ranks of the royal army there was much discontent. Some of the soldiers were even showing approval of Jack Cade's demands and they started to turn mutinous. They demanded the death of Lord Say, the former treasurer, Lord Dudley and several of their lower-ranking captains. Lord Say was an exceptionally unpopular man in Kent and, to protect their lives, the king sent him and Dudley to the Tower. He told the soldiers that the two men were to be tried for their crimes but this did nothing to appease their anger. The band of rebellious soldiers started to ransack the city of London and, scared of where this might lead, their commanders disbanded them. Henry VI, fearing for his safety, fled to Kenilworth castle and left London to its own fate.

On hearing about the mutiny in London, Jack Cade and his men advanced on the city on July 2. They forced their way over London Bridge with Cade defiantly cutting the ropes of the drawbridge with his own sword. The mayor and the aldermen met in haste, but realizing that Cade had so many supporters by now, they knew that they could do nothing to resist him.

Up until the attack on London, Cade had been able to keep control of his men, but as soon as they saw the rich pickings that were on offer in the city, he was soon powerless to stop their looting. They started to ransack the city, stealing whatever they could, killing anyone who got in their way. Cade's men were joined by an equally unruly mob from Essex, which had set up camp close to the Tower of London. To try to prevent them from attacking the Tower, Scales offered them Lord Say and William Crowmer. The mob were delighted to have the hated treasurer in their grasp and impeached him in Guildford. Say demanded a trial, but of course the verdict was a foregone conclusion and he was beheaded in Cheapside. Crowmer suffered the same fate but was not allowed the privilege of a trial. A third man, John Bailey, was also executed because, it is thought, that he had too much information about Jack Cade. The three heads were put on display at London Bridge, replacing the heads of criminals that had been put there to mark their shame.

In the meantime the rebels' hatred of Queen Margaret, who was just as unpopular as her husband, Henry VI, was causing further unrest in other parts of the country. The Bishop of Salisbury, William Ainscough, who had married the couple, paid for performing the deed with his life. He was dragged from his church at Edington by a separate band of rebels in Wiltshire, and stoned to death.

The Queen's chancellor, William Booth and her confessor, Walter Lehart, Bishop of Norwich, were both attacked in their own dioceses but managed to escape with their lives.

Back in London Jack Cade and his men had certainly outstayed their welcome. The people of the city were horrified by their behaviour, looting and killing innocent citizens. The mayor and the aldermen, who had renewed energy, raised some troops and set out under the cover of night. The inhabitants of London had also banded together against the rebels and so with the royal army's help, the streets were soon cleared.

However, a vicious fight broke out over the possession of London Bridge and the battle went on right through the night. Many people lost their lives in the fight and bodies were thrown over the side of the bridge into the river below. By dawn Lord Scales had regained possession of the northern half of the bridge and was determined to renew his assault for the other half. However, the Bishop of Winchester, William of Waynflete had arrived with a bag full of blanks forms of pardon. Scales agreed that these should be offered to the militants if they would abandon the rebellion and return to their homes.

Many of the rebels who were exhausted and shaken by the assault on London Bridge, agreed to accept the bishop's pardons, and around 2,000 men in total agreed to his terms. The bishop was quite prepared to pardon John Mortimer but, as no man could have more than one pardon, Jack Cade went unpardoned. This meant that the government was quite entitled to take proceedings against him.

THE DEATH OF JACK CADE

Jack Cade left London and headed for Rochester with his remaining men. In his pocket was the pardon for John Mortimer and, on arrival in Rochester, he demanded that parliament endorsed the bishop's pardons. However, the government considered Cade to be a traitor and had issued a reward of 1,000 marks to anyone who could catch him either dead or alive.

In July Cade was trapped and killed in Haywards Heath, West Sussex. His body was later taken to London where it was quartered and displayed in different cities as a reminder to any future would-be rebels. His head was placed on a pike on London Bridge along with other members of his rebellion.

AFTER THE REVOLT

Cade's death did not put an end to the troubles because, even though the Duke of York returned un-invited to England, events continued to take a down-wards turn. York was determined to take a more leading royal in the royal courts, but from 1450 up until 1461, politics became increasingly unpleasant. It eventually turned into a civil war with the dispute between York's family and the reigning Lancastrians going from bad to worse.

York knew he had to do something to rescue the situation and he decided to organize demonstrations in his own favour to take place all over England. York marched through Kent, which was still unsettled from Cade's rebellion, into London in the hope of taking power by force. However, his plan failed miserably and he failed to gain any major support.

In 1453, York had another chance to take control when Henry VI had a mental breakdown. York com-peted for leadership with Queen Margaret and this time York was successful. York was officially an-nounced as protector of the realm, and for the next couple of years was officially in charge. But these were years of conflict and the first phase of what became known as the War of the Roses.

Jack Cade is remembered in Shakespeare's play *Henry VI, Part 2*, which gives an account of the contest between the York and Lancaster families and also of the rebellion.

Although Cade's rebellion was not an outright

success it did contribute to the breakdown of corrupt royal authority. He was not just a rebel, but a man with considerable military knowledge and organization. It was not just a random revolt but a serious attempt by politically aware citizens to assert their right to use armed protest. In the 15th century the only way the common population could make themselves heard was through the use of arms, and Jack Cade and his men felt justified in fighting to try to break the monopoly of the corrupt realm.

THE BASTARD OF FAUCONBERG

This chapter is a continuation of the rivalry between the House of York and the Lancastrians and is an addendum to the rebellion by the Earl of Warwick against King Edward. The Kentish Rising, which took place in May 1471, was led by Thomas Neville, the illegitimate son of William Neville, Lord Fauconberg and Earl of Kent. Neville was a sailor who became more generally known as the *Bastard of Fauconberg* (or Falconbridge). In 1454, he received the freedom of the City of London for his part in ridding the North Sea and the English Channel of pirates. His cousin, Richard of Warwick appointed him Vice-Admiral of the Fleet and played an active role in placing Edward IV on the throne. When his cousin changed allegiance, Neville remained on his side, and his eventual attack on London in May 1471 was part of a two-part attack by Lancastrian forces. The Lancastrians were led by Queen Margaret of Anjou. She wanted to regain the throne for her husband, Henry VI, who was being held prisoner in the Tower of London.

THE BASTARD AND THE PIRATES

Sea trade in the middle ages was a dangerous business and the only way that merchants could protect themselves from attacks by pirates was by travelling together in groups. An intensification of the conflict with the Hanseatic League in 1470 forced Edward IV to form a new fleet under the Earl of Warwick. The Hanseatic League was a league of merchant associations within the cities of Northern Germany and the Baltic. Edward appointed Lord Howard and the Bastard of Fauconberg to command a fleet against the Hanseatic pirates; a mission that lasted for ten weeks and was financed by the citizens of London.

When Warwick swapped allegiance with the king he had helped put on the throne, the Bastard of Fauconberg took several ships and went to Warwick's aid. Edward knew he had to act quickly because, once before, having command of the seas had allowed Warwick and his father to beat the Lancastrians. Edward closed off the entrance to Calais and appointed Lord Rivers to take a fleet to head off Warwick's ships. The English fleet was joined by a fleet from the Low Countries and they raided the port of Harfleur, where both Warwick and the Bastard of Fauconberg had set up their base. They managed to block the entrance to the port for a while, but a storm forced them to break up and Warwick and the Lancastrians managed to slip out and cross the English Channel.

It took a while for the news to reach Edward IV and, having managed to escape the Hanseatic pirates at sea, he headed to a small port in the Low Countries, called Alkmaar. However, due to low tides, Edward was unable to enter the port and was now at the mercy of the pirates. He was rescued by Lord Gruthuyse, who was one of the leaders of the Low-Countries fleet. Gruthuyse forced the pirates to retreat and took Edward IV to a place of refuge.

Back in England in October of 1470, Warwick reinstated Henry VI on the throne and, to repay his loyalty, Henry made Warwick Keeper of the Seas. Warwick appointed the Bastard of Fauconberg to act as his deputy but, once in command of his fleet, Fauconberg committed an act of piracy by robbing a fleet of Portuguese merchants. The Portuguese had been allies with England since the end of the 14th century, and consequently they were taken completely by surprise by the attack.

Edward IV was angry at having been driven out of England by his arch rival Henry VI and, using money supplied by the Duke of Burgundy, managed to obtain a fleet of ships. He landed in Yorkshire and assembled a small army, gathering reinforcements as he marched south towards London.

Warwick's men, a mixed force of around 9,000 men, took up a position of attack on Hadley Green just outside of Barnet in Hertfordshire. Edward, with about 8,000 men, arrived in Barnet on the evening of April 13 and marched close to Warwick's men. In was exceptionally dark and Warwick's army fired their cannons randomly at the position where they believed their enemies were camped, but they completely missed their target.

The real battle started at dawn while the ground was still covered with a thick mist. The battle lasted between three and four hours and ended with an victory for Edward. The Earl of Warwick was killed in battle and Henry VI was taken captive again.

THE BATTLE OF TEWKESBURY

Queen Margaret landed at Weymouth on April 14, with her son Edward and a small French army. She hadn't gone far when the devastating news reached her that her ally, the Earl of Warwick, had been killed at the Battle of Barnet that same day. The Lancastrians did not let the loss of their leader deter them; they gathered fresh troops and headed north-west accompanied by the Duke of Somerset and the Earl of Devon. Margaret was hoping to recruit a large army from the west country and Wales and then march on to face the Yorkists.

Edward IV rallied his forces and left London to head off Margaret and Somerset before they crossed the Severn at Gloucester. However, Somerset's army had been forced to stop at Bristol to get more supplies and weapons, and this delay was to prove fatal.

Edward's army almost caught up with the Lancastrians at Sodbury, but Somerset had taken his forces north towards Gloucester in the hope of getting across the Severn as quickly as possible. Edward warned the Governor of Gloucester to hold out against the anticipated attack for as long as possible, so when Gloucester closed its gates Somerset was forced to go even further north towards the river crossing at Tewkesbury. Edward led his men in a beeline towards Tewkesbury, knowing that if the army could not cross at Gloucester this would be their next destination.

Realizing just how close Edward's army was, Somerset chose not to cross the river and placed his exhausted men in the most advantageous position he could find. They had no choice; they just had to turn and fight.

Edward's army was outnumbered by some 2,000 men so he broke his troops into three divisions led by himself, Gloucester and Lord Hastings. The Yorkists opened fire first with guns and arrows. Somerset responded but his gun fire was not strong enough and he was forced to make a flanking manouevre to the left of the king's central division. However, Somerset's men were soon pushed back by Gloucester towards the town and river, where many soldiers drowned trying to make their escape. The Lancastrians lost as many as 2,000 men, including Prince Edward, who was the last legitimate descendant of Henry IV.

When Queen Margaret heard of the death of her son and the disastrous battle at Tewkesbury, she fled, but she was captured and brought before Edward at Coventry. She was held prisoner for four years until Louis XI of France paid a ransom for her release.

Although the Battle of Tewkesbury doused the hopes of the Lancastrians, on May 12, the Bastard of Fauconberg presented himself at the gates of London Bridge at the head of 17,000 Kentish men in the hopes of reviving their cause.

THE KENTISH RISING

The Bastard of Fauconberg landed in Kent in May with around 300 men, claiming to have been given a naval command by Henry VI. Fauconberg received a warm welcome, not just from the people of Kent, but also from the surrounding counties of Essex and Surrey. His army grew until he had about 3,000 men.

On May 12, Fauconberg arrived at the gates of London Bridge and asked for permission to march through the city of London. He said he had come to dethrone Edward and restore the rightful king, Henry VI. He promised that his men would cause no trouble and that he held a commission from the Earl of Warwick.

The Mayor of London sent Fauconberg a letter saying that as Warwick had been killed at the Battle of Tewkesbury, his commission was no longer valid. It also told him of the total annihilation of the Lancastrian cause and that they would not grant him permission to enter London. They urged Fauconberg to lay down his arms and acknowledge Edward as king.

It is not clear whether Fauconberg chose to believe the contents of the letter but, undeterred, he decided to make an assault on London. He planned it carefully; attacking it at three separate points. He removed the cannons from his ships and laid them along the shore-line to afford some cover for a large number of his men who were preparing to cross the river. Another section of Fauconberg's army attacked London Bridge by setting fire to a number of small buildings in the hope that they could enter the city without having to breach one of the gates.

The artillery situated in the Tower fired cannons at Fauconberg's men, but the majority of their shots missed their target causing little damage. In the meantime Fauconberg's men had reached the north bank of the river and attacked Aldgate and Bishopsgate. A contingent of Essex rebels arrived to help with the assault on Aldgate, but the citizens retreated through the gate and the portcullis was lowered. Many of Fauconberg's men were trapped inside and killed by the inhabitants of Aldgate. The London citizens fought hard and when they had overcome the rebels, they raised the portcullis and charged out of the city.

The attack on Bishopsgate fared no better; Earl Rivers led a small force from the Tower assisted by the Earl of Essex, who proved to be a formidable force. Fauconberg's men, realizing that they were completely overpowered fled to Mile End, Stratford and Blackwall, with the London citizens in hot pursuit. The rest of the army on the south bank, who had made little progress with their attack on London Bridge, had been outmanouevred by the London citizens and withdrew to Blackheath.

The Bastard of Fauconberg, seeing that he could not take London, left to meet with Edward IV, probably trying to negotiate his pardon. Knowing that the majority of his men were dead, he told his fleet to wait for him at Mersey and he marched on to Kingston-upon-Thames. When he arrived he was met by Lord Scales and Nicolas Fanute, the Mayor of Canterbury, who persuaded him to return to his defeated men. Fauconberg agreed and marched back to Blackheath, where he told his men to break up and go back to their homes peaceably.

On May 21 Fauconberg returned to his fleet of around 600 sailors, and sailed round the coast to Sandwich. He waited for Edward IV to arrive, who was triumphant after his victory at Tewkesbury, and handed over his entire fleet of 56 ships. The king pardoned him, knighted him and made him Vice-Admiral of the Fleet.

That night Henry VI died at the Tower, no doubt killed at the request of Edward. The king followed his younger brother, Richard of Gloucester, to start the pacification of Kent. Edward himself went into Kent where he punished the rebels severely. Some were hanged to encourage the others to pay fines, which the king demanded before he would give them a pardon. Edward was in desperate need of funds and the £2,000 he gathered was a welcome addition to his deflated treasury.

In September, the Bastard of Fauconberg was taken prisoner at Southampton and transported to Middleham Castle in Yorkshire, where he was beheaded on September 22, 1471. There is no specific reason why he was killed, but his head was placed on a spike on London Bridge with his face turned pointedly towards Kent, as a cruel reminder to everyone not to take on the might of the realm. Various citizens of London were knighted for their part in valiantly defending their city. So despite his brave fight for the Lancastrian cause,

Fauconberg had very little effect. In many accounts the Bastard of Fauconberg has been referred to as a swashbuckling adventurer but, despite his antics at sea, he was a loyal fighter for the Lancastrians and did his utmost to change the course of history.

HANS BOHEIM

Hans Boheim lived in Niklashausen in Southern Germany and was better known as the 'Piper' (or Drummer) of Niklashausen. He was a simple cowherd who, in his spare time, played as a musician at local weddings and festivities. By all accounts Boheim was an illiterate, uneducated man, and yet he had deep-rooted views on the political situation in Europe in the 15th century. He had a burning desire to overcome the oppressive feudal system and to rid Germany of the institutions that were bleeding the peasants dry.

The European feudal system was divided into categories, the highest social class being the wealthy landowners, the territorial princes and the Church. Next came the lesser nobles, who were tenured to the territorial princes. Beneath these, and the lowest in the hierarchy, were the peasants who rarely owned their own land, but held tenure from the landowner. Owning land, whether as a prince, a noble or a peasant, was the foundation of a man's social status. There was a large quantity of land available and yet a considerable number of the population did not have any rights to it. Peasants were also being impoverished by crippling taxes and bad government, and so it is not surprising that by 1476 conditions had reached an all-time low and there was a rising ebb of discontent.

THE VISION

Hans Boeheim was sitting on the banks of a small stream called the Tauber on March 24, 1476. While here, he received a visitation from the Virgin Mary, who told him to burn his musical instruments and to dedicate the remainder of his life to preaching the Gospel to his neighbours.

Boeheim abandoned his former way of life and his preaching soon attracted an enormous following. People streamed from the surrounding villages, making the pilgrimage to the altar of St Mary at Niklashausen, where Boeheim gave his sermons.

Boeheim would probably not be remembered today had it not been for the second visitation from the Virgin Mary, whose instructions were a lot more controversial. Boeheim claimed that she had told him that there should be no social class and that all men should be equal, cleansing themselves of any sins. They should earn their daily bread by hard toil, and what they earned they should share with their neighbour. Boeheim started to preach that the main obstacle that stood in the way of the people's salvation was the feudal system. He demanded the abolition of all worldly and clerical authority – popes, emperors, dukes and the like. Feudal taxes were also to be abolished and land was to become common property.

Boeheim's preachings attracted a lot of attention and his popularity grew among the common folk of Germany. The peasants flocked in their thousands to Niklashausen from kilometres around – men and women, young and old – many bearing offerings which they laid at the altar. Those who could afford it brought costly clothing and jewellery and soon the universal greeting between the pilgrims was 'brother' and 'sister'. Boeheim was hailed as the new Messiah and his congregation fell on their knees before him, tearing shreds from his garments to keep as sacred relics.

Their enthusiasm was not shared by the authorities who, because of the large crowds he was attracting, started to take his movement seriously. The priests in the surrounding villages called him a sorcerer and devil worshipper and tried, in vain, to stop their parishioners from making the pilgrimage to Niklashausen.

The mass of believers continued to increase and before long a revolutionary sect began to emerge. Boeheim's Sunday sermons were now attracting as many as 40,000 people, but little did his followers realize that Boeheim was in secret communication with the priest of Niklashausen and with two knights, Kuns of Thunfeld and his son, Michael. He appointed Thunfeld and his son as leaders of the planned insurrection.

PEASANTS' REVOLT

On the Sunday before the day of Saint Kilian (July 8), Hans Boeheim gave a sermon in front of a large gathering. He concluded this sermon with the following words:

And now go home, and weigh in your mind what our Holiest Madonna has announced to you, and on the coming Saturday leave your wives and children and old men at home, but you, you men, come back here to Niklashausen on the day of St. Margaret, which is next Saturday, and bring with you your brothers and friends, as many as they may be. Do not come with pilgrims' staves, but covered with weapons and ammunition, in one hand a candle, in the other a sword and a pike or halberd, and the Holy Virgin will then announce to you what she wishes you to do.

The bishop of Würzburg, Rudolph of Scherenberg, received news that there was to be a peasants' revolt, and he wasted no time in taking action. He sent 34 mounted men by nightfall to the village of Niklashausen and burst in on the sleeping Boeheim. They stole him out of his bed, tied him to the back of a horse, and took him to the bishop of Würzurg.

However, about 4,000 pilgrims had already arrived at Niklashausen in preparation for Saturday and, on hearing the news that their precious leader had been kidnapped, hurried after the horsemen. The pilgrims caught up with the bishop's men close to the Castle of Würzburg. One of the bishop's knights was wounded, but the others succeeded in taking Boeheim inside the castle, so their rescue efforts failed.

By the following Sunday, news had spread fast that Boeheim had been taken captive, and about 34,000 peasants assembled at Niklashausen. Some were disheartened and simply returned to their villages, but under the leadership of Kunz of Thunfeld and his son, about 16,000 pilgrims left for the castle at Würzburg. They marched through the night holding burning candles in one hand and weapons in the other.

They arrived early the next morning and gathered outside the walls of the castle. The castle's marshal came out to greet them and asked them what they wanted. The peasants ordered the marshal to release their leader, Boeheim, and said that if he refused they would have to use force. The marshal paused, and because he didn't give them an answer straight away, the peasants showered him with stones, forcing him to retreat within the safety of the castle walls.

This angered the bishop and he ordered his men to open fire on the peasants. After a short while the bishop ordered his men to cease firing and, after giving the peasants (false) promises, the pilgrims agreed to withdraw and started to disperse. The bishop did not remain true to his word, and as the pilgrims started to leave in straggling parties, he ordered his knights to pursue them and attack them from the rear. The peasants defended themselves bravely against such a cowardly onslaught. Twelve were killed and many others sought shelter in the Church of a neighbouring village. The bishop's knights followed them and threatened to burn the Church down, causing the peasants to surrender. They were taken back to the castle dungeons were they remained for several days.

The majority of the peasants were released, with the exception of Hans Boeheim and the man who had killed the bishop's knight when they first attempted to rescue Boeheim. These two men were beheaded outside the castle gates and the body of Boeheim was burnt to ashes, which was the normal treatment of a heretic.

The appointed leader of the revolt, Kunz von Thunfeld, fled the area and was only allowed to return home after surrendering all of his lands to the bishop. Germany remained quiet for a few years, but at the end of the century peasant rebellions started afresh.

In 1970, German film director, Rainer Werner Fassbinder, directed and starred in a television adaptation of *Niklashauser Far, Die,* which was based on the life of Hans Boeheim, one of history's tragic medieval heretics.

BUNDSCHUH
MOVEMENT

The Bundschuh movement, which lasted from 1493 to 1517, was a series of localized peasant rebellions in southwest Germany, and it played an important part in the German Peasants' War of the 15th and 16th centuries. It got its name from the peasant shoe (*Bundschuh*), meaning 'tied shoe', which was displayed on the flag the peasants used when they went into battle.

The first organized peasant movement under the banner of the Bundschuh movement took place in 1493 in Elsass. Seeking relief from oppressive taxes, unfair justice systems, high debts, costly ecclesiastic privileges, serfdom and many prohibitions, a band of peasants and burghers planned to seize the town of Schlettstadt and plunder its monastery. Under the leadership of a man called Jacob Wimpfeling, a German Renaissance humanist and theologian, the band of rebels planned to spread their movement throughout the area of Elsass, taking one town after another.

This was the first time that the banner was to be used, the design of which was the result of careful deliberation. It was decided that as a knight was distinguished by his use of spurs, so the peasant rising should be symbolized by their common shoe with long leather strings, the so-called Union Shoe. The hope was that when they displayed their banner, that anyone capable of fighting, would rush to their cause and join the movement. Membership into the movement was connected with strange initiation ceremonies and severe threats were issued to deter anyone from turning traitor.

Despite the movement's secret meetings and promises of loyalty, they still suffered from betrayal, when one of their members warned the local authorities of their planned attack on Schlettstadt. The authorities immediately intervened by sending a body of knights to seize anyone suspected of belonging to the conspiracy. Many members of the movement were taken captive and put in front of a tribunal. Their punishment was cruel, some were placed on the rack, others quartered or decapitated and some were crippled by having their hands or fingers removed.

Members who survived the torture fled to nearby Switzerland, where the Bundschuh thrived. Although the movement was now somewhat dispersed over the countryside, they succeeded in continuing their meetings. There were many minor skirmishes but it wasn't until nine years later, in 1502, that the opportunity arose for a mass uprising.

THE SECOND ATTEMPT

A branch of the Bundschuh had successfully re-organized itself in the bishopric of Speyer with about

7,000 recruits. Their movement extended into the regions of the Upper and Middle Rhine, with members mainly from the smaller villages rather than towns. Their headquarters was at Untergrünbach and its aim was to completely overthrow the existing ecclesiastical and feudal system. Their plan was to seize the lands and property belonging to the clergy and nobles and divide it up among the common people, forcing the abolition of taxes and serfdom. Another of their aims was to have no other authority apart from the emperor.

As they prepared to rise against the authorities, the movement was once again betrayed. A peasant taking confession, revealed the secret to a priest, who in turn revealed it to the authorities. Realizing how large the movement had grown, ecclesiastics, princes and nobles quickly arranged counteraction. The Bundschuh became the object of severe persecution. Anyone who was suspected of having been involved with the movement had their property confiscated, their wives and children were driven out of the country, and the men themselves were, in many cases, quartered alive. The more prominent members of the movement were tied to horses' tails and literally dragged to their place of execution.

Other bands of Bundschuh quickly gathered and, although their numbers were not sufficient to start an effective revolt, they did manage to hold the knights off long enough to allow many of their members to escape into Switzerland or other neutral territories. Others, who had been able to remain undetected, stayed in their own villages.

THE THIRD ATTEMPT

The Bundeschuh remained underground for a period of ten years, and it was not until 1512 that there were murmurs of new action. One of the leaders, who had managed to go unnoticed in the former suppression of the movement, was Joss Fritz, a former soldier. Fritz lived in Untergrünbuch where his job was a ranger, which gave him the freedom to wander from country to country. During the ten years of peace he never forgot the Bundeschuh, or what it stood for, and with his military background proved, Fritz to be a formidable leader.

In 1512, Fritz moved to a small village called Lehen, which was a few kilometres from the town of Freiburg, in Breisgau, where he took the position of a forester. From his new home he started to gather together the shreds of the remaining Bundeschuh and started encouraging new recruits. He moved stealthily, not wishing to attract any unwanted attention from the authorities. It was at this point that Fritz caught the attention of people of different classes – knights, priests, burghers, plebeians and peasants – all of whom listened intently to what he had to say. Slowly he talked them all round to his way of thinking – a new freedom, a permanent peace and a chance for the peasants to become equal citizens.

Fritz started regular meetings of the Bundeschuh in a meadow called the Hardematte, which lay just outside his village and was surrounded by woods. It was here that Fritz started to sew his seeds of rebellion.

These meetings led to the formation of a committee of people who were most dedicated to Fritz's cause, and gradually these men recruited more and more members, while Fritz himself travelled the country spreading his gospel.

The new rebellion broke out in the spring of 1514, when newly imposed taxes on wine, meat and bread were hitting the peasants hard. Their first target was the city of Schomdorf and about 5,000 members of the Bundeschuh arrived at the city. They demanded to see Duke Ulrich, who had been taxing the peasants to meet the costs of his luxurious court. The duke promised to abolish the new tax if the peasants would move on. However, the leaders were wary and felt that this was just a delaying tactic, so that the duke could have time to rally his knights and collect the taxes by force. The peasants decided to strike a blow on the valley of Rems as soon as possible, to let the duke know that they were serious about their demands. Soon the entire territory was under revolt and Ulrich was compelled to give in. He sent a letter to princes in the cities that had not been affected by the rebellion, asking for their support.

Meanwhile, the Diet (legislature of the German empire), which represented the cities and many delegates of the peasants, convened in Stuttgart. The peasants who were encouraged by their success in Rems and the surrounding districts, made their demands. They told the meeting that they wished to depose and punish three members of Ulrich's hated coucil – Lamparter, Thumb and Lorcher – add four knights, four burghers and four peasants to the duke's council and finally that they wished to confiscate the monasteries and any payments in favour of the state treasury.

In response the duke rode with his knights and councillors to Tuebingen, where he continued the meeting without the presence of the peasants. The burghers, who were now being threatened by the duke's military, betrayed the peasants and on July 8, the Tuebingen agreement came into being. This agreement imposed a large amount of the Ulrich's debt on the country, disposed of the peasants and finally inflicted a penal law on insurrection.

The peasants, on learning about the agreement, cried out that Ulrich had committed treason. However, Ulrich was gaining in strength after his debts had been taken away by the estates and, with added military aid, the new agreement was soon accepted all over the country.

The only area to offer resistance was the valley of Rems, where the Bundschuh still fought for their independence. They formed a peasant camp on the mountain of Koppel, but as time went by and food was becoming scarce, the peasants were soon driven home by starvation.

Ulrich's army turned force against the peasants and attacked the valley of Rems, plundering its cities and villages, which was contrary to the terms of the new agreement. They took 600 peasants captive, beheaded 16 of them and the remainder received heavy fines that went straight into Ulrich's coffer. Ulrich issued a number of penal laws against any future peasant gatherings and a special union was formed for the suppression of any future insurrections. Many of the leaders of Bundschuh had managed to evade being captured and gradually, one by one, made their way back home.

FURTHER OUTBREAKS

In the spring of 1514, a peasant war broke out in Hungary. There was a crusade being planned against the Turks and, with promises of freedom, many serfs joined the ranks. The 60,000 command was to be led by György Dózsa, who had already distinguished himself in a previous Turkish conflict. The Hungarian knights and nobles did not approve of the crusade, which threatened to deprive them of both their land and their slaves. They followed the bands of peasants going to join the crusade, and physically took back their serfs, punishing them for running away from their masters. When the army of crusaders heard about this, they were incensed, and their hatred of the nobility was heightened by revolutionary speeches. Dózsa shared this anger and soon the army of crusaders turned into an army of the revolution.

Dózsa set up camp with his followers in a field at Rakos, near Pest. Hostilities soon broke out with the surrounding villages. Nobles fell into the hands of the insurgents and castles were burnt to the ground. After their initial successes, Dózsa decided to divide his forces up into five separate columns. Two were sent to the mountains, a third remained on the field at Rakos to guard the capital and the fourth and fifth columns were led by Dózsa and his brother Gregor against Szegedin.

Back in Pest the nobility gathered an army, which was joined by the middle classes of Budapest. Together they attacked the field at Rakos, overcoming the peasants and executing many in a barbarous way. The remainder were sent home after having either their nose or ears removed.

Dózsa, on learning about the atrocities at Rakos, withdrew his forces from Szegedin and struck out at Bishop Csaky and the Count of Temeswar, who were on their way with troops to defend the town. The peasants fought hard for two days and their bravery was soon rewarded with victory. Dózsa and his men demanded vengeance for their comrades, and they impaled the bishop and hanged the royal treasurer from the gallows. Unfortunately, it was only Dózsa's group that met with success and the remnants of the other columns travelled to join the victorious army.

Dózsa issued a proclamation to abolish nobility, demanding equality to all men before God. Dózsa succeeded in recruiting a new army, many of whom were experienced cavalrymen. He moved his men to a powerful fortress at Temeswar, but the siege lasted over two months and soon his men were demoralized. While they were waiting for reinforcements, two columns of the Dózsa's army in Upper Hungary were defeated by the nobility, and the Transylvanian army, under the lead of Johann Zapolya, moved in against them.

A long and vicious battle ensued, and after several hours of fighting one branch of Dózsa's army took flight. Dózsa tried his hardest to encourage his remaining soldiers, and stood in the midst of them striking the nobles down until his sword broke in his hand. Dózsa was taken captive with about 40 of his officers and thrown into the castle dungeons, where they were left to starve. His brother, Gregory, was beheaded. After 14 days in the dungeons, only ten men were left alive. The ten men were led out into the open with Dózsa in the lead. Dózsa was led to an iron throne which had been made red hot and, loaded down by chains, he was made to sit down. They placed a red-hot crown on his head and a red-hot sceptre was thrust into his hand. The remaining nine men were told their lives would be spared if they were prepared to eat the flesh of their leader. Three, who were repulsed by the idea of cannibalism, refused and were immediately hacked to pieces. The other six, who were determined to survive, agreed. The last word that Dózsa uttered was 'Dogs!', as his former allies tore his flesh apart with red-hot pincers.

Any peasants who had survived capture, reassembled, but soon fell into the hands of their enemies. Their corpses were hung in thousands along the roadside or at the entrances of burnt-out villages. Records show that as many as 60,000 peasants were either massacred or fell in battle.

After this series of such decisive defeats and the mass atrocities that were carried out by the nobility, the Bundschuh movement virtually died out. However, by 1517 the Bundschuh was back in full swing in the Black Forest. Joss Fritz, reunited with many of his old comrades starting to recruit new members and the conspiracy started all over again.

PART THREE

EARLY MODERN FREEDOM FIGHTERS

THE PEASANTS' WAR

The Peasants' War in southern and central Germany lasted from 1524–25 and was the climax of a series of local rebellions that dated from the 15th century. These earlier revolts were all suppressed, but they were not as well organized or indeed as widespread as the rebellion of 1525. The revolt of the peasants, was closely connected with the Protestant Reformation in the regions, although, originally, their demands were more economic than religious.

Until the end of the 14th century, the peasants had enjoyed a reasonably comfortable existence. Although they didn't actually own their land, they were able to rent it at reasonable rates for fixed periods of time. However, conditions gradually grew worse as economic conditions became detrimental to the peasant class. The social structure of Germany was divided up into separate classes – princes, the lesser nobles, the prelates, the patricians, the burghers, the plebeians and finally, at the bottom of the hierarchy, the peasants. The princes were not really answerable to anyone and had the right to enforce taxes and borrow money as they needed it. The constantly rising costs of administration and the maintenance of their military meant that they were continually having to raise the cost of living for their subjects. The lesser nobility and clergy, who were not liable to pay any taxes, were generally in support of their princes. The main burden, therefore, fell on the peasants, who were often forced into slavery through increasing tax demands. The growing importance of having a strong military started to diminish the role of the lesser nobility. Their luxurious lifestyle took what little income they had as the cost of living continued to rise. To try and maintain a good standard of living they started to extort as much money as they could out of their territories. Rivalry broke out among the different sections of society and the ones that suffered the most were the peasants.

The peasants supported all the other levels of society not just through direct taxation but also in the production of agriculture and the raising of livestock. The peasant was responsible to whoever owned his land, whether it was a bishop, a prince, a town or a noble, and his time was spent tending his landowner's estate just so that he could earn enough to pay the extortionate taxes. Peasants were not allowed to hunt, fish or take wood from the forests, but they did have to sit back and watch their hard work being destroyed as nobles hunted across their precious crops. If a peasant wished to marry, they had to obtain the permission from their lord and were also forced to pay a heavy tax. When a peasant died, whatever they owned automatically became the property of his landlord. The only way out of this state of servitude was for the peasants to physically fight for their rights.

THE FIRST RISING

The first rising, in August 1524, took place in the county of Stühlingen and, although it was not well planned, its scale and ferocity showed that the peasants were to be taken seriously. It was as a result of restrictions put on them by the nobles, who wanted to restrict rural assemblies as much as possible, including festivals, village gatherings and even weddings. This was because the nobles sensed a growing discontent among the peasants and were worried about the outcome.

The peasants certainly weren't without military power as they had been forced to defend their villages many times over the past years, so they were well equipped with crossbows, guns and cannons. The tension finally erupted into the first real act of rebellion under the lead of a former *landsknecht* (mercenary) by the name of Hans Müller. On August 24, he led 1,200 peasants to the nearby town of Waldshut to take part in St Bartholomew's Day celebrations, gaining the alliance of the townspeople.

Müller tried unsuccessfully to recruit some Swiss mercenaries to help them attack Stühlingen castle. He knew that if his band of rebels was to be successful he would need a proper command structure and so between them they elected their own captains, sergeants and corporals to take control. Luckily for the peasant army, the nobles were not quick in responding, and the poor financial situation of the Hapsburg empire worked in their favour, as the nobles had not been able to fund a strong military army. By September, Captain George von Frundsberg, had planned a counter-attack. He asked the peasants to lay down their arms and ask their God for forgiveness, which was completely unacceptable to the peasants and a battle broke out. After this initial battle many of the peasants returned to their land to prepare for harvest, but a small hardcore group remained with Müller for the winter period.

At about the same time another group of peasants was reaching boiling point in Nuremberg over the strict enforcement of tithes. Refusing to pay, they burnt large quantities of grain that had been set aside to meet the extortionate payments. The council in Nuremberg responded by strictly enforcing the tithes.

In the autumn of 1524, there were small outbreaks of violence in Allgäu, Klettgau, Hegau, Thurgau and near the town of Villingen. The Swabian League, which was a peace-keeping force comprised of princes, nobles and cities, attempted to counter the attacks, but their armies were busy supporting Charles V in his war with Italy. The shortage of available fighting men was not helped by the fact that the Duke of Württemberg was hiring mercenary forces to try and retain some former territory from the Hapsburgs.

THOMAS MÜNZER

The radical reformer, Thomas Münzer (1489–1525), was born in Stolberg in Saxony. He studied for priesthood and was ordained in May 1514 at St Michael's in Braunschweig. Münzer was greatly influenced by Andreas Karlstadt and Martin Luther, and he agreed with their opposition to the Catholic Church's abusive use of power. He became a prominent figure in the German peasant war.

During the winter months Münzer had been busy spreading his gospel among the peasants of Klettgau. His influence was instilling a burning hatred of the nobility and their archaic feudal system, and by spring 1525 the rebellion had engulfed the majority of the south. The peasants had a strong desire to spread the Reformation in the rural areas, and not just the cities. They wanted to educate people on 'divine law', which had been drafted in a document called the *Twelve Articles in Memmingen*. These articles made the following demands:

1 The right of each community to choose and depose its own pastor.
2 An end to the small tithes of cattle for lay and ecclesiastical lords.
3 Release from serfdom.
4 Free access to fish and game.
5 Free access to firewood as needed.
6 An investigation of excessive tenural services.
7 Strict observance by the lords of the agreements made with their servants.

8 New rent assessments, based on equity and justice.
9 The basing of legal judgments, that is, punishments, on customary law rather than on constantly appearing arbitrary new laws.
10 The return of expropriated common fields.
11 Abolition of the death tax.
12 The Bible and 'divine law' justifies these demands.

The demands in themselves were revolutionary. To abolish serfdom would mean that the feudal lords would lose their main financial support. The restoration of tithes was an attack on the upper classes as it deprived them of almost one-half of their income. The right to choose one's own pastor would purge the nobility of its proprietary churches and thus take away their control. In fact the idea was so revolutionary that Martin Luther drafted a reply to the peasants in a pamphlet entitled *Admonition to Peace; A Reply to the Twelve Articles of the Peasants of Swabia*. In the pamphlet he gave cautious encouragement to the peasants, and condemned the oppressive practices of the nobility that had incited many of the riots. However, as the war continued, and especially as atrocities at the hands of the peasants increased, the revolt became an embarrassment to Luther, who subsequently turned against the revolt.

By the end of April 1525, it is estimated that as many as 300,000 peasants were armed and prepared to fight for their rights. The peasant rising also attracted the attention of some rebellious knights who had previously revolted about the power of the Church.

These men included, Stephan von Menzingen, Götz von Berlinchingen and Florian Geyer, who all decided to take part in the revolt.

THE MAIN RISING

At the start of the rebellion, peasants were equipped with little other than converted pieces of farm machinery and any personal weapons they might own. They had to try to steal artillery from captured cities and many arsenals were taken by force. Some of the cities supplied the peasants with weapons, just to avoid a major conflict, and by the summer of 1525, the peasant army were well equipped and ready to fight.

Although the peasants were now fully armed, they lacked military experience and seemed unable to keep up their formations when the battle was at its height. Their pikes were not long enough to be effective against the enemy's cavalry, and the peasants, themselves, had no cavalry to speak of.

In contrast, however, the peasants who had been trained by Thomas Münzer were skilled in military tactics and were able to withstand the resistance from the Landsknechte. When Münzer's army reached Mülhausen, they were quick to back up the peasants' grievances, and he issued them with a white banner with the words 'The Word of God is Eternal' emblazoned across the front.

When the peasant force met the Imperial army at Frankenhaüsen, they were promised a negotiation of terms if they were prepared to hand over their leader,

Münzer. While they were discussing what to do, a rainbow appeared in the sky, which the peasants took to be a sign from God. The peasants charged at the Imperial army. However, they were immediately butchered, losing approximately 5,000 men, against an Imperial loss of only six. Both Münzer and Pfeiffer were captured and tortured to extract confessions and were eventually executed.

Martin Luther, who had originally shown some sympathy for the peasants' cause, published a second pamphlet entitled *Against the Murderous, Thieving Hordes of Peasants*. He urged the nobles to quell the rebellion at any cost.

Within about six weeks the majority of the peasant movement was suppressed and, although fighting continued into the following year in isolated areas, it had little, if any, effect. The nobles fined any known rebel that had supported the peasant war. A peasant could only escape this extra payment if there was proof that he or she had no knowledge whatsoever of the revolt.

However, the repercussions did not end there. The cruelty that followed the peasants war was atrocious. It is estimated that more than 100,000 peasants were killed in the revolt itself, and there is no record of how many were slaughtered or tortured in the aftermath. The Swabian League, which was an association of Swabian cities and other powers in southwest Germany for the protection of trade and regional peace, set up a compensation programme, whereby their members were paid by the peasants own money. Peasants were forced to sell their personal belongings to meet this obligation and the nobles took a tighter hold following the end of the revolt. Their optimistic struggle to gain political rights ended in an even tighter control on the part of the higher social classes.

WILLIAM TYNDALE

Almost a century after John Wycliffe translated the Bible from Latin into English, Englishman William Tyndale translated the first English Bible, which was taken directly from Hebrew and Greek. Unlike his predecessor, who had to write his manuscript by hand, Tyndale was able to take advantage of the newly discovered printing press.

In 1454 the Christians were driven out of the capital of Constantinople (modern-day Istanbul), following a battle with the Turks. Many Greek scholars came to live in Europe and, instead of reading the Latin Bible, which had been used up until that time, they started to show an interest in the Greek New Testament. This made people realize that it would be beneficial to have a Bible in the language of the people, so that it was available for everyone to read. The invention of the printing press in 1440, by the German inventor Johannes Gutenberg, allowed for the first time the mass production of printed books. It involved a method of printing from movable type, including the use of metal moulds, a special press and oil-based inks, and this form of printing survived until late into the

20th century. With the study of languages ever-increasing, the dreams of having a new Bible soon became a reality.

William Tyndale was born c.1494, probably near Dursley in Gloucestershire, and was a descendant of an old Northumbrian family. Tyndale received an excellent education and enrolled in Oxford University in 1505, and later moved to Cambridge University. He was a bright student who excelled in languages and became fluent in Hebrew, Greek, Latin, Spanish, French, Italian, English and German. At the young age of 21, he received a Masters Degree and was a strong supporter of the movement for reform in the Catholic Church.

Tyndale was born into an era where Christians had fought and suffered considerably for their faith. In 1408, a Convocation at Oxford had ordained a law that forbade the translation of Scripture into English. It also warned if anyone was caught reading such a book, they would be excommunicated. However, many Christians held the Bible dear to their hearts and continued to read it in secrecy and many copies of Wycliffe's original Bible had survived the Roman persecution.

On top of this, in the 15th century the pope was an exceptionally powerful person, and a Bible in English that everyone could read was something he definitely didn't want. Tyndale, however, had a passion to produce a pure English translation of the Scriptures and, against all odds, he dedicated his life to this purpose.

HIS MISSION

When Tyndale left Cambridge University, he took the post of chaplain and tutor to the children of Sir John Walsh at Little Sodbury Manor. Walsh was a well-known warrior who had been knighted as the king's champion during the coronation of Henry VIII. Walsh often invited church dignitaries into his home and it was round the dinner table that the names of Martin Luther and Erasmus first came to Tyndale's attention. Luther had recently published important works on the Reformation, while Erasmus had published his Greek and Latin New Testament in 1516.

Filled with his desire to spread the Scripture, Tyndale preached in the open air at Little Sodbury and in the surrounding villages, where he gained many friends among the laity but not the church leaders. He was incensed that the ordinary person was suppressed by the Roman dignitaries and he kept raising the question whether the Bible belonged solely to the hierarchy of the Church, or whether it was meant for the average Christian as well.

While still employed by the Walshes, Tyndale translated one of the works of Erasmus – *Enchiridion Militis Christiani (Christian Soldier's Manual)*, which contained considerable truths about the Christian faith. Becoming more and more unpopular with his fellow clergymen, Tyndale was arrested for ministering the Word and charged with spreading heresy. He was eventually released by the bishop's chancellor on the understanding that he did not continue to preach publicly.

Worried that his kind employer might get into trouble for harbouring a dissenter, Tyndale decided it was time to leave Little Sodbury Manor. With the aid of financial help from Sir John Walsh, Tyndale moved to London where he found the opportunity to preach at a church in St Dunstan-in-the-West. It was here that he met Humphrey Monmouth, an Alderman in the city.

Monmouth listened intently to the words of Tyndale, and realized that his beliefs were similar to his own. At the end of his sermon, Monmouth approached Tyndale and discovered that he was penniless and had nowhere to stay. Monmouth took pity on him and offered him to stay at his house, which is where he was introduced to John Frith, an English protestant priest. Frith was educated in Greek, and so with his help, Tyndale worked day and night for six months to fulfil his dream – to translate the Bible into English.

Tyndale sought the help of Bishop Cuthbert Tunstall, but like many church officials, he was uncomfortable with the idea of an English translation. After this, Tyndale was met with considerable persecution, and his friends advised him to flee from London. Fearing that he would be arrested again for heresy, and realizing that England was not the place to complete his translation, Tyndale left England, with the help of Humphrey Monmouth, and fled to the continent.

HIS TIME ABROAD

Little realizing that he would never return to England, Tyndale left for Hamburg with parts of his translation on paper and some still in his head. As soon as he left the English shores, his true friend Monmouth was arrested and sent to the Tower of London. He was charged with harbouring a nonconformist, which in those days was a very serious offence, but after an abject appeal to Cardinal Wolsey, he managed to obtain his release.

Tyndale found friends among the Christian people during his time on the continent, who offered him places to continue his task. By 1525 Tyndale had completed his manuscript and had managed to find a printer in Cologne to set his copy in type. Tyndale was determined to stay in Cologne until the printing of his precious Bible was complete, but his efforts were nearly destroyed.

Two of the printers who were employed in setting up the type for Tyndale's Bible were overheard at the local tavern, talking indiscreetly about what they were doing. Their bragging was overheard by John Cochleus, a Romanist who was a bitter enemy of Martin Luther and the Reformation. Plying the two printers with wine, Cochleus learned the whereabouts of the 3,000 copies of Tyndale's first printing. Cochleus informed the authorities, who banned the printers from any further work on the project.

Tyndale and a companion, William Roye, were able to get away with the majority of the printed sheets, and fled up the Rhine to the city of Worms. Cochleus, when he realized that his plan had been foiled, sent a description of Tyndale's translation to prominent religious leaders in England and urged them to be on the lookout. Cochleus carefully decribed the format of the printing so that the authorities would be aware when it arrived in England.

WORK IN WORMS

Worms was the city associated with the name of the great German Reformer, Martin Luther. It is thought that Tyndale and Luther met up on several occasions, sharing the same doctrines on religion. In Worms, Tyndale saw how they were gradually breaking the shackles of Rome and he longed for the same thing to happen in his own beloved country.

Tyndale settled down once again to continue his translation from Greek into English, using Luther's German version of the Bible as an occasional reference. By 1525 Tyndale had completed his translation of the New Testament and it was ready to go to a new printer.

Having been tricked once by Cochleus, Tyndale made a clever move and had two versions of his Bible printed in different formats. He hoped that if the Catholics discovered the larger books, he still might be able to sneak the smaller ones past the authorities. The Bibles arrived in England, using every way possible to conceal them – in bales that looked like cloth, in sacks of flour and even in barrels. They arrived safely in England and it wasn't long before the Catholic bishops learned that Tyndale's new Bible was being sold throughout the country. The East Coast ports were being watched carefully, and some Bibles did not reach their destination as bundles were found by officers and burnt. As soon as one bundle was destroyed, however, more Bibles arrived and the authorities could do nothing to stop them.

Henry VIII and the ecclesiastical authorities were incensed at the arrival of the Bibles and didn't know how to stop them. The Archbishop of Canterbury then came up with a bright idea. He decided to buy up all the copies that were printed, through a German merchant named Packington. This would mean that there would be no more copies arriving in England. What he didn't know was the merchant was already a good friend of Tyndale.

Packington knew that Tyndale needed money to pay the printers for the work they had already done, so he thought he had found a way of getting him out of trouble. Packington set up the deal with the bishop – the bishop had the books, Tyndale had the much-needed money and the finances to start his second edition of the New Testament.

TYNDALE THE MARTYR

Tyndale, who knew he had made many enemies, stayed in hiding on the continent and continued writing Christian literature. *The Obedience of a Christian Man* boldly argued that ordinary Christians should be able to have and understand the Word of God without being dependent on corrupt religious leaders.

One of Tyndale's most bitter opponents was Sir Thomas More, who was commissioned by Henry VIII to refute the heretic's arguments and discredit his character. More wrote nine books against Tyndale the reformer, which ultimately defended the authority of the pope and the Roman Catholic Church. Thomas More also tried to prove that Tyndale's translation of the New Testament was full of error and his attack on the reformer was relentless.

Meanwhile, Tyndale was enduring a life of exile just for the sake of his beliefs, aware that it would be his death sentence if he were to return to England. Afraid to venture out on the streets, Tyndale yearned to return to his beloved country. His enemies sent people to befriend Tyndale to try and persuade him to come home, but he wasn't stupid and knew that once he stepped foot on English soil he would be arrested and killed.

Tyndale was eventually betrayed by a man called Henry Phillips, who he considered to be a true ally but who, in fact, had been sent by the pope to try to trap him. One evening in 1534, waiting until it was nearly dark, Tyndale stepped out for an evening walk. A band of officers from Brussels attacked him, tied him up and took him to the dungeons at the castle of Vilvorde, 29 km (18 miles) from Antwerp. For almost six months Tyndale was kept prisoner in the damp, dark and windowless cell. He asked permission to use a candle at night and for a cloak to keep out the cold, but all his requests were denied. There was no trial, there were no questions, he knew he was there to die.

On October 6, 1536, Tyndale met the death of a heretic. He was taken from his prison, tied to a stake, strangled and then his body burnt to ashes. His last prayer to God, which was answered, was 'Lord, open the King of England's eyes'.

One year after his death, the English Bible received royal recognition and a year after that every parish church in England had received their own copy. So the reformer who eventually got his way never got to see his Bible in general use, not just in England, but all over the world. Tyndale was certainly a pioneer, a man who was dominated by an overpowering passion. He was a freedom fighter in every sense of the word, giving himself up to a lonely life so that he could complete his burning desire. In the end he achieved everything he set out to do – a Bible in clear, simple English that everyone could understand. He worked selflessly for the love of God in a constant struggle to free his countrymen from the previous religious restraints.

MARTIN LUTHER

The English Reformation started in the Reign of Henry VIII on October 31, 1517, when a German monk by the name of Saint Martin Luther nailed his *95 Theses* on the 'Power and Efficacy of Indulgences' to the church door in Wittenberg, Germany. The opening paragraph read:

> *Out of love for the truth and the desire to bring it to light, the following propositions will be discussed at Wittenberg, under the presidency of the Reverend Father Martin Luther, Master of Arts and of Sacred Theology, and Lecturer in Ordinary on the same at that place. Wherefore he requests that those who are unable to be present and debate orally with us, may do so by letter.*
>
> *In the Name our Lord Jesus Christ. Amen.*

The reason Luther took this action was because of a dispute over who was entitled to money generated by wandering papal indulgence sellers. The theory behind Luther's *Theses* was that people could only be saved by their faith, and no amount of purchased indulgences could alter this fact.

The logic behind indulgences is hard for modern people to understand, but in fact they made a great deal of sense. The idea is based on the medieval Catholic doctrine in which sinners must not only repent their sins, they must also confess these sins and pay some sort of retribution. In other words, the sinner needed to undergo some kind of punishment or task so that his or her sin would be completely absolved. The punishment often took the form of doing charitable deeds, such as feeding the poor or looking after the sick, which showed the sinner was repentant in his behaviour towards fellow human beings.

Indulgences, which were granted by the pope, forgave individual sinners, not for their sins, but for the secular punishment applied to those sins. These indulgences had become big business and were earning certain unscrupulous people a lot of money. Although Luther's was a drastic view in the 16th century, little did he realize what a lasting and radical effect it would have.

THE YOUNG LUTHER

Martin Luther was born on November 10, 1483, in Eisleben, Germany, to a rugged miner Hans and his wife Margarethe. He was baptized the following morning, on the feast day of Saint Martin of Tours, after whom he was named. The following year the family moved to Mansfeld where his father had obtained a job working in the copper mines. Having come from a very poor background, Hans was determined to see that his son had a sound education. Luther was sent to a school run by a lay group called the Brethren of Common Life. In 1498, he attended a school in Eisenach where he stayed until 1501. At the age of 18 he went to the University of Erfurt, obtaining a Bachelor of Philosophy in 1502 and a Master's Degree in 1505.

His father's greatest wish was that his son should become a laywer, and in accordance with this, Luther enrolled in the law school at the University of Erfurt. History differs greatly on the reasons why Luther left law school so suddenly in 1505 and entered an Augustinian monastery. One reason is the possible brutal bullying he received both at school and at home drove him into the monastery. The second reason is that a lightning bolt struck the ground next to him as he was returning to school one day. He was terrified, but realizing that his life had been spared decided to devote his life to God. The third reason was that a close friend was brutally attacked and killed and that the anguish caused him to retreat. Although the true motive will always be a matter of controversy, the reason he gives in a letter to his father is, 'When I was terror-stricken and overwhelmed by the fear of impending death, I made an involuntary and forced vow.'

LIFE IN THE MONASTERY

Luther entered the monastery on July 17, 1505. Although little is recorded about his monastic life, it does appear that Luther dedicated himself to trying to please God, whether through fasting, flagellation, long hours in prayer or constant confessions. He became aware of his own sinfulness and described this part of his life as one of deep spiritual despair.

Luther's superior in the monastery, Johann von Staupitz, tried his hardest to explain to Luther what the 'love of God' actually meant, and told him that he was trying too hard. At one time Luther sat for six hours in the confessional with Staupitz, trying to remember every sin that he had ever committed. In the end his mentor decided that the young Luther needed more work to distract him from his internal disputes, and he told his young monk to pursue an academic career. In 1507, Luther was ordained as a priest.

Luther started teaching theology at the University of Wittenberg in 1508 and earned a Bacherlor's degree in Biblical Studies on 9 March and the following year a Bachelor's degree in the *Sentences* of Peter Lombard. Lombard was a celebrated theologian and bishop of the 12th century, whose *Four Books of Sentences* was a compilation of biblical texts on the entire field of Christian theology. This was the main textbook of theology in the Middle Ages, and Luther was greatly influenced by his writing. Martin Luther was given the title Doctor of Theology by the university on October 19, 1512, for his teachings of the Scripture and the early Church.

The demands of teaching and lecturing made Luther study the Scriptures in depth, and it led him to question the contemporary use of terms such as *penance* and *righteousness* in the Roman Catholic

Church. The Bible started to take on a new meaning, and he believed that the church had lost sight of the true meaning of Christianity.

LUTHER'S *95 THESES*

In addition to his teaching at the university, Luther also preached at the city church, St Mary's. Luther started to preach to his parishioners that salvation was a gift from God, and that Christ died on the cross to forgive sins in return for faith and trust. It was in the Scriptures that Luther found the answers to questions that troubled his soul, answers that lit the way for the Reformation.

Luther was also asked to preach occasionally at the castle church in Wittenberg, which was the site of one of Europe's largest collection of relics. The relics had been gathered by Elector Frederick the Wise and were considered to be holy. Pilgrims believed that if they viewed the entire collection of relics at Wittenberg they would reduce their time in Purgatory.

In 1517, the Dominican friar Johann Tetzel arrived in Germany, selling indulgences in an attempt to raise money for the ongoing construction of St Peter's Basilica. Although Elector Frederick kept Tetzel out of his domain, Luther's parishioners went against his preachings and crossed the border to buy indulgences. Luther saw this trade in indulgences as an abuse that could mislead people away from the true meaning of confession and true repentence.

At first, Luther approached the problem cautiously, but his *95 Theses* were in part due to the sale of these indulgences. Luther changed the course of history by nailing his *Theses* on the church door at Wittenberg, accusing the Roman Church of heresy. Other men before him – John Wycliffe, John Hus, Thomas Linacre and John Colet – had already put their lives on the line for their beliefs, forming the foundations of Reform upon which Luther was now acting. Although the original *Theses* were written in Latin, they were quickly translated into German and within two weeks, the text had quickly spread throughout Germany, and within two months throughout Europe.

Luther wrote a letter to his superior, Archbishop Albrecht of Magdeburg on October 31, 1517, to express his concerns, and included a copy of his *95 Theses*. The archbishop didn't reply to Luther's letter, but instead forwarded it to Rome, believing the document to be heretical due to its criticism of the pope.

REPERCUSSIONS

At first Pope Leo III treated the matter with disdain, believing that it was merely a matter of dispute between the monks. Local church officials, however, were not so keen to let the matter rest, and they urged the pope to take action. Three months after the *Theses* first appeared on the church door, the pope ordered the Augustian Order to suppress Luther and his heretical preaching. The Order of St Augustine, also known as the Augustinians, is one of the five great mendicant religious orders founded in the Middle Ages. In April 1518, Luther was given the chance to defend his case at a meeting of the Augustinians. One of the members on the committee was the Dominican monk Martin Bucer, who listened intently to Luther's new teachings before officials of the Augustinian order. Bucer was converted to Luther's beliefs and eventually withdrew from his order in 1521.

On August 7, 1518, Luther was given 60 days in which to appear in Rome to renounce his heresies. At this point, Luther's ally Frederick the Wise intervened and arranged a meeting with the papal legate, Cajetan, in Germany. Instead of helping, this meeting made matters worse, as Cajetan would not give in and threatened Luther with with all kinds of papal punishment. Luther stood firm, believing that the pope would take his side once he understood what Luther was trying to say. By November, Luther realized that this was not going to happen, and he appealed openly for a general council of the Church to amend the errors of the Church and the pope.

As nothing satisfactory had resulted from the meeting with Cajetan, and Luther was temporarily silenced, another voice was heard, that of Doctor Eck. Eck challenged Luther's friend, Doctor Carlstadt, to a public dispute on the contested points of theology and indulgences. This aroused Luther once more to speak out, and a public discussion, which lasted several weeks, was held at Leipsic. Doctor Eck spoke for the papacy, while Luther and Carlstadt supported the Reformation. It was through these discussions that the mind of Europe was prepared for the great revolution that was soon to take place.

The next two years were filled with activity and, following the rejection of Rome, Luther started his appeals in earnest to try and reform the Church. At this time he wrote three major works – *Address to the German Nobility, Babylonian Captivity of the Church* and *The Freedom of a Christian* – thereby emotionally cutting himself off from Rome.

Because of these works, the inquisition against Luther was reopened in 1520. The peak of the inquisition came on June 15, when the pope issued the Papal Bull of excommunication, the famous *Exsurge Domine,* which ordered Luther to recant his teachings. This meant that Luther was now officially excluded from the ancient Catholic Church.

Luther reacted in protest and, on December 10, 1520, he burnt the Papal Bull along with other books on church law. As the flames rose, Luther is said to have yelled:

*Because you, godless book, have grieved or shamed
the holiness of the Father, be saddened and consumed
by the eternal flames of Hell.*

The repercussions in Rome were considerable and on January 3, 1521, the pope had Luther excommunicated. Luther, however, had an ally in the emperor, who felt forced to accept his views due to the large amount of pro-Luther support in his empire. He was also influenced by various princes, who were hoping to weaken the pope's political influence through Luther. Because of this, Luther was guaranteed a safe passage on his trip to the Imperial Diet of Worms (a general assembly [a Diet] of the estates of the Holy Roman Empire).

THE TRIP TO WORMS

Luther started his trip to Worms, a small town on the Rhine river, on April 2, 1521. On his journey he preached in the towns Erfürt, Gotha and Eisenach, and in each place he was welcomed enthusiastically by the people. At Worms Luther was asked to renounce his teachings in front of the emperor, the young Charles V, but Luther saw no proof that his views were wrong and said:

> *Unless I am convinced by Scripture and plain reason*
> *– I do not accept the authority of the pope and*
> *councils, for they have contradicted each other - my*
> *conscience is captive to the Word of God. I cannot and*
> *I will not recant anything for to go against conscience*
> *is neither right nor safe. God help me. Amen.*

After negotiations failed, the emperor issued his Edict of Worms and declared Martin Luther an outlaw. Luther was dismissed, but because he held a letter of safe conduct, he was not arrested. The letter guaranteed him 21 days of safe travel and Luther headed home on April 25.

After Luther's allies left Worms, the emperor imposed an Imperial Act (*Wormser Edikt*) which simply meant that, being an outlaw, Luther could be killed by anyone without the threat of punishment. Luther had powerful friends among the princes of Germany, one of whom was Frederick the Wise. Frederick arranged for Luther to be kidnapped on his way home from Worms. Luther himself was fully aware of the plan, which not only allowed him to disappear from public view for a while, but also guaranteed his safety.

Luther was seized by masked horsemen and taken to the secluded castle of Wartburg, which was located on a high cliff overlooking Eisenach. During his 300 lonely days at Wartburg castle, Luther changed his appearance from a monk to a knight, assuming the name Knight George. He wore a cloak and dagger, let his hair grow long and went hunting with other knights in the castle. This period of his life turned out to be very productive, as he continued his work on the translation of the Bible from Greek into German and wrote countless letters and religious tracts. Luther's version of the New Testament was eventually printed in September 1522, which gave the Germans a uniform written language. It is still being used today in its basic form.

Letters and pamphlets started to appear, signed by the now infamous Martin Luther. The emperor was unable to track them down, but he had his suspicions. The emperor wrote to Frederick the Wise, asking the whereabouts of the heretic, but Frederick replied saying that he had no knowledge as to where he was. In fact Frederick was not lying, as he had given strict instructions that no one should tell him where Luther was being kept so that he would not betray his friend.

Although Frederick remained a loyal Catholic throughout his life, he still regarded Luther as one of his subjects and protected him not so much on religious, as on political grounds.

RETURN TO WITTENBERG

Luther came out of exile at Wartburg in March 1521, and return to Wittenberg. Although Luther had launched a revolution, at the beginning he almost lost control of it. He found himself in conflict with other reformers with whom he disagreed and, who he felt, had become too radical. Luther had to work hard to bring the Reformation movement back to a more moderate line. Luther was still considered to be an outlaw by the emperor and the Catholic Church, but the Reformation had rooted itself so deeply by this time, it seemed unlikely that Luther would be arrested.

Luther continued to spread his beliefs in the following years and in his work *Of the Worldly Authorities, and How Much Obedience one owes Them,* he formulated the basis for his political ethics. He worked diligently to explain his beliefs and offered guidance to anyone who sought his counsel. He wrote books on pastoral care, on the proper conduct and mode of life for a Christian and many other topics. As Lutheran Churches grew, Luther started to write guidelines for their ministers and a new order of social service was achieved by the introduction of a community money box. One of Luther's most important duties was the reform of the school system. The Reformation called for well-educated pastors, teachers and civil servants and Luther, in his work entitled To the *Councilmen of all Cities within German Territories; Christian Schools Ought to be Kept Up*, stated that the authorities were obliged to provide a good education for young people.

LUTHER AND THE PEASANTS REBELLION

The Peasants Rebellion was closely connected with the Protestant Reformation, and the rebellious commoners took great strength from Luther's preaching, believing that he supported their cause. Some of Luther's statements gave them good reason for thinking that he was on their side, but they were wrong. Possibly fearing that the rebellion might have a major impact on his religious reforms, he became their enemy and the peasants had to turn to more radical religious figures. One of these was Thomas Münzer, a religious fanatic who was out to overturn the feudal system and replace it with an egalitarian order.

Luther continued to preach even within areas of unrest, and he stood firm against his use of force. He encouraged the peasants to free themselves from the religious ties of the authorities, not their economic or political influence. His experience with the peasants led Luther to write his controversial work entitled *Against the Murderous and Thieving Hordes of Peasants*.

Initially the rebellion spread quickly and knights and territorial lords were at a loss to know how to suppress it. However, the peasants were eventually defeated in

1526 at the battle of Frankenhausen, and the rebel leaders were executed.

LUTHER AND THE NUNS

Luther's teachings on the goodness and necessity of marriage caught the attention of Katherine von Bora and other nuns who lived at Marien-thron Cistercian monastery in Nimbschen. In secret they read passages from Luther's sermons, as it was a punishable offence if they were caught. Knowing that they could not voluntarily leave the monastery, some of the nuns wrote letters to their families asking for help. Their families were poor, however, and were unable to offer assistance, so the nuns poured out their hearts in a letter to Martin Luther. They used Leonhard Koppe, a 59-year-old merchant who delivered fish to the monstery, to discharge the letter from them.

When Luther received the letter, he struggled deeply with his conscience, but finally came up with a plan. Luther asked Koppe for his help, and even though he knew he risked his reputation, career and his own life if he aided in the escape, Koppe agreed to the plan. They left in the early hours of the morning and, using Koppe's team of horses to pull a covered wagon filled with fish barrels, they managed to get inside the gates of the monastery. The wagon left the monastery with empty fish barrels, this time carrying 12 runaway nuns.

Three of the nuns returned to their families, while the remaining nine travelled through the night to the Augustinian monastery in Wittenberg, where Luther lived. Having helped the nuns escape to a new life, Luther felt responsible for their well-being. He helped six of them find a home, a husband, or a job, while three, including Katherine, remained at Wittenberg. Katherine's family were ashamed of her conduct and did not want her back, so Luther arranged for her to live with the family of the city clerk, Philipp Reichenbach.

Katherine became friends with a young man by the name of Jerome Baumgärtner, who was a former student of the University of Wittenberg. They fell in love and they talked of getting married. Jerome was forced to return home to Nuremberg, but promised to return to Wittenberg before the end of the month. Despite the fact that Katherine wrote him numerous letters, he never replied, and it was apparent that his prosperous family did not consider a runaway nun with no money to be an ideal match for their son.

Luther, who still felt responsible for Katherine, suggested that a pastor, Dr Kasper Glatz, who was a man in his sixties, would make a suitable husband. Katherine immediately snubbed the suggestion, which Luther considered to be rather prudish.

Still wanting to see his protégé married, Luther wrote to Jerome Baumgärtner to see if he would change his mind. On October 12, 1524, Luther wrote:

If you want your Katie von Bora, you had best act quickly, before she is given away to someone else who wants her. She has not yet conquered her love for you. I would gladly see you married to each other.

Baumgärtner did not reply to Luther's letter and in the spring of 1525, announced his engagement to a beautiful 14-year-old girl from a wealthy family. Katherine was devastated by the news and Luther arranged for her to go and live with his friends, Lucas and Barbara Cranach, along with the Schönfeld sisters, who had also escaped from the monastery.

LUTHER MARRIES

Because Luther had been excommunicated by the pope and outlawed by the emperor, he did not consider himself to be a suitable candidate for marriage. And yet, despite opposition from many of his friends, he still asked Katherine to be his wife. Katherine was 16 years his junior, and many of Luther's friends felt that the union would bring about the downfall of the Reformation. They married on the evening of Tuesday, June 13, 1525, and Katherine moved into Luther's home at Wittenberg. Luther became a devoted husband to 'Katy' – as she had become affectionately known – and father to their six children: Hans, Elizabeth, Magdalena, Martin, Paul and Margaretha. The family grew as the household also included one of Katherine's relatives and, after 1529, six of Luther's sister's children. To help with the running of the house, Luther also housed students, and he became famous for his talks around the dinner table. The students were eager to hear what he had to say and his views became the basis for the Protestant interest in good marriages and families.

Luther continued with his reforms of the Church, and one of the most important changes was allowing the parish to take both the wafer and the wine during Holy Communion. On top of Church reforms, Luther also continued to write many books, including song-books – *Smart Songbook* and the choral *A Mighty Fortress is Our God.*

LUTHER'S LAST YEARS

During his years as a reformer, Luther had suffered from many ailments, which had caused him a lot of discomfort. After 1536 Luther started to experience more serious bouts of illness. These included tinitus and kidney and bladder stones, which caused him a lot of pain during the remainder of his life.

Luther remained busy during the later years of his life, with lecturing at the university and serving as dean of the theological faculty. He struggled with continuing illness and physical problems, causing him to be short-tempered, which showed in his final writings.

Martin Luther eventually died of natural causes on February 18, 1546, in Eisenben, the city of his birth. He was buried in the castle church at Wittenberg directly underneath the pulpit.

Luther's last written statement was found in his pocket just before his burial, which stated:

No one who was not a shepherd or a peasant for five years can understand Virgil in his Bucolica and Georgica. I maintain that no one can understand

Cicero in his letters unless he was active in important affairs of state for twenty years. Let no one who had not guided the congregations with the prophets for one hundred years believe that he has tasted Holy Scripture thoroughly. For this reason the miracle is stupendous in John the Baptist, in Christ, in the Apostles. Do not try to fathom this divine Aeneid, but humbly worship its footprints. We are beggars. That is true.

Martin Luther will always be remembered, as Lutheranism remains to this day the dominant religion, not only of Germany, but also in the countries of Scandinavia. He was a man who was in the right place at the right time, who despite much opposition, managed to get his message across. He left behind him a legacy of his irrepressible fascination with the study of God and God's relationship to mankind. There is no doubt that the reformation, with Luther's aid, changed the Church fundamentally, forever.

HULDRYCH ZWINGLI

Huldrych Zwingli was a prominent leader of the Swiss Reformation (1516–31). After Luther and Calvin, Zwingli was the most important early Protestant reformers and was active in extending the reform to other Swiss cities, such as Basel, Sankt Gallen and Bern. What Martin Luther had preached in Germany, Huldrych Zwingli taught in Zürich and even his preaching was more radical. He was involved in controversy not just with Catholic opponents, but also with the Lutheran reformers because he denied the presence of Christ in any form in the Eucharist. Zwingli gained much public support because his beliefs were simple and straightforward – the Bible is the truth and anything that is not in the Bible is not truth. He began a large Reformation movement that resulted in the demise of Catholicism in Switzerland, making him extremely unpopular with Roman officials.

HIS EARLY YEARS

Huldrych Zwingli was born on January 1, 1484, in the village of Wildhaus in the Toggenburg valley in

Switzerland. His father was a free peasant who was a village magistrate and his mother, Margaret Meili, was the sister of the abbot of Fischingen in Thurgau. His uncle, Batholomäus Zwingli, was the priest of Wildhaus and later went on to become dean of Wesen.

The young Zwingli was educated in Basel and then in 1496 in Bern, where his master, Heinrich Wölfin, inspired in him a love for the classics and music. In addition to music, Zwingli studied poetry, philosophy, astronomy, physics and the ancient classics and he acquired his BA degree in 1504 and Master of Arts in 1506. His musical talent caught the attention of the Dominicans, who tried to entice him into entering a monastery. However, his father and uncle managed to dissuade him, and he moved on to further study at the University of Vienna. He read theology and became deeply influenced by the lectures of Reformer Thomas Wyttenbach. Under Wyttenbach, Zwingli started to learn the truth about the Gospel and at the age of 22 he was ordained by the Bishop of Constance.

Zwingli was appointed parish priest of Glarus in 1506, where he proved that he was a good pastor. He served as a chaplain in the Swiss army where he accompanied mercenaries on several campaigns. However, this period of his life convinced him that the mercenary system was a great evil, a view that was bound to provoke hostility at Glarus, and in 1516 he moved to a new position in Einsiedeln. The ten years spent at Glarus laid the foundations of Zwingli's work as a reformer and in Einsiedeln he continued his studies of the Bible and the classics.

At this point Zwingli was influenced by Desiderius Erasmus, a prominent Dutch humanist. Erasmus exposed the abuses of the Church, and did more than any other single person to advance the revival of learning. In Einsiedeln, Zwingli had the opportunity to preach his new convictions to pilgrims, but continued his denouncement of the mercenary trade. His early publications were more political than religious, being aimed at what he deemed the degrading Swiss practice of hiring out mercenaries in war. Zwingli's literary works, while still in Glarus, found him an ally in the Swiss cardinal, Mattias Schinner, and he was given an annual pension from Rome.

STRENGTHENING HIS BELIEFS

Zwingli's opposition to foreign military service and his growing reputation as a fine preacher and learned scholar led to his election in 1518 as people's priest at the Great Minster (Grossmünster) in Zürich. This post, although providing him with a minimal income, gave him the scope he needed to extend his preaching. It wasn't really until he was a priest of the Great Minster that Zwingli started to publicly question the dogma of the Roman Catholic Church.

In 1519, the plague struck, Zürich killing one-quarter of the population. Zwingli stayed to minister to the sick and dying. He too was struck down with the plague and nearly lost his life. This, followed by the death of his brother in 1520, strengthened his beliefs in spiritual and theological elements, which had hitherto been somewhat overshadowed by his humanistic convictions.

Having fully recovered from his illness, in 1520, Zwingli was given permission by Zürich's governing council to preach the true Scriptures, and these sermons helped to stir the revolts against fasting and clerical celibacy that initiated the Swiss Reformation. Boosted by his success as a politician and his social efforts during the plague of 1520, Zwingli's prestige and importance began to increase.

Following the arrest of some printers for eating meat during lent, Zwingli rose to the defence, which started the reforms in Zürich. Zwingli also challenged the practice of clerical celibacy when he broke his vows by marrying a widow of high standing in the community, Anna Reinhard, in 1522. They managed to keep their marriage a secret from all but their closest friends until 1524, when they had a public ceremony. It was a good partnership that resulted in four children, adding to the three Anna already had from her previous marriage.

THE REFORMATION

It was after his recovery from the plague that Zwingli started his reform in earnest. The reform in Switzerland came about in a different way in that the reformers petitioned the city magistrates to implement certain reforms. The magistrate would then call a public meeting or disputation, to which Roman Catholic theologians and reformers were invited. Both were required to defend their beliefs and it wasn't uncommon for the councils to rule that the debate had to be conducted on the basis of Scripture alone.

The first of these disputations was held on January 29, 1523, in Zürich in front of an audience of over 600 people. Just prior to the disputation, Zwingli had published his *67 Articles*. This document was an important historical document because it constituted the earliest declaration of the Reformed faith. The first few points from the *Article* will indicate some of the basic beliefs of Zwingli:

All who say that the gospel is nothing without the approbation of the Church, err and cast reproach upon God.

The sum of the gospel is that our Lord Jesus Christ, the true Son of God, has made known to us the will of his heavenly Father, and redeemed us by his innocence from eternal death, and reconciled us to God.

Therefore Christ is the only way to salvation to all who were, who are, who shall be.

Christ is the head of all believers who are his body; but without him the body is dead.

All who live in this Head are his members and children of God. And this is the Church, the communion of saints, the bride of Christ, the Ecclesia catholica.

Christ is our righteousness. From this it follows that our works are good so far as they are Christ's, but not good so far as they are our own.

This first disputation ended in a complete victory for Zwingli and his followers, and ended with the Council instructing Zwingli to continue his preaching of the true, divine Scriptures. Their victory came about basically because the Catholic Church had no significant or knowledgeable theologians who could stand up in an open debate and oppose the reformers.

Disputations were held all over Switzerland and the reformers won victory after victory. Lent was abandoned; clerical celibacy was declared unbiblical; Zürich was cleansed of organs, images and relics; churches were severed from the control of the papacy; monasteries were dissolved; fasting was prohibited; the mass was replaced; the Lord's Supper was held at regular intervals and preaching of the Bible was ordered in all of the churches.

Zwingli was one of the first Protestants to oppose using musical instruments during church services. Most of the Reformed movement agreed with the banning of music, although none actually followed the elimination of music. In some branches of Presbyterian Churches, singing without the accompaniment of music, continues to be the practice up to the current day.

Zwingli wrote the *12 Theses of Berne* for a disputation held in Berne in January 1528. Through the efforts of Berthold Haller, Valerius Anshelm, Franz Kolb and other friends of Zwingli, Berne adopted the Reformation. In fact Berne was the first canton to follow Zürich into the Reformation, and the city's enthusiasm resulted in their drive to spread the movement further west.

THE ANABAPTISTS

With the Reformation now firmly established in Zürich, it wasn't long before it was being spread to other parts of Switzerland. In each case, the Reformation came about because of the actions of a leading reformer who represented Zwingli at the disputations. However, these new doctrines were not introduced without opposition.

Anabaptism came to the fore in Zürich during Zwingli's work there and was a tremendous threat to the Reformation. The name *anabaptist* derives from Greek meaning 're-baptism'. The term was applied to a number of revolutionary groups during the Reformation, and their members questioned the validity of infant baptism. The first such group was organized by Felix Manz and Conrad Grebel in 1525, and it became known as the 'Swiss Brethren'. Many of the early Anabaptists were heavily influenced by the beliefs of Zwingli, but they were impatient to implement more radical changes to Christian practises. Zwingli was prepared to negotiate and make certain concessions, but the Anabaptists were not so easily subdued.

Zwingli and his followers were fiercely opposed to the Anabaptists and although he had meetings with several of their leaders, he was unable to suppress their views. So, with the co-operation of the secular magistrates, the reformers persecuted the Anabaptists. They were banished from Zürich and those who fought back were either tortured or imprisoned, and one of their leaders, Felix Manz, was drowned.

Zwingli had a more difficult fight against the

Anabaptists than he had with Rome, and they remained a threat to the Reformation throughout the remainder of the 16th century.

THE MARBURG COLLOQUY

The Marburg Colloquy was a meeting held in the city of Marburg in October 1529. It attempted to resolve the differences between Lutherans and Zwinglians over the matter of the Lord's Supper and issues relating to transubstantiation.

Besides the two main characters, Martin Luther and Huldrych Zwingli, the other main reformers at the disputation were Johannes Agricola, Johannes Brenz, Martin Bucer, Caspar Hedio, Justus Jonas, Philipp Melanchthon, Johannes Oecolampadius and Andreas Osiander. They all attended at the request of Philip I of Hesse, whose motive was to unite the protestant states in a political alliance.

The public colloquy began on October 2 and on October 4, again at the behest of Philip of Hesse, Luther drew up his *15 Articles of Faith* which were based on the *Schwabach Articles* put together before the colloquy. Surprisingly, the reformers agreed on 14 of the articles, allowing for slight modifications, but it soon became apparent that Luther and Zwingli would continue to differ on the fifteenth – the Eucharist. At the end of the disputation a conciliatory statement was issued:

Although we are not at this present time agreed, as to whether the true Body and Blood of Christ are

*bodily present in the bread and wine, nevertheless
the one party should show to the other Christian love
as far as conscience can permit.*

Zwingli and Luther left the Marburg Colloquy
without having reached an agreement. Soon after the
disputation, there were rumours of critical remarks
about each other's beliefs and subsequent articles
written by Zwingli convinced Luther that he had not
been sincere in accepting the Marburg Articles. Their
unresolved differences led to further problems and on
top of this the Roman Catholics were not about to see
Switzerland become entirely Protestant.

PERSECUTION

Opposition by the Catholics took the form of extreme
persecution of any Protestants who remained in
Catholic cantons, even resulting in one Protestant
being burnt alive. The Protestants, who were not
prepared to be treated so badly, announced they
would go to war with the Roman Catholics. The
Catholics themselves were in no military position to
fight and tried to pacify the situation.

Zwingli was in no mood for peace talks and urged
his men strongly to take the opportunity to go to war
while the Catholics were in a weakened state.
Zwingli's beliefs were not shared by all the Protestant
cantons and the resulting delay cost them them dearly,
as the Catholics used the time of peace to strengthen
their armies to prepare for war.

In October 1531, five Catholic cantons, amounting to approximately 8,000 men, joined together for a surprise attack on Zürich, goaded by Protestant blockades that had inflicted much suffering on the Catholics. The Protestants, who had amassed about 1,500 men, were unprepared for the attack. They were quickly defeated, and Zwingli, who had accompanied the troops as their chaplain, lost his life along with a total of 500 other Protestants.

As Zwingli was bending down to tend to a dying soldier, he was hit on the head by a stone. He managed to struggle to his feet, but repeated blows and a final thrust from a lance, left him lying on the ground close to death. Seeing how bad his wounds were, he cried:

What matters this misfortune? They may kill the body, but they cannot kill the soul.

He was placed under a pear tree by his friends and for the rest of the day sat with his hands folded in prayer and his eyes firmly fixed towards heaven. As evening drew close, several men from the victorious army passed by and asked if he wanted to confess his sins to a priest, but he shook his head, refusing their help. One of the soldiers passing by, recognized him in the light of his torch, and as he struck him with his sword he shouted: 'Die, obstinate heretic!'

The Catholic soldiers were delighted that the controversial reformer was dead. They quartered his body, burned the pieces to ashes, and then mixed them with the ashes of pigs and scattered them to the four winds.

The death of Zwingli halted the spread of the Reformation in Switzerland.

FAITHFUL REFORMER

Zwingli was something of an anomaly because, on the one hand he remained faithful to the Scriptures, but on the other hand he never really shook himself free from his humanism. Humanists believed that the Greek and Latin classics contained all the lessons needed to lead a moral life. Zwingli's humanist mentor, Erasmus, remained a strong influence on him right up until his death.

Huldrych Zwingli had prepared the way for the Reformation in Switzerland, where Calvinism finally took over. Calvinism is a system of Christian theology and an approach to Christian life and thought that was introduced by John Calvin, a French Christian theologian.

Zwingli was succeeded by Heinrich Bullinger, who was elected as the pastor of the Great Minister on December 9, 1531. Bullinger worked hard to salvage the remains of Huldrych Zwingli's democratic reforms after Zürich's military defeat in 1531.

JOHN KNOX

John Knox played a pivotal role in the reformation of the Church in Scotland. There is little documented about the first 30 or more years of his life, but it is generally accepted that he was born *c.*1512 in a small town south of Edinburgh, called Haddington. His father, William Knox of Haddingtonshire, is believed to have been a farmer and was known to have fought at the Battle of Flodden in September 1513.

Knox was educated at the Haddington burgh school, and the first record of his university days is on the register of Glasgow University, where he enrolled in 1522. Knox studied theology under the famous scholar John Mair (John Major), who was a native of East Lothian. Although it is uncertain whether he actually graduated from university, it is apparent that Knox had a good knowledge of Latin, Greek and Hebrew and was certainly familiar with the works of classical writers.

CONVERSION TO PROTESTANTISM

John Knox was ordained as a priest in 1536, and by the end of 1543 he was still ministering as a Catholic clergyman. He held the post of private tutor to the family of Hugh Douglas of Longniddry for several years, and he was also responsible for the education of the son of a neighbour, John Cockburn of Ormiston. The young John Knox was probably influenced by the interests these two families had in the new religious ideas that were sweeping Europe at the time.

During Knox's youth there was a lot of unrest in Scotland, and many people were angry with the goings-on within the Catholic Church. The Church was considered to be too greedy, owning more than half of the property and land, and gathering an annual income that was far greater than that of the crown. Many of the Catholic priests and bishops led immoral lives, one of them being Cardinal David Beaton, who was known to openly consort with concubines, and had sired several illegitimate children.

In the early 1540s, Knox was influenced by converted reformers, and in particular the preaching of a man called Thomas Guilliame. He decided to join them, and by the end of 1545, Knox converted to Protestantism, something that he had been thinking about for a considerable time. It is believed that Knox's conversion was a result of a friendship formed with a man named George Wishart. Wishart was a member of the famous Pitarrow family and a powerful Protestant preacher, who became a confidant and mentor of John Knox. Knox became almost obsessed with Wishart and was known to have followed him everywhere. He acted as his bodyguard, carrying a sword to defend him, if necessary, from the leader of the anti-Protestant movement, Cardinal Beaton.

While Wishart was preaching the Protestant Reform in 1546, he was betrayed to Beaton and imprisoned in the dungeon at the castle in St Andrews. Knox was with him on the night of his arrest and was prepared to stay with him during his confinement. Wishart persuaded Knox against the idea and told him to return home. Wishart was subsequently tried for heresy, condemned to death and burnt at the stake outside the castle walls.

Several weeks later a party of 16 Protestant nobles conspired against the Cardinal and managed to gain entry to the castle by deception. They found Cardinal Beaton in his room, killed him and hung his body from the battlements. Although Knox took no part in the murder, he was delighted when he heard the news of Beaton's death, as he felt it was a fitting revenge for the death of his closest friend.

After Beaton's death the first congregation of the Church of Scotland was formed in the castle, and it became a place of refuge for many Scottish Protestants, one of them being John Knox. Knox was asked to take the office of preacher and, although he declined at first, he eventually agreed to what he felt was a 'divine call'. However, this was to be a short-lived ministry as the castle came under siege in 1547.

DAYS OF CONFINEMENT

For a few months they were able to hold out against the pro-Catholic French forces, but at the end of July 1547 they took possession and Knox and some of the other refugees were imprisoned.

They were taken to Rouen, where they were forced to row in the French galleys. For 18 months Knox was a galley slave and was subjected to untold hardships and miseries, which affected his health for the rest of his life. Even though his life was tough, Knox was still able to write a theological treatise and preach to his fellow prisoners. The French made several attempts to have Knox renounce his Protestant faith, but he never faltered in his beliefs and never gave up hope of returning to Scotland.

One incident during the months on the galley reveals the strengths of the Protestant preacher, even though he was bound by chains. The French brought a picture of the Virgin Mary on board the ship and forced the slaves to kiss it one by one. When they came to Knox they thrust the picture into his face but he refused to kiss their idol. Outraged at what they had asked him to do, Knox flung the picture into the water, saying 'Let our Lady learn to swim'.

In 1549 he was free to leave, through the intervention of the English government. Aware that he would be vulnerable in his beloved Scotland, Knox decided to live in England under the reign of Edward VI. He was given a state licence, which allowed him to preach at Berwick, where he stayed for a period of two years. His reputation as a preacher quickly spread and he was transferred to Newcastle, where he was appointed as the royal chaplain.

FORCED TO FLEE

The next strategic event to affect John Knox was the accession to the throne of Queen Mary ('Bloody Mary'), who was possessed in her quest to return England to the Roman Catholic Church. In 1555, John Rogers and Thomas Cranmer were both burnt at the stake for heresy. Mary went on to burn reformers at the stake by the hundreds, simply for committing the 'crime' of being a Protestant. This era was known as the Marian Exile, and many refugees fled from England with little hope of ever seeing their home or friends again. One of these exiles was Knox, who fled to Geneva. It was here that he became acquainted with John Calvin, the French reformer and theologian. Calvin was impressed with Knox's fervour and in return Knox was equally impressed with the preachings of Calvin. In a letter to a friend, Knox described Calvin's Geneva as:

> . . . the most perfect school of Christ that ever was in the earth since the days of the Apostles. In other places I confess Christ to be truly preached; but manners and religion to be so seriously reformed, I have not yet seen in any other place besides.

Knox accompanied other Protestant refugees to Frankfurt am Main, where he soon became tangled up in controversy. The Protestants were finding it difficult to agree on an order of worship, and arguments became heated and resulted in a group of worshippers storming out of a church, refusing to worship in the same place as Knox.

Knox returned to his beloved Scotland for several months, where his enlightened preaching furthered the Protestant cause. As a result, a number of Scottish nobility banded together and formed a group called 'The Lords of the Congregation'. They vowed to make Protestantism the religion of the land, and this became the political backbone for the reforming of a nation. Knox was a leading figure in the reformation, and he preached extensively for nine months in Scotland before he was forced to return to Geneva.

A TIME OF WRITING

During this time away from his homeland, Knox started to write prolifically. He published many controversial pieces, including *Admonition to England*, in which he venomously attacked the people who allowed Catholicism back in England. In his article entitled The *First Blast of the Trumpet Against the Monstrous Regiment of Women*, Knox contended that a female monarch such as Queen Mary Tudor was 'most odious in the presence of God', and that she was a traitor and rebel against the true God. In his *Appellations to the Nobility and Commonality of Scotland*, he made it clear to the ordinary person that it was their right, indeed their duty, to rebel against unjust rulers. He was later to say directly to Mary of Queen of Scots, 'This sword of justice is God's, and if princes and rulers fail to use it, others may.'

Knox returned to Scotland in 1559, where he took up his preaching once again to increase Protestant militancy. Within just a few days of his arrival, he preached a controversial sermon at a church in Perth, which caused a major riot. The sermon was against Catholic idolatory and soon the parishioners were demolishing idols and destroying religious houses.

In June 1559, Knox was appointed the minister of Edinburgh church, where he continued to inspire his parishioners. Sometimes he would get so heated during his sermons that he would pound the the pulpit in his excitement.

KNOX AND MARY QUEEN OF SCOTS

John Knox finally ended his 13 years of exile in July 1559 and never left Scottish soil again. Knox was instrumental in the Reformation in Scotland, and his manifestos in 1560 had more input than any other individual. Worship was changed forever by Knox's Liturgy, or the *Book of Common Order*, and the Scottish Parliament accepted the reformed confession drawn up by Knox and several other people. It appeared that the time of conflict had passed.

What Knox didn't realize at the time was that he had one final conflict to fight, and this time it would be fought with words. Knox certainly had a way with words, and he said them in a way that made people listen to him. This time his words were aimed at the young Mary Queen of Scots, cousin to Bloody Mary.

The death of Mary's young husband, Francis II, in

December 1560, left Mary in a difficult position. Still only 18 years of age and unwilling to stay in France, she decided to return to Scotland and take her chances with the Protestant reformers. Mary was a Catholic and somewhat out of place in the rugged countryside of Scotland. She came to rule a country that had been changed by reformation, and it was obvious that the man she faced, Knox, had a considerable amount of influence over the people.

Knox and his parishioners were horrified when she tried to restore the Roman mass, which Parliament had already outlawed, and the Catholics were also concerned that she was not totally true to their cause. Knox and Mary had a total of five confrontations, and each time she underestimated the power of Knox's words. On a number of occasions, Mary ordered Knox before her for statements he made in sermons. Knox was adept at speaking, and each time God gave him the wisdom to answer her accusations and Mary left frustrated. She tried desperately to win Knox over by womanly ways, but he was not to be swayed. She finally prohibited Knox from preaching altogether after he demonstrated political authority and warned those who persecuted the Church of Christ misused their authority.

Mary married her first cousin Henry Stewart, Lord Darnley, on July 29, 1565. This marriage was not acceptable to the Protestants and, with the aid of some nobles, they raised a rebellion. However, Mary quickly suppressed it. Mary felt betrayed by her Protestant advisors and she immediately withdrew her support from the reformed Church.

Mary did not lead a virtuous life, and by the end of 1566 she had befriended James Hepburn, Earl of Bothwell, and was trying to find a way of dissolving her marriage to Darnley. Darnley was mysteriously murdered on February 10, 1567, at Kirk o' Field, and at the time Bothwell was believed to be the chief instigator.

Bothwell obtained a divorce from his wife and on Mary 15, 1567, he and Mary were married according to the Protestant rite. This marriage alienated even some of Mary's closest supporters, many of whom despised Bothwell, and little did she realize that her actions were to be her own downfall.

Just five years after landing on Scottish soil, Mary Queen of Scots knew that her enemies outnumbered her allies, and she abdicated the throne and fled to England. Mary left her infant son, James VI, in charge of the throne of Scotland and she appointed James Stewart, Earl of Moray, as regent until James was old enough to rule himself.

On July 29, Knox travelled to Stirling to preach at the coronation of the newly appointed king. At the coronation, Knox became closely connected with the regent, the Earl of Moray. Under Moray, the Reformed Presbyterian Church of Scotland was finally established. Knox played a significant part in this and at last was able to see something come of his years of arduous work.

THE FINAL YEARS

Knox's remaining years were not peaceful, as many Protestants were committed to keeping political ascendancy in order, one of the chief instigators being Moray. Moray made many enemies, some of whom even threatened him with his life. His enemies finally succeeded in assassinating him in 1570, and the constant threat of the stability of Scotland had taken its toll on Knox.

After the murder of Moray, Knox's political power diminished, and his health started to weaken. Towards the end of his life in 1570, he wrote:

And so I end; rendering my troubled and sorrowful spirit in the hands of eternall God, earnestlie trusting at his good pleasure; to be freed from the cares of this miserabill lyfe, and to rest with Christ Jesus, my only hope and life.

In 1572, Knox suffered a severe stroke, which left him in a weakened condition, and he was forced to retire from St Andrews. It was at this time that he wrote his last work, *An Answer to a Scottish Jesuit.* Knox was granted his wish to end his miserable life, when he died of natural causes on November 24, 1572. It was only after his death that his cause finally triumphed. Knox was always true to his cause, a man of one heart, a man who believed totally in God. He believed that God's Kingdom was his only home and, although a bigoted and ouspoken man, Knox always managed to wield enormous influence. His influence shaped not only the course of the Scottish Church but also Protestantism in the English colonies in North America, where it became the dominant religious force.

John Knox was clearly a man of incredible courage and determination and a mourner who stood over his open grave commented:

Here lies a man who neither flattered nor feared the flesh.

HIS WORK CONTINUES

The work of John Knox did not stop with his death, and his beliefs were soon taken up by a man named Andrew Melville. Like Knox, he had been greatly influenced by the ideas of Calvin during his years spent in Geneva. It was Melville who took up the Calvinist cause associated with Protestantism, and who standardized the structures of Presbyterian worship. Melville also took the place of Knox in defending the achievements of Protestantism in Scotland against the royalists, gradually gaining the confidence of James IV.

SIR WALTER RALEIGH

Sir Walter Raleigh is certainly a fascinating character, who has been portrayed as a genius, an idealist, a pirate, a statesman, a scientist, a writer, a gentleman and even a rogue. One of the greatest events to occur in modern history has been the expansion of western Europe, bringing with it the influence of distant places. Raleigh played a pivotal role in the expansion of England into the New World and fought hard for colonization. His career can definitely be described as exciting; fighting for his fellow Protestants in France and exploring the New World with his half-brother, Sir Humphrey Gilbert. He became a favourite of Queen Elizabeth I and spent much of his time in court with her. Raleigh grew up with a hatred of the Catholic Church and, when Elizabeth came to the throne in 1558, he was able to express it openly. He gained the title Captain of the Guard for his part in foiling the 'Babington' conspiracy – aimed at replacing Queen Elizabeth I with Mary, Queen of Scots – which ended up with him owning a 16,000-ha (40,000-acre) estate in Ireland. Courage was one of Raleigh's main characteristics, and through his endeavours he had a great impact on Renaissance society and made it easier for future explorers.

THE YOUNG RALEIGH

Walter Raleigh was born *c.*1554 at Hayes Barton in East Devon. Raleigh's father, Walter Senior, had moved to Devon on his marriage to Joan Drake, who was a distant relative of the famous sailor, Sir Francis Drake. He rented Hayes Barton in the village of East Budleigh, which consisted of a large house and estate, on which he set up as a farmer. His business rapidly grew and soon he had the grazing rights on both Lympstone and the local Woodbury Commons. In 1530, Joan died, after which Walter had a short-lived marriage to a daughter of a Genoese merchant. His third wife was Katherine Champernowne, whose brother was the Vice Admiral of Devon. Katherine bore Walter a daughter and two sons – Carew and their youngest, Walter.

Little is known of Raleigh's childhood until the age of 15, when he joined a troop of horsemen led by the Compte de Montgomerie. During his time with the horsemen he witnessed the murder of Catholics in their caves at Languedoc in France and on August 24, 1572, the St Bartholomew's Day massacre, where French Protestants were massacred by French Catholics in Paris. By the time Raleigh returned to England he was well aware of the misery that could be caused by religious fanatics in the pursuit of power.

In 1572, Raleigh was sent to Oriel College, Oxford, to further his education. He studied Aristotle and became proficient in oratory and philosophy. However, the young Raleigh soon tired of the discipline inflicted on him at Oxford, and in 1575 he left to study law and current affairs in the Middle Temple in London. He lived in the fine rural area of Islington, and it was here that he started to associate with the nobility and also caught the attention of Queen Elizabeth I. At this time, the most influential person in his life was his half-brother, Sir Humphrey Gilbert, and it was through him that Raleigh first heard of John Dee's vision of founding a Tudor Empire in North America.

During Raleigh's youth England was having a rough time, as there was a deepening crisis with the late Queen 'Bloody' Mary's husband, King Philip of Spain. The Spanish Papal monopoly in the Americas had been hindered by John Hawkins of Plymouth, who had started a lucrative trading of slaves between Africa and the Caribbean. This trade led to several battles between Hawkins and Francis Drake and, on one occasion, more than 100 men were surrendered to the Spanish. The Spanish treated their captives cruelly, making them work for up to eight years in the galleys. Others were lashed, strangled or burnt at the stake.

THE FIRST MISSION

In 1578, Sir Humphrey Gilbert was given a patent from Elizabeth asking him to:

> ... *discover and take possession of any remote, barbarous and heathen lands not possessed by any Christian prince or people.*

This was just the type of adventure Raleigh and his half-brother had been waiting for, and they embarked with Gilbert captaining the *Anne Archer* and Raleigh in the *Falcon,* with Simon Fernandez as master. The *Falcon* was only a small vessel less than 23 m (75 ft) long with a crew of about 70 men. In the cramped conditions, Raleigh eventually reached the Cape Verde Islands having had to face 12-m (40-ft) waves and storms that nearly destroyed their inadequate vessel. Large numbers of his crew died, and the *Falcon* was driven back to Plymouth after a failed engagement with Spanish warships in the Atlantic.

A second expedition the following year was equally disastrous and Raleigh and his half-brother found themselves having to look elsewhere to make a living. Raleigh returned to live in London where, along with his friend Sir Thomas Parrot, they got into trouble and were called before the council for a minor affray. They were sent to Fleet Prison for six days as a cooling-off period, and Raleigh was sent to Marshalsea prison after being involved in a fight. During his time in Marshalsea, Raleigh befriended the rich and dangerous Edward de Vere, Earl of Oxford.

Using his association with the Earl, Raleigh attached himself to the Court in London and gained employment as captain of a company of 100 soldiers. Raleigh and his troop were sent to southern Ireland to suppress a rebellion that was taking place in Munster of the Desmonds. The rebellion was between the Earl of Desmond dynasty and their allies against the efforts of the Elizabethan government to extend their control over the province of Munster. Although the primary reason was to do with the independence of feudal lords from their monarch, the rebellion also had an element of religious conflict. Raleigh played a significant role in the defeat of the rebels, but in so doing he resorted to massacre to achieve his goal.

THE QUEEN'S FAVOURITE

Raleigh returned to England in 1581 and immediately became a favourite of Queen Elizabeth. She rewarded him richly with grants and monopolies, among these grants was 16,000 ha (40,000 acres) of Irish land which had been forfeited by the Desmonds after they were defeated at the rebellion. The land included the beautiful castles of Lismore (near Cork) and Waterford. On top of these privileges, the queen conferred on him the distinction of a knighthood. Raleigh, now in his late twenties, was 183-cm (6-ft) tall and an exceptionally handsome man, who had a powerful air of authority. He was fashioning himself as the perfect Elizabethan courtier, and he soon became adept at talking politics. Raleigh was driven by a strong ambition and intellect and Elizabeth was determined to keep him close by, and he was to remain in her court for the next ten years.

In 1578, Gilbert obtained from Queen Elizabeth the charter he had long been after, to form a colony in North America. His first attempt failed and cost him his whole fortune; but, after further service in Ireland, he sailed again for Newfoundland in 1583. In August of that year he managed to take possession of the harbour of St John and founded his colony, but on the return voyage he went down with his ship, the *Squirrel*, in a storm south of the Azores.

After the death of his half-brother, Raleigh planned a third expedition with John Dee and Thomas Harriot, who was an outstanding English mathematician. They set sail in May 1584 and landed on the North Carolina coast at Roanoke Island on July 13. The party of explorers considered the island to be a paradise and found the natives to be friendly. After spending several weeks among the generous natives, Raleigh convinced two of the natives, Wanchese and Manteo, to return with him to England.

They arrived home in September and Elizabeth was delighted with Raleigh's report. She decided to name her new possession *Virginia*, after the fact that she was a virgin queen.

THE FIRST COLONY

The following spring, Raleigh sent a colony of 108 people to Roanoke Island, but this time he decided to stay at home. This new expedition was commanded by Raleigh's cousin, Sir Richard Grenville, and he set off from Plymouth, England, on April 9, 1585, to find out more about the New World. In total there were seven ships and among the party were Philip Amadas, Ralph Lane and Simon Ferdinando, who had been on the previous expedition, and the two natives Wanchese and Manteo.

During this expedition the explorers managed to gather valuable information into how the native Americans lived. Sunflowers and pumpkins flourished on the fertile land as did the tobacco plant, which the natives dried and smoked. Although tobacco had been grown in England as early as 1565, it was Raleigh who eventually made it fashionable.

Grenville, armed with all the details of how to farm the local crops, started to build his settlement on Roanoke Island. Grenville then returned to England, leaving Ralph Lane in charge. Lane sent a party of men, including Harriot and White, to Chesapeake Bay to make the first maps of North America and what is now called Virginia. However, this expedition relied heavily on being supplied food by the natives and this led to many disputes. Because Raleigh was in England, he had difficulty in arranging a relief expeditio. The men were eventually rescued from the harsh conditions by Sir Francis Drake. Unfortunately, in their hurry to leave Raonoke Island, many of the records were destroyed by uncaring soldiers, and they even left three men behind by accident. The remainder of the party arrived back in England on July 28, 1586.

During their absence, Raleigh remained a true and loyal servant to Elizabeth and was instrumental in uncovering the Babington Plot. During the years that Mary Queen of Scots remained captive in England, several attempts were made to place her on the English throne. The most significant of these was the Babington Plot, which ultimately led to Mary's trial and her execution in 1587. The person for whom the plot was named was Anthony Babington, and he, along with his conspirators, were hanged, drawn and quartered at Tyburn and Walter Raleigh was given his lands as a reward.

RALEIGH AND THE ARMADA

Despite being disappointed over the abandonment of the Raonoke Island project, Raleigh was appointed Vice Admiral of Devon in 1588. However, he was beginning to lose favour in the Queen's court as the young and impetuous Robert Devereux, the Earl of Essex, was becoming Elizabeth's prime favourite. There was little time to dwell on his misfortunes, as Philip II of Spain launched 130 ships against England in 1588. This was the Great Armada, the largest fleet Europe had ever seen, and it consisted of 19,250 troops, 8,350 sailors and 2,080 galley slaves. It is fairly certain that Philip II did not really wish to rule England as part of the Spanish empire, but, as a zealous Catholic, his deepest wish was to return England to the 'true Church'. The pope agreed to support the invasion, and excommunicated Elizabeth, absolving her subjects from any duty to obey her.

Raleigh immediately attended a council of war to discuss the best way to defend England. At the council were his old friends Lord Grey, Sir Richard Grenville, Admiral Lord Howard of Effingham and Ralph Lane, who was now Master General of the Forces. Raleigh set up his headquarters in Plymouth, where he managed to raise an army of 5,560 soldiers and 96 cavalry.

Raleigh himself captained the *Ark Royal,* which was the flagship of the English fleet.

The battle started when the Spanish sailed up the Channel to Calais, where they were met by a collection of English vessels. Under the cover of darkness Raleigh set fireships adrift, using the tide to carry the blazing ships into the Spanish vessels. There was confusion and the Spanish were forced to cut their cables, and those ships that were not destroyed by the fire, sailed for the open sea.

On Monday, July 29, the two fleets met again in a battle off Gravelines. The English once again emerged victorious, although there was little damage done to the Spanish fleet. The Duke of Medina Sedonia was now determined that the Armada should return to Spain, but their exit was hampered by the English, who blocked the Channel with their ships. This meant that the only route open to the Spanish was north around the tip of Scotland and down the coast of Ireland. It was then that the unpredictable weather took a hand in the proceedings.

Hit by severe storms, the Spanish fleet soon experienced heavy losses and by the time they reached Spain, the Armada has lost half of its ships and almost three-quarters of its men. Much of the English victory was down to the forethought and quick actions of the now 34-year-old Walter Raleigh, once again fighting for the freedom of his country and queen.

COURT RIVALRY

Back in England the conquering of the Spanish Armada was greeted as a victory for the Protestant cause. Special services of thanks were held throughout the country, praising God for his intervention by creating the storms that brought about the downfall of the Spaniards.

Despite this triumph, Raleigh was still being rivalled by the Earl of Essex for his position in court, which resulted in quarrelsome rivalry between the two men. At the height of his career, Raleigh angered Elizabeth when she found out that he had seduced one of her maids of honour, Elizabeth Throgmorton. Raleigh was thrown into the Tower of London, and Elizabeth Throgmorton was removed from the queen's court. Raleigh was released on a passionate plea for clemency, coupled with the fact that he agreed to marry Elizabeth Throgmorton. The wedding took place in the Tower itself, and proved to be a a great success, with husband and wife remaining devoted to each other for the rest of their lives.

Raleigh decided to retire from his position in court and went to live on an estate in Dorset with his new wife. In 1594 they had a son, but Raleigh was beginning to get restless and yearned for adventure. In 1595 he set out on a voyage in search of gold to South America, attracted by stories that he had heard of the mines at El Dorado. Although he found no gold, he did write an account of his voyage called *The Discoverie of Guiana*, which even to this day is a fine example of Elizabethan adventure.

RALEIGH BACK IN FAVOUR

Eight years had passed since the victory over the Spanish Armada and the King of Spain had spent the time planning his vengeance on England. With his treasury now replenished, he prepared another mighty fleet with which to invade England.

Although Raleigh had planned to return to Guiana, when he heard the news of the latest Spanish Armada, he knew that he would be needed to fight for his country and queen. The queen gathered her council and discussed the best way to break the Spanish power. Remembering Raleigh's advice, of eight years earlier, they fitted out an English fleet ready to attack the Spanish ships who were anchored in their own harbour of Cadiz, in southern Spain. Lord Burghley, who was the Chief Minister, decided that attack was their best means of defence, and he sent Raleigh and his rival, Essex, to Cadiz. Elizabeth, who was uncertain about the decision, acted cautiously, but eventually she agreed and sent 5,000 sailors, 65,000 soldiers and raised £30,000 to finance the operation.

The English set sail from Plymouth on June 11, 1595, with Lord Admiral Howard captaining the *Ark Royal*, Essex as joint commander of the *Duc Repulse* and Raleigh in *Warsprite*. Some of the bravest men who had fought in the previous victory over the Armada, were missing from this trip – for example, Sir Richard Grenville, who had died a hero while fighting for his country. Sir Francis Drake, one of the most daring of the sea captains, was also dead.

The English fleet sailed into Cadiz harbour with Raleigh staying outside to attack any ships that tried to escape. The English commanders made the decision to land the soldiers and capture the town of Cadiz before attacking the fleet anchored in the bay. When Raleigh sailed into the harbour he found Essex already offloading his soldiers, and due to an exceptionally rough sea, he had already lost 15 of his men.

Raleigh, realizing that they had no chance of victory if they didn't attack the ships first, demanded Essex to change his plans, humiliating him in front of all crew. Raleigh was given the post of honour, which meant his ship, the *Warsprite*, would lead the vanguard.

Night fell and the Spanish, who were aware of the presence of the English fleet, continued to feast and make merry, confident that they would drive them out of the harbour. As soon as dawn broke Raleigh led his fleet to attack the enemy. As the *Warsprite* passed below the walls of Cadiz, the fort and the galleys opened fire. Leaving the remainder of his fleet to deal with the galleys, he sailed on to deal with the larger galleons, the *St Philip* and the *St Andrew*. Raleigh was determined on revenge as it was these two ships that had cost his old friend, Sir Richard Grenville, his life.

The battle was fierce and long and at the last the Spanish knew they could fight no more. So, setting fire to the *St Philip*, they jumped into the sea and swam for the shore. It was a great sea victory for the English, which left the ground clear for Essex to land his soldiers and capture the city of Cadiz. Even though Raleigh had been badly injured during the long sea battle, he was so keen to take part in the capture of the city, he insisted that his men carry him ashore on their shoulders. However, he was overcome by pain and was forced to return to his ship.

When the people of England heard the news from Raleigh that they had defeated the Spanish on their own shores, they were elated and lined the streets to welcome their victorious soldiers and sailors home. English men, who had been forced to work as galley slaves, were rescued from their life of misery. When everyone heard that Raleigh had led the fight, he was heralded as a hero. Due to the incompetence of the Earl of Essex during the battle, Raleigh was back in favour with Elizabeth and reinstated as Captain of the Guard.

From 1600 to 1603 Raleigh was Governor of Jersey and was made responsible for modernizing the island's defences. He named the fortress that protected the approach to St Helier as *Fort Isabella Bellissima*, or Elizabeth Castle, after his beloved monarch.

DEATH OF QUEEN ELIZABETH

The death of Elizabeth I on March 24, 1603, saw mounting problems for Raleigh. The new king, James I, suspecting that Raleigh may have been against his coronation, revoked Raleigh's many privileges and offices. In July 1603, Raleigh was accused, falsely, of taking part in conspiracies against the life of James I, and was condemned to death.

After an unfair trial he gained public sympathy and instead of execution he was confined to the tower, where he remained for 13 years. During his time of confinement his wife and son were allowed to live with him, and he was also visited by a great many scholars and poets. Raleigh spent his time writing and completed a book called *The History of the World* for the king's son, Prince Henry.

In 1616, Raleigh convinced the king to release him so that he might lead an expedition to the Orinoco river in South America, to bring back gold from a mine he claimed to have discovered on an earlier visit.

He was granted permission to leave England, but he disobeyed the king's ordered by fighting the Spaniards, which cost him the life of his son, Walter. Raleigh returned to England empty-handed and King James, who wanted to stay on good terms with Spain, had him arrested once again. The King of Spain wrote King James a letter saying that Raleigh could be spared execution in Madrid, but it would please his 'Most Catholic Majesty' if the deed could be carried out in London.

This time there was nothing he could do to prevent his fate, despite the fact that he defended himself stoutly. The Lord Chief Justice explained to Raleigh that his treason could not be pardoned and, despite being a brave and wise Christian, Raleigh was executed on October 29, 1618. Cheerful right up to the last, Raleigh touched the blade of the executioner's axe and said:

This is a sharp medicine, but it is a sure cure for all diseases.

Sir Walter Raleigh will always remain one of those popular figures from Elizabethan England, along with names such as Drake, Hawkins and other famous sea adventurers. He made no secret of his enmity against Spain, which endeared him to the public and his execution at the Spanish ambassador's instigation, only enhanced his popularity. He must also be remembered for his unfaltering loyalty to his country and his queen, for which he fought at all costs regardless of his own safety. He has been portrayed as many things – a genius, a pirate, a statesman, a writer, a gentleman and even a rogue – but he was truly a powerful figure of the Elizabethan Age.

It is said that the ghost of Walter Raleigh strolls around the grounds of Sherborne Castle and sits under a tree that bears his name. It was here, reportedly, that a worried servant threw a pitcher of beer at Raleigh in an attempt to extinguish the smoke coming from his pipe.

Raleigh's wife had her husband's head embalmed and kept it with her until her death. Their son, Carew, inherited his father's head and it was buried with him in his grave.

JOHN PYM

John Pym was undoubtedly the most prominent member of the House of Commons in the events leading up to the English Civil War. He fought a campaign against the Roman Catholics and led parliament against the Earl of Strafford and Archbishop Laud, fearing that their politics would restore Catholicism to England. Pym was also instrumental in setting up a network of parliamentary committees that were to run the country for the next 17 years. He organized a number of tax reforms to support the parliamentary war efforts and arranged an alliance with Scotland based on English acceptance of the Solemn League of Covenant, which was signed on on September 25, 1643.

INTRODUCTION INTO POLITICS

John Pym was born in 1584 and was the eldest son and heir of Alexander Pym of Brymore in Somerset. The family's roots went right back to the 13th century and the time of Henry III. Alexander Pym died shortly after the birth of his son and his widow later remarried Sir Anthony Rous, who was a client of the Earl of Bedford.

ABOVE: *61 AD, Queen Boudicca of the Iceni, a British tribe which rose in revolt against the Romans, attempting to rouse her countrymen.*

ABOVE: *c.1530, Martin Luther (1483–1546), German theologian and religious reformer, who changed the world considerably.*

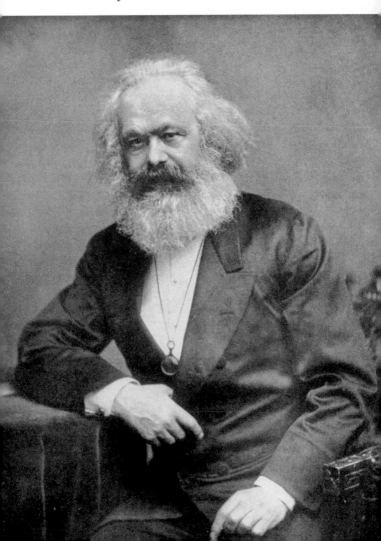

BELOW: *The philosopher, social scientist, historian and revolutionary, Karl Marx (1818–1883), was without doubt the most influential socialist thinker to emerge from the 19th century.*

ABOVE: *English suffragette, Estelle Sylvia Pankhurst (centre) (1882–1960) was the daughter of the famous Emmeline Pankhurst who founded the Women's Franchise League.*

ABOVE: *The legendary Ernesto Che Guevara (1928–1967) who was executed in Bolivia on October 8, 1967. Although communism may have lost its fire, Guevara remains the potent symbol of rebellion and revolution.*

ABOVE: *South Africa's first black President, Nelson Mandela. Nobel Peace Prize winner in 1993, Mandela joined the African National Congress in 1944 and was engaged in resistance against the ruling National Party's apartheid policies for many years.*

ABOVE: *A human rights activist, poses outside the offices of Burma Campaign in the UK with a poster of Aung San Suu Kyi, who remains under house arrest in Yangon following her clashes with the Burmese government.*

The young Pym metriculated from Broadgates Hall, which is now known as Pembroke College, and went on to study in Oxford, in 1599. From there he joined the Middle Temple in London in 1602, but although he had a sound knowledge of the law, he was never called to the bar.

In May 1604, Pym married Anne Hooke of Bramshott in Hampshire, who was the daughter of John Hook and Anthony Rous's sister, Barbara. This marriage, and the influence of the Rous family, had a profound affect on his views about Puritanism and gave him a fierce opposition to Catholicism and Arminianism. Arminianism was, basically, the belief that God gave man the choice to accept Him or reject Him. Pym obtained a position in the Exchequer and became receiver-general of the king's (James I) revenue for Hampshire, Wiltshire and Gloucestershire. This post gave him a valuable insight into the world of business and finance, which set him on the path to his political career.

His first real appointment in politics came in 1614 when, under the patronage of the Earl of Bedford, Pym was elected MP for Calne in Wilshire and again in 1621. Pym made his first great speech on November 28, 1621, stating that the Roman Catholics should be subjected to restrictions, not because of their religion, but because of their politics.

In 1621, James I decided to dissolve parliament before it was recalled for a second session. This was due to an escalating war in the Holy Roman Empire, and a militant parliament in England put pressure on the king to mount an effective defence against the Spanish and Imperial forces. James resisted, wishing to maintain his empathy with Spain, and it subsequently became necessary to take evasive action. Motivated by a genuine desire for peace, the king provoked a confrontation with the House of Commons in order to give him a pretext for dissolving parliament. John Pym was one of the ministers who was placed under house-arrest in January 1622 for criticizing the king's policies. At first he was confined to his house in London and then to Brymore, where he associated himself with Francis, the 4th Earl of Bedford.

In 1624, Pym took over a new seat, representing Tavistock in Devon, and he stayed in this position for the remainder of his political career.

The already ailing James I died in March 1625 and was succeeded to the throne of England, Scotland and Ireland by his eldest surviving son, Charles I. Charles's first parliament assembled in June 1625, and it was here that Pym emerged as an outspoken enemy of Catholicism and a firm supporter of those who opposed the king's discretionary use of power.

THE EARL OF BUCKINGHAM

George Villiers was a firm favourite with James I after they first met in 1614. His fast advancement up the ranks to Earl of Buckingham in 1619 provoked a lot of bad feeling, and Villiers soon attracted a lot of enemies. The reputation of the king was damaged considerably when he allowed Buckingham to involve himself in matters of policy and decision making. This alienated powerful groups in parliament, who became more and more displeased with some of the king's decisions.

When James I died, Buckingham could easily have been left out in the cold, but he had cleverly spent time with Charles when he was prince, winning him over to his way of thinking. Buckingham simply moved over to his new king and became his chief minister.

Right from the start of his reign parliament had not been happy to give Charles a free rein, unlike his father. He was attacked severely for his religious policies and was openly critized as being incompetent. Buckingham, who was tainted with the same brush as the new king, started to take the blame for the poor decisions made by Charles.

Like his predecessors Sir Walter Raleigh and Sir Francis Drake, Buckingham attempted to seize the Spanish port of Cadiz and burn the fleet anchored in its harbour. Although his plan was tactically sound, his troops were ill-equipped and badly trained, and finding a warehouse full of wine, they simply became drunk and the attack was called off.

When Parliament, led by radicals John Pym and Sir Edward Coke, attempted to impeach him for his failure of the Cadiz expedition in 1625, the king simply had parliament dissolved before they could put Buckingham on trial.

This led Buckingham to declare war on France, which meant he had to face the two most powerful dynasties in Europe – the Hapsburgs of Spain and Germany and the Bourbons of France. His advance on

France in 1627 was a disaster, resulting in the loss of 4,000 men out of a total of 7,000.

The following year Buckingham started to organize another attack on France. However, he was killed on August 23 by a naval officer, John Felton, who held a personal grudge against the earl.

PYM AND THE EARL OF WARWICK

Pym caught the attention of the Earl of Warwick through his financial abilities, and he was employed in 1627 to manage his affairs and estate. It was through the guidance of Warwick that Pym was appointed as treasurer of the Providence Island Company, who sought to raise money for a Puritan colony on Providence Island in the West Indies. This appointment brought Pym in direct contact with several Puritan magnates, who eventually became leaders of the Parliamentarians in the 1640s. These men included Lord Brooke, Lord Saye and John Hampden.

Lord Brooke was a sympathizer with the Scottish Covenanters' resistance to Archbishop Laud's religious reforms and refused to give any support to the king during the Bishops' Wars of 1639 and 1640. Brooke was an active supporter of godly ministers and set out his own radical religious views in his work entitled, *The Nature of Truth*, published in 1640. He also attacked the power of the bishops in his paper *A Discourse on Episcopacy*, and when the Long Parliament met in 1640, Brooke was outspoken in his demands for the exclusion of bishops from the House of Lords.

Like Brooke, Saye sympathized with the Scottish Covenanters and supported Pym's activities in the House of Commons. He remained a determined opposition leader in the House of Lords.

John Hampden sat as MP for Buckinghamshire in April 1640, where he collaborated with John Pym and other opposition MPs in trying to overturn the Ship Money judgement. Ship Money, one of the most unpopular of Charles's taxes, was an ancient custom that called for coastal towns to pay for the upkeep of naval defences in times of emergency. Hampden was elected to the Long Parliament later that year and continued to work with Pym in opposing the King's attempts to reintroduce Roman Catholic practises into the English Church.

THE SHORT PARLIAMENT

The Short Parliament got its name because it was dissolved after only three weeks. It was the fourth parliament of Charles I reign, and it was assembled due to the crisis brought about by the Bishops' Wars against Scotland.

The parliament assembled on April 13, 1640, and many members of both Houses criticized the king's methods of taxation and his religious reforms. John Pym emerged as the leading spokesman for the opposition and on April 17, he gave a two-hour speech saying that the Commons would not release any funds to continue the war unless the grievances over the king's policies were addressed. His approach was clever, trying not to appear to confrontational. He appealed to the House of Commons to join the Lords in an attempt to get to the bottom of the nation's problems. Although Charles tried to split parliament by appealing to the House of Lords, Pym's speech had left a deep impression, and Charles announced a dissolution of parliament on May 5, 1640.

Following the dissolution Pym and his colleagues spent all their efforts trying to convince the king to recall parliament. Pym with the aid of Oliver St John, raised a petition signed by 12 peers, calling for a new parliament to redress their grievances. Oliver St John rose to fame in 1637 by serving as a legal representative to Saye and Hampden when they challenged the legality of King Charles I's imposition of Ship Money. Pym, accompanied by Hampden, travelled the region trying to raise support and getting an idea of public opinion. An appeal to the nation raised a total of 10,000 signatures from the citizens of London.

THE LONG PARLIAMENT

While Pym was busy getting signatures, Charles was making every effort to implicate him in treason, which failed miserably. Eventually Charles was forced to summon the Long Parliament in November 1640, and Pym was nominated as the leader of the political opposition to the king.

Pym's main criteria was to try to establish a balance between the power of the Crown and the power of the parliament. Like other Puritans, Pym believed that

Charles was trying to destroy the Protestant faith in England. The first step Pym took towards saving the nation's freedom and religion was to arrange the prosecution of the king's principal advisors, the Earl of Strafford and Archbishop Laud. He played a leading role in setting in motion impeachment proceedings in March and April 1941, which eventually led to Strafford's execution on May 12. Next he set about abolishing the courts of High Commision, the Star Chamber and any other archaic institutions that allowed the king to rule without parliament.

Other members of parliament persuaded Pym to support the abolition of episcopacy, which is the government of the Church by a hierarchy of bishops. Many protestants regarded it with suspicion after the Reformation, but it became a cornerstone of religious policy in the reign of James I. Charles I and Archbishop Laud were both strong supporters of episcopacy. The greatest fear that Pym had was that the king would use his military strength against parliament. This became even more prominent when the king raised an army against the Irish Uprising, which reached its peak in October 1641. Pym realized that if the king could raise an army against the Irish, it could easily be used to quell the Parliamentarians.

THE GRAND REMONSTRANCE

Part of Pym's strategy for gaining parliamentary control was the Grand Remonstrance, which was a list of grievances against Charles I, consisting of over 200 clauses. The Remonstrance was drafted by Pym and his supporters between August and November 1641 and listed all of the king's faults and the actions that parliament had already taken. It urged that the power of the Bishops should be restricted and that the Church should be reformed by a synod of Protestants. It also demanded that parliament should be instrumental in the appointment of any future king's ministers.

The king tried to pacify Pym by offering him the position of Chancellor of the Exchequer, but Pym was true to his cause and flatly refused to be bribed. The debate went on into the night on November 22, 1641, and after a lot of heated exchanges, parliament succeeded in passing the Remonstrance by a narrow margin of only 159 votes to 148. Any protestors were shouted down, which almost resulted in a riot. Allegedly Oliver Cromwell said that if the Remonstrance had not been passed he would have sold everything he owned and gone to live in America.

For the first time in the history of Parliament, opponents to the Remonstrance formed a Royalist party. The completed Remonstrance was presented to Charles I on December 1, 1641, and even though he ignored it for as long as possible, when Pym took the step of having it printed and circulated, the king realized that he needed to take action.

Charles I arranged for the arrest of five prominent members of parliament – John Pym, John Hampden, Denzil Holles, Sir Arthur Haselrig and William Strode. Of course this did nothing to improve his status and in fact did great political damage to his cause. The House of Commons considered it to be a direct attack on Parliament itself, and the King's reputation never recovered. The situation became volatile and there were even rumours of civil war, forcing the king and his family to flee from London. Meanwhile, Pym and his many followers returned to Westminster in triumph.

THREAT OF CIVIL WAR

In 1642, the threat of civil war looked inevitable, and Pym became one of the leading figures involved on the Committee of Safety. The Committee was first established on July 4, 1642, as a means of communication between the members of parliament in Westminster and their armed forces fighting on the field. It consisted of five members of the House of Lords – the Earls of Essex, Northumberland, Pembroke and Holland, and Viscount Saye and Sele. Also included were ten members of the House of Commons, headed by Pym. However, disagreements over strategy rendered the Commission ineffective and little military success was achieved under its direction.

With the relationship between parliament and the king at an all-time low, Pym started to organize finance for the Parliamentarian war effort. He arranged loans from city merchants, introduced a land tax and also proposed excise duties for the first time in England. It was Pym's organizational skills that guided the nation throughout the Civil War and the Commonwealth years.

In 1643, Pym proposed a coalition between the Scottish Covenanters and Parliament against the king.

This coalition was sealed with the signing of a document called the *Solemn League and Covenant* on September 25, 1643. It was both a military and religious alliance, with the main aim of overwhelming the Royalists, who seemed to be in a strong position to win the English Civil War. Pym was the first English Parliamentarian to sign the document, and this was to be his last political achievement.

John Pym died of cancer on December 8, 1643, just two weeks after the final terms of the alliance had been completed. He was given a state funeral and his body was buried in Westminster Abbey. His death deprived parliament of one of the greatest statesmen of his, or indeed, any other century. His skills as a leader were the result of the confidence he exuded during his speeches, along with his courage and resolution at critical moments. His fight for the parliamentary and religious cause were endless, and he will always be remembered as a true party leader and a freedom fighter for his country.

After the Restoration in 1660, his body was exhumed and buried in a communal grave with other leading parliamentarians in St Margaret's churchyard in Westminster.

A Parliament is that to the Commonwealth which the soul is to the body. It behooves us therefore to keep the facility of that soul from distemper.

JOHN PYM

OLIVER CROMWELL

Oliver Cromwell rose from humble beginnings to become one of Britain's greatest political and military leaders. He can be considered as a freedom fighter and a soldier of liberty because his actions were purely out of an intense passion for his country. When Britain was on the verge of anarchy, Cromwell emerged to give his country a lasting legacy – parliamentary democracy. At the height of his career Cromwell was offered the crown of England, which he politely turned down.

Cromwell was born on April 25, 1599, in Huntingdon to a relatively poor family. He was baptized at St John's Church in Huntingdon when he was only four days old, and as a young boy he studied at a free school which was attached to the Church. Cromwell later went on to spend a year at Sidney Sussex College, Cambridge, where he became popular because of his abilities in sports rather than his academic skills. His spell at Cambridge University was cut short when his father died in 1617. He was needed back home to manage the family's estate and help his mother look after his seven umarried sisters.

Cromwell made a living by farming and also collecting rents from his native Huntingdon. In August 1620, he married Elizabeth Bourchier, who was the daughter of a London merchant, Sir James Bourchier. His income was modest and he needed to support an ever-growing family. The marriage was a long and happy one and produced nine children.

CROMWELL ENTERS POLITICS

Cromwell was elected as MP for Huntingdon in 1628, and this was his first introduction to the opposition to the current king, Charles I. During the late 1620s, Cromwell suffered a period of mental illness, which seemed to have had the effect of awakening his religious beliefs. His religious fervour made him suspect, along with fellow Puritan reformers and dissenters, that Charles I was sympathetic towards the Catholic church, which had a profound influence on Cromwell's future political career.

In 1631, Cromwell was once again down on his luck when his fortunes started to decline. He was forced to sell most of his estate in Huntington, and he leased a farmhouse in St Ives, where he worked as a farmer for the next five years. In 1636, Cromwell's uncle, Sir Thomas Steward died, leaving no heir to his fortune. Cromwell came into what amounted to quite a significant inheritance, which turned his fortunes round. He was now the owner of a house next to St Mary's Church in Ely and also inherited the position of local tax collector for the two parishes of St Mary's and Holy Trinity. Cromwell's new, improved social status was just the rung he needed in his climb up the political ladder.

His first major political role was in 1640, when he was elected as a freeman of the borough of Cambridge and also MP for Cambridge in the two parliaments. Cromwell came into prominence as a speaker during the first week of the Long Parliament. He made a long and passionate speech about the wrongful imprisonment of a man named John Lilburne. Lilburne had been arrested for his involvement in the illicit printing and distribution of unlicenced Puritan books and pamphlets. As soon as Cromwell met Lilburne he was incensed at the injustice and drew attention to his case by denouncing the tyranny of the bishop. Parliament immediately ordered his release and he immediately became active in the revolutionary fervour that was taking place in London.

During the following months Cromwell was prominent in his parliamentary attacks on epispopacy. Although he was not such a fluent speaker as John Pym, his fervour and passion gained him a reputation as a solid supporter for the opposition leaders Pym, and his own cousin, John Hampden.

CROMWELL THE SOLDIER

The outbreak of the first civil war in August 1642 was the start of Cromwell's military career. He became an active and committed officer in the parliamentary army and led one of the earliest military actions of the war with a band of 200 volunteers, trying to stop Charles from taking the silver plate of the Cambridge colleges. Cromwell was initially a captain in charge of a small body of 60 mounted troops, and in October 1642 his cavalry joined the army of the Earl of Essex. His natural abilities as a military leader came to the fore when he fought at the Battle of Edgehill, where he was so impressed by the skills of the Royalist cavalry, it made him realize that his Parliamentarian horsemen needed far more disciplined training. On his return to East Anglia, Cromwell was more careful in his recruitment of new 'god-fearing' men and the provisioning, training and disciplining of the army were to be constant demands for the new leader. He believed this was the only way to an army's success.

His leadership came to the fore in a minor battle at Gainsborough in July 1643. Cromwell assisted in securing the majority of East Anglia for parliament by 1643, and he was rewarded with the post of governor of Ely. He was also promoted to colonel and given control of his own regiment, with whom he was to enjoy numerous successes. These victories quickly raised Cromwell's reputation, and by 1644 he was second in command of the Eastern Army, with the rank of lieutenant-general.

The largest battle of the civil war took place at Marston Moor in 1644, and what nearly became a Parliamentarian defeat, was turned around by the skill of Cromwell, defeating the highly disciplined cavalry of Prince Rupert and Lord Goring.

The redesigning of Parliament's army was initially proposed by Sir William Waller and Thomas Fairfax after the defeat at Cropredy Bridge in June 1644, and it was endorsed by Cromwell in a speech in the House of Commons in December. The Self-denying Ordinance swept away the existing military high command and the New Model Army Ordinance was passed on February 19, 1645. The New Model Army was the first ever national army and a forerunner to the modern British army. Cromwell was officially appointed as lieutenant-general, second in command to Thomas Fairfax.

Their first great victory was mainly due to Cromwell's strategy when the 22,000-strong army won a decisive battle at Naseby in 1645. Despite the fact that he had received no official military training, by 1646 Cromwell was generally recognized as the greatest soldier in England.

When civil war flared up again in 1648, Cromwell commanded a large part of the New Model Army, which crushed a rebellion in South Wales and then defeated a Scottish royalist army at Preston.

THE EXECUTION OF CHARLES I

Following his defeat at the hands of the Parliamentarians, Charles was put on trial in London on January 1, 1649. The accusations against him were:

Tyrant, traitor and murderer; and a public and implacable enemy to the Commonwealth of England

His trial was to be in front of 135 judges who would determine his guilt, but on the day only 68 turned up. Those who were absent were not happy about being associated with the trial of a king, an opinion that was shared by many members of Parliament. In fact, the only people allowed into Parliament were those who Cromwell considered to be supporters of the trial. This Parliament became known as the 'Rump Parliament' and of the 46 men allowed in – known supporters of Cromwell – only 26 voted to actually carry out the trial on Charles.

Of the 68 judges who turned up, not one was prepared to be the Chief Judge, and the unenviable job was given to a lawyer by the name of Richard Bradshaw. He knew that the trial was not going to be popular with the public and feared for his life. To protect himself from attack he made himself a special hat, which he lined with metal.

The hall where the trial took place was filled with soldiers, both to protect the judges and to ensure that the king didn't escape. Charles refused to defend himself, stating that he did not recognize the legality of such a court. He also refused to remove his hat as a sign of respect to the judges, which confirmed their decison that he was arrogant and therefore a danger to the public.

Bradshaw announced the verdict:

. . . he, the said Charles Stuart, as a tyrant, traitor, murderer and public enemy to the good of this nation, shall be put to death by severing of his head from his body.

When Charles heard the court's decision he finally started to defend himself, but he was told that his chance had gone and the King of England was bundled out of the court by the guarding soldiers.

It was a cold day in January 1649, when Charles I stepped out before a silent crowd and climbed the steps to the scaffold. The unthinkable had happened: a Christian nation had actually put their own king to death. It is hard to believe that a Puritan like Oliver Cromwell, a man who was so devoted to the Bible, could have been primarily responsible for the death of Charles I. However, in his defence he truly believed that his actions were for the liberty and rights of his people and country, not for his own political gains.

THE RUMP PARLIAMENT

After the execution of Charles I, the English Commonwealth was governed by the Rump Parliament, whose members wanted to promote Puritan godliness. Cromwell continued to lead major military campaigns, which culminated in the defeat of another Scottish Royalist army at Worcester in September 1651. Cromwell was now lord general, or commander-in-chief, of all the parliamentary forces.

After their victory, Cromwell became unhappy with the Rump Parliament, who seemed lethargic in formulating any new representative. He soon lost his patience, and on April 20, 1653, he led a body of musketeers to Westminster and forcibly expelled the Rump Parliament.

Cromwell had no plans to take over control of the Parliament and the Rump was replaced by the

Nominated Assembly, which met for the first time in July 1653. Cromwell was pleased with the new Assembly and he expected them to govern the commonwealth in the godly and righteous ways he admired so much. In December of the same year, moderates made a move to dissolve the Assembly and wanted to hand power over to Cromwell. Cromwell made it quite clear that he did not want to take over as king, and proposed a revival of the old title of Lord Protector.

This seemed to please the moderates and he was duly appointed Lord Protector for life and installed at Westminster Hall. This decision displeased many republics and religious radicals, who thought that it went against the principles for which the civil wars had been fought. In April 1654, Cromwell moved into Whitehall Palace, which was the former residence of King Charles I.

THE DEATH OF A LEGEND

In 1658, Cromwell's health went into a sharp decline, not helped by the death of his favourite daughter, Elizabeth, from cancer. Oliver Cromwell died on September 5, 1658, after a bout of malarial fever, which had afflicted him for over 20 years. Although Cromwell nominated his eldest son, Richard, to take over, the Protectorate had ended within a year of Cromwell's death, and it was subsequently followed by the restoration of the Stuart monarchy.

Whether you consider Cromwell to be a hero or a villain, he is certainly one of the most enigmatic figures in the history of England. He certainly inspired the beginnings of a democratic society, even if his methods were somewhat brutal. It cannot be denied that Cromwell was a stalwart representative of the Puritan ideals, and to him we owe much of our religious and political liberty.

Although Cromwell was given a truly regal funeral ceremony, to this day there are still doubts as to where his remains lie. At the direction of the Council, his corpse was embowelled and embalmed on the day after his funeral, but then it effectively vanished from public view. It was assumed that his corpse had been quietly buried somewhere within Westminster Abbey. In 1660, Parliament ordered the exhumation and post-humous execution of several regicides (people who were known to deliberately kill a monarch) and in 1661 Westminster Abbey was searched for the remains of three men – Cromwell, Henry Ireton and John Bradshaw. Three corpses were produced and taken to Tyburn, where they were hanged and then decapitated on January 30, which coincided with the 12th anniversary of Charles I's execution. Their heads were displayed on poles above Westminster Hall, and their headless corpses, including the supposed trunk of Oliver Cromwell, were simply dumped at dusk in an unmarked pit beneath the Tyburn gallows.

STENKA RAZIN

StepanTimofeyevich Razin, better known as Stenka Razin, was a Cossack leader who led a major uprising against the nobility and Tsar's bureaucracy in southern Russia. He is also the hero of a popular Russian folk song written by Dmitri Sadovnikov, which was later dramatized in the first Russian feature film in 1908, entitled *Ponizovaya Valnitsa*.

THE COSSACKS

The Cossacks were a military order that formed in what we now know as southern Russia and the Ukraine, possibly as early as the 14th century. The word Cossack comes from the Ukrainian word 'Kozak', and they were basically a rough band of fugitives, outlaws and vagabonds who organized themselves into effective military groups.

Most of their income came from farming and raising livestock, but this was supplemented by raids on the Turks, Poles and Jews, or indeed any other group that lived in their close vicinity. The Cossacks themselves were divided into two groups – the Don Cossacks and the Zaporozhian Cossacks – and each group was ruled by a chieftain or 'ataman'.

Russia was no stranger to revolts, because a nobleman by the name of Bohdan Khmelnitskyi (sometimes spelt Chmielnicki) who later became a Cossack ataman, led a rebellion against the Poles in 1648–54). He believed that the Poles had sold the Cossacks into the hands of Jewish slave masters. Khmelnitskyi made a pact with the usually hostile Tatars, descendents of the Mongol invaders who had occupied Russia for over 200 years. However, the Tatars soon betrayed the Cossacks, and in order to protect themselves the Cossacks made an alliance with Russia, which led to parts of the Ukraine coming under Russian domination.

The Cossacks played a large part in the expansion of Russia in the 17th century. They used to press into new regions of Siberia, which at the time were only occupied by tribes of hunters. Having taken control, the Cossacks established settlements and collected tributes – usually in the form of furs – which were paid to Russia and used as trade with the nations of Europe.

In the course of time the Cossacks grew in numbers and built themselves into a nation of professional soldiers. They established numerous posts and settlements, protecting Russian towns and villages from the raids and invasions of the militant Mongol and Tartar tribes from the south and the east.

SERFDOM

The origins of serfdom in Russia can be traced back to the 11th century. Under the rule of Ivan III of Russia (1462–1505), peasants lost the right to free movement and were restricted under a strict code of laws. By 1658 it became a criminal offence to try to escape from serfdom, and Russian landowners eventually gained unlimited ownership over Russian serfs. This included the right to sell them and even to assign marriages, so in effect, they had become slaves, bound to the land by harsh policies tied to imperial rule. There were numerous rebellions against this bondage, most often in conjunction with Cossack uprisings, and this is where our freedom fighter enters the history books.

Stenka Razin rose to be an ataman of the Don Cossacks and the first we hear of him is in 1661, when he went on a diplomatic mission to the Kalmyk Tatars. In the same year, he went on a pilgrimage to the Solovetsky Monastery, which was situated on an island in the White Sea. The monastery was in its day one of the main cultural and spiritual centres of Russia and an important centre of the Orthodox faith. Its cultural influence was considerable and thousands of pilgrims travelled to it every year from all over Russia and many other countries too. Razin was thought to have made the pilgrimage in an effort to 'benefit his soul'.

In his early years with the Cossacks, Razin was little more than a rebel and a pirate, leading his warriors from his headquarters in Panshinskoye on looting missions on the lower reaches of the Don River. In 1667,

Razin started to expand his missions to the shores of the Caspian Sea, and there he pirated imperial and merchant ships that sailed up and down the Volga River carrying grain and other goods.

Russia had suffered heavy financial losses during its long war with Poland, and this had put heavy demands on its people, forcing them to pay ever-increasing taxes. Many of the peasants, hoping to escape from the burdens of enforced conscription and taxes, fled south to join the bands of Razin's Cossacks. Others that had joined the peasants were people of the lower classes, who were fed up with the oppression imposed by the Russian government.

With his reinforced band of rebels, Razin went on to destroy the great water caravan which consisted of treasury barges and those belonging to wealthy Moscow merchants.

After taking possession of 35 galley ships, Razin sailed down the Volga to the city of Astrakhan, which was near the mouth of the river. He captured many forts on the way, which devastated the country. At the beginning of 1668 Razin vanquished the governor, Yakov Bezobrazov, who had been sent to attack him from Astrakhan.

EXPEDITION TO PERSIA

In the spring of 1669, Razin set off on an expedition that was to last 18 months. Leading his fleet into the Caspian Sea, he sailed to Persia (Iran), where he plundered and massacred the inhabits of the great emporium of Rasht, Derbent, Yaitsik and Bakú. Using not just his martial excellence to overcome the cities, he often resorted to trickery, getting his men to pose as merchants or pilgrims to gain the confidence of the local inhabitants. During these raids, Razin accumulated vast sums of money, making him and his men a force to be reckoned with. He successfully defeated a Persian fleet sent to destroy him, even though they tried every tactic to stop the Cossacks from escaping. The Persian fleet had chained their ships together, so when one of Razin's cannonballs set fire to some gunpowder in the hold of one of the ships, it subsequently capsized, taking down the rest of the fleet with it.

STENKA GETS MARRIED

By 1669 Razin had firmly established himself on the island of Suina and was honoured and revered by his men. During one of their missions, Razin captured a Persian princess with whom he fell deeply in love. He married his princess, but this caused consternation among his men, fearing that their love-sick leader would now lose his warring spirit. Sensing a mutiny, and wishing to remain loyal to his band of rebels Stanka raised his wife above his head and dropped her over the side of the boat into the waters of the Volga River, where she subsequently drowned. This story became the topic of a folk song entitled *Stenka Razin*.

In August 1669, Razin and his men reappeared in Astrakhan, he was greeted warmly by the people who wanted to hear all about his fascinating adventures. He was approached by Tsar Alexei Mikhailovich, who offered him a pardon if he would stop his killing and plundering. Razin agreed to the amnesty for a while, but in 1670 he defaulted and seized the city of Astrakhan, making it the capital of his republic.

Astrakhan was mostly occupied by nomadic people and a place where the atmosphere was somewhat predatory, which was a perfect base for Razin's rebellion.

THE REBELLION

As was to be expected, the continuing restraints of serfdom added fuel to the already smouldering fire of a peasant revolt. Peasants who had been heavily exploited and financially burdened by the tsar were ready to take up arms against the government. The rebellion took place at the height of Razin's popularity, at a time when he had more than 200,000 followers. In 1670, fed up with the tsar's enforced taxes and treatment of the peasants, Razin marched on Moscow and openly rebelled against the government, deposing Tsar Alexei I.

Like other revolutionary leaders before him, Razin claimed to be fighting the boyars – members of the highest rank of the Russian feudal system – and landlords, but not the crown. Razin made triumphant progress when his forces took Samara, Saratov, Penza, Cherkassk, Tsaritsyn and other cities. Razin was proclaimed as their 'saviour' by the peasants and native tribes, but his victory was to be short-lived.

After three weeks of considerable bloodshed, Razin

left Astrakhan with 200 barges full of troops in an effort to increase Cossack territories along the Volga, hoping to make his entry into Moscow easier.

His army was not well equipped and badly organized, and in October 1670, they met their match when they encountered the royalist forces at Simbirsk. After a fierce and bloody siege, Razin and his rebels were forced to flee down the Volga, leaving the bulk of his followers to face their victors. Those who were not fortunate enough to escape, were either flogged, maimed or killed.

Despite this overwhelming defeat, the rebellion was by no means over. Razin, having strengthened his forces and armed with inflammatory proclamations, he managed to cause unrest among members of the modern governments of Nizhny Novgorod, Tambov and Penza. His plan was to oust the boyars and officials that had dominated for so long. It was quite easy to win people over to his way of thinking, especially when Razin proclaimed that they would have a much freer and fuller life under an established Cossack rule, with its belief of absolute equality.

By the beginning of 1671 the rebel forces were starting to weaken, gradually being broken down by the opposition. Razin's reputation suffered considerably after he abandoned his men at Simbirsk and even some of his own settlements were now refusing him entry. The Don Cossacks, hearing of his waning popularity, also turned their backs on their former ataman.

In 1671, Razin and his brother Frol were captured at Kaganlyk, which was his last remaining fortress. They were taken to Moscow, where they were tortured.

Razin was quartered alive in the middle of Red Square and the parts of his body were marched around the city of Moscow, impaled on spikes. This was a warning to any future rebels who thought they could take on the might of the government and the ruling tsar.

Although the death of Razin ultimately ended the peasant revolt, unrest among the local tribes continued well into the 1680s.

> *From beyond the wooded island*
> *To the river wide and free*
> *Proudly sailed the arrow-breasted*
> *Ships of Cossack yeomanry.*
>
> *On the first is Stenka Razin*
> *With his princess by his side*
> *Drunken holds in marriage revels*
> *With his beauteous young bride.*
>
> *From behind there comes a murmur*
> *'He has left his sword to woo;*
> *One short night and Stenka Razin*
> *Has become a woman, too.'*
>
> *Stenka Razin hears the murmur*
> *Of his discontented band*
> *And his lovely Persian princess*
> *He has circled with his hand.*

His dark brows are drawn together
As the waves of anger rise;
And the blood comes rushing swiftly
To his piercing jet black eyes.

'I will give you all you ask for
Head and heart and life and hand.'
And his voice rolls out like thunder
Out across the distant land.

Volga, Volga, Mother Volga
Wide and deep beneath the sun,
You have never such a present
From the Cossacks of the Don.

So that peace may reign forever
In this band so free and brave
Volga, Volga, Mother Volga
Make this lovely girl a grave.

Now, with one swift mighty motion
He has raised his bride on high
And has cast her where the waters
Of the Volga roll and sigh.

Now a silence like the grave
Sinks to all who stand and see
And the battle-hardened Cossacks
Sink to weep on bended knee.

'Dance, you fools, and let's be merry
What is this that's in your eyes?
Let us thunder out a chantey
To the place where beauty lies.'

From beyond the wooded island
To the river wide and free
Proudly sailed the arrow-breasted
Ships of Cossack yeomanry.

PART FOUR

18TH AND 19TH CENTURY FREEDOM FIGHTERS

YEMELYAN PUGACHEV

The name of Yemelyan Pugachev became a personification of the spirit of the peasant revolution in Russia. Using his longstanding grievances against Catherine II, Pugachev gained followers not just among the peasants but with the Cossacks and many other minority groups as well. He fought to restore freedom to the serfs and his exploits were retold in the famous book by Alexander Pushkin entitled *The Captain's Daughter* (1836).

The rebellion instigated by Pugachev was perhaps the most serious outbreak of peasant resistance in the history of Russia. Pugachev, under a clever guise, was able to assemble an army of 10,000 men and face the crown on behalf of the downtrodden peasants.

BACKGROUND

Born around 1740, Yemelyan Pugachev was the son a Don Cossack landowner. He married a Cossack girl by the name of Sofia Nedyuzheva in 1758 and was the veteran of several wars, including the Seven Years' War (1756–63). In the first Russo-Turkish war (1768–74), Pugachev, who by this time was a Cossack, served under Count Peter Panin and fought in the siege of

Bender. Invalided out of the army, Pugachev spent the next few years as a relative nomad, and on several occasions was arrested by the authorities as a deserter from Catherine's army.

Like her predecessor, Peter the Great, Catherine II was aggressive in her expansion of the Russian empire. She used a combination of threat and intimidation to accomplish this and, although her empire almost doubled, with it came a multitude of problems, not least the social antagonisms of the peasants. Her marriage to Peter III, was over in all but the name, and her popularity with the lower classes diminished as she became more and more conservative and increasingly hostile towards criticism of her policies.

The situation between Peter III and Catherine deteriorated to such an extent that he was imprisoned by the consort and later mysteriously murdered at the castle of Ropsha on July 18, 1762.

PLANNING THE REBELLION

Pugachev apparently held an uncanny resemblance to the murdered Tsar Peter III, and he used this to his advantage. Taking into account the fact that Russia was engaged in a major war against Turkey, and that few troops were stationed in the eastern part of the country, Pugachev put his ruse into action.

Acting in a manner befitting a tsar, Pugachev claimed himself Emperor Peter III, alleging that he had managed to escape the plot of his wife, Catherine, to have him killed. He established a sort of imperial court, copying the one already in existence at St Petersburg. Here he quickly built up his own bureaucracy and started to assemble an army, copying that of Catherine's. He even persuaded some of his top commanders to take on the supposed position of dukes and courtiers to complete the deception. Considering he was nothing more than a defector, his skills at organizing an army were nothing short of remarkable. He built up his own War College and arranged a fairly polished system of messengers and spies. Pugachev himself was illiterate, but he enlisted the help of local priests to write his royal decrees in local Russian and Tatar dialects. These documents were copied and sent out to the masses, asking them to serve the tsar faithfully. For those who obeyed. he promised better conditions and a lowering of taxes, those who went against him were threatened with death.

Pugachev sent out his generals to carry out a mass recruitment drive for his army in both Tatar and Bashkit settlements. They were given strict instructions to recruit at least one member from each household and to seize as many weapons as they could procure.

To try to build up his reputation, Pugachev sent out messengers to a city or village he planned to visit, to warn them in advance that they were going to receive a visit from the tsar. The priests would be instructed to bring out salt and water and ring the church bells to signify his arrival. In this way, Pugachev ensured a heroic welcome.

THE START OF THE REBELLION

In 1773, Pugachev's army was ready to go into action, having amassed around 10,000 men. They attacked and occupied Samara, but Pugachev's greatest victory was the taking of Kazan. At the start of the rebellion Pugachev's men managed to capture territory that stretched from the Volga River up to the Ural mountains.

At the beginning of October 1773, Catherine and her generals merely regarded Pugachev and his rebels as nothing more than a troublesome problem, and they offered a mere 500 roubles for Pugachev's head. By the end of November Catherine started to realize that he was making more headway that she would have liked, and she increased the reward to 28,000 roubles to anyone who brought him back dead or alive.

By the start of 1774 Catherine realized that the troublesome Cossack army had developed into a real threat. All the forts on the Volga and Ural were in the hands of the rebels, the Bashkirs had joined forces with them, and there was considerable unrest among her subjects.

However, not everything went Pugachev's way. Although many people actually believed Pugachev to be Peter III, there were a few minority groups, such as the Bashkir and Tatar, whose loyalties were not so certain. In January 1774, Bashkir and Tatar generals attacked the city of Kungur, which left Pugachev's army with little food and ammunition. Many of his fighters deserted him, and one general took his entire unit with him.

When Pugachev's army seized Kazan they virtually

destroyed all of the churches and monasteries and massacred anyone who was unprepared to join the rebellion. Catherine, now taking the situation seriously, ordered General Peter Panin, who had earlier conquered Bender, to take his army and suppress the rebels. Despite the fact that Panin had a large army, which far outnumbered those of the Cossack, the start of his mission was fraught with difficulties. Lack of transport, discipline and gross insubordination of his poorly paid soldiers meant that he made no progress for months. Meanwhile, Pugachev and his ubiquitous band were victorious in nearly every engagement.

August 1774 was a completely different situation, when General Mikhelson managed a crushing defeat of the rebels near the town of Tsaritsyn. Pugachev lost the majority of his men, who were either killed or taken prisoner. Panin, who had managed to pull his troops into some sort of semblance, finished the job when he captured Penza.

By early September the rebellion was all but crushed and Pugachev was finally betrayed by his previous allies when he tried to flee to the Urals. Aleksandr Suvorov had him placed inside a metal cage and sent to Moscow for public execution, which took place on January 11, 1775.

PUGACHEV'S EFFECT ON RUSSIA

Even though Pugachev's rebellion fizzled out as quickly as it started, it did have quite a lasting effect on Russia. Catherine, who considered herself to be a wise monarch, passed new laws to strengthen control over regional administration. However, the horrors of the revolt, actually forced her to rescind previous reforms, and she revised her legislation on the institution of serfdom. Pugachev's rebellion was certainly a warning to the extreme conservatism of Catherine's reign. It served to point out, even if it was forcefully and tragically handled, the chasm between the different levels of society, and it certainly added to the alliance between the crown and the gentry in future years.

FRENCH REVOLUTION

The 18th century became known as the age of enlightenment because of fresh ideas that were starting to break down the old traditions. This new way of thinking set the stage for the great revolution that was to come in France. The French Revolution, which took place between 1789 and 1799, saw major changes in France, Europe and western civilization in general. The monarchy in France was replaced by republicanism and the Catholic Church was forced to make some major reforms.

As conflicting ideas started to clash, the Revolution turned into a scene of conflict and bloodshed. Their slogan became 'Liberté, égalité, fraternité ou la mort!' – Liberty, equality, fraternity or death! – which outlived the Revolution and became the cry of many future militants wishing to overthrow their oppressive governments. Many people came to the fore during the French Revolution, fighting for their country and what they believed should be the way for the future.

COMTE DE MIRABEAU

The Comte de Mirabeau (Honoré Gabriel Riqueti), generally referred to as just Mirabeau, was a French statesman, writer and popular speaker during the time of the Revolution. He was a moderate, believing in the constitutional monarchy modelled by Great Britain. France was ruled by Louis XVI in 1789 and, although a kind, considerate king, he had little knowledge of what the common people really wanted.

Mirabeau was born on March 9, 1749, in Le Bignon, near Nemours, and was the eldest son of the economist Victor de Riqueti, who was the Marquis of Mirabeau. When Mirabeau was three years old he suffered a bad attack of smallpox, which nearly cost him his life and left him with a badly pock-marked face. He was educated at a military school in Paris and, on leaving in 1767, he received a commission in a cavalry regiment that had been commanded by his grandfather some years before.

Mirabeau became renowned for his amorous antics and was even imprisoned at the request of his own father. During the 18th century it was possible for an individual to obtain *Lettres du Cachet* if a person had displeased an aristocrat, and having received such a letter the person was subject to a term of imprisonment. He was released to serve in Corsica with the rank of sublieutenant, where he managed to distinguish himself and redeem himself, temporarily, with his father.

In 1772, Mirabeau married an heiress, Marie Emilie, daughter of the Marquess de Marignane. Mirbeau's father arranged the alliance in the hope that it would stop some of the scandal surrounding his son. It wasn't long, however, before his father was forced to take action again when his wayward son would not control his extravagant ways. He forced his son to go into exile into the country to get him out of the way of his creditors, and it is here that he wrote his earliest work, *Essai sur le despotisme* (Essay on Despotism).

Mirabeau was known to have a violent temper, which led to an argument with a country squire who he felt had insulted his sister. His father once again presented him with a *lettre du cachet* and his exile was changed into imprisonment at the Château d'If in 1774. When he was moved to the castle of Joux in 1775, Mirabeau had a lot more freedom and was not so closely watched, and it was during this period that he met, Marie Thérèse de Monnier, who became affectionately known as 'Sophie', and the couple fell in love. Sophie, however, was already the wife of an older man, and together the couple sought exile in Switzerland. Mirabeau's desertion of his wife and subsequent affair meant that he was facing serious charges and was even under a death sentence.

May 1777, he was seized by the French police and imprisoned by a *lettre de cachet* in the castle of Vincennes. During the early part of his confinement, Mirabeau is famous for sending indecent letters to his beloved Sophie and also the obscene *Erotica Biblion* and *Ma conversion*. A fellow inmate was the Marquis de Sade, who was also famous for his erotic writings, but the two men detested each other.

Mirabeau was finally released in 1782, managing to get his death sentence overturned. He went looking for Sophie, only to find that she had taken comfort in the arms of a young soldier and had subsequently taken her own life following his premature death. Mirabeau then demanded that his wife return to live with him, which she refused. Following a lawsuit with his wife and a virulent attack on the ruling powers, Mirabeau was once again forced into exile and fled to Holland.

During his time in Holland, and later in England, Mirabeau became involved with the literary and political circles. Mirabeau started to mend his ways when he met Mme de Nehra, who was the daughter of a Dutch statesman, Zwier van Haren. She was a refined and educated woman, who was able to appreciate the better points of Mirabeau's character. Strengthened by her love, and his adopted son, Lucas de Montigny, Mirabeau settled down and was admitted into the best leading Whig and political society in London.

Wishing to return to Paris, Mirabeau sent Mme de Nehra ahead of his to make peace with the authorities on his behalf. He followed shortly after, with the hope of gaining employment with an old literary friend of his, Durival, who at that time was the director of finances at the department of foreign affairs. One of the roles of this position was to subsidize political pamphlets, but Mirabeau blew his chances by writing a series of controversial papers after he undertook a secret mission to Berlin in 1786.

During the late 1780s, the French Royal State was suffering major financial difficulties, mainly due to its involvement with foreign wars. Trying to alleviate the burdens of an archaic system of taxation and privileges, Louis XVI summoned an assembly of the States

General. This was an assembly of the clergy, the nobility and the commoners, with an effort to implement the necessary reforms. It was this meeting that set in motion the great French Revolution of 1789.

When the States General were summoned, Mirabeau hoped that he would be appointed as a deputy for the nobility of Provence. However, to obtain this post he needed the backing of his father, with whom he had never had a good relationship. With no backing, and having spoken quite openly against the privileged classes, Mirabeau was not elected deputy, but was offered to represent both Marseilles and Aix-en-Provence. Realizing that he would be unable to represent both, he chose Aix-en-Provence.

Already an avowed enemy of despotism, Mirabeau was a firm supporter of the monarchy and executive power, and he wished to help establish a representative government. With little money, and having been rejected by his own social class, Mirabeau abandoned his title so that he might sit with the commoners and help the cause of his people. He used his intelligence to gain some political experience and became a great orator. He certainly had the gift of speech and he was able to turn people towards his way of thinking.

He persuaded the Third Estate to divide up and give itself a new name, the National Assembly. He proposed that without the backing of the National Assembly, the nobles and clergy of the States-General should not be allowed to pass any new laws. On the day of its birth, the National Assembly was joined by more than 100 clergy. Louis XVI and his nobles were displeased when they learned of the new assembly, fearing that Mirabeau and his deputies were now growing too bold.

Wishing to teach them a lesson, the king ordered that the great hall in which the Third Estate met should be closed, and none of the members of the National Assembly should be allowed to enter. Although the deputies were aware of the king's order, they didn't believe that he would actually carry it out and turned up at the usual time outside the hall.

When they arrived they saw carpenters at work building a platform, and the deputies were told that no one, save the president and secretaries, could enter the building. It was a cold and dark morning, and the weather did nothing to improve the mood of the National Assembly. After much discussion and wandering about, their president, assisted by Dr Guillotine, managed to find an empty building in an abandoned tennis court of Old Versailles. They quickly gathered their members and assembled in the rough shelter. It was here that the deputies took an oath, which became known as the 'Oath of the Tennis Court', declaring that they would never give up until they had carried out the work the people had sent them to do. This was to reform the corrupt government of France.

Crowds had followed them into the old building in the tennis court and, after hearing them swear to the oath, loud cheers resounded round the derelict shelter. The National Assembly did not believe that it was the king that had turned them away, but his crooked advisers, and in their enthusiasm they shouted 'Long live the king! Long live the king!'

A few days later Louis went to meet the members of the National Assembly. Many members of the clergy and a few nobles were among the gathering, in particular, the Duke of Orleans. He was disloyal to the king, and hoped to be promoted to the post of Lieutenant-General of the Kingdom, in an effort to take away the power of Louis XVI. Two other rebellious characters at the meeting were the Marquis de la Fayette and also Maximilien Robespierre, who had already proved himself to be a great orator. Mirabeau, his face disfigured from his childhood illness, sat firm and resolute.

When Louis arrived, realizing what he was up against, he was forced to grant all their demands, but with one proviso. That was that all the members were to go home and never meet up again as the National Assembly. Although the nobles cheered on hearing his words, there was complete silence from the deputies. When the king left the tennis court with his nobles, the Third Estate made no effort to leave.

The king, suspicious that the Assembly would pay no need to his order, sent a messenger back to the tennis court. When he saw the members still seated, he said abruptly, 'You heard the king's orders?'

Mirabeau jumped to his feet and with a powerful and overpowering voice, answered, 'Go tell those who sent you that we are here by the will of the people, and that we will only be driven out at the point of the bayonet.' The king's messenger made a hastry retreat.

The king, who was not strong enough to oppose the Assembly single-handed, formed his three orders into one single body in June 1789. Versailles went mad, excited crowds ran through the streets, carrying torches and cheering the royal family. At last they felt all their troubles would now be over. However, they rejoiced too soon. The queen, along with many members of the nobility and clergy, were completely opposed to the deputies of the National Assembly, and they soon convinced the king that he had been foolish to give in so easily to their demands. They convinced Louis that if he was to keep any sort of power he must use force against the Assembly, and Louis sent his soldiers to seize Paris.

The Parisians could not believe what they heard and were even more shocked when they learned that the king was paying no attention to the National Assembly. This meant that the king wanted to take complete control with the help of the nobles. The people of Paris despised the nobles, and they rallied round taking up arms against the king's army. They quickly tore up the pavements and barricaded the city against the soldiers. The commoners lined the streets, were ribbons of red, white and blue, which their wives had quickly sewn into their jackets. These colours became known as the Tricolour, the emblem of the French Republic.

The news of the rebellion travelled quickly back to Versailles, and realizing that his troops could not be trusted, the king sent no one to disperse the rebels. In fact, many of his troops had already joined the people in the streets of Paris.

It wasn't long before the people realized that the king was not going to take any retaliatory action, and they decided to take the matter into their own hands. The Bastille was the chief fortress and prison in Paris, and the people saw this as a sign of the king's power. With an excited cry, 'To the Bastille! To the Bastille!', the crowds set off to destroy the old fortress.

The governor of the Bastille, who was old but brave, was uncertain how to handle the situation when he saw all the people outside the walls of the fortress. At first he ordered the cannon to be fired on them, but seeing that this only made the crowd more incensed, he changed his mind and foolishly opened the gates. He hoped to talk the crowd into retreating, but the people were determined and saw this as an opportunity to rush in and destroy the enormous building. It wasn't long before the whole fortress was nothing but rubble.

The mob ruthlessly murdered the governor and his officers, and now completely mad with excitement, the mob placed their heads on the tops of pikes and paraded them triumphantly through the streets.

Back in Versailles, the king was unaware of what had taken place at the Bastilles, and it wasn't until one of the nobles rushed into his apartment that he learned of the terrible events that had taken place.

Bewildered, the king asked why the people had taken such action. His courtier simply replied, 'Sire, it is a revolution!'

Mirabeau's health had been greatly affected by the extremes of his youth, and his recent strenuous activities led to his death on April 2, 1791.

His public mourned the loss of a great representative, and he was given a magnificent funeral. As a statesman, Mirabeau failed in his main objective of reconciling the monarchy with the Revolution, but as an orator he was unsurpassed. His work with the National Assembly was for the freedom and rights of the common people and a fight against the social class from which he was rejected.

MADAME AND MONSIEUR ROLAND

The atrocities of the French Revolution brought many famous women to the forefront, one of them being Jeanne Marie Roland de la Platière (better known as Madame Roland). Jeanne Marie was born in Paris in 1756, the daughter of an artist, and made rapid progress in the arts and literature. She was largely self-taught and acquired a liking for the works of Plutarch, which she continued to cherish throughout her life.

In 1781, she married Monsieur Roland, a man who was 20 years her senior, but every bit a match for her intelligence and strength of character. Early in her marriage, Jeanne Marie divided her time between the education of their young daughter and helping her husband as inspector of manufactures. Together they travelled to England and Switzerland, and it was here that they realized that France was still restricted by the old Bourbon régime.

She started to write political articles for the *Courrier de Lyon* and, when the family moved to Paris, Mme Roland soon started taking a more active role in politics. She opened her house to revolutionaries such as Brissot, Pétion, Robespierre, Mirabeau and other leaders of the popular movement.

When the French struggle for liberty started in 1789, the Rolands threw themselves into the Revolution with great verve, and Monsieur Roland was elected as the representative of Lyon to the National Assembly. The Rolands attached themselves to a moderate party called the Girondists, who were less violent than their fellow Jacobins. Within the Girondist ministry, Monsieur Roland was appointed as Minister of the Interior (or Home Secretary) and he became an unpopular figure in the court of Louis XVI when he appeared wearing inappropriate costume. He wore a round hat and had strings in his shoes instead of buckles, and this departure from court costume was interpreted by many as symbolic fall of the monarchy. By now the ravages of the Revolution were in full swing, urged on by the Jacobins. However this new bloodthirsty turn of events was distasteful to both the Rolands and the Girondists in general.

On September 2, 1792, news reached Paris that the Duke of Brunswick's Prussian army had invaded France. On September 3 and 4, inflamed by radical propaganda, ongoing food shortages and fear of the invasion, crowds broke into the prisons, where they attacked the prisoners, including refractory clergy, who were feared to be counter-revolutionaries who would aid the invading Prussians. This became known as the September Massacres. Following these events, Monsieur Roland boldly attacked the action of the

Parisians in the National Convention, but it was obvious by this time that the Jacobins, along with Robespierre, Marat and Danton, were becoming too powerful for him. These men were also particularly bitter towards Madame Roland, whose outspokenness had often impeded their progress. The Girondists considered the Rolands' lives to be in danger, and they arranged for them to be moved to a secret location. This, however, did not fit in with the plans of Madame Roland, who was not prepared to take a back seat and she announced:

I am ashamed of the part I am made to play. I will neither disguise myself nor leave the house. If they wish to assassinate me, it shall be in my own house.

On May 31, 1793, almost 40,000 Jacobins marched against the National Convention, believing this to be the best way of putting down the Girondists. On the morning of June 1, Madame Roland was arrested and thrown into Abbaye prison. Her husband managed to escape to Rouen, but Madame Roland would never see him again, nor indeed her liberty.

During her three months' imprisonment she was treated with respect by her gaolers and given the privilege of writing materials and occasional visits from close friends. She wrote her memoirs during this time of hardship, entitled *Appel à l'impartiale postérité,* and considered taking her own life, but her courage took over and she decided to face her fate bravely. Many of her close associates had already gone to the guillotine and eventually she was brought to trial for being an accomplice of the Girondists.

A few days prior to the trial, Madame Roland's advocate, Chauvieu, came to visit her in prison to talk about her defence. Half way through the meeting, however, Madame Roland removed her ring and said:

Do not come tomorrow to the tribunal; you would endanger yourself without saving me. Accept this ring as a simple token of my gratitude. Tomorrow, I shall cease to exist.

She appeared at the trial dressed from head to toe in white, with just her beautiful black hair in contrast. She maintained a regal dignity despite the insults that were thrown at her, but she already knew the outcome.

She was taken to meet her executioner on November 8, 1793 and, before placing her head on the executioner's block, she bowed before the clay statue of liberty in the Place de la Révolution, saying the famous remark for which she is remembered:

O Liberté, que de crimes on commet en ton nom! (Oh, Liberty, what crimes are committed in thy name!)

On hearing of her death, her husband committed suicide in his dingy lodgings just outside Lyon, realizing that he, and indeed France, had lost possibly the most remarkable woman of the French Revolution.

GEORGES DANTON

George Jacques Danton was born on October 26, 1759, and was a prominent figure in the early part of the French Revolution. He was not renowned for his good looks, but this was put down to the fact that he was kicked in the face by a bull when he was just a child. As an adult he was said to be exceptionally tall and muscular, with a mop of coarse, black hair. He had a powerful voice, which he used to his advantage when making speeches and had been likened to that of thunder and a lion's roar. His strength of character lay in his courage and audacity, and his career began as a barrister at the Paris bar. While in Paris he befriended Mirabeau, Camille Desmoulins, Robespierre, Marat and others who became famous for their devotion to revolutionary ideas.

We first hear of Danton in the Revolution as president of the famous club of the Cordeliers. The club got its name from the old convent of the order of the Cordeliers, where they held their meetings, and it was one of the more radical debating societies in Paris. Danton joined the Girondists and each day he grew in popularity as they realized the power he had over people when he was making a speech. With the aid of Jean-Paul Marat, Danton and the Cordeliers were not frightened to speak out about the need for freedom for the French people, and they vehemently proclaimed the need for some radical action.

Danton was not involved in the two earlier events of the Revolution – the storming of the Bastille and the forcible removal of the court from Versailles to the Tuileries). However, in the spring of 1790, he could be heard publicly speaking to urge the people to prevent the arrest of his ally, Marat. Danton was elected to be the commander of the battalion of the National Guard, and at the start of 1791 he was elected to the post of adminstrator of the *départment* of Paris.

On June 20, 1791, Louis XVI, Marie-Antoinette, their children and their servants attempted to flee Paris in secret, with the hope of reaching Luxembourg, where they planned to join the Austrian troops. However, their attempted escape was foiled when they were recognized, and the royal party was forced to return to Paris. As the king rode through the streets, accompanied by the National Guard, he was met with silence and hostility. Before he had left, the king had issued a proclamation explaining his rejection of the Revolution's 'complete anarchy'. With this statement, the people of Paris felt that he had renounced the right to lead the French nation.

Despite his treachery, the king was not deposed and the Cordeliers, as usual, outspoken in their opinions, cited him as a traitor. The Cordeliers drew up a petition against the king and organized a mass signing on July 17. They placed the petition on the altar where that year's Fête de la Féderation had taken place. However, when they discovered two suspicious characters hiding beneath the altar, the crowd immediately organized an impromptu lynching. This action was just what the authorities had been waiting for, and the mayor, Bailly, declared martial law.

The result was the Massacre at Champs de Mars, which took place as a direct result of French peasants and workers being unsatisfied with the outcome of the Revolution. They didn't believe that it had benefitted the middle classes, and they feared that Louis XVI would return to his original power and rule France under a constitutional monarchy. When the National Guard approached the Champ de Mars, the waiting crowds greeted them with a barrage of stones. The guardsmen immediately opened fire and killed about 50 people. The authorities then clamped down on the clubs that had organized the signing of the petition, and they closed down the radical newspapers. Danton fled to England and Desmoulins and Marat went into hiding, while many others were taken into custody.

In Paril 1792, war was declared against Austria, and to add to the political problems of the last two years, France now had to face the horror of war. The royal family sought refuge with the Legislative Assembly, while Danton did his utmost to give courage to a nation under threat:

Legislators! It is not the alarm cannon that you hear: it is the pas de charge against our enemies. To conquer them, to hurl them back, what do we require? To dare, and again to dare, and without end to dare!

In just a few weeks, 14 republic armies were repelling the allied forces with such a remarkable success, that the people of France were left with their mouths wide open. The next thing to happen was that Danton and Robespierre came face to face as rivals for the leadership of Paris. The two men were totally different in character and this period of history, which lasted from September 1793 until the fall of Robespierre in 1794, became known as the Reign of Terror. Its main purpose was to get rid of any adversaries of the Revolution and to protect France from foreign invaders. France was governed by the Committee of Public Safety, in which Danton and Robespierre were both influential members. In a period of just nine months, 16,000 'supposed enemies' were sent to the guillotine. All the time there was a shift in power within the committee itself from Danton to Robespierre. On the one hand Danton had a strong, physical presence and was an incredible public speaker, on the other hand Robespierre was less passionate, but he was an ambitious and hard-working man.

Danton's downfall was when he started questioning the extremes to which Robespierre was going in the Reign of Terror. Danton, who felt that his power was slipping away from him, resigned from office and retired to the country with his young wife. Rosepierre was not happy to let Danton escape so easily from his duties, and he recalled him to Paris. When the two met, Robespierre accused Danton of embezzling public money and accused him of being a tyrant. Fearing for his life, his wife and close friends pleaded with him to run away, but his response was:

*Whither fly? If freed France cast me out, there are
only dungeons for me elsewhere. One carries not his
country with him at the sole of his shoe.*

Robespierre showed no mercy and Danton was
denounced as a traitor and arrested on March 31, 1794.
He was brought to trial on April 2, and he defended
himself with his usual wise, but scornful words, but was
silenced on the grounds that he would incite the
people to revolt. Without one witness being called
against him, Danton was declared guilty. His last
words to his executioner were:

*You will shew my head to the people it is well worth
shewing!*

As his head fell, on April 5, 1794, the executioner,
Samson, caught it in his hands and carried it round the
scaffold to the sound of crying and howling that came
from the crowds.

In 1794, the French armies had defeated their
enemies, which meant that the Reign of Terror could
come to an end. Robespierre, however, continued saying that he wanted to purge France of anyone who was
corrupt, and it didn't end until Robespierre was
executed on July 28, 1794.

JEAN-PAUL MARAT

A prominent, if somewhat sinister, figure, Jean-Paul Marat was a fought for the 'lower classes' during the French Revolution. From the beginning to the end of the Revolution Marat stood on his own, suspicious of whoever was in power at the time, letting no one get in his way to make a better life for the French – a life with no poverty, no misery and no persecution.

He was a Swiss-born scientist and physician who spent much of his time in the UK, but he is best known as a fiery journalist and an activist who was prepared to use violent measures against any enemies of liberty. He was a member of the radical Jacobin faction and helped to launch the Reign of Terror, in which he compiled the 'death lists' of those suspected of being enemies.

Marat was born on May 24, 1743, and was the eldest child of Jean-Paul Marat, a native of Cagliari in Sardinia, and Louise Cabrol of Geneva. When his mother died in 1759, Marat set out on his travels and later studied medicine in Bordeaux. After he qualified he settled in Paris where he used his knowledge to help people suffering with eye diseases.

He moved to London to practise medicine and wrote several controversial papers during this time. One of which was *The Chains of Slavery*, published in 1774, in which he urged people to reject the British king's friends as candidates for parliament.

In 1776, he sailed to France where, despite his anti-royalist views, his reputation as a doctor soon won him a position as physician to the guards of the comte d'Artois, and afterwards Charles X of France. He was soon in great demand as a court doctor among the aristocracy and was earning a comfortable living.

In July 1788, Marat fell ill and, expecting not to survive, wrote his last will. He pulled through, and with his body and soul revived, he decided to throw himself into the Revolution and fight its enemies.

At the onset of the French Revolution, Marat decided to put his medical life behind him and concentrate on a new political one. He devoted himself to politics when the Estates-General assembled for the first time in 150 years. He fought ceaselessly right from the start, showing incredible boldness as far as his own safety was concerned. He trusted no one and was quite scathing in the pamphlets he wrote, for example against the famous Necker, Minister of Finances.

He published his first newspaper on September 12, 1789, entitled *Le Publiciste Parisien* (The Parisian Publicist), but just five days later it was changed to the legendary *L'Ami du Peuple* (The Friend of the People). Between the years 1789 and 1793, Marat produced 914 copies of his newspaper, which he used as a weapon against anyone who tried to hamper the progress of the Revolution.

Because of his outspoken views, Marat was often forced to go into exile for his own safety, but he never stopped the publication of the paper that made him so popular with the people of France. Marat attacked the most influential and powerful groups in France, which resulted in his imprisonment from October 8 to

November 5, 1789. In January 1790, he narrowly escaped being arrested again for his aggressive attack on the Marquis de La Fayette, but he escaped by fleeing to London. It was here that he wrote his famous scathing papers on Necker, a minister of Louis XVI, entitled *Denonciation contre Necker*.

In such a brief story, it is impossible to go into any great depth on his political works, of which he wrote more than 10,000 pages, or indeed the number of attacks he had to suffer. Marat returned to Paris in May 1790, but after printing derogatory articles about some of France's most powerful citizens, fearing reprisal, Marat was forced to hide once again, this time in the cellars and sewers, where he contracted a debilitating skin disease.

In September 1792, Martat was made a deputy by the people of Paris, but his election did not stop his ceaseless fight against the enemies of the Republic.

In January 1793, the National Convention condemned Louis XVI to death, and from then until May, Marat was involved in an unrelenting struggle with the Girondins. Marat, having uncovered anti-revolutionary tactics by the Girondists, was then accused by the faction of some concocted crime. His trial took place on April 24, 1793, but thanks to his own eloquence and adept way of stating the truth, he was declared not guilty and escaped the guillotine. He left the Tribunal Révolutionnaire in triumph, carried high on the shoulders of his closest friends.

The fall of the Girondins on May 31 was a great triumph for Marat, but this was to be his last. The skin condition that he had contracted during his time in the subterranean sewers was starting to take a toll on his health, and the only way to ease the pain was by sitting in a warm bath.

He used to sit in the comfort of the water for many hours, writing his journal, and one evening on July 13, he heard a young woman begging to be allowed to speak with him. She said she had brought news from Caen, where the escaped Girondins were trying to rouse France against Paris. Marat told his servant to let her in, and he asked her the names of the deputies at Caen. After writing their names on a piece of paper, she said, 'They shall be soon guillotined', and stabbed Marat through the heart with a knife she had just purchased from a shop across the street. Marat called out, '*A moi, ma chere amie!* (Help me, my dear friend!)' but within minutes he was dead, slumped over the side of the bath.

The 25-year-old girl's name was Charlotte Corday, and she was a Girondin, who had come to avenge the death of a friend. She was arrested and sent to trial and was executed on July 17.

Marat's funeral was attended by the entire National Convention and his ashes were placed in the Hall of Spectacles. Jacques-Louis David painted *The Death of Marat* in 1793 as a fitting memorial to the death of a close friend. Although Marat was perhaps too bloodthirsty in the pursuit of his beliefs, it must be remembered that he also suffered untold persecutions in his pursuits as a freedom fighter.

THOMAS PAINE

A man with a grand vision, Thomas Paine used his writings as a powerful weapon against the monarchy, feudal lords, dictators and indeed any repressive social structures. His controversial opinions on politics and religion would eventually destroy his success, but throughout his life his writings inspired passion. He brought the ideas of the American Revolution to the common farmers in a form that they could easily understand, and he was one of the first men to advocate a world peace organization.

HIS EARLY LIFE

Thomas Paine was the son of a Quaker corset maker, who was born on January 29, 1737, in Thetford, Norfolk. Paine grew up around farmers and uneducated people, and he left school at the age of 12 to become an apprentice corset maker. At 19, Paine became a merchant seaman, serving for a short time before returning to England in April 1759 to set up his own corset business in Sandwich, Kent.

Paine married Mary Lambert in September 1759, but this was to be an unhappy time in his life. His business collapsed and, following a move to Margate,

Kent, his wife went into an early labour and neither the baby nor Mary survived.

PAINE THE WRITER

In 1761, Payne returned to Thetford, where he was employed as a supernumerary officer, and the following year he became an excise officer in Grantham, Lincolnshire. Unfortunately he didn't excel at this position, getting discharged twice in four years and upsetting his superiors by asking for higher wages. In 1772, he wrote his first paper entitled *The Case of the Officers of Excise,* which was perhaps a sign of what was to come. The document argued for a pay rise and better conditions for excise officers.

In 1774, Paine went to London, where he became acquainted with Benjamin Franklin. Franklin told him of the benefits of living in America and helped Paine emigrate to Philadelphia. This was the turning point in Paine's career: he had found his niche and his work in journalism got him noticed. He had several articles published in the *Pennsylvania Magazine,* the most notable of which was one advocating the abolition of slavery.

He published *Common Sense* in 1776, which was a strong defence of American Independence from England and attacked the British monarchy. During the war, Paine joined the Continental Army but wasn't a successful soldier. However, he did produce a paper called *The Crisis,* which was an inspiration to the army itself. In 1781, Paine travelled to France to raise funds for the American cause.

After independence Paine ceased fighting for the Revolutionary cause and returned to Europe to try his hand at other ventures. These included trying to invent a smokeless candle and also work on an iron bridge. During this time he continued to write his pamphlets on political issues and in 1776, he published *The Rights of Man*, which was probably his most influential work. This book was in response to criticism of the French Revolution and argued for equal political rights. He suggested that all men over the age of 21 should be allowed to vote, which would mean that the House of Commons would be able to pass laws that were favourable to the majority. It recommended progressive taxation, family allowance, old age pensions and maternity grants, and it called for abolition of the House of Lords.

The British government were outraged by Paine's latest book, and he was subsequently outlawed in England as an antimonarchist. His book was instantly banned and Paine was charged with seditious libel. Before he could be arrested, Paine fled to France. He announced that he did not wish to make any profits out of his latest book, and that anyone had to right to reprint it if they so wished. *The Rights of Man* went on the printing presses again, but this time in a much cheaper format, making it available to the working classes. Even though the book was banned in England, it still managed to sell over 20,000 copies.

One influential man who obtained a copy of *The Rights of Man* was the English poet and novelist Thomas Hardy. In 1792, Hardy founded the London

Corresponding Society, with the aim of achieving the vote for all adult males in the UK. His views followed those that had been expressed by Paine.

THE AGE OF REASON

In 1792, Tom Paine became a French citizen and was elected as a member of the National Convention. Paine's downfall came when he upset French revolutionaries with his opposition to the execution of Louis XVI. He was arrested and detained in prison from December 28, 1793, until November 4, 1794, under the threat of execution. During his imprisonment he wrote and distributed the first part of what was to become one of his most controversial books, the anti-church work called *The Age of Reason*.

Paine was eventually released from prison because the American minister, James Monroe, put pressure on the French government. Soon after his release, *The Age of Reason* was published, which had a tremendous impact due to the fact that it questioned the validity of Christianity. Paine openly criticized the Old Testament, stating that not only was it untrue but it was also immoral, and claiming that the Gospels contained many inaccuracies.

Paine stayed in France until 1802, then he returned to America following an invitation from Thomas Jefferson. However, *The Age of Reason* had upset a lot of people, and Paine discovered that he had lost much of the popularity he had gained during the War of Independence. Unable to return to Britain, Paine, who had been abandoned by his friends and derided by the American public, died a lonely man on June 8, 1809, at the age of 72 in New York City.

HIS LEGACY

There is no doubt that Thomas Paine's literary works had a great influence on his contemporaries, and especially those connected with the American Revolution. Throughout his life he showed a dedication to the liberation of all those people who are oppressed not only by political extremes but also by religion. He always felt compelled to write for any cause that had its roots in reason and humanity. He didn't tolerate brutality in any form, and he saw the execution of human beings as being totally unnecessary, ardently stating, 'Kill the king but spare the man'.

There is a statue that stands in King Street in Thetford, the place of his birth, of Paine holding a quill and his book *The Rights of Man*. There is also a museum dedicated to him in New Rochelle, New York. Although towards the end of his life he was hated by many of his fellow countrymen, today he is remembered as the 'World's Citizen' and the 'People's Philosopher', and rightfully so, for all his self-sacrificing work to liberate the oppressed.

THE MARQUIS
DE LAFAYETTE

The Marquis de Lafayette was a national hero in both France and the American colonies for his part in the French and American Revolutions. He was motivated by his native France's hatred of England and his sympathy for the political ideals of the American Revolution. He fought for the cause of liberty and it was his actions that helped corner the British forces at Yorktown, which led to their eventual surrender to General Washington on October 9, 1781. His struggle for political independence was of considerable value and this has earned him a place in history as a respected freedom fighter.

His full name was Marie Joseph Paul Yves Roch Gilbert du Motier, but he is better known as the Marquis de Lafayette. He was born on September 6, 1757, at the château of Chavaniac in Auvergne. Before he was even two years old, his father, who was a colonel of the grenadiers, was killed at Minden in 1759. His mother died when he was only 12, and just a few weeks later he lost his grandfather as well. So by the age of just 13, he was left an orphan with a considerably healthy inheritance. Lafayette joined the Royal Army when he was 14, and just two years later married Marie Adrienne Françoise de Noailles, who was the daughter of the duc d'Ayen, one of the most influential families in the area at that time.

INTRODUCTION TO AMERICA

Lafayette's first introduction to America came on August 8, 1775, when he came into contact with the Duke of Gloucester at a dinner party. The duke spoke with sympathy of the struggle going on in the colonies to secure their independence. Lafayette felt an excitement rise inside him when he thought about fighting for the American cause, and he immediately made plans to travel to America. Knowing that his family and the king would try to stop him, Lafayette sought the help of his friend the Comte de Broglie, who in turn introduced him to the Baron Johan de Kalb, both of whom were seeking to travel to America.

Lafayette offered his services to America as a volunteer, and through an American agent in Paris, Silas Deane, he was able to obtain passage with several other French officers. They landed near Charleston in South Carolina on June 13, 1777. Later that summer Lafayette went to Philadelphia and was welcomed warmly by the Congress. Not only did he represent the highest rank of French nobility, but he had also come to fight for the American cause without pay and as a volunteer. He was commissioned as a major general, and later that year met General Washington, which turned into a lifelong friendship. They became so close that Washington asked Lafayette to be his son's godfather, naming him Georges Washington-Lafayette.

Lafayette's first battle under Washington's command was on September 11, 1777, at Brandywine. Although he only participated in the latter part of the battle, he showed such courage and determination that he was given the command of a division, something which he had earnestly desired.

Although Lafayette never had many troops under his command, he proved to be a wise and astute leader. His retreat from Barren Hill on May 28, 1778, was commended as masterly. He fought at the Battle of Monmouth on June 28 and he also received a formal recognition from Congress for his services in the Rhode Island expedition in August of that year.

In 1778, Louis XVI recognized the Independence of the 13 colonies and signed treaties with America, and the United States of America was formed. Louis sent over an expeditionary force to the USA and 6 million French pounds to George Washington. This was promptly followed by a declaration of war by Great Britain, and Lafayette was asked to return to France to consult his king as to his future service. He applied to Congress for a furlough to return home, and on October 21, Lafayette was granted permission to return to his native land. Although it was easy for Washington to replace the major general, it was not so easy to find another man who was so devoted to fighting for the American cause.

RETURN TO FRANCE

When Lafayette arrived in France he went straight away to the palace at Versailles to see his wife and family. However, since he had left France without the permission of the king, Lafayette knew he could not go to the royal court until he had been forgiven. His father-in-law went to see the minister, Maurepas, on his behalf and was told that Lafayette must undergo a period of exile before he could return to court. He was exiled to the Hotel de Noailles for a period of eight days, in which time he was not permitted to leave or receive any visitors, with the exception of his family. The king, when he learned of the young man's exile, felt it was unfair punishment for someone who had been praised so highly for his services in America. At the end of his punishment, Lafayette was summoned by the king, congratulated and was given the commission of colonel in the French cavalry. He also received a sword from the Congress of the United States, an honour that was appreciated by the king and his government.

As soon as Lafayette returned to France, he made every effort to secure financial and military support for Washington and his armies. On June 12, 1779, Lafayette wrote a long letter to Washington saying that he hoped to return to America soon with the necessary aid. So keen was he to help his friends overseas, Lafayette even bought supplies out of his own private funds to give to his own troops when he returned.

After much discussion the French troops were put under the command of Count de Rochambeau, while

Lafayette returned to America to command his own troop under the watchful eye of Washington.

Lafayette returned to his beloved America on March 19 on board the French frigate, *Hermione*, and arrived in the port of Boston after a 38-day voyage. He immediately reported to Washington and then handed over official papers to the French representatives of the government. In the summer of 1780, the Americans received a major boost to their cause when 5,500 French troops, commanded by Rochambeau, arrived at Newport, Rhode Island. France had been sending supplies to the colonies all along, but after France and England declared war against each other in 1778, Louis XVI sent troops and naval assistance to them to engage the enemy. With this added strength, Washington and Lafayette believed that their fight for independence was nearly at an end.

THE FINAL BATTLE

The final major action of the American Revolution was the Siege of Yorktown, which ended with the surrender of British troops on October 19, 1781. American and French land forces, under the command of Washington, collaborated with a French fleet commanded by Admiral François Joseph Paul, comte de Grasse, who managed to surround and overcome the British forces commanded by Lieutenant General Charles Cornwallis. The siege lasted 20 days, and the surrender by Cornwallis resulted in the resignation of the British prime minister Lord Frederick North.

North accepted the terms of the Treaty of Paris, signed on September 3, 1783, which officially ended the war. Lafayette played a significant part in the success of Yorktown, and this was to be the termination of his military career in America.

Lafayette applied for a leave of absence to return home to France, and before he sailed home Washington wrote him a personal letter:

> *I owe it to your friendship and to my affectionate regard for you, my dear Marquis, not to let you leave this country without carrying with you fresh marks of my attachment to you, and new expressions of the high sense I entertain of your military conduct and other important services in the course of the last campaign, although the latter are too well known to need the testimony of my approbation.*

Lafayette returned to France on December 23 on board the US ship *Alliance*, and on arrival he was duly honoured as a hero for his work in America, which bonded a strong tie between the two countries. Back in public life, Lafayette played a prominent role in plans to abolish slavery. He worked closely with Benjamin Franklin and Thomas Jefferson, still working on behalf of American interests.

After 1782, Lafayette becamed totally absorbed with the question of reform in France, and he was one of the first people to recommend a National Assembly. He worked ceaselessy towards the establishment of a constitutional monarchy in the years leading up to the

French Revolution, something which lost him a lot of support from the French nobility. When France was attacked by the European coalition in 1792, Lafayette was given the command of the French Revolution Army. Fearing the Jacobin factions that had taken over control of the French government, Lafayette, like many other nobles, fled to Belgium. The Austrians, however, thought Lafayette was the cause of an anti-monarchy revolt in France and imprisoned him for five years. He spent one year at Magedeburg and the other four at Olmutz, and he was eventually freed by Napoleon in September 1797. After his release, although he was quite prepared to accept Bonaparte's position, he declined any role in the Emperor's regime.

Lafayette returned to France in 1800 and found that his personal fortune had been confiscated, and he was forced to live off his property in Lagrange until the US Congress came to his rescue. As a reward for his services to America he was given 46,500 ha (11,500 acres) of land along the Ohio River.

In 1815, he was elected to the Chamber of Deputies and, as one of its vice presidents, he worked for the abdication of Napoleon after the Battle of Waterloo. Although Lafayette played no major role in the politics of France, he did become a focal point of resistance to the Bourbon kings. In 1830, he became the leader of a revolution that dethroned the Bourbons and helped make Louis Philippe the constitutional monarch of France.

Lafayette made a long visit to the USA from July 1824 to September 1825, attending an inaugural banquet of the University of Virginia at the invitation of Jefferson. He also visited Lafayette Square Park in Missouri, which was named in his honour.

On his return to French soil, Lafayette spent over $200,000 of his fortune in support of the colonies in the Revolution. Lafayette continued to maintain strong ties with his friends of the American Revolution and he made his last speech on behalf of Polish political refugees in 1834.

THE LOSS OF A GREAT MAN

Lafayette died in Paris on May 20, 1834, and was buried in Le Jardin de Picpus cemetery in Paris, under American soil taken from the foot of Bunker Hill. In 1917, General Pershing paraded his army in front of Lafayette's tomb and held a special ceremony, at which he said the famous words, 'Lafayette, we are here!' His grave bears an American flag, which even the Nazis left alone when they entered Paris during World War II.

In July 2002, the US Congress voted to make Lafayette an honorary citizen of the USA. There are only five other people who have received this honour – Winston Churchill, Mother Teresa, Raoul Wallenberg and the founder of Pennsylvania, William Penn and his wife Hannah. It is easy to understand why the USA was so eager to express its appreciation of General Lafayette, because his patriotism has never been equalled and the fact that he spent more than half of his considerable personal fortune for the cause of American liberty.

TIPU SULTAN

Tipu Sultan is probably one of the most fascinating characters to come out of the 18th century. He was a freedom fighter par excellence, and one of the first to fight for his country, India. Sultan had a vision and purpose to his life, and that was to free India from the enslavement of the colonials. For many years the colonials stayed in power by enforcing social and cultural practises that were designed to convince the subaltern classes to accede to their power. The colonials considered any uprisings to be mutinies and any freedom fighters to be usurpers or terrorists. Although Sultan's reign was short, he fought not only for political freedom, but also for social, economic and cultural freedom, to try to give his people a better standard of living. Tipu lived and died to personify the value of freedom and the enhancement and prosperity of his state.

HIS CHILDHOOD

Tipu Sultan was born on November 20, 1753, in Devanahalli, about 75 km (45 miles) east of Bangalore. His father, Hyder Ali, was an Indian general and sultan of Mysore in southwestern India from 1759. He was in command of the army in Mysore and became ruler of Mysore State in 1761, rivalling British power in the area until his defeat by Sir Eyre Coote in 1781 during the Anglo-French wars. From the age of 15, Sultan accompanied his father on various military campaigns, having received training in the art of warfare from an early age. He was a devout Muslim with a fascination for learning, and it was said that his personal library numbered in excess of 2,000 books. He spoke several different languages and was educated in both mathematics and science.

THE MYSORE WARS

India was in a state of confusion in the second half of the 18th century due to the rise of colonial power. The British East India Company, which was established in 1600, held a dominant position and was making large profits from India. By 1720, 15 per cent of Britain's imports came from India. The only state to actually offer resistance to the colonial expansion was Mysore, and this resulted in four Mysore wars. Tipu Sultan was to take part in all four of these wars against the British, and in two of the conflicts he imposed serious blows on his enemy severely damaging their reputation as an invicible power.

Apart from the British, Sultan and his army were also involved in several clashes with their neighbours, the Marathas and the Niza. These neighbours had joined forces with the colonials in their fight against

Mysore because they were opposed to the rise and growth of Mysore as an independent powerful state. Realizing that the Marathas and the Niza were against Sultan and his army, the British took full advantage of the situation by joining with them as allies against Mysore.

In 1769, the British suffered heavy losses in the First Anglo-Mysore War, and the East India Company sued for peace. The British and the Mysores signed a treaty in which they both agreed to help one another if either were attacked by a third party. However, when Mysore was attacked by the Marathas in 1771, the British refused to help Sultan's father, Hyder Ali, so he turned to the French for their military support. Subsequently, when the British wanted to attack the French at Mahe in 1780, Ali did not offer any support, which caused the British to declare war against Hyder Ali.

Tipu Sultan, who was gaining more and more military experience, was sent to the northern part of Mysore in 1772 to try to recover the territories that had been taken over by the Marathas.

In July 1780, Sultan joined forces with the Marathas and Nizam, having managed to change their allegiance. Together with Sultan's father, they marched on Carnatic with 80,000 men and 100 guns. In October, they captured Arcot, inflicting a crushing defeat on the British army under the command of Colonel Braille. The whole detachment was destroyed, with the British soldiers either being killed or taken prisoner.

TIPU SULTAN BECOMES RULER

The British were now scared of Sultan's growing strength. After the death of his father on December 7, 1782, in the Second Anglo-Mysore war, Tipu Sultan was left to continue the war against the British. He was enthroned as ruler of Mysore on May 4, 1783, in a simple ceremony that took place at Bednur.

Sultan inherited a powerful empire from his father, which was about 644 km (400 miles) in extent. He gradually built on his empire by constructing roads and encouraging agriculture with improved drainage systems. He introduced new industries and supported foreign enterprise with the aim of making his kingdom the most prosperous state in India.

Tipu Sultan adopted the tiger as his emblem and tiger motifs and tiger stripes decorated his personal possessions, including jewellery, weapons and textiles. His obsession was so great that his armoury included mortars shaped like sitting tigers, cannons with tiger muzzles and hand weapons decorated with gold tiger heads, or inlaid in gold with tiger masks formed by an arrangement of Arabic letters meaning 'The Lion of God is the Conqueror'. He even had a throne made out of solid gold in the shape of a life-size tiger, and through this obsession he became nicknamed the *Tiger of Mysore*. He was a generous ruler who treated his subjects well. He encouraged learning and the arts and also allowed his subjects complete freedom of worship.

Just like his father, Sultan was a brave warrior, and in

1783 the British were once again defeated when Brigadier Matthews, appointed by the Bombay government, was captured. The Second Anglo-Mysore war came to an end with the Treaty of Mangalore. Under the terms of the treaty, both parties decided to restore each other's conquered territories and to release all the prisoners. However, both Mysore and the British treated the treaty as little more than a temporary truce. It was an important document in the history of India, as it was to be the last time that the Indian power would dictate their terms to the British. The first Governor-General of India, Warren Hastings, called the treaty a 'humiliation' and pleaded with the king to punish the Madras government, claiming that the honour of the British nation had been violated. Not prepared to bow down to this form of degradation, the British did everything in their power to overturn Sultan's power.

However, it was not just the British that were disappointed with the Treaty of Mangalore. There were seeds of unrest among the Marathas who, having acted as mediators, believed they would be rewarded with the return of some of their territories. They were jealous of the new power that Sultan had achieved, and both the Marathas and the Nizam fought with Sultan's army for the next two years, from 1785 to 1787. The war ended, this time with the Treaty of Gajendragadh, in which Sultan ceded Badami to the Marathas, hoping to win their support against the British.

However, Sultan was to be disappointed with the outcome of the treaty, because, far from joining him to remove the British from India, both the Marathas and the Nizams allied with the British. The outcome was the start of the Third Anglo-Mysore war, which lasted for two years, from 1790 to 1792. The war came to an end when Sultan was eventually outwitted by Lord Cornwallis, and he was defeated in his own capital of Seringapatam. He was forced to sign a humiliating treaty and had to surrender half of his kingdom. He was unable to pay the substantial indemnity enforced on him by the British, and two of his sons were taken as hostages to Madras. This was a major blow to Tipu Sultan, and he wasted no time in building up his power once more.

THE SULTAN'S DOWNFALL

Sultan was soon able to pay the indemnity and his sons were returned to him. With renewed vigour Sultan started to reinforce his relationship with the French, the Turks and the Afghans. Napoleon made plans to travel to India to help Sultan, but just as all his plans were coming together, fate took the upper hand. Napoleon was defeated in a battle at Accre in Syria and was forced to return to France. It was the discovery of correspondence between Sultan and Napoleon that made the British angry and precipitated the Fourth Anglo-Mysore war. With the Nizam and Marathas not showing any true allegiance, and the fact that his state was now surrounded by British territories, Sultan stood alone in his fight against the British. Passes that were once open to Sultan and his father were now closed, and he felt as though he were caged in just like the tiger that he so loved. Lord Wellesley, a British soldier and statesman, planned to launch an atack on Sultan's capital from Madras and Bombay, determined to wipe out his independent state.

Sultan, realizing that his army was probably going to be outnumbered, prepared for the attack, bravely saying:

It's better to live a day as a tiger than a lifetime as a sheep.

After a prolonged period of fighting, the British made a direct assault on Srirangapatna on the morning of May 4, 1799. Sultan, mounting his horse, rode right into the thick of the battle with just a few of his most faithful soldiers. When the palace was eventually sieged, the commander-in-chief of the Mysore army, Sultan, was nowhere to be found. After much searching his body was found where the fighting had been fiercest, lying beneath a pile of dead and wounded soldiers. He had been shot in the head and stripped of his jewels. Wellesley refused to believe that Sultan was dead, which showed the fear and awe the British had of the brave and tactical soldier. He was given the funeral of a hero with full military honours.

HIS LEGACY

Tipu Sultan was not only a proud Mysorean, an even prouder Indian, but also a brilliant and fair ruler. Although he was eccentric at times, he was certainly a martyr to the cause of a free India. He laid down his life defending his country and state against the British and was in fact the only Indian prince who took on the might of the British army and died on the battlefield.

Part of Sultan's legacy includes the invention of military rockets, which he used to great effect against the British invaders of his domain. Today, however, his famous 'rocket court' in Srirangapatna lies in ruins. As a freedom fighter he was unsurpassed, but unfortunately his death paved the way for the rapid expansion of the British power in India.

SIMÓN BOLÍVAR

Simón Bolívar earned himself the title of 'El Liberator', or 'The Liberator', for his incredible achievements on behalf of his beloved South America. He dedicated his life to the independence of the then Spanish colonies and the dream of unification for Latin America. Even today he is heralded as South America's greatest hero and freedom fighter, and many streets and cities – and even the county Bolivia – bear his name.

Simón José Antonio de la Santísima Trinidad Bolívar was a descendant of a family of Basque origin that had been established in Venezuela since the end of the 16th century. He was born in Caracas on July 24, 1783, to Colonel Juan Vicente Bolívar y Ponte and Concepción Palacios Blanco. Having been born into an aristocratic family, Bolívar and his two older sisters and brother, María Antonia, Juana and Juan Vicente, received an excellent education from private tutors. These included the great intellectuals Andrés Bello and Simon Rodríguez, who introduced him to the works of the Enlightenment as well as those of classical Greece and Rome.

Bolívar lost both his parents by the age of nine, and was left in the care of his uncle, don Carlos Palacios.

Badly affected by the death of his parents, Bolívar became a restless child, which resulted in him running away from his uncle's house to live with his sister María Antonia and her husband in 1795.

Bolívar loved to study, and he formed a close relationship with his tutor, Símon Rodríguez, who was the headmaster at an elementary school in Caracas. He occasionally went to stay with Rodríguez and his family, which added to his already blossoming wealth of knowledge.

At the age of 14, Bolívar joined the White Militia in the Aragua Valley, which had been commanded by his father as colonel several years before. He proved to be a natural soldier and was quickly promoted to the rank of second lieutenant.

In 1799, Bolívar travelled to Spain with a close friend, Esteban Escobar, stopping en route in Mexico City. It was here that they met the viceroy of New Spain who was quite astounded with the strength of Bolívar's views on Spanish American independence. When Bolívar arrived in Madried in June of that year he went to stay with his uncle, Esteban Palacios. Here he devoted himself passionately to his studies, widening his knowledge of history, classical and modern literature, mathematics and French. His social life was full of parties and dances, and it was at this time that he met his future wife, María Teresa. They married on May 26, 1802, and the newlyweds returned to Venezuela to set up home. However, their happiness was to be short-lived as María died of yellow fever in January 1803.

HIS VOW TO FIGHT FOR FREEDOM

Bolívar was deeply affected by the death of his young wife and vowed never to remarry, a pledge which he kept for the rest of his life. After the shock of losing his wife, Bolívar returned to Spain with his old friend and tutor, Sémon Rodríguez. It was while in Europe that he witnessed the crowning of Napoleon Bonaparte as emperor of France and later the coronation of Napoleon as the king of Italy. It was during his visit to Italy that Bolívar was to make the vow to fight for the freedom of South America, while he stood on top of Mount Aventin in Rome.

Meanwhile, great changes were taking place in Europe and Bolívar decided to return to Venezuela. Napoleon invaded Spain and deposed the king. In his place he appointed his brother, Joseph Bonaparte, as king of Spain, which was an unpopular decision and launched a revolt in Spain known as the Peninsular War. The colonies in South America refused to accept the new king and set up 'juntas' (governing councils) to rule the colonies. These juntas not only refused to accept Joseph as the new king, but were also not prepared to take orders from representatives of the deposed, or genuine king.

Bolívar was appointed as lieutenant colonel of the junta and the Caracas junta declared its independence from Spain. Bolívar was sent to Great Britain on a diplomatic mission, along with Andrés Bello and Luis López Mendez. Their mission was an attempt to get aid from Great Britain, but they only managed to get a promise of neutrality.

Bolívar returned to Venezuela on June 3, 1811, at the time when the First Republic of Venezuela was declared. However, the people of the country were not united in their beliefs and the republic only lasted one year due to constant counter-rebellions. Bolívar tried to suppress one of the rebellions at Puerto Cabello, but he failed miserably and fled to Cartagena in New Granada (present day Colombia). It was while he was here that Bolívar, the devout republican, issued one of his most famous papers in 1812, his *Cartagena Manifesto*. In his manifesto, Bolívar stated that the revolutionary government's primary role was to restore order. Bolívar argued that without law, order and stability, the ensuing chaos would destroy what the heroes of the revolution had been fighting to establish.

Bolívar managed to convince New Granada to help liberate Venezuela, as their causes were both the same. He said that if Venezuela was free it would secure the freedom for New Granada. His manifesto was a success and in 1813 Bolívar led an army back to Venezuela and managed to recapture Caracas. Bolívar set himself up as dictator, but this was a short-lived role as the nation was still divided in their loyalties.

A group of royalists known as *llaneros,* or plainsmen, led by a man named José Tomás Boves, defeated Bolívar in a series of battles, and once again he was forced to flee. This time Bolívar took refuge in Jamaica, and it was here that he wrote his famous *Jamaica Letter*. He arrived in Kingston in May 1815, where he was personally welcomed by the governor. His letter, dated September 6, 1815, analyzed the causes of the patriot movement's failure and also outlined his ideas for a republic government and unity for Latin America. The letter was actually a lengthy response to a letter received from a South American gentleman who lived on the island, in which he empathized with Bolívar's struggle for liberation.

While living in Jamaica, Bolívar survived an assassination attempt by his servant, Pio, who had been bribed by Spanish agents. He stabbed another man who at the time was lying in his master's hammock. Having survived the attack, Bolívar left Jamaica and travelled to Haiti in December 1815. Here, he gathered troops and supplies with the blessing of the Haitian president, Petion, who only made one request of Bolívar. The request was that he free all the slaves of the countries he intended to liberate.

Bolívar, having got what he wanted, returned to Venezuela in 1816 to finish what he had started. His first few battles were not successful, but little by little Bolívar gained more support and popularity. By 1816 he had retaken Venezuela, and he gradually started to unite the different factions and gained the support of the powerful *llaneros*. As promised to Petion, Bolívar started to free the slaves, although he received a lot of opposition from the slave-owners themselves and even some of his own military commanders.

Bolívar's greatest victory was the Battle of Boyaca, which took place on August 7, 1819. The battle itself took place near the city of Bogotá, and it was the major turning point in the fight for independence in Spanish South America.

Using the city of Angostura – which is now renamed Ciudad Bolívar – as the headquarters of his new national revolutionary government, Bolívar created the Congress of Angostura in 1819. Bolívar was made the president of Venezuela and on December 17, he declared the formation of the Republic of Gran Colombia, which was a federation of the present-day Venezuela, Colombia, Panama and Ecuador. During those years royalist opposition was eliminated, and following the defeat of the Spanish forces at the Battle of Pichincha on May 23, 1822, all of northern South America was liberated.

LIBERATING PERU

Flushed with success, Bolívar prepared to take his army across the Andes in an attempt to liberate Peru. Before attempting his next journey, Bolívar met with the great Argentine liberator, José de San Martín on July 26, 1822, to discuss their strategy. San Martín had already succeeded in liberating Argentina and Chile, and had fought several battles in Peru. The meeting was held in secret and there are no records of what was actually said between the two great revolutionaries, but the outcome was that San Martín pulled out of Peru, resigned his presidency of Argentina and basically left Peru for Bolívar to conquer.

Bolívar succeeded in taking Lima in September 1823, was appointed dictator and followed this with other victories. The battle that sealed his final victory in Peru was the Battle of Ayacucho on December 9,

1824, when Bolívar destroyed the last remnants of the Spanish army in South America. On August 6, 1825, Antonio José de Sucre called the Congress of Upper Peru, which created the Republic of Bolivia in honour of Bolívar.

FINAL EFFORTS

Following his success in Peru, Bolívar attempted to unite the Spanish nations of South America at the Congress of Panama in June 1826. The Congress was attended by four American states – Mexico, Central America, Colombia and Peru. They attempted to draw up a treaty that would bind all parties to mutual defence in an effort to settle future disputes in peaceful ways. However, there were too many differences between the countries to allow for any sort of agreement, and the treaty was only ratified by Colombia and consequently never became effective. Although Bolívar made several futile attempts to establish smaller federations, he was not so successful in the role of governor as he was in the role of leading revolutionary.

There were many uprisings until 1829, when both Venezuela and Ecuador both left the republic. Bolívar, whose health was already failing, resigned when Sucre, the man that he had been grooming to be his replacement, was assassinated.

Bolívar left in 1830 and planned to live the rest of his life in exile in Europe. However, before he was able to make the journey he suffered from a bout of tuberculosis and died on December 17, at the age of 47.

CAPTAIN SWING RIOTS

The Swing Riots that took place between 1830 and 1831 were the first large-scale demonstration of agricultural labourers, and they were a response to a long period of poverty and political change in rural southern England. The Napoleonic wars had caused a lot of instability, and the onset of an agricultural depression made an already appalling situation even worse. Cereals, especially wheat, and certain areas of livestock farming suffered from a sharp fall in market prices. Many farmers were left destitute, and matters took an even worse turn with the gradual introduction of machinery, particularly threshing machines. Workers soon realized that many of their jobs would quickly be replaced by this new technology, both on land and in the factories.

The worst areas hit by poverty were the so-called 'Swing Counties' of Sussex, Hampshire, Suffolk, Norfolk, Berkshire, Wiltshire, Oxfordshire, Buckinghamshire, Gloucestershire, Bedfordshire, Cambridgeshire and Kent. The situation deteriorated at the beginning of the 19th century and when the great radical William Cobbett started a tour of Britain on horseback in 1821, he was appalled at what he found and made his views known when he published a series of articles in the *Political Register*. Despite being warned about writing controversial material, Cobbett continued to write in the *Political Register,* and in July 1831 he was charged with seditious libel after writing an article in support of the Captain Swing Riots. Cobbett was so successful in conducting his own defence, the jury failed to find him guilty.

By 1830 the working man had had enough of poverty and hunger, appallingly low wages, bad conditions and incredibly long hours of work. The increase in population, which was proportionately high at this time, contributed further to the pressures of trying to make a living in agriculture. Added to this were the gangs of travelling Irish agricultural workers, who were resented by the local populations for taking away any work that was available to them.

Although the government was aware of the problems of poverty in the rural areas, the responsibility lay with the local parishes and consequently they took no action. By 1830 many of the rural areas were simply at breaking point, and this led to them taking direct action, starting in Kent, which quickly spread across the country.

THE SWING LETTERS

The Captain Swing riots got their name when a number of landowners received threatening letters from a mythical 'Captain Swing'. These letters were first made public when they appeared in *The Times* on October 21. Most of the letters threatened arson as a reprisal and were sent to landowners and farmers and were signed 'Swing' – the supposed, although probably fictitious, leader of the protests.

THE ONSET OF RIOTS

Although there had been isolated outbreaks of arson throughout 1830, the actual 'Swing Riots' began in June of that year with the firing of hayricks, barns and houses in the Kent area. The already tense situation was exacerbated by the news in July of revolutions that were taking place in France and Belgium. The first threshing machine to be destroyed was in Canterbury, which subsequently led to many farmers destroying their own machinery.

Following the death of George IV in June 1830, there was a parliamentary election that resulted in a new Tory government led by the Duke of Wellington, who promised reform. At first government did little to stop the riots, other than those taking place close to London. The Home Secretary, Sir Robert Peel, said he would prefer to leave the matter to local magistrates but, as the trouble spread rapidly, there was fear that Britain was following France and Belgium in a full-scale revolution.

The riots were gradually building in momentum as the harvest got under way and by November 18 the trouble had spread from West Sussex into Hampshire. From then on it spread at an alarming rate. It reached its peak on November 25 when there was fighting near

Tisbury and in the Wylye Valley between rioters and the yeomanry. During all the riots, this was the only occasion that anyone was killed, John Hardy of Tisbury was shot, and several others were wounded.

Now realizing that the situation was serious, the government started to take notice and chastised the magistrates for being too lenient towards the rioters. The government set up a special commission to deal with the worst affected counties – Hampshire, Berkshire, Buckinghamshire, Dorset and Wiltshire. They arrested as many troublemakers as they could and, as a result of the subsequent trials, at least nine men or boys were hanged, 450 were transported and another 400 were imprisoned. Further trials took place at the Assize and County Courts, which led to a further 19 being executed, 600 imprisoned and 500 transported to Australia for a term of seven or 14 years, and some even for life.

REPRISALS

The local Justices of Peace who had enforced the law and given such severe penalties still had to live in the communities after the trials, and even though some had divided loyalties, they were treated with disdain by the locals. The villagers quickly organized petitions to save the condemned men and their actions met with limited success. Although public sympathy was mainly on the side of the rioters, a motion put forward in parliament for a general pardon was heavily defeated by the House of Commons.

Due to public pressure in 1834, the British government was forced to reconsider the issue of pardons, and later that year a few were issued. In 1835, a further 264 were pardoned and by the mid-1840s the majority of the rioters were released, with the exception of those who had committed further crimes while they were exiled in Australia.

Although the riots played their part in changing attitudes and reforms, the political and social reforms of the 1830s offered little comfort to the poor rural workers. The population continued to rise, which led to many labourers leaving the countryside to search for work in the cities.

In 1833, Prime Minister Earl Grey set up a Poor Law Commission to examine the system in Britain for the working classes. Their report, published in 1834, made several recommendations to parliament, and as a result the Poor Law Amendment Act was passed. This act reduced the amount of benefit available to the unemployed, forcing those who claimed to go into the newly constructed workhouses. The act stated:

1. No able-bodied person was to receive money or other help from the Poor Law authorities except in a workhouse.

2. Conditions in workhouses were to be made harsh to discourage people from wanting to receive help.

3. Workhouses were to be built in every parish.

4. Ratepayers in each parish had to elect a Board of Guardians to supervise the workhouse, to collect the Poor Rate and to send reports to the Central Poor Law Commission.

5. The three-man Central Poor Law Commission would be appointed by the government and would be responsible for supervising the Amendment Act throughout the country.

These harsh, new amendments inspired a further series of riots and arson, but nothing was really done to improve the conditions of the impoverished living in the countryside for many many years to come. The only real victory to come out of the Captain Swing Riots was that steam threshing machines did not really come into use until the middle of the century.

The Swing Riots were caused by the failure of the ruling classes to recognize the basic needs of the working classes, who were subjected to an unacceptable life of misery, squalor and degradation and manipulated by the people who were in power. The rebellion itself illustrated how people can only take so much before they are forced to take action and fight for their legal rights. According to the author E. L. Woodward, who was famous for his *The Age of Reform, 1815–70*, said:

> . . . *were only asking for a living wage; there was no organized plot and no co-ordination between the various outbreaks.*

NAT TURNER AND THE BLACK SLAVE REVOLT

Nat Turner's slave rebellion was by far the bloodiest and most effective in the history of slavery in the USA. The vicious attack by black slaves led to more stringent slave laws in the South and put an end to the organized abolition movement there. Over the years, Nat Turner became a figure of controversy, seen by some as a vicious fanatic and by others as a hero and freedom fighter for black resistence.

THE VISIONS

Nat Turner was born on a plantation in Southampton County, Virginia, on October 2, 1800. Turner's mother and grandmother had been brought to North America from Africa and they both had a deep hatred of slavery and all its restrictions. From birth Turner was the property of Benjamin Turner, from whom he took his name. Although a strange child, Turner was intelligent and seemed to have a natural ability to read, assisted by his master's son. Even as a young boy Turner was committed to his Christian faith and was often seen to be praying or fasting. Turner believed he received messages from God through visions, which greatly influenced his adult life. When Turner was only three or four years old, his mother overheard him telling some other children about an experience that had happened before he was born. When she questioned him about the event, his answers confirmed that he did in fact know all the details of what had happened. As he grew older, and his visions increased, among the other slaves on the plantation he became known as 'The Prophet'. Encouraged by his parents, Turner eventually came to believe that he had been chosen by God to lead his people out of slavery.

In the New World (the Americas), slavery emerged as a system of forced labour, which was designed to encourage the production of staple crops, including sugar, tobacco, coffee and cotton, depending on the location. The vast majority of the slaves were of African origin while, in contrast, their masters were mainly Europeans and their descendants.

In 1821, Turner ran away from his master only to return 30 days later, following a vision in which the Spirit told him to 'return to the service of my earthly master'. The following year his master, Benjamin Turner, died and he was sold to Thomas Moore. Three years later he had his second vision, in which he saw bright lights in the sky. Unable to understand their significance, Turner prayed to God to give him an answer.

. . . while labouring in the field, I discovered drops of blood on the corn, as though it were dew from

*heaven, and I communicated it to many, both white
and black, in the neighbourhood; and then I found
on the leaves in the woods hieroglyphic characters
and numbers, with the forms of men in different
attitudes, portrayed in blood, and representing the
figures I have seen before in the heavens.*

Turner had this third vision on May 12, 1828, when
he said the Spirit had spoken directly to him and said
he should take on and fight against the 'Serpent'.

*. . . And by signs in the heavens that it would make
known to me when I should commence the great
work, and until the first sign appeared I should
conceal it from the knowledge of men; and on the
appearance of the sign . . . I should arise and prepare
myself and slay my enemies with their weapons.*

At the beginning of 1830, Turner moved once again
to another plantation to work for Joseph Travis, who
was the new husband of Thomas Moore's widow.
Turner liked his new master, who he considered to be
far more humane to his slaves than any other slave
owner in the country.

TIME TO TAKE ACTION

In February 1831, there was an eclipse of the sun, and
Turner took this to be the sign from God to take
action. He chose four slaves who he completely
trusted, Henry, Hark, Nelson and Sam, and confided in

them about what he planned to do. He told them that he wanted to fulfill his dream to liberate his people and they decided to delay the insurrection until July 4, giving them plenty of time to make proper arrangements. They had to further delay the revolt because Turner was taken ill, and it wasn't until August 13 that he received his final sign. The sun had taken on an eerie bluish-green tinge, and believing this to be another omen from the Spirit, Turner arranged to meet his colleagues on August 21, just one week later.

When Turner arrived in the woods on the appointed Sunday, he found two more men standing with his four colleagues. He asked his friends who these men were, and when they answered that they were two people whose liberty was dear to them, Turner relaxed. They spent 11 hours deliberating and planning their revenge on those people who had kept them in bondage for so long. They decided they would attack under the cover of night and that the massacre was to be swift to create terror among the other slave owners, hopefully eliminating the need for any further bloodshed. They returned home to gather weapons.

BLOOD IS SPILLED

During the next 24 hours Nat Turner and his gang of black slaves moved swiftly and stealthily from house to house with avowed resolution. Starting with the Travis household, they killed the entire family while they were asleep in their beds. Then they moved to the next house, killing all the white people they met, and so the massacre continued, sparing no one, man, woman or child. From each house they stole arms and ammunutions, and from every plantation they found new recruits willing to join their cause. Gradually their numbers increased first 15, then to 40 and eventually as many as 60 black slaves joined Turner's revolt, many riding on horses they had stolen from their masters.

Having killed all the white families in the immediate area, Turner decided to march towards Jerusalem, which was the closest town and the county seat. Aware that a few of the white slave owners had managed to escape, Turner realized that it wouldn't be long before word of their rebellion spread to Jerusalem, so time was at an essence. On the way several of his men wanted to stop at the plantation of a Mr Parker, just 5 km (3 miles) outside Jerusalem, to enlist a few more of their friends. Turner said the delay could prove to be dangerous, but he eventually relented. This proved to be a fatal move.

Turner waited at the gate with a few men, while about 40 others went up to the house about 800 m (2,640 ft) away. They seemed to be gone too long, and so Turner went to hurry them up, not realizing that a party of around 18 armed, white men had gone to disperse the slaves waiting at the gate. When the rest of the slaves came out of the house, they were confronted, for the first time, by armed men who started firing at them. The slaves scattered, leaving some of their colleagues lying wounded on the ground. Turner, Hark and about 20 other slaves managed to escape on horseback and fled to a nearby plantation owned by Major Ridley. They spent the night in the slave cabins and by morning they were joined by further slaves, increasing their numbers once more.

Still determined to reach Jerusalem, Turner set off with his band of rebels, attacking one more house on the way. By the time, however, the news had spread fast and they were met by state and federal troops in one final skirmish. One slave was killed and the remainder scattered, including Turner. At the end of the rebellion, the slave rebels had slaughtered at least 55 white people in their fight for liberty.

NAT TURNER'S CONFESSION

Nat Turner hid for two days and two nights, waiting and praying that his men would join him. Soon he realized that no one was going to come and that the insurrection had hopelessly failed. Making himself a hideout in the woods, Turner eluded capture for a further six weeks, however he was eventually discovered and captured on October 30. He was taken to the county jail, which is where he dictated his famous *Confession* to Thomas R. Gray.

Turner was tried at Southampton County Court and sentenced to execution. On November 11, he was hanged and skinned. The state executed a total of 55 slaves, banished many more and a few were acquitted who could prove they took no part in the revolt. The white slave owners were reimbursed by the state for the loss of their slaves.

The rebellion actually did more harm than good for

the liberty of the black slaves. There was a considerable amount of tension after the court case, and fearing further retribution, as many as 200 black people were murdered by white lynch mobs. Added to this, Virginia, which had been considering abolishing slavery, voted to retain it by a close vote, affected by the recent uprising. An official repressive policy was drawn up that supported a curtailment of black people, both slave and free.

Mr Gray published Nat Turner's *Confession*, and it is thought that as many as 50,000 copies were printed. *The Confessions of Nat Turner* (1967), a novel by William Styron, won a Pulitzer Prize for fiction in 1968.

Nat Turner is still considered a hero by many African Americans worldwide, and there is no doubt that no other single person had such an effect on the community of slave owners.

WILLIAM WILBERFORCE

William Wilberforce is perhaps one of the best-known British campaigners against both the slave trade and slavery. He was a philanthropist and a founding member of the RSPCA (Royal Society for the Prevention of Cruelty to Animals). He once wrote about himself,

> *God Almighty has set before me two great objects, the suppression of the Slave Trade and the Reformation of Manners.*

Unhappy with the way that slaves were treated, not just on their horrific sea journeys to Britain, but also once they were bought by their masters, Wilberforce fought selflessly for their freedom and rights.

Wilberforce was born in Hull on August 24, 1759, and was the only son of a prosperous merchant, Robert Wilberforce. He was a sickly child and showed little promise at school except for his skill in elocution. His father died when Wilberforce was only nine years old and his mother, who was unable to take care of him, placed him under the care of a paternal uncle who lived in Wimbledon. His aunt and uncle took him regularly to their evangelical Anglican parish church, and the stories and sermons, especially those of Rev. John Newton, affected him deeply. It turned out that Newton had once been the captain of a slave ship, and his influence on the young Wilberforce was incalculable. He told him stories of the terrible conditions in which the slaves were transported from West Africa. They were restrained by chains with no sanitation facilities, and by the time they reached their destination they were ravaged by poor nutrition and seasickness. Once on shore they were fattened up, oiled to make their skin shine and then paraded naked in front of potential buyers. Britain was the world leader in the trade of slaves, and supplied as many as three million to the New World in a relatively short period of time.

One story Newton told the young boy was about a British slave trader who literally threw 132 slaves overboard during a violent storm in an effort to lighten his vessel. When he arrived in England he had the gall to submit an insurance claim for loss of cargo. Although people were outraged with his behaviour, the man received no punishment. This embedded deep in Wilberforce's heart the feeling that nothing would be done unless a leading figure from parliament made a stand for abolition.

In October 1766, Wilberforce entered St John's College at Cambridge University, where he largely wasted his time, possibly due to the large inheritance he had been left by the death of his grandfather. However, he managed to achieve his required qualifications and also got noticed for his eloquent skills in public speaking. He was given a prominent seat in parliament at the earliest age possible, 21, and, although at first he did not involve himself with any particular cause, his conversion to evangelical Christianity in 1785 changed his approach to the morals of politics. In 1786, he attempted to put through the House of Commons a bill to amend the criminal law. But the Lords were not prepared to accept the bill and this was something that was constantly repeated throughout his fight for abolition.

Wilberforce forged a close friendship with the prime minister, William Pitt the Younger, and proved to be of great assistance to him in his struggle against the majority of the House of Commons. In 1787, Wilberforce founded the Proclamation Society, which aimed at reforming public manners and also the suppression of vice.

Later that year, and at the suggestion of the prime minister, Wiberforce became the parliamentary representative of the abolition movement, due partly to his association with Thomas Clarkson, a British campaigner who had written many essays on abolition. Clarkson took on the role of fact finder and rode around the country gathering evidence against the trading of slaves. On his periodic returns to London, Clarkson passed on his information to the Abolition Committee, who in turn passed it on to William Wilberforce. Wilberforce and Clarkson were now seen as the leaders of the antislave trade movement. While Clarkson travelled to get his evidence, Wilberforce took every opportunity to expose the evils and horrors of human trading to members of the House of Commons. The majority of Wilberforce's Tory colleagues in the House of Commons opposed any changes to the slave trade, and he had to rely on the support of Whigs such as Charles Fox and William Grenville. Wilberforce persisted in his fight and even when his first bill, in 1791, was defeated by a majority vote of 163 to 88 votes, he was not dispirited.

In 1805, the House of Commons finally passed a bill that made it illegal for any British subject to transport slaves, but this bill was blocked by the House of Lords. However, Wilberforce had an ally in Lord Grenville and his foreign secretary, Charles Fox, who were both strong opponents of the slave trade. While Fox and Wilberforce led the campaign in the House of Commons, Grenville had the job of persuading the House of Lords. It wasn't until 1807, following a passionate speech by Lord Grenville, that the bill actually got passed. It was backed by a huge majority in the House of Commons and Grenville had won the hearts of the House of Lords.

The Abolition of the Slave Trade bill became law on March 25, 1807, after which time any British captains found to be breaking that law could be fined £100 for each slave on board. Like most illicit traders, however, they managed to find a loophole, and if any slave ships were in danger of being searched, the captains would simply throw the slaves overboard to avoid paying the fine. Many of Wilberforce's fellow campaigners felt the only way to stop the transportation of slaves completely was to make it totally illegal, but Wilberforce disagreed. He felt that if it was made illegal, both the slaves and their owners would suffer unless it was a gradual process. He made his view clear in a pamphlet that he wrote in 1807:

It would be wrong to emancipate (the slaves). To grant freedom to them immediately would be to insure not only their masters' ruin, but their own. They must first be trained and educated for freedom.

Thomas Fowell Buxton, who was one of the campaigners for making it illegal, formed the Society for the Mitigation and Gradual Abolition of Slavery in 1823. Both Clarkson and Wilberforce were vice presidents, although the majority of the work was carried out by younger members, such as Buxton.

Wilberforce retired from the House of Commons in 1825 and, due to failing health, settled away from public life in Highwood Hill, near Mill Hill, just outside the city of London. He died on July 29, 1833. Just one month later parliament passed the Slavery Abolition Act, which granted every slave in the British empire their freedom. It would be many more years before American slaves were granted the same freedom.

Thomas Clarkson retired to Ipswich, where he died on September 26, 1846. The resolve and courage of both Clarkson and Wilberforce never abated, and they fought for the emancipation of slaves right up to the end of their lives.

KARL MARX

Karl Marx is best remembered as a revolutionary communist whose inspirational works had a major influence on the modern world. Although he did not live to see his ideas actually take form, his writings did form the theoretical base for modern international communism. Marx's social, economic and political theories were taken up after his death, and until quite recently approximately half the world lived under his regimes. Although, technically he shouldn't be labelled as a freedom fighter, he has been included because our understanding of society has been so greatly enhanced because of his perseverence and struggle to achieve a better world.

AN INFLUENTIAL TIME

Karl Marx was born on May 5, 1818, and grew up in the city of Trier, in modern day Germany. He was the son of a successful Jewish lawyer, Hirschel Marx, who came from a long line of rabbis, but who also struggled with his own religion. To avoid anti-Semitism and so that he would not lose his job as a respected lawyer, Hirschel changed his name to Heinrich and joined the official denomination of the Prussian state, Lutheranism. This afforded him various advantages, despite being one of a small minority of Lutherans in a predominantly Catholic area.

When Karl Marx was 17, he enrolled in Bonn University to study law. Much to his father's disgust, the young Marx spent much of his time socializing and ran up huge debts. After finding out that his son was wounded in a duel over nonpayment of his debts, his father took the matter into his own hands, paid what his son owed, and moved him to Berlin University. While studying at Bonn, Marx became engaged to Jenny von Westphalen, who was the daughter of Baron von Westphalen, a prominent member of Trier society. The baron was to be a considerable influence on the young Marx, giving him an insight into Romantic literature and politics.

The move to Berlin appeared to be a wise choice, as Marx buckled down to his studies. One of Marx's lecturers, Bruno Bauer, had a great influence over the young man with his views on atheism and radical political opinions, which had frequently got him into trouble with the authorities. Bauer introduced Marx to the works of Wilhelm Friedrich Hegel, who had been a professor of philosophy at Berlin until his death in 1831. Marx was impressed with Hegel's theories, especially his view that 'a thing or thought could not be separated from its opposite'. That is to say, for example, that a slave could not exist without its master, and vice versa. Marx became a member of the Young Hegelian movement, a group that included Bruno

Bauer and David Friedrich Strauss and which was prominent in Berlin at the time.

Heinrich Marx died in 1838. Without his support Karl Marx had to make his own way in the world and decided to become a university lecturer. He obtained a Ph.D in philosophy from the University of Jena in 1841, and he approached his mentor Bruno Bauer to see if he could have any influence in finding him a teaching position. Unfortunately, Bauer had been dismissed from Berlin University as a result of his outspoken atheism and so was unable to help his ex-student.

MARX BECOMES A JOURNALIST

Marx decided to try his hand at journalism, but his radical views meant that most editors were unwilling to publish his work. Marx moved to Cologne in 1842 and managed to obtain an editorial position with the radical newspaper *The Rhenish Gazette*. This was a publication associated with the Cologne Circle, and after an article by Marx where he defended the freedom of the press, the group were so impressed that, in October of that year, they appointed him as editor of the newspaper.

During his time in Colone, Marx met the radical Moses Hess, who considered himself a socialist. Marx began attending socialist meetings that were organized by Hess, and it was here that he learned of the injustices suffered by the working classes in Germany. Because of what he heard in these meetings, Marx decided to write an article on the poverty of Mosel wine farmers, which also was quite scathing about the government. It was published in *The Rhenish Gazette* in January 1843 and, because of this, the newspaper was closed down by the Prussian authorities. Marx continued writing as a freelance journalist, but because of his radical and outspoken articles, and his fear of being arrested, he decided to leave Germany.

Before moving to France, Marx married his long-term girlfriend, Jenny von Westphalen. The couple settled in Paris, where Marx was reunited with his old tutor, Bruno Bauer and the Young Hegelians. He wrote a fundamental piece entitled *On The Jewish Question*, which was a highly critical piece regarding civil rights and political freedom. It was written from an atheist standpoint and contained several criticisms regarding the Jewish and Christian faiths. Marx was offered a job as editor of a new political journal called *Franco-German Annals,* and through this post he became acquainted with the Russian anarchist Michael Bakunin, and the radical son of a wealthy German industrialist, Friedrich Engels. Fate brought Marx and Engels together, and the two friends devoted their life's work to the common cause. These two men were the first to show that the working class and its demands are a necessary outcome of the present economic situation.

It was during his time in Paris that Marx mixed with people of the working class for the first time. He was shocked by their poverty and the conditions under which they lived, but he was impressed by their camaraderie and their support of one another. After a few months Marx became a communist and put his feelings down on paper in an article written for the *Franco-German Annals*. Applying some of Hegel's theories, Marx wrote about what he had experienced in Paris and argued that the working class would eventually be the emancipators of society. When the journal was published in February 1844, not only was it immediately banned in Germany, but it also upset the journal's owner, Arnold Ruge, who objected to Marx's attack on capitalism.

In the same year Marx wrote the *Economic and Philosophical Manuscripts*, which were not published until after his death. These manuscripts covered a wide range of topics including material on private property and communism, but they are noted most for his opinions on 'alienated labour'. First, that the worker is alienated from what he produces. Second, the worker is alienated from himself, and it is only when he is not working that he can feel truly himself. Finally, Marx believed that in a capitalist society people are alienated from each other, believing that society is too competitive and that people are actually competing against each other. He believed that communism was the solution to this problem as this would enable the 'fulfilment of his potentialities as a human'.

MARX AND ENGELS

During their time in Paris, Marx and Engels had become close friends, sharing many of the same views. Engels, who had just completed a book on the lives of industrial workers in Britain, said of their friendship, that they were on complete agreement in all theoretical fields. They decided to work together and this proved to be a beneficial partnership. While Marx was at his best when working on troublesome abstract ideas, Engels excelled at writing for a mass audience.

While the two men were working on an article together, *The Holy Family,* Marx heard that the Prussian authorities were putting pressure on the French government to expel him from the country. Marx received an order deporting him from France on January 25, 1845, but wishing to continue their work together, Engels and Marx decided to move to Belgium. This country would offer them more freedom of speech than any other European country, and there was already a large community of political exiles, including Marx's old associate Moses Hess.

Marx had no career as such and Engels supported him and his family using the royalties from a recently published book entitled the *Condition of the Working Class in England.* With this money, and the help of sympathetic donations, Marx was able to devote himself to an intensive study of history, economics and political theories. He wanted to understand how a capitalist society worked and how the working class people could bring about a socialist revolution. Unlike other philosophers, Marx was not just interested in discovering the truth. He wanted to know how he could go about changing the way we live in our world.

In July 1845, Marx and Engels made a brief visit to Britain, where they spent the majority of their time in libraries consulting literary works. Marx visited London, where he met many political exiles from Europe, including the Chartist leader, George Julian Harney.

On their return to Belgium, Marx concentrated on finishing his book *The German Ideology*. This was basically a historical work on a theory that it is human activity, rather than thought, that plays a crucial role in the way we live. Marx was unable to find a publisher to produce his new book, and like most of his work, it was not printed until after his death.

THE COMMUNIST MANIFESTO

In January 1846, Marx set up a Communist Correspondence Committee, with the idea of linking socialist leaders together from different parts of Europe. Encouraged by Marx's ideas, socialists in Britain set up the Communist League, which was an organization of German immigrant workers who set up their headquarters in London. Marx and Engels were the major theoreticians, and Marx formed his own branch in Brussels in December 1847. The main aim of the league was to see the overthrow of the old bourgeois society based on social antogonisms, and replace it with a new society without classes and the ownership of private property.

Following a meeting at the London branch, Marx and Engels were commissioned to write a pamphlet outlining their views. *The Communist Manifesto*, which was based on a first draft produced by Engels called the *Principles of Communism*. The pamphlet, which consisted of around 12,000 words, was completed by Marx in a period of six weeks. It was written for a mass audience, and as soon as it was published in 1848, a wave of revolutions broke out all over Europe. Briefly, the manifesto outlined the struggle between the two different social classes: the bourgeousie and the proletariat.

As soon as *The Communist Manifesto* was published, the government expelled Marx from Belgium. After first visiting Paris, Marx and Engels returned to Cologne, where they set up a newspaper called the *New Rhenish Gazette*. Not deterred by past opposition, the two men used the newspaper to encourage the revolutionary fervour they had already witnessed in Paris. Having witnessed police brutality first hand in Colone, Marx set up a Committee of Public Safety in an effort to protect the public from the power of the authorities. Their newspaper continued to publish radical articles on revolutionary activities that were taking place in various parts of Europe. This included a story on the seizure of power in Austria by the Democrats, which resulted in the emperor fleeing his country.

Thoughts of a worldwide revolution soon subsided after the army managed to help the Austrian emperor return to power, and any attempts at revolt in Dresden, Baden and Rhur were quickly suppressed by the authorities. Marx and Engel's newspaper was suppressed and Marx learned that he was again to be expelled from the country in which he lived.

Marx fled to France, which he believed was on the brink of a socialist revolution. However, within one month of his arrival the French police drove him out of Paris and he sailed for the only country willing to accept him, Britain. His family settled in London, and a few weeks later Marx's wife gave birth to their fourth child. Although the Prussian authorities urged Britain to expel the revolutionary, Prime Minister John Russell, who believed in freedom of speech, refused to comply to their demands.

LIFE IN LONDON

During the first half of the 1850s, the Marx family lived in virtual poverty in a small flat in the Soho area of London. Marx and Jenny already had four children and in the next few years they had two more. Of these only three survived. Engels was still helping the Marx family financially with an income from his family business in Germany, and although the two men were now apart, they kept in constant touch throughout the next 20 years.

In 1852, Marx was given the opportunity to write for the *New York Daily Tribune* by Charles Dana, the socialist editor. He was also commissioned by another US radical, George Ripley, to write for the *New American Cyclopaedia*. The money from his articles and a small inheritance from his mother-in-law, enabled the Marx family to move to less squalid conditions to Kentish Town.

In 1856, Jenny's health started to deteriorate after contracting smallpox and giving birth to a stillborn child. Although she survived, Jenny was left deaf and badly scarred. During the last decade of his life, Marx also suffered from declining health and was incapable of sustaining the powerful writings of his earlier years. Despite all his problems, Marx continued to write and in 1867, the first volume of *Das Kapital* was published. This was a detailed analysis of capitalism and dealt with the issue of revolution.

In 1871, aided by his eldest daughter, Eleanor, Marx began work on the second volume of *Das Kapital*. Taking guidance from her father, Eleanor already had a complete understanding of the capitalist system and went on to play a major role in the future of the British labour movement.

THE DEATH OF MARX

Karl Marx died on March 14, 1883. At his graveside, his closest friend, Engels, paid tribute to a great man who had made ground-breaking achievements in his lifetime. The works of both Marx and Engels cover a wide range of topics and give a complex analysis of history in terms of class structure within society.

Marx was indeed one of the greatest 'thinkers' of modern times and will always be remembered for defending the ideals of a free society with uncompromising passion for over 50 years. Both Marx and Engels were primarily concerned with freedom of mankind, reviving the ancient concept of communism, so that human beings could fulfill their cooperative roles within society without the fear of being exploited.

THE PARIS COMMUNE

The story of the Paris Commune of 1871 is an important one because it was the first revolution where the working class played a pivotal role in their effort to improve society. The Commune itself was a result of an uprising in Paris following the Franco-Prussian war. The war, which was started by Napoleon III in July 1870, was disastrous for the French and ended with Paris coming under siege. In September over 80,000 untrained and ill-equipped men were pitted against the overpowering Prussian army. The French were quickly surrounded and defeated. Napoleon and over half of his army, were captured, along with the Paris defences, as the Prussians swept the capital.

The attack on Paris left an already discontent public in a state of unrest, as the gap between the rich and poor widened. The Parisians were not prepared to accept the Prussian victory, and there was considerable resentment of the new government at Versailles. The people of Paris felt they should be self-governing, with its own elected council, something which was already in operation in the smaller French towns. Already feeling the effects of food shortages, the citizens of Paris procured a number of cannons to defend themselves and placed them on the Paris ramparts. The wealthy inhabitants of Paris saw this as a major threat, and feared that this would lead to a revolution.

Adolphe Thiers, head of the national government, had managed to negotiate peace terms with the Prussians, but still had the problem of regaining control of Paris. He needed to convince the citizens that the war was over and, more importantly, Thiers needed to disarm the National Guards. This was not an easy task as Thiers only had about 12,000 troops left after the siege, against several hundred thousand National Guard.

THE REVOLUTION IS IGNITED

It was the government's attempt to capture the guns of the National Guard that sparked off the revolution. Thiers's plan was to occupy strategic positions in the capital, seize the guns, and arrest anyone known to be a revolutionary. Thiers, along with some of his ministers, went to Paris to supervise the operation. Everything went to plan at first, until the city started to wake in the early hours of the morning.

It was all too much for the citizens of Paris after all the hardship they had already suffered. The alarm was given and the whole city of workers, both men and women, turned out to defend the city, jeering at the soldiers. The National Guard didn't really know what action to take, and Thiers's troops, who were waiting for transport to remove the cannons, found themselves outnumbered. The situation became serious when the troops positioned at Montmartre, refused to open fire on the crowds and chose to arrest their own commander instead. The rebellion spread rapidly, and aware that he was unable to rely on the support of his own men, Thiers panicked and decided to abandon Paris. Before leaving he left an order that the entire army were to retreat to Versailles.

The retreat was chaotic, and as the troops tried to withdraw, several regiments were left behind in Paris. The government abandoned the capital, many of the officers who were left behind were arrested, while others without anyone in command, just sat out the period of the Commune.

NATIONAL GUARD TAKES CONTROL

By 11.00 p.m. on March 18, 1871, the National Guard had rallied their men together and managed to take control of the town hall at the Hôtel de Ville. The central committee of the National Guard was now, in effect, the only form of effective government in Paris. The central committee entered into negotiations with the mayors and arranged for elections for a Commune which were to be held on March 26.

Eight days later the citizens of Paris cast their votes, totalling 227,000 voters, representing a proportionately high number of the densely-populated working class community. The Commune was officially installed into the Hôtel de Ville just two days later on Tuesday, March 28. It had 92 members, including a high proportion of skilled workers and professional people.

Many of the members were political activists and the elected president of the council, was a revolutionary socialist by the name of Louis Auguste Blanqui. Although Blanqui was elected a member of the insurgent government, his detention in prison prevented him from taking an active part. The majority of the members of the Commune lacked any political experience and without veteran revolutionist Blanqui, who could have given them his guidance, the whole party lacked any political direction. This was a major problem but, despite internal differences, the Commune did manage to get off to a good start. Within the Commune, all elected council members were paid an average wage and had equal status to other Commune members.

The formation of the Commune excited contemprary anarchists, believing that if Paris could manage to organize itself without the help of the state, this could be applied to the rest of the world. The Paris Commune led by example, in creating a new type of state – the 'Worker's State'. The proclamations were pinned up for everyone to read:

- separation of the church
- no more night work in the bakeries
- no payment of back rents for the poor
- priests were to be arrested
- abandoned factories were to be reopened
- fines against workers were to be abolished

Meanwhile, back in Versailles, Thiers and his reactionary government, with the help of some Prussian officers, were already planning their attack on the Paris Commune. Thousands of captured French soldiers were to be released and prepared for armed combat.

READY FOR COMBAT

The Communards, who knew that an attack was imminent, made preparations. Both men and women laboured hard to erect barricades in the streets, to protect themselves from invasion. On May 21, the government troops poured into the city and were met with seven solid days of street fighting. The Communards fought valiantly, but eventually were driven into one small section of Paris. Every house became a fortress and every street a battlefield.

The last stand against the government's army took place at Pere-Lachise cemetery in Montmartre, where there was no proper defence. The army blew open the gate and amidst heavy rain there was hand-to-hand fighting among the tombs. Those Communards not killed in the fighting were lined up against a wall in the eastern corner of the cemetery and shot. The massacre continued for several days and by Sunday, May 28, the Paris Commune had completely collapsed, literally drowned in its own blood. At the end of the fighting as many as 40,000 people – men, women, children, old and sick – had been killed. Bodies were unceremoniously dumped in mass graves, while the victorious bourgeoisie simply looked on.

Those Communards who had managed to escape

death were later tracked down and given mock trials. One by one the Communards were found guilty and were either executed or sent to work as slaves in the colonies. Many died of fever and overwork, all as a result of the revenge of the victorious bourgeoisie, who wanted to punish the Parisians for their part in helping to form the first government of workers.

Even though the battle was over, the repercussions continued, as anyone who was connected to the Commune, or who was simply in the wrong place at the wrong time, was shot. Far more people died during that last week in May, than in any of the battles of the Franco-Prussian war, or indeed any previous massacres in the history of France.

Karl Marx had followed the events surrounding the Paris Commune closely and, immediately after its fall, he spoke to workers throughout the world urging them to learn from what had happened. He said:

> *Working men's Paris, with its Commune, will forever be celebrated as the glorious harbinger of a new society.*

WHAT THE COMMUNE SYMBOLIZED

The Paris Commune only lasted for a period of 71 days and was brought down by a combination of its own weakness and lack of decision and the treachery of the bourgeoisie in an uncontrite alliance with the Prussian army. There are many lessons to be learnt from the history of the Commune, not in the least, the murderous brutality with which the fighters of the Commune were shot, tortured and deported. For Marx the symbol of the Commune itself was of inestimable value. It proved to the world that not only were the working class people of Paris heroic, noble and devoted to their cause, but they were also the forerunner of a 'new society'. Even though France had not signed a peace treaty with the Prussians, the Commune was prepared to appoint a German working man as their Minister of Labour. Marx saw in their actions the innovative responses of the revolutionary proletariat to the corrupt practises and ideology of the bougeois society.

The anniversary of the Paris Commune on March 18, is one of the milestones of the advancing working class. Since 1871, it has been a day of celebration of the working class in every single country.

Because of Marx's studies, Lenin was later able to recognize the significance of the Soviets and to establish them as the basis of the new workers' state. So, in October 1917, 46 years after the Paris Commune, the workers of Russia, under the leadership of the Bolshevik Party, are helping it come alive again. In fact, the Paris Commune has been the subject of reverence for many communist leaders, including Chairman Mao, who would often refer to it in his speeches to his people.

The revolution of 1871 will always remain a popular event in the history of the working man because it was made by the people themselves. Out of the great masses of people who lived in Paris at that time, arose

many defenders, heroes, martyrs, but most importantly, many heroic freedom fighters. It was a revolution of
the lowest classes who marched forward with a positive spirit to conquer their rights.

CHARLES BRADLAUGH

Charles Bradlaugh was a political activist, an atheist, and possibly one of the most famous controversial public figures of the 19th century. He spoke out on many unpopular topics of the time such as birth control, Republicanism, atheism, reform, peace and anti-imperialism – views which placed him in conflict with many powerful people and institutions. Bradlaugh was not frightened to fight for what he believed to be the rights of the common man. He will be best remembered, however, for having founded the National Secular Society in 1866 and for his pioneering work to make contraception widely available to women of all classes.

EARLY LIFE

Charles Bradlaugh was born on September 26, 1833, in a working-class area of London, Hoxton, the son of a poor legal clerk. His education was rudimentary and he only stayed at school until he was 11, leaving to work as an office errand-boy and later as a clerk to a coal merchant in an effort to contribute to his family's meagre income. In his youth, Bradlaugh saw enough of the worst side of Victorian urban squalor to make him want to fight for better conditions.

For a short while he was a Sunday school teacher, but was suspended when he expressed his concerns regarding discrepancies between the *39 Articles of the Anglican Church* and the Bible, to the local vicar. Not only was he accused of atheism, but he was also thrown out of his family home. He went to live with Elizabeth Carlile, the widow of Richard Carlile, who had been put in prison for printing Thomas Paine's *Age of Reason*. Through Elizabeth he was introduced to George Holyoake, who encouraged Bradlaugh to speak publicly about his atheism. By the age of 17 he had published his first pamphlet entitled, *A Few Words on the Christian Creed*.

An early attempt to start his own coal business failed, due to the lack of funds and, attracted by the idea of foreign travel, Bradlaugh enlisted as a soldier with the Seventh Dragoon Guards. His dreams of adventures overseas were dashed when he was stationed in Dublin, and it was here that he made a vow to fight for Irish freedom. He was allowed leave to visit his dying father, and managed to buy himself out of the army in 1853.

Bradlaugh returned to London and found a job working in a law office. He was now a committed free-thinker and republican and was starting to gain prominence in a number of liberal and political groups. He rapidly gained recognition as a speaker and in 1855 led a group of demonstrators to Hyde Park to oppose a restrictive Sunday Trading Bill.

Bradlaugh was no stranger to opposition, and his

skill at using the legal system to his own advantage, proved to be one of his greatest strengths.

Bradlaugh joined Joseph Barker, a Sheffield Chartist, to form a secularist newspaper, *The National Reformer*, in 1860. However, the two men disagreed over the introduction of material relating to contraception, and Bradlaugh became sole editor.

Bradlaugh proved to be a natural leader and, when the National Secular Society was founded in 1866, he became its first president and remained in that position for the next 20 years.

BRADLAUGH MEETS ANNIE BESANT

Annie Besant was a woman whose unorthodox religious views included first atheism and freethought and later theosophy. After leaving her husband, Annie Besant completely rejected Christianity and became a member of the Secular Society. Bradlaugh, who was the leader of the Secular Society at that time, formed a close relationship with Besant, and gave her a job working for the *National Reformer*. During the next few years, Besant wrote many articles on issues such as women's rights and marriage.

In 1877 Besant and Bradlaugh published *The Fruits of Philosophy*, which was a book by Charles Knowlton advocating birth control. They were both charged with publishing material that was 'likely to deprave or corrupt those whose minds are open to immoral influences'. Although they argued with the court that it was kinder to prevent the conception of children than to mistreat them after they were born, they were both found guilty and sentenced to six months in prison. However, their sentence was overturned by a Court of Appeal due to a legal technicality.

Annie Besant continued her activism throughout the 1880s and often wrote and spoke against unhealthy industrial conditions and low wages for young women working in factories. In 1887 she wrote a pamphlet in 1887 with Charles Bradlaugh entitled, *Why I Do Not Believe in God*, which was widely distributed by the secularists and is still considered one of the best summaries of arguments defending atheism. In 1888 she led the Match Girls' Strike, due to the horrific pay and conditions of the women working at the Bryant & May match factory. Bryant & May reacted by trying to force their workers to sign a statement that they were happy with their working conditions. A group of women refused to sign the statement, and the company responded by sacking the organizers of the militant group. The workers' reaction was immediate – 1,400 of the women at Bryant & May went on strike.

BRADLAUGH AND POLITICS

Bradlaugh was appointed Member of Parliament for Northampton in 1880, but became involved in a controversy when he requested that he be allowed to *affirm* as opposed to taking the religious Oath of Allegiance. His request was turned down and, because a member had to take the oath before being allowed to take their seat, Bradlaugh effectively forfeited his place in

Parliament. Angry at not getting his own way, Bradlaugh attempted to take his seat regardless and was arrested and briefly imprisoned in the Clock Tower of the Houses of Parliament, where for centuries the monarchy had imprisoned challengers.

The Conservative leader, Benjamin Disraeli, who was by no means a friend of Bradlaugh's, successfully argued for his release, realizing that such medieval treatment could possibly make the man into a martyr.

With his seat now vacant, a by-election was called and once again he was re-elected as the member for Northampton. This farcical process was to continue for a further six years. Bradlaugh would enter the chamber and try to take his seat, being greeted with abuse and catcalls from his fellow MPs. The situation was totally ridiculous. Bradlaugh offered to affirm rather than swear the oath, a view which was supported by the prime minister, William Gladstone.

However, Bradlaugh had made many enemies with his views on women, the monarchy, reforms and God. Whenever it came to the vote the MPs always upheld the speaker's decision and the Archbishops of Canterbury and Westminster and leading figures from the Church of England and the Roman Catholic Church argued strongly against the very idea of an atheist actually serving as an MP.

Bradlaugh received support from William Gladstone, George Bernard Shaw, John Stuart Mills, along with thousands of people who signed a public petition. On February 7, 1882, Bradlaugh presented Parliament with a petition of 241,970 signatures, which demanded that he be allowed to take his seat. Once again he was refused access, which was a remarkable denial of democracy.

Eventually, in 1886, a new speaker was appointed to the House of Commons, Sir Arthur Wellesley Peel. He conceded that Bradlaugh should be allowed to take his seat in Parliament after making a non-religious affirmation, as it was his own business as to how he affirmed his allegiance to the House.

In 1886, Bradlaugh was finally permitted to take the oath and took his seat. He became an active member of parliament, enthusiastically supporting causes which he knew would not only lose him votes but would also make him even more unpopular with his fellow MPs. Despite this he managed to hold his seat while fighting for Home Rule in Ireland, Republicanism and his criticism of the royal family and Britain's foreign policies.

Bradlaugh had been prematurely aged by his fight to gain a seat in Parliament and, ironically, he did not live long enough to benefit from his greatest parliamentary achievement. In 1888 Bradlaugh's Oaths Amendment Act enabled non-religious affirmations to be given as an alternative to the religious oath in every circumstance where one was required, for example in Parliament, in courts and on certain legal documents. It was a major step forward in establishing the freedom of conscience.

He took such an interest in Indian affairs, that Bradlaugh became known as 'the member for India'. In 1890, at the suggestion of his doctor to take a rest from politics, Bradlaugh sailed to India and was received in

Bombay with great acclamation. He received banners and scrolls for his research into the question of famine in Ganjam which, through his persistance for a proper investigation, had saved thousands of lives.

THE LOSS OF A GREAT ORATOR

Even in his last years Bradlaugh was not free from the litigation and conflicts that had sapped most of his strength. His relationship with Annie Besant had dwindled, as her allegiance swapped from socialism to theosophy. Bradlaugh's last pamphlet was entitled, *Humanity's Gain from Unbelief,* which was published in 1888. He wrote of a time when religion would eventually fade away, even though he knew it would be a gradual process:

No religion is suddenly rejected by any people; it is rather gradually outgrown. None sees a religion die; dead religions are like dead languages and obsolete customs: the decay is long and – like the glacier march – is perceptible only to the careful watcher by comparisons extending over long periods . . .

With his health failing rapidly, Bradlaugh resigned as president of the National Secular Society. In Janury 1891, the kidney disease from which he had suffered for many years, worsened and he died on January 30, 1891. There were so many people, from ordinary working men and women to MPs, that wanted to pay their last respects, that a special train had to be laid on from Waterloo to Brockwood (the place of his burial in a family plot). Among the mourners was a young Indian student by the name of Gandhi. A group of Nottingham secularists sent some flowers bearing the inscription:

Brave, honest, incorruptible, thorough

Years later, George Bernard Shaw said, of Bradlaugh's iconoclastic reputation:

Though Charles Bradlaugh preached the gospel of Rationalism, he acted throughout his life in the most irrational manner. Instead of choosing the line of least resistance . . . he chose the line of greatest resistance. When he met one of these idols, instead of taking off his hat and filling his pockets – which was the sensible, rationalistic thing to do – he hit the idol as hard as he could, and very often knocked it down.

Despite his radical views, Bradlaugh proved himself to be a great orator and eventually won a tremendous amount of support. It is fair to say that his free thinking and selfless outspokenness, paved the way for the democratic reforms of the 20th century.

GEORGI GAPON

Georgi Gapon was one of the leaders of the failed Russian Revolution of January 1905. Born in Russia in 1870, he followed his father into the Church to become a priest and began to work among the poor of St Petersberg. At this time, as Russia began the process of industrialization, the Russian peasantry were being herded into cities to work in factories where conditions were abysmal: typically, employees worked 11-hour days, operating dangerous machinery, often injuring or killing themselves. Appalled at the injustice of this situation, Gapon became a socialist and established a union to improve the lot of the factory employees: The Assembly of Russian Workers.

APPEAL FOR JUSTICE

By the turn of the century, the assembly had gained thousands of members. In 1904, four of its leaders were sacked from the Putilov Iron Works where they worked, and Gapon decided to bring his members out on strike. Over 100,000 factory workers in St Petersburg withdrew their labour, causing a furious reaction among the owners.

In the belief that Tsar Nicholas II was, at heart, concerned for the welfare of his people but perhaps ignorant of their true plight, Gapon drew up a petition to present to him at his palace. The petition called for an increase in workers' wages, which had declined in real value as the price of goods in Russia had gone up. It also called for an eight-hour day; the right for all workers to vote in elections; and the cessation of the unpopular Russo-Japanese War, which had involved the Russian peasantry and working classes in further misery, poverty and suffering.

Gapon, who drafted the petition along with other colleagues, wrote:

We workers, our children, our wives and our old, helpless parents have come, Lord, to seek truth and protection from you. We are impoverished and oppressed, unbearable work is imposed on us, we are despised and not recognized as human beings. We are treated as slaves, who must bear their fate and be silent. We have suffered terrible things, but we are pressed ever deeper into the abyss of poverty, ignorance and lack of rights.

Gapon hoped that the tsar, or 'little father' as he was affectionately known by the people, would take pity on the workers and grant them essential human rights when he realized how dreadful their conditions of labour had become.

HACKED TO DEATH

However, Gapon's faith in the tsar's essential benevolence proved to be misguided. When he marched to the palace with his petition, signed by over 150,000 people, the tsar's police and Cossack troops opened fire on the crowd. Over 100 workers were killed, and about 300 more were injured. The massacre became known as Bloody Sunday and went down in history as the moment when the seeds of the Russian Revolution were sown.

According to Gapon's description, as the small procession of workers moved along towards the Winter Palace, a group of Cossack soldiers on horseback suddenly appeared, galloping towards them with their swords unsheathed. As they bore down on the crowd, the Cossacks waved their swords in the air and brought them down, slicing through the bodies of men, women and children, who 'dropped to the earth like logs of wood'. Undeterred, the procession continued on, but the Cossacks then turned their horses around and attacked from the rear.

Next, a group of soldiers opened fire on the protesters, who were carrying images and icons of the tsar to show their loyalty. Onlookers were outraged that the authorities would fire on portraits of the tsar, but the shooting continued, until over 100 of the workers were dead.

TRUST BETRAYED

Prior to leading the march, Gapon had sent a letter to the tsar reassuring him that the workers came in peace.

'The people believe in thee,' he said. 'They have made up their minds to gather at the Winter Palace tomorrow at 2 p.m. to lay their needs before thee. Do not fear anything. Stand tomorrow before the party and accept our humblest petition. I, the representative of the workingmen, and my comrades, guarantee the inviolability of thy person.'

It seems that his letter was ignored; even though Gapon headed a peaceful procession, which included the wives and children of the workers, the Russian military and police met the protest with violence. Whether or not Tsar Nicholas himself ordered the troops to open fire or not remains debatable; entries in his diary suggest that he felt that the disturbance had to be quelled by force, although he was sad about the fatalities that occurred as a result. In retrospect, his action in allowing the troops to fire on the crowd was the biggest mistake he ever made, in that it opened the door to a revolution that eventually swept away the Romanov dynasty entirely and established a Soviet state in its place.

The writer Maxim Gorky offered Gapon refuge in his house directly after the massacre, and he later described how his guest that night told him that he had completely lost his faith, not only in the tsar, but in God and the established church altogether.

AFTERMATH

Realizing that there was no hope for justice for the Russian people while the tsar was still on the throne,

Gapon escaped to Geneva, Switzerland, where he abandoned his belief in progress through peaceful liberal reforms and joined the Socialist Revolutionary Party (SRP). Sadly, he was assassinated by members of the party on a visit to Finland in 1906. They believed him to be in the pay of the Russian authorities, spying on exiled Russian revolutionaries, but there is little evidence to show that this was the case.

After the Bloody Sunday Massacre, unrest continued not only within Russia, with general strikes in its industrial cities, but also in Poland, Finland and Georgia. There were general strikes in all the major cities of Russia, and a number of workers' councils, called *soviets*, set up revolutionary governments and assassinated thousands of officials. There was also a great deal of conflict between revolutionary and anti-revolutionary factions, leading to civil war.

Faced with this situation, the tsar was forced to issue his *October Manifesto*, which promised democratic elections in the future. However, these promises were not kept, and it became clear that the tsar had no real will to make any reforms: he was just doing his best to save his own skin as circumstances dictated. Even though a parliament or '*duma*' was introduced, it had few real powers and in essence Russia remained the same, with an extremely wealthy monarchy and nobility supported by a labouring mass of poverty-stricken factory workers and peasants.

A LESSON IN CIVIL WAR

As the Russian authorities struggled to recover from the failed revolution of 1905 and maintain order, a number of leading revolutionaries such as Leon Trotsky were arrested. Many radicals also escaped abroad, where they began to plot the overthrow of the monarchy in Russia. There were many different ideas about how to bring this about, and the various factions disagreed about what form the revolution should take; however, there was general agreement that a new regime had to come into being, and little sympathy left for the tsar. As Lenin wrote in an article on Bloody Sunday at the time:

The working class has received a momentous lesson in civil war; the revolutionary education of the proletariat made more progress in one day than it could have made in months and years of drab, humdrum, wretched existence.

His words proved prophetic: from the Bloody Sunday massacre of 1905 on, it became clear that the monarchy's days were numbered. Whether violent revolution could have been avoided in the long term had Tsar Nicholas II responded more intelligently and compassionately to Georgi Gapon's initiative is unclear: although Gapon believed, at least to begin with, that the interests of the monarchy and the working people could be reconciled, there were other radicals (such as Lenin) who argued that their interests were absolutely incompatible, and that the monarchy would have to be done away with if a reasonable, fair and just social order was to be established in Russia.

Whatever the truth of the matter, Gapon's name has gone down in history as a freedom fighter who believed that reform could be achieved peacefully, and that the monarchy could adopt the attitude of an affectionate 'little father' to his people. In the event, Gapon was proved wrong, and his action set in motion the Russian Revolution, which became one of the bloodiest revolutions of all time. However, Gapon's initial faith in peaceful protest as a way of improving and changing the working conditions of ordinary people to this day remains touching and inspiring. He was a brave, gentle man devoted to furthering the cause of justice for all, who was sadly betrayed not only by the tsar, whom he had respected, but by his revolutionary comrades, who turned on him and assassinated him a year after the events of Bloody Sunday.

THE SUFFRAGETTES

The Suffragettes, or suffragists as they were sometimes called in the USA, fought a long, hard battle at the turn of the 20th century to gain the right for women to vote. They argued that women in society had numerous responsibilities, from raising families to holding public posts. If women broke the law, they were punished just the same as men; and if they earned a living, they were taxed in exactly the same way as their male counterparts, while having no say in how their money was spent by the state. Moreover, many wealthy women ran great estates and employed male workers, who were allowed to vote, while they could not.

The suffragettes, who were mostly highly educated women from middle-class backgrounds, argued that this situation was intolerable, and that in any modern society that called itself democratic, women should have the vote. Their fight for recognition became one of the central elements of the feminist movement, making people aware that as adult human beings, women had the same intellectual and moral faculties as men, and therefore had the right to be treated equally to men in every way.

MILITANT ACTION

The suffragette movement began in the UK in 1897 when Millicent Fawcett, a follower of the political philosopher John Stuart Mill, founded the National Union of Women's Suffrage. Prior to this, she had worked for the London Suffrage Committee. Fawcett, who was married to a high-ranking minister in the British government, went on to conduct several important campaigns: for example, to outlaw the white slave trade and to improve conditions and wages for low-paid women workers. However, neither she nor her husband could persuade the prime minister of the day, Herbert Asquith, to legislate for votes for women. Asquith and his cabinet were convinced that women would be unable to understand the workings of parliament, and, like children, should be excluded from voting because of their mental incapacity. Fawcett, a highly intelligent, well-educated woman who had helped found Newnham College in Cambridge, and whose daughter was a talented mathematician, became increasingly frustrated by this, but she refused to respond to calls for militant action, believing that peaceful, constitutional reform was the only way forward.

The intransigence of the prime minister angered many women suffragists, who felt that since their arguments were being ignored by the politicians, the time had come to take direct action. In 1903, Emmeline Pankhurst and her two daughters, Sylvia and Christabel, founded a new, more militant organization, the Women's Social and Political Union, whose members later became known as the Suffragettes. The group's actions began fairly peacefully: typically, their members disrupted political meetings and when they were arrested, they refused to pay a fine and were sent to prison, attracting a great deal of publicity.

FIRE BOMBING CAMPAIGN

However, when no change came about as a result of these actions, the situation soon escalated into violence. The Suffragettes began to burn down churches, as a protest against the Church of England's support for their exclusion from the vote. They hired boats and loudhailers to sail up the Thames and shout abuse at politicians sitting in the Houses of Parliament; they chained themselves to the railings of Buckingham Palace; and they broke the windows of fashionable shops in Oxford Street. They also launched attacks on politicians and fire bombed their homes. When they were arrested for these crimes, they went on hunger strike, causing a problem for the prison officials and the government, who did not want to be blamed for the death of these women in their custody.

In order to deal with this problem, Asquith passed the Prisoners' Temporary Discharge for Health Act in 1913, which became known as the 'Cat and Mouse Act'. According to this legislation, instead of being force fed in jail, women prisoners on hunger strike could be released once they became weak. The thinking behind this was that, if they died once outside custody, the state could not be blamed. An added advantage for the government was that, in their weakened state, they would not be capable of any more activism. Moreover, if they recovered, the police could immediately re-arrest them on any small pretext so as to prevent them launching further attacks.

TRAMPLED TO DEATH

Not surprisingly, after this, the Suffragettes' actions became even more desperate. The situation reached a crisis point when, at a horse race in 1913, a suffragette named Emily Davison threw herself under the king's horse as it took part in the race. Davison was badly injured and died in hospital several days later. It was not clear whether Davison had meant to commit suicide, or whether she had just wanted to disrupt the race; and some believed that the horse could have stopped to avoid Davison, but instead that the rider galloped on towards her regardless, killing her on purpose. Whatever the truth of the matter, the Suffragettes now had a martyr, and the depth of their commitment had to be apparent to all. At the same time, there were criticisms that Davison's action showed the Suffragettes to be insane, and some felt that her death had done the campaign for women's rights more harm than good.

Whether the crisis of women's suffrage would have deepened after this event remains debatable, because the issue was suddenly overshadowed by a much bigger problem:World War I. In August 1914, during a long, hot summer, it was announced that Britain and Germany were at war.

THE WAR YEARS

In response, to show their patriotic support for Britain, Emmeline and Christabel Pankhurst decided to stop their campaign for the right to vote for the duration of the war. The more radical Sylvia, who had split with her mother and sister some time before over the issue of violence, in particular the fire bombing campaign, refused to support the war initiative, and announced her continuing commitment to pacifism.

At the end of the war, the Representation of the People Act of 1918 was passed by Parliament, granting limited voting rights to women. Only women over 30 who owned or occupied property over a certain value, or who were educated at university, were allowed to vote. Two years later, in 1920, similar rights were granted to women in the USA, under an amendment to the Constitution. Eventually, in 1928, British women were granted the same voting rights as men.

Many believe that it was the experience of war, rather than the activism of the Suffragettes, that finally helped secure the vote for women. During World War I, women showed that they were capable of all kinds of difficult and distressing work, such as nursing wounded soldiers on the battlefield and keeping communities going in times of extreme hardship. The notion of women as fragile creatures who could not cope mentally or physically without the support of men could no longer be sustained. Not only this, but tragically, so many young men had been killed during the war, that a new female workforce was needed to keep the economy running. Thus, in the end it was necessity, rather than moral argument, that finally gave women the vote in Britain.

FREEDOM AND EQUALITY

In the USA, the story was somewhat different, since the struggle for women's right to vote was won piecemeal, state by state, until in 1918, President Woodrow Wilson announced that women's suffrage was urgently needed as a 'war measure'. Prior to this, there had been great resistance to the idea, and it was only the deep commitment of campaigners such as Fanny Wright, Elizabeth Cady Staton and Susan B. Anthony that helped to keep the pressure on to secure women the vote in the USA.

From 1913 on, activists such as Alice Paul introduced militant methods such as the hunger strike to the USA, but in general constant political lobbying rather than direct violent action seemed to be effective, slow as it often was. After several failed attempts to introduce new legislation for women's right to vote into the Senate, the Nineteenth Amendment was certified by the Secretary of State on August 26, 1920. This was after the state of Tennessee had finally ratified the bill, becoming the final state in the union to do so.

Thus it was that, on both sides of the Atlantic, the battle for the rights of women to vote in elections was won: by a combination of direct action, political lobbying and steadfast commitment to the idea of equality. None of this could have been achieved without tireless campaigning of feminists around the world: whether thinkers, writers, journalists, organizers or activists. These women were determined to make their voices heard and take part in the running of their communities and countries, and despite the many obstacles in their path they refused to be intimidated. Some of them did not live to see the fruits of their labours; but their work ensured that future generations of women would be free to live as equals to men in a democratic society – a right that we now take for granted, both in Europe and the USA.

FAMOUS SUFFRAGETTES

<u>SUSAN B. ANTHONY</u>

Susan Brownell Anthony was one of the pioneers of the American movement for female suffrage. The daughter of a cotton manufacturer, she was born in Adams, Massachusetts in 1880. Her father Daniel, a Quaker, was a staunch campaigner against the slave trade and brought his children in a strict atmosphere. Susan was taken out of school when a teacher refused to educate her properly because she was a girl, and she went on to receive an excellent education at home. On leaving home, she became a teacher in a girl's academy and started to campaign for women's rights for suffrage and equal pay, as well as becoming a leading antislavery activist. She also believed in Prohibition and gave many speeches in support of it. In 1869, she formed the National Woman Suffrage Association with Elizabeth Cady Stanton and toured the USA, making speeches on women's right. She died on March 13, 1906, and is remembered as one of the great feminists of the 19th and early 20th century.

ELIZABETH CADY STANTON

Elizabeth Cady Stanton was one of the leading lights of the early feminist movement in the USA at the turn of the 20th century. Born in Johnstown, New York, in 1815, she was the daughter of a well-known attorney who later became a judge. As a young woman, she married political activist and journalist Henry Brewster Stanton, and with him campaigned for the abolition of slavery, known as the abolitionist movement. She was also active in the temperance movement, which called for a ban on alcohol. She argued that drunkenness was grounds for divorce, and attracted a great deal of controversy for her views, which included the belief that religion was an oppressive force in society and that abortion was a form of infanticide. In 1851 she met Susan B. Anthony and together the pair founded the National Woman's Suffrage Association. She was an early campaigner for racial equality as well as women's rights, and a critic of those who advocated the vote for black people but not for women. Stanton herself had six children, most of whom she cared for herself, and she continued to travel the world campaigning until her death in 1902.

LUCY BURNS

The American feminist Lucy Burns was a founder member, along with Alice Paul, of the National Woman's Party. Born in Brooklyn, New York, in 1879, to an Irish Catholic family, she excelled at academic work and studied at Vassar, Yale and Oxford. While a student in Britain, she became involved in feminist politics, joining the Women's Social and Political Union, and was sent to prison. On returning to the USA, she continued to fight for women's rights, adopting a more militant stand than most of her colleagues. Dissatisfied with other feminist lobbying organizations, she set up the National Women's Party, which favoured direct action such as picketing the White House. She conducted a public campaign of criticism against Woodrow Wilson, nicknaming him 'Kaiser Wilson' because of his refusal to give women the vote, which in her view made him as bad as the German ruler. She was also an outspoken critic of the war. In prison, she went on hunger strike and was thought to have been force fed and tortured while there. However, she fearlessly continued her political activism, and spent more time in jail as a result than any of her other colleagues. Despite the ups and downs of her life, she lived to a ripe old age and died in 1966.

CARRIE CHAPMAN CATT

Founder of the League of Women Voters, Carrie Chapman Catt was one of the leading members of the American women's rights movement. Born in 1859 in Wisconsin to a farming family, she then moved to Iowa. Although her father refused to spend money on educating her at college, she managed to pay her own way through teaching. She later became a school superintendent, one of the first women ever to do so in the USA. After marrying newspaperman Leo Chapman, she worked as an editor, and she became active in the Iowa Woman Suffrage Association. After the death of her first husband, she married George Catt, and continued her political activities, giving speeches and organizing rallies across the USA. She eventually took over from Susan B. Anthony as the leading light of the US movement for women's suffrage, and she became the first president of the International Woman Suffrage Alliance in 1904. She died in 1947, after a life spent furthering the cause of women's rights.

ALICE STOKES PAUL

A close friend of women's rights campaigner Lucy Burns, Alice Paul helped to lead the US campaign for women's rights. She was born in 1885 into a farming family of Quakers at Mount Laurel, New Jersey. She did well at school, and went on to study in New York before moving to Britain to continue her studies at the London School of Economics. While there, she met Lucy Burns, who was to become a lifelong friend, and together the pair joined the Women's Social and Political Union. As a result of her political activism, she was arrested and imprisoned several times. She took part in a hunger strike, undergoing the traumatic experience of being force fed. On returning to the USA, she continued to campaign for female suffrage, forming the National Women's party and trying to attract attention to the cause by direct actions such as demonstrations, picketing and hunger strikes. Her picketing of the White House, in which activists stood silently with banners demanding the vote for women, is thought to have been the first act of civil disobedience ever recorded in the USA. Paul was arrested and sent to jail, where she organized a hunger strike. In 1920, the campaign for women's suffrage at last achieved success, and women were granted the right to vote in federal elections. Alice Paul died in 1977, and has gone down in history as a champion of equal rights and civil liberties.

IDA B. WELLS

Ida B. Wells was a leading African-American civil rights campaigner, who not only fought for women's rights as a suffragist, but spoke out against all forms of racism, particularly the barbaric practise of lynching. Born to a slave family in Holly Springs, Mississipi, Wells' early life was one of great hardship. As a teenager, her parents and brother died of yellow fever, and Wells took over the job of caring for her other siblings, finding work as a teacher. Later, she moved to Memphis, where she became involved in politics, leading a campaign against segregation on public transport there. She then began to support the campaign for women's suffrage and wrote editorials against lynching in an antisegregationist newspaper. She married attorney Ferdinand Lee Barnett and went on to have four children, but returned to political life to help form the National Association for the Advancement of Colored People (NAACP). She died in 1931 and is remembered as one of the great pioneer activists of the civil rights and women's movement.

FANNY WRIGHT

Fanny Wright was an early radical, a Scotswoman who formed her own commune in the USA during the 18th century. She questioned some of the most fundamental concepts about the status and behaviour of women, and she attempted to create a community in which women were allowed freedoms in education, sexuality and even dress codes that were hitherto unheard of.

Wright was born in Dundee in 1795, the daughter of a linen manufacturer. Sadly, her mother died when she was young, and she was brought up in a succession of relatives' homes. One of these relatives was a well-known progressive philosopher, James Milne, who taught his young protégé to question basic assumptions about society. Milne's teaching made a lasting impression on Wright, who later became a political writer, publishing a book praising the egalitarian 'society and manners' of the USA in 1818 following a visit there.

Wright returned to the USA and went on to become involved with the socialist community of Robert Owen in Indiana. In 1892, she set up her own community, Nashoba, near Memphis, Tennessee, attracting outrage by buying slaves from local landowners and setting them free to farm their own land there. She also encouraged sexual freedom, believing that miscegenation was the key to solving the slavery issue in the

USA. Another of her radical ideas was to develop new dress codes for women: instead of tight bodices and stiff petticoats, she advocated loose tops, pantaloons and short dresses. (This style was later promoted by feminists such as Amelia Bloomer, who famously gave the pantaloons their modern name.)

Eventually, Wright's considerable personal fortune began to run out and she was forced to abandon the community. However, she continued to write on subjects such as the abolition of slavery, women's suffrage, birth control, racial equality and reform of the marriage laws. Her own marriage to French doctor Guillaume Darusmont ended in divorce when he tried to take control of her estate and the earnings from her writings. She eventually died in 1852 and was buried in Cincinatti. Her tombstone records:

I have wedded the cause of human improvement,
staked on it my fortune, my reputation and my life.

SUN YAT-SEN

Sun Yat-Sen is regarded as 'the Father of the Revolution' in modern-day China and Taiwan. He holds a unique place in Chinese history as a personal and political inspiration to all, including parties and individuals who are implacably opposed to each other. His own life was one of constant disappointment, hardship and exile from his homeland; as a result of his political activities, he spent a great deal of time abroad, and when he finally did achieve the establishment of a Chinese Republic in 1912, his position as president was immediately usurped. Moreover, by the time he died in 1924, China was in chaos, as warlords fought for control over the country.

However, Sun Yat-sen's 'three principles of the people' – nationalism, democracy and socialism – and his personal example of courage and commitment continued to live on after him. His political philosophy became, at least theoretically, the basis for the Nationalist government established by Chiang Kaishek in 1928, and many of his teachings were also adopted by the Chinese communist party. To this day, Sun Yat-sen is the one political figure to be revered both by the Chinese and the Taiwanese; for, as well as embodying the people's aspiration to unity, he stands as a testament to endurance in the face of failure.

EDUCATION OF A REVOLUTIONARY

Sun Yat-Sen was born on November 12 1866, to a peasant family in the small village of Cuiheng in the province of Guangdong, near Macau and Hong Kong. He attended school there, and then left to live with his prosperous older brother Sun Mei, in Honolulu, Hawaii. Sun Mei had emigrated to Hawaii as a labourer, and had since become a well-to-do merchant there. He financed the education of young Sun Yat-sen, who attended a Christian boarding school and proved to be an excellent scholar.

However, when Sun Yat-sen returned to China, he became extremely critical of what he saw as its backward culture, especially its traditional religion, and spoke out against the old-fashioned values of his homeland. Legend has it that, in frustration, he damaged a statue of one of the Chinese gods in his village, and became so unpopular there that he had to leave.

UNDERGROUND SOCIETY

As a young man, Sun Yat-sen went to Hong Kong, where he converted to Christianity and studied medicine. He began to practise medicine in Hong Kong, and he also entered into an arranged marriage with Lu Muzhen, a girl from his village back home. The couple had three children, including a son who later became an important official in the Nationalist party. During his stay in Hong Kong, Sun joined the notorious Triad organization, who later funded his revolutionary activities.

Instead of merely advancing his own career, as other westernized Chinese émigrés had done, Sun began to develop plans for advancing his country. He believed that China's immense natural resources could be harnessed to new technology to benefit the people, and he wrote to many government officials to explain his ideas. However, these officials were mostly drawn from members of the Chinese gentry, and they looked down on Sun because of his lowly origins and his lack of a classical education. He found that no one in power would listen to his ideas, so he began to form an underground group, the Revive China Society, to overthrow the government by force.

POLITICAL EXILE

In 1985, Sun attempted to mount a coup in Southeast China, but it failed. As a result, he was exiled not only from China, but from Hong Kong, which was ruled by the British at the time. For a while, he went to Japan, but the Japanese government also banned him. Thus, for over a decade, Sun was forced to live in the West, in the USA, Canada and Europe, where he spent his time fundraising for the revolution and for uprisings taking place in China.

By the turn of the century, Sun had developed a political philosophy, which he called the *Three*

Principles of the People: nationalism, democracy and socialism. He believed that the government of China should be in the hands of the Chinese, not a foreign imperial power; that China should be a republic, not a monarchy, with a government elected by the people; and that all land should be nationalized, to prevent landlords from gaining too much power. Under Sun's proposals, people would not be able to own their land, but would be allowed various rights over it, by permission of the state.

REVOLUTIONARY COUP

In 1905, Sun audaciously proclaimed his Three Principles, together with a plan for a period of 'political tutelage', in which the Chinese people would be educated to take part in democracy. In 1911, partly because of the pressure Sun continued to exert on Chinese political life, even from abroad, the notorious Manchu dynasty collapsed. Sun was made provisional president of the new Chinese Republic. He immediately transformed his revolutionary organization into a political party, the Kuomintang, or Nationalist Party. In China's first ever elections, held in 1913, the Kuomintang won a landslide victory.

However, there were powerful military and economic groups in China who were determined to keep Sun out of power, and shortly after his victory, he was forced into exile once again. The Kuomintang disbanded and its members were expelled from parliament. Undeterred, Sun continued to try to organize another coup from abroad, together with his new wife, Soong Ching-ling. Soong Ching-ling was a young woman who came from a wealthy Chinese family and had been educated in the USA. She was highly politicized and helped him to plan the coup. (Sun also remained married to his former wife, refusing to take Soong as a concubine, under the accepted rules of Chinese society.)

DEATH OF A HERO

In order to expand their military base, Sun and Soong made links with Soviet Communists, who provided a great deal of technical backup for their revolutionary political organization. He found some support in Northern China and set about expanding his base in southern China. In 1924, he travelled to meet military leaders in Beijing, but became ill there. He was found to have liver cancer, and a year later, he died.

Sun's body was preserved and kept in a temple in Beijing, where it was visited by many people, from high-ranking dignitaries to ordinary working folk. There were public memorial ceremonies, in which his image was broadcast on to large screens and his speeches were played on loudspeakers. He became a national hero overnight. Yet it was over three years before his successor, Chiang Kai-shek, managed to establish the rule of the Kuomintang, with the aim of creating a unified China. Under Chiang Kai-shek, renewed unrest broke out, as a result of Chiang's efforts to oust the communists from the party, once the new government was established.

LEGACY OF A FREEDOM FIGHTER

To some degree, the fact that Sun never actually held power for any length of time meant that his reputation remained unsullied by the realities of confrontation and compromise that any political leader experiences. He did not establish a regime long enough to make mistakes, and therefore, his enemies were few – especially after his death. As a result of this, his legacy became extremely important in China, and he was revered among all the different political factions in the country. The Kuomintang adopted his writings as their central ideology, as did their bitter enemies, the communists, who cited Sun's insistence that the revolution be carried out with the help of the communists as evidence of his commitment to their ideology. Thus, even though Sun's own life was largely one of disappointment and failure, to this day he remains a hero of the people, both China and Taiwan.

After the death of Sun Yat-sen, his successor Chiang Kai-shek used Sun's doctrine of 'political tutelage' – a period in which the population would learn to become part of a democracy – to establish a virtual military dictatorship in both countries. Many regarded this as contradicting the spirit of Sun Yat-sen, although there were also those who supported it as an interpretation of the master's philosophy. Not surprisingly, in modern times, the reputation of Chiang Kai-Shek has became tarnished by the many conflicts that took place under his reign, particularly the Taiwanese fight for independence, and there is little evidence of his legacy in

Taiwan and China today. Instead, it is Sun Yat-Sen's image that now adorns public places in Taiwan, from schools to law courts, and it is also seen on the bills and coins of Taiwanese currency. In China, Sun is also remembered everywhere; most major cities have streets named after him, as well as parks, schools and other public places. Ironically, it is the leader that did not attain power, rather than the one that did, who is revered in modern-day China and Taiwan.

Thus it is that, at least in principle, Sun Yat-sen remains the one unifying figure among Asian peoples driven apart by a turbulent history of war and conflict – though, sadly, he never lived to see the extent of his influence himself.

THE RUSSIAN
REVOLUTION 1917

The Russian Revolution was a massive uprising in which the corrupt, incompetent monarchy that had governed the country for hundreds of years was overthrown and was replaced by an elected Provisional Government. Only a few months later, after numerous conflicts between different revolutionary factions, the Bolsheviks displaced the Provisional Government and established the Soviet Union. The new Communist regime, which became known as the USSR, went on to develop a sizeable empire in opposition to that of the USA, and the two superpowers continued a 'cold war' policy of arms proliferation, espionage and counter-espionage that lasted for decades. During this time, within the country itself, the promise of the revolution was betrayed by a succession of despotic party leaders – most notably, Joseph Stalin – and millions of ordinary citizens died or lived out miserable lives as a result of a series of oppressive economic and social policies. Eventually, in 1991, the totalitarian Soviet regime crumbled, leaving behind a legacy of poverty, social fragmentation, technological backwardness and numerous other problems that continue to beset Russia and Eastern Europe to this day.

MEDIEVAL CONDITIONS OF LIFE

After so many years of autocratic rule by the Romanov Dynasty, why did the revolution occur in 1917? There were many reasons. Firstly, Tsar Nicholas II was a detested ruler who seemed to have no inkling of the fact that in order for the dynasty to survive, he would have to move with the times. He made no effort to modernize the country in terms of agriculture and industry, resulting in a situation where the Russian peasantry and factory workers faced medieval conditions of life that were much worse than those of their European counterparts. Not only this, but the tsar's failure to run a modern economy with an infrastructure of proper roads and railways meant that there were constant food shortages in the country, and thousands starved to death each winter. Moreover, the experience of World War I had been an appalling one for Russia: as a result largely of military incompetence, thousands of Russian soldiers died unnecessarily. It did not help the tsar's cause that, during the war, he had decided to take personal control of the army.

BLOODY SUNDAY

While the tsar was away losing the war, he left the running of the country to his wife Alexandra, who was unprepared for such a role and made many foolish decisions. She also became extremely unpopular through her favouring of the monk, Grigori Rasputin, whom she believed to have magical powers to cure her son's haemophilia. Rasputin brought shame on the Russian court through his licentious, coarse behaviour, and was generally regarded as, at best, a vile drunkard and womanizer, and at worst, an evil monster. There were even rumours that he was sleeping with Alexandra, although it is now thought that this was not the case.

The misery and frustration of the Russian people reached a peak on Bloody Sunday, when Russian workers, led by Georgi Gapon, marched to the tsar's winter palace to demand justice and were shot in cold blood by the army. The fact that the tsar had responded so brutally to this peaceful plea for mercy angered the public, who responded with a series of massive strikes that further crippled the economy.

ROYAL FAMILY SHOT

In an attempt to mollify his critics, Tsar Nicholas promised to set up a democratic parliament, known as the Duma. However, he then passed laws making the Duma ineffective and retaining power for himself, which infuriated the Russian aristocracy and middle classes. In 1916, the Duma issued the tsar with a warning that he must agree to a constitution. The tsar ignored this, and the following year, revolution broke out. The streets thronged with workers protesting about food shortages, and before long there were riots.

The police and soldiers initially tried to quell these, but eventually large numbers of them joined the rioters. The mob took over the imperial buildings of St Petersburg, and the tsar was forced to abdicate. He and his family were arrested, and a year later, after being held prisoner, they were all shot by a firing squad.

SPONTANEOUS REVOLT

Immediately after the tsar's abdication, a Provisional Government took power under the leadership of Alexander Kerensky, who made the mistake of continuing to send soldiers to fight the Germans in World War I. After more heavy defeats, Kerensky lost popularity, and by October, other political leaders were waiting to take control.

Thus, in its initial stages the revolution was not the work of any one person, but was a spontaneous uprising of the Russian peasantry, workers, soldiers and middle classes against a tyrannical autocracy that refused to allow the kind of progress and democratization that had become the norm in other parts of Europe.

CIVIL WAR

On November 7, 1917, the leader of the Bolsheviks, Vladimir Illich Lenin, led a coup against the Provisional Government, and he succeeded in establishing a Soviet Government, with the Bolshevik party in power. In it early stages, this was a democratic government, in which members of other parties contested the power of the Bolsheviks through the soviets, which were people's local councils. However, it was not long before conflicts between the different parties reached a crescendo, and a serious of strikes and rebellions broke out once more. Eventually, the entire country became enmeshed in a hugely damaging civil war between the 'Reds' – the radical, revolutionary elements – and the 'Whites' – the more liberals and conservative elements. The USA, Japan and several European powers, fearing revolutions in their own countries, poured money in to back the Whites, which arguably resulted in the isolationist perspective of the communists who eventually gained control: their experience of the civil war led them to a deep distrust of foreign powers, whom they saw as meddling in Russia's affairs entirely for their own advantage.

'SOCIALISM IN ONE COUNTRY'

Later, under Stalin, the communist party developed a doctrine of 'socialism in one country', which was entirely contrary to Lenin's early ideas of international solidarity between workers, and it ultimately led to terrible human rights abuses as Stalin's totalitarian regime held sway and the USSR began to lose contact with the rest of the world.

THE FREEDOM FIGHTERS

The Russian Revolution was not the work of any one individual, but took place for a variety of reasons, as outlined above. However, there were leaders whose vision and commitment were important factors in the revolution, and who helped to shape its destiny. Of these, the two towering figures are Vladimir Illich Lenin, whose Bolshevik party staged a coup and took over from the Provisional Government, and Leon Trotsky, who became the leader of the Red Army, and following a power struggle with Joseph Stalin, was removed from office and exiled.

Today, many argue about the exact ideology of these leaders, and how the USSR might have developed if, for instance, Lenin had not died when he did, and if Trotsky, rather than Stalin, had won the struggle for power. Some believe that the oppressive, totalitarian nature of the USSR was already revealing itself before Lenin died, and that Trotsky would also have been a ruthless leader had he taken power; others think that both these men might have presided over a much more democratic, progressive Soviet Union.

Whatever the case, it cannot be denied that both Lenin and Trotsky were, at least in their early years, committed revolutionaries who underwent considerable personal hardship in the pursuit of their beliefs. In their long years as political activists, they were both dedicated to improving the lot of the Russian people, and as such, must be called freedom fighters – even if, once in power, the realities of conflict, both domestic and foreign, meant they were unable to retain their high ideals for long.

LENIN

Vladimir Ilyich Lenin was one of the towering figures of the Russian Revolution, the man who masterminded the country's transition to a Communist state, became its first leader and propounded the theory of what was later called Marxist Leninism, a 20th-century adaptation of the economic, political and social theory of Karl Marx.

EXILED TO SIBERIA

Lenin was born in Simbirsk, now Ulyanovosk, on April 22, 1870. His original surname was Ulyanov, and his father was a civil servant. He grew up in a household where freedom of thought and democracy were prized, and the whole family were involved in politics. When he was a teenager, his father died suddenly of a cerebral haemorrhage. The following year, another family tragedy occurred: his elder brother Alexander, who had taken part in a plot to assassinate the tsar, was hanged for treason.

From then on, the young Vladimir resolved to avenge his brother's death, and when he became a university student, he immediately involved himself in radical politics. He was a brilliant student, but his study of Marxism further convinced him of the need to overthrow the oppressive regime of the tsar, and before long he was expelled. However, he later managed to complete his studies, and when he graduated, he began to work in a lawyer's practice. Once again, however, his revolutionary fervour led him into political activism, and he was arrested, imprisoned and exiled to Siberia.

THE COUP

After this, Ulyanov was no longer able to live in Russia, so he began to travel Europe as an exile, publishing writings on the need for revolution in his homeland, founding the newspaper *Iskra*, and adopting a new surname: Lenin. It was during this period that he met and married Nadezhda Krupskaya, a political activist like himself. Together the pair worked tirelessly for change in Russia, and Lenin became the leader of the Bolsheviks (meaning 'majority'), a group with a strong socialist and internationalist outlook.

When spontaneous revolution finally occurred in Russia in 1917, toppling the tsar and the aristocracy, Lenin hurried back to his homeland to take part. This was during the World War I, and Lenin was helped to travel home by the German government, who were hoping that Lenin would agitate to take Russia out of the war. For this reason, there were claims that Lenin was a spy in the pay of the Germans.

Despite this and other obstacles, Lenin managed to stage a coup, ousting the Provisional Government that had been set up after the revolution and taking power with his Bolshevik party. Ironically, the 'majority' Bolsheviks were actually a minority group, and the takeover of power was not at all democratic; however, the Bolsheviks considered they had a right to govern, as the 'vanguard of the proletariat', showing a totalitarian trend that did not augur well for the future.

CIVIL WAR

After the victory of the Bolsheviks, Russia underwent a massive civil war. During this time, their Red Army brutally put down all opposition, showing their complete disregard for human suffering and their determination to win power at all costs. Some have argued that the Bolsheviks were forced to take this position because of the chaos that ensued in the country, and particularly because of the involvement of foreign powers in the conflicts, which put the revolutionaries in a very vulnerable position. However, most agree that well before Lenin died, the Bolshevik regime had become very illiberal and dictatorial, laying the ground for the horrific purges that later took place under Stalin.

ASSASSINATION ATTEMPT

Once the civil war was over, Lenin set about building a new structure for the country's government, based on 'soviets', or local councils, in which ordinary people could have their say and influence the running of their workplaces and society in general. However, the radical nature of Communist theory did not square with the reality, which was anything but democratic. Instead of taking part in decision-making, peasants and factory workers were forced to work longer hours than ever, in an effort to rebuild the country after the shattering political upheavals it had experienced. Before long, it became clear to the people that the new regime was no socialist utopia, but merely a different form of dictatorship.

There was an attempt on Lenin's life in 1918, when he was shot and bullets lodged in his body, one of them narrowly missing his heart. Medical science at the time was not advanced enough to remove the bullets safely, so he had to live with these injuries, which damaged his health severely. In 1922, he had a stroke, and he finally died two years later.

CULT OF THE PERSONALITY

Today, there is much speculation about how the Soviet Union would have developed had Lenin not died. In many ways, he was a pragmatic thinker who tried to adapt the theories of Marx to fit the realities of post-revolutionary Russia. For example, he developed a model he called the New Economic Policy to allow for some private enterprise within communism, that is, what we now call a mixed economy. It is also clear from his writings that he had grave doubts about the way the increasing bureaucracy of the Bolshevik party, and about Stalin's suitability to succeed him. Lenin always disliked pomp and circumstance, and he criticized what he called the 'cult of the personality', whereby leaders were treated as heroes. He believed himself to be a man of the people and always adopted a simple, working man's dress. However, after his death he was worshipped by millions almost as a god, in a way that he would doubtless have found loathsome. And the Soviet Union came to be known as the most brutal and unjust regime of the 20th century.

LEON TROTSKY

Leon Trotsky was second only to Lenin as one of the leaders of the Russian Revolution, in which the old order was replaced by a Communist state. He was a brilliant thinker and a courageous fighter who led the Red Army of the Communists to victory in the civil war that ensued after the revolution. A key figure in the birth of the Soviet Union, after the death of Lenin he lost power to Joseph Stalin and was forced to leave the country. He continued to criticize Stalinism until his assassination in 1940.

EXILE TO SIBERIA

Trotsky was born Lev Davidovich Bronstein on October 26, 1879, in the Ukraine. The son of a Jewish farmer who had high ambitions for his children, the young Lev was sent to the home of a family friend in the city of Odessa to attend school. He turned out to be a gifted scholar and quickly learned the polished manners of his peers. He also developed an interest in revolutionary politics, and as a young man he began to set up political parties to further his cause.

It was not long before Lev was arrested and imprisoned for his activities. Like many of his contemporaries, such as Lenin, he was exiled to Siberia, but he later escaped. He travelled to Europe under the false name of Trotsky and began a life of exile in London, where he met Lenin and joined him in producing the newspaper Iskra.

PLOTTING THE REVOLUTION

There was much debate about how the revolutionaries should proceed in their goal of overthrowing the Tsar's regime Russia, particularly as the conditions of the country did not correspond with those advocated by Marx. Marx had envisaged revolution occurring in a highly developed, industrialized nation such as England, whereby the working people or 'proletariat' would take control. Russia, by contrast, was a peasant economy. Thus, Lenin, Trotsky and their colleagues had to adapt the ideas of Marxism to fit the Russian situation, and not surprisingly there was a good deal of controversy as to how this should be done.

Eventually, two major factions emerged: the Bolsheviks, led by Vladimir Lenin, and the Mensheviks, led by Julius Martov. Broadly speaking, the Bolsheviks argued for an elite revolutionary group of intellectuals who would take control, while the Mensheviks envisaged a more open, democratic revolution, in which the middle classes would play an important part. Trotsky joined the Mensheviks.

RED ARMY LEADER

In 1905, Trotsky went back to Russia, where he became involved in the failed Russian Revolution that took place that year. Together with other revolutionary leaders, he set up the St Petersburg Soviet, a local council, with the aim of ruling the city. However, the leaders were arrested and imprisoned. In 1907, Trotsky was once more deported to Siberia, and once more he escaped. He returned to London, where he met Stalin, and set up the newspaper *Pravda*.

On hearing the news of the overthrow of Tsar Nicholas II in 1917, Trotsky immediately travelled back to his homeland. The Bolsheviks, led by Lenin, ousted the Provisional Government that had been set up to replace the tsar, and Trotsky was appointed to the Central Committee. The following year, Lenin put Trotsky in charge of the Russian military and the navy. In this capacity, Trotsky set up the Red Army. Although many criticized the army as a force that brutally put down all opposition, it became crucial to winning the civil war that ensued after the revolution.

EXILED REVOLUTIONARY

Trotsky continued to play a central role in the new government until the death of Lenin in 1922. At this stage, there was a power struggle between Trotsky and Stalin for control of the party, which Trotsky lost. In 1928, Stalin forced Trotsky into exile. From his position outside the Soviet Union, Trotsky constantly criticized the regime, developing a theory of 'permanent revolution' that emphasized the internationalist perspective of socialism.

Trotsky's status as an expelled communist meant that it was hard for him to find a home, and thus he travelled the world as an exile before settling in Mexico in 1937. Here he met many important radical thinkers, artists and political figures, and he continued to write and publish. However, he was constantly harassed by the Stalinist secret service, and on August 20, 1940, he was assassinated by Ramon Mercader, a Spanish communist, who came to his home posing as a political follower and attacked him with an ice pick. The following day, he died. After his death, Trotsky's political legacy remained an important rallying point for many socialist disillusioned by the brutal regime of Stalin and subsequent leaders of the Soviet Union.

THE MEXICAN
REVOLUTION 1910

The Mexican Revolution took place when the people of the country rose up against the oppressive regime of General Porfirio Diaz and overthrew his dictatorship. In his place, they elected Francisco Madero, who went on to establish a liberal democracy in the country. However, once in power, Madero failed to carry out the land reforms that the people had hoped for and thus lost their support. Instead, Mexicans turned to folk heroes such as Pancho Villa in the north, and Emiliano Zapata in the south, to champion their fight for justice and equality, and a period of civil war broke out. During this time, the USA backed the counter-revolutionary forces, and sought to impose a regime beneficial to itself, such as it had enjoyed under Diaz' regime. However, its attempts to quell the revolution ultimately failed, and in 1917, after a great deal of chaos and bloodshed, the Constitution of Mexico was signed, which remains in force to this day.

THE RULE OF THE TYRANT

The issue that sparked the revolution was the election of November 1910. The country had been ruled for many years by General Porfirio Diaz, who had rigged elections to secure his position and had suppressed any opposition to the regime, either by force or by bribery. At the same time, Diaz had endeavoured to develop Mexico's poor, agricultural economy into a modern, industrialized one. In order to do so, he had sought foreign investors, particularly the USA, which came to dominate the mining, oil and transport industries. In addition, he had allowed private investors to purchase vast tracts of public land, including land belonging to Mexico's native populations. Not only this, but much of the food grown in Mexico was being exported abroad, to the degree that many of its own people were starving. Both in rural areas and in the city, workers had to put up with appalling rates of pay and conditions and were forbidden to organize labour unions.

Diaz was expecting to win the November election in 1910, as he had always made sure to do, but this time there was a candidate who attracted the people's attention: Francisco Madero. Madero came from a well-to-do background and had made a name for himself by publishing a book in which he called for free elections in Mexico. Diaz had allowed Madero to stand against him at the elections, so as to pretend that there was a genuine democratic system operating in the country, but never thought that Madero had any real chance of winning. However, when Madero's candidature became a focal point for factions hostile to the government, and it became clear that he was a real threat, Diaz had his opponent thrown in jail. Once the election was over, Madero was released and went to Texas to plan the overthrow of the tyrant Diaz.

'LAND AND LIBERTY'

Unfortunately, it turned out Madero was more of a political theorist than a realist, and he was more concerned with constitutional issues than with the pressing economic problems of Mexico in terms of poverty, foreign ownership and social reform. When Madero returned to Mexico to begin the revolution, he found that his supporters had not organized a proper army, so he retreated to Texas again and waited until the rebels fighting in the name of revolution had finished their work. Thus, it was the rebels – men such as Emiliano Zapata, Pancho Villa and Pascual Orozco – who really achieved the overthrow of Diaz, rather than Madero himself.

Adopting the slogan 'land and liberty', the rebel forces, made up of armed cowboys and ranch hands, attacked privately owned estates, ranches, railways and federal troops, with the aim of restoring land back to the people. On May 10, 1911, they captured the town of Cuidad Juarez near the border with Texas, prompting the resignation of Diaz, who fled to Europe. In November of the same year, democratic elections were held in Mexico, and Madero won a landslide victory.

CIVIL WAR

Before long, it became clear that Madero and the band of revolutionaries had different aims in mind. Unwisely, Madero refused to disband Diaz' military force as the revolutionaries wanted to do, but instead tried to disband the rebel forces. Madero was also slow to implement land reforms. Angered by what they saw as the betrayal of the revolution, Zapata and Orozco mounted major rebellions against Madero.

Not only did Madero have enemies in the revolutionary camp, but the loyalists he had allowed to stay in the country also bitterly opposed him. A series of revolts took place, which Madero initially succeeded in quelling, but eventually a full-scale civil war broke out, with the revolutionaries on one side and the loyalists of the old regime on the other. Within a short time, Mexico City became a war zone as the opposing groups struggled to gain control, and during the intense conflicts that followed, thousands of civilians as well as soldiers lost their lives.

POWER SEIZED

Among the loyalist forces was General Victoriano Huerta, who seized power in the capital and ordered the execution of Madero on February 22, 1913, claiming that the former president had been killed in an accidental shooting. In response to Huerta's coup d'état, a group of revolutionaries, including Zapata, Villa, Alvaro Obregón of Sonora and Venustiano

Carranza of Coahuila, banded together under the name of 'The Constitutionalists' to demand a democratically elected government.

Huerta's other enemy was the US government under Woodrow Wilson, who completely opposed his undemocratic seizure of power. Wilson began by refusing Huerta financial and military aid, hoping that he would capitulate and agree to democratic elections in Mexico. When he did not, Wilson sent US troops to occupy the port of Veracruz and allowed the revolutionary forces to procure arms from the USA. In July 1914, under mounting pressure from all sides, Huerta was forced to step down and was replaced by Venustanio Carranza.

REBEL WARS

Sadly, the new president was not able to stabilize the country. The revolutionary factions were unable to sink their differences, and while Villa and Zapata continued to fight for land redistribution, Carranza and Obregon opposed it. The fighting intensified, and before long, another huge civil war broke out, which claimed the lives of over 200,000 Mexicans.

By 1914, it looked as though Villa and Zapata would be able to take control of Mexico City; however, the following year, Obregón rallied, and the USA officially recognized Carranza as president. This provoked further hostilities between the USA and revolutionary forces in northern Mexico, which continued until 1917. Eventually, Zapata was killed in the fighting, while

Villa retreated to the state of Chihuahua in the north, where his forces continued to occupy both urban and rural areas.

PRECARIOUS PEACE

Under the presidency of Carranza, a constitution was established that provided for land reform, minimum wages, improved working conditions, unionization and restrictions on Church and foreign ownership of land. However, even though these gains looked important on paper, Carranza actually did little to see that the constitution was put into practise, and he became extremely unpopular. In April 1920, he was assassinated by supporters of Alvaro Obregón, who then took over power.

Despite the violent start to his rule, Obregón went on to preside over a period of relative stability in Mexico, initiating a far-reaching educational programme and reopening trading and diplomatic relations with the USA. After suppressing a major revolt by Adolfo de la Huerta, who wanted to succeed him to the presidency, Obregón eventually handed over power to his chosen successor, Plutarco Elías Calles.

LEGACY OF THE REVOLUTION

In the years that followed, the Mexican government trod a precarious line between improving economic conditions for the inhabitants of the country and placating their powerful neighbour on their border, the

USA. Successive governments also had to deal with the Catholic Church, which instigated its own rebellions and proved a constant source of conflict with the state. Under Calles, sweeping reforms were made, and the country's infrastructure of roads and services was improved. Calles also oversaw the founding of a mainstream political party, now called the Partido Revolucionario Institucional (PRI), which has ruled the country ever since.

In many ways, the Mexican revolution was an upheaval that caused untold chaos, bloodshed and misery over a period of many years. However, despite this, there is no doubt that the freedom fighters who led the revolution of 1910 liberated the country from centuries of despotic rule, in which society was divided into an elite of extremely wealthy landowners and a mass of poverty-stricken workers who had little hope of a decent life for themselves and their families. Over the decades that followed, basic systems of health care, education and transport were established, and working conditions and wages improved dramatically. This was the legacy of the Mexican revolution, and even though Mexico today continues to be a country beset by myriad problems, including overpopulation, poverty, illiteracy and high levels of child mortality, there is a real sense in which the freedom fighters of the 20th century helped to sweep away the old order and establish a modern state where justice, freedom and equality became, if not a reality, a goal for everyone.

PANCHO VILLA

Pancho Villa was one of the most colourful, flamboyant figures of the Mexican Revolution. Born a peasant, he began his long career of riding and fighting as a cattle rustler and bandit. When the revolution of 1910 broke out, he was recruited by the revolutionary leader Abraham Gonzales to lead the war in the northern part of Mexico. A brave, charismatic leader, Villa led his ragged band of men to victory many a time, and by the end of the war he had become a national hero. However, during his lifetime he killed many opponents and made many enemies as well as friends. When he retired from the battlefield, relatives of those who had died sought vengeance, and Villa became the subject of numerous assassination attempts. In 1923, one of these attempts was successful; as he was driving his car through the town of Parral, Chihuahua, he was shot and killed. Nobody ever found out who his assailant was.

HEAD FOR THE HILLS

Pancho Villa's real name was Doroteo Arango Arámbula, and he was born on June 5, 1878. There is some dispute as to the facts about his early life, because he appeared on few official records, but it is thought that he grew up in San Juan del Rio in the state of Durango. His parents, Agustin Arango and Maria Micaela Arámbula, were landless peasants, and he briefly attended the local church school, but he had to go to work when his father died. With his mother and four young siblings to support, Doroteo had to provide the family income and laboured as a sharecropper.

At 16, Doroteo moved to Chihuahua, but he was forced to return when his sister was raped by the son of a wealthy local landowner. Legend has it that Doroteo shot the culprit and then headed for the mountains to avoid the law, taking a stolen horse with him. From that time on, he became a bandit, living a travelling life with a horde of rough and ready compadres in the mountains of northern Mexico and making his living by cattle rustling and stealing from wealthy travellers.

POLITICAL EDUCATION

As a country boy, Doroteo knew the mountainous region around Chihuahua well, which helped him to survive while he was on the run. After a few years, he teamed up with a band of ruffians under the leadership of one Ignacio Parra. Parra was killed in a police shoot-out, whereupon the fearless Doroteo took over his role, changing his name to Francisco Villa after a notorious local bandit, who was said to have redistributed the goods he stole from the rich to feed and clothe the poor.

Up to this point, Villa had been a mere bandido, eking out a living as best he could by stealing cattle, killing enemies and hiding out in the mountains. However, he then encountered one of Francisco Madero's followers, Abraham Gonzales, who was trying to win the people of Chihuahua over to his cause. During this period, Villa's horizons broadened, and he began to understand the causes of the intense poverty and hardship he saw around him.

Gonzales explained that the 'hacendados', or wealthy owners of great estates in the area, had stolen land from the peasants there, supported and encouraged by the corrupt government of Porfirio Diaz. This had been going on for decades, but Madero and his followers were now taking a stand against Diaz in an attempt to gain justice and democracy for the Mexican people, and to give the land back to its rightful owners.

REVOLUTION AND COUNTER-REVOLUTION

Villa decided to throw his lot in with Madero's party, and he proved a valuable military asset in the revolution that followed. At the Battle of Juarez, Villa and others led the fight against the military forces of Diaz' regime and successfully defeated them. Madero went on to become President of Mexico, and the stage was set for the radical democratization of the country. However, in the event this did not take place as planned, and as it turned out, Villa's task was far from over.

Madero was slow to implement the land reforms that the revolutionaries had hoped for, and he seemed less concerned with improving the conditions and wages of the rural 'peons', or peasant labourers, than with reorganizing the political system in Mexico. Life for the ordinary people of the country did not improve a great deal; indeed, Madero began to make links with the wealthy landowners and seemed disinclined to alienate them. Thus it was not long before a group of radicals, led by Pascual Orozco, became tired of Madero's failure to address the burning issues of the day and sought to throw him out of office. Along with a loyalist general, Victoriano Huerta, Villa fought against Orozco's men to protect Madero; however, Huerta then assassinated Madero and seized power himself. Huerta also assassinated Abraham Gonzales, who had been Villa's chief guide and mentor at the outbreak of the revolution.

CHARISMATIC LEADER

Not surprisingly Huerta now became Villa's sworn enemy, so he and a number of other revolutionary leaders, including Alvaro Obregón and Emiliano Zapata, banded together under the leadership of Venustiano Carranza to overthrow the new regime. Once more, Villa marched on Ciudad Juarez, this time with only a tiny band of men and little in the way of weapons or ammunition. However, using his consider- able charm and skills of persuasion, Villa went on to recruit many new soldiers for his army, who began to raid haciendas and rob trains in order to raise cash to fund their cause.

Not only did Villa attract a loyal following of soldiers: women also flocked to his side, and he earned a reputation as a serious womanizer. According to some reports, during his life he married over 20 times and had a succession of torrid affairs as well.

ROBBING THE BANK

Villa's military skills brought him great success, and after a series of hard-won battles, he became the governor of the state of Chihuahua. This position enabled him to raise more funds, which he did with great bravado, confiscating the gold reserves held in bank vaults and forcing wealthy local people – under threat of execution – to sell their goods and land for worthless paper money that he had specially printed. By these means, he managed to amass enough money to buy everything his army needed and also rebuild the infrastructure of the state, including the railways.

Villa's army was highly successful in defeating loyalist forces, and he began to be seen as the saviour of the revolution. However, at this stage he fell out with the leader of the revolutionary forces, Carranza, whom he saw as trying to gain power for himself at the expense of his compadres. Villa eventually split completely with Carranza and his group, after which his career as an army leader waned. He began to lose battles and have difficulty in financing his army. When President Carranza began to forge links with the USA, under the leadership of Woodrow Wilson, Villa felt completely betrayed.

ASSASSINATION

Villa reacted by launching attacks on American interests in Mexico, and in one instance, he led a raid across the border into the town of Columbus, New Mexico. This took place on March 9, 1916. US President Wilson responded by sending 6,000 troops on a 'punitive expedition' under General John Pershing to capture Villa and his men. However, despite this large force, Villa managed to evade his captors, and eventually the hunt was called off. Legend has it that Pershing telegraphed Washington before giving up the chase with the word:

Villa is everywhere, but Villa is nowhere.

After 1919, when Villa conducted his final raid on Ciudad Juarez, he retreated to the northern territories, where he had massive support from the local population. The following year, he negotiated peace with the incoming president, Adolfo de la Huerta, and he began a period of semi-retirement, living on a large farm, or 'hacienda'. In 1923, he was assassinated as he drove through the local town of Parral.

TRUTH OR LEGEND?

Many people were suspected of Villa's murder, for in his lifetime he had made a lot of enemies, but no one was ever arrested for the crime or charged with murder. Thus, the final end of one of Mexico's greatest freedom fighters remains a mystery to this day.

After his death, legends and stories about Villa became part of Mexican folklore. Some were true, some near the truth and some complete fabrications. For example, it was said that Villa loved to dance, so much so that he was once late for a battle after an all-night session. It was also reported that he enjoyed ice cream, to the extent that he once stopped to buy some before going on to shoot an enemy. Tales of his exploits in battle also abound; apparently, on one occasion he escaped General Pershing and his soldiers by asking his men to sew him up inside the body of a dead horse. However, by all accounts, Villa was not a drinker; surprisingly, he never touched alcohol at all.

But not everyone today sees Villa as a great leader. There are those who believe that he was an uneducated, bloodthirsty thug, who enjoyed violence and was not motivated by anything other than personal gain. There may be some truth in this view; but while it is certainly the case that Villa was a rough and ready individual who was no stranger to violence, he does seem to have pursued a radical course of action throughout his life, fighting for his people against those who sought to betray the ideals of the revolution.

EMILIANO ZAPATA

Emiliano Zapata is known as one of the great liberators of Mexico. Under the slogan of 'Land and Liberty', he fought for the rights of the peasants who had had their land taken away from them under the regime of Porfirio Diaz. A major instigator of the Mexican Revolution in 1910, he was determined to see that the principles of freedom, justice and democracy were upheld once the old regime was swept away, and he became a thorn in the side of the liberals and moderates, such as Carranza, who then gained power. His career ended in 1919, when he was brutally murdered by a general loyal to the Carranza government.

CORRUPTION IN HIGH PLACES

Emiliano Zapata Salazar was born on August 8, 1879, in the small village of Anencuilco, Morelos. He grew up as part of a large family on a farm, working as a sharecropper and training horses. As a young man, he was sent to the army to do his military service and then returned home to become active in the political life of the village as president of the council.

During this period, many native communities such as the Mayans had had their land taken away from them by 'hacendados' – wealthy landowners who ran huge estates and exported most of their produce abroad. Having stripped the local people of their land, they then forced the poverty-stricken communities to labour on the farms as 'peons'. Under the corrupt government of Porfirio Diaz, who had ruled Mexico for many years, the 'hacendados' were encouraged to continue squeezing land and rights away from the peasants, through officials who presided over this process in each of the country's rural districts. The peasants could not register their protest through the democratic system, and they had few other rights. Although Mexico was nominally a democracy, in practise, the elections were run purely for show and no candidate was allowed to stand who would not support Diaz and his government.

FLAMBOYANT HERO

Zapata was outraged by the situation, which had persisted for many years by the time he became active in village politics. His parents were not poor peasants – in fact, he came from a successful, independent family of ranchers who had at one time supported Diaz – but he was acutely aware that the governments corrupt, unjust practises were strangling the life out of Mexico's rural communities and that something had to be done to reverse the process. As a speaker of Nahuatl, the language of the indigenous people in his area, he quickly rose through local politics to represent the interests of Native Americans, and he became involved in their struggle to gain back their land and rights.

Although Zapata dressed like a rich man, often wearing flamboyant riding costumes whenever he made a public appearance, the people of Anenecuilco trusted him, and indeed, he always remained loyal to their cause. During his time as leader of the village council, Zapato helped many families to win back their land, sometimes risking his own life to do so. He witnessed many conflicts and he saw first hand how viciously the landowners fought to retain their stolen land. Initially, he worked within the law, unearthing old title deeds to confiscated territory and pressurizing government officials to comply with them. However, as it became clear that the system was completely corrupt, Zapata began to take over the lands by force, using bands of armed men to do so.

TRIUMPH AND FAILURE

Zapata was not the only radical to become disgusted with the 'Porfiriato', as Diaz' regime had become known. Many others, including Francisco Madero, a liberal intellectual, had made their views known, and Zapata began to make alliances with these groups. When, in 1910, the country finally erupted into revolution, Zapata immediately formed an army in Morelos and joined forces with other revolutionary leaders including Pascual Orozco and Pancho Villa, to overthrow Diaz and replace him with Madero.

At the battle of Ciudad Juarez the following year, the revolutionary forces finally won their fight, and Madero went on to become President of Mexico. However, it was not long before Zapata realized he had made a mistake in supporting Madero. It soon became clear that the new president had no intention of making sweeping land reforms; he was a moderate who was more concerned with the political apparatus of government than restoring justice to the people. Because of his outspoken views, Zapata was forced to flee, and he went into hiding in the mountains, where he developed a far-reaching plan of land reform: the Plan de Ayala.

'LAND AND LIBERTY'

Adopting the slogan of an anarchist thinker named Ricardo Flores Magon, 'Land and Liberty', Zapata assembled an army with revolutionary leader Pascual Orozco and came down from the mountains to do battle against Madero and his forces. However, Madero was assassinated – not by the revolutionaries, but by another faction, a military force loyal to the Diaz regime led by General Victoriano Huerta. Zapata and his men were forced to retreat to their homelands; this time, they went on to ally themselves with a new rebel group, that of Pancho Villa.

Unable to defeat Huerta on their own, Zapata and Villa joined forces with Venustiano Carranza, a moderate whose central aim was the imposition of a constitution in Mexico. The Constitutionalists, as they became known, went on to depose Huerta, but once again, the so-called moderate turned out to be a wolf in sheep's clothing: within a short time, Carranza had appointed himself president, even though he had not been elected. When Zapata protested, Carranza responded by putting a bounty on his opponent's head, and Zapata was forced to flee to his home state. Just as before, he had been robbed of the chance to put his radical land reform programme into action, and the peasants had been cheated out of their revolution.

BOUNTY HUNTERS

Zapata remained in Morelos, where he held considerable power, until 1919, when he was tricked into a meeting with a general loyal to Carranza, Jesus Guajardo. Guajardo invited him for a meeting at the Hacienda de San Juan in Chinameca, Ayala, on the pretence that he was considering becoming a rebel. When he arrived there, Guajardo's soldiers opened fire on him, and he was shot dead. The body was taken to the Carranza administration so that the bounty would be paid; however, legend has it that the bounty hunters only received half of what they were due.

Not surprisingly, after the death of their leader, the army that Zapata had built up over the decades began to dwindle. Some of the soldiers joined other revolutionary groups, while others gave up the fight. However, today the legacy of the freedom fighter still lives on in southern Mexico, where a series of revolts have taken place in recent years.

ZAPATA'S LEGACY

In 1994, a group of revolutionaries calling themselves the Ejercito Zapatista de Liberacion Nacional (EZLN) mounted several major protests against the continuing oppression of the indigenous people of the region. The Zapatistas, as they are known, are mainly Mayan in origin, and have pioneered a largely nonviolent campaign of resistance to the exploitation of the Mayan people, using modern technologies such as the Internet to do so. In addition, they have aligned themselves to ecological and anti-globalization movements, and see themselves as part of a wider protest against the destruction of native cultures and the earth's resources by world capitalism. In this way, the radical reforming zeal of Emiliano Zapatista has been kept alive.

Among some Mayan communities Zapatista has gained the status of a god. He is known as 'Votan' or 'Wotan' Zapata, after the Mayan god who is believed to have come down from the mountains with his twin brother, Ikal, to teach the people self-defence. There are some communities in Morelos who believe that Zapata was not murdered but that he sent an envoy posing as himself to the meeting with Guajardo. Legend has it that after the death of the envoy, Zapata escaped to a foreign country, where he continued to live to an old age.

A TRUE FREEDOM FIGHTER

There are critics of Zapata who believe that he was a semiliterate peasant who enjoyed the bloodshed and violence of his life as a bandit and had no real grasp of politics whatsoever, but was co-opted by the leading intellectuals of his day into fighting their battles for them.

However, this account does not really square with the facts. While it is certainly true that Zapata was often betrayed by the intellectuals he allied himself with, he did so for his own ends and not out of political naivety. Moreover, it is well established that Zapata came from a family of independent farmers who were politically – if not formally – educated. This enabled him to propose the most radical and imaginative social reforms that the country had ever known under the Plan de Ayala.

For these reasons, Emiliano Zapata is still seen in Mexico, and around the world, as a hero: one of the few freedom fighters in history to remain true throughout his life to the cause of justice for his people.

TAN MALAKA

Tan Malaka was an Indonesian communist leader and political activist who spent most of his life fighting to free his people from colonialism. He was exiled by the colonial Dutch government of the East Indies, as Indonesia was then called, but after many years was able to return to his homeland. With the establishment of a nationalist government, Malaka briefly came to power in 1946 with a nationalist coalition. However, he was later imprisoned and forced to flee his country once more. In 1949, Malaka was captured and executed by supporters of Sukarno, the nationalist leader whose government he had also criticized.

PLOTTING REVOLUTION

Datuk Ibrahim Gelar Sutan Malaka was born in Suliki, Western Sumatra, around 1895 (his exact date of birth is unknown). He was a member of the Minangkabau people, who are noted for their matrilineal society, in which property and land are passed down from mothers to daughters while men attend to political and religious matters. Tan Malaka, as he became known, was deeply influenced by the Islamic religion of his people, who also follow what they call 'adat', ethnic traditions. 'Adat' is an ancient system of spiritual beliefs linked to ancient animistic rituals, which also includes elements of Hindu culture. Among the Muslims of Minangkabau, these different belief systems are merged, in a fashion that Malaka later drew on to develop his political theory, in which he sees Islam as being compatible with communism.

As a young man, he trained as a teacher at a college run by the Dutch in Bukittinggi. It was here that he learned Dutch. He excelled at his studies, so much so that the elders of his village gave him financial assistance to move to the Netherlands and continue his education. There he attended a government teacher training school in Haarlem, where he began to read Marx and other socialist writers. He also met many Dutch and Indonesian teachers and students, with whom he discussed the problems of his native country. During this time he became convinced that the only way to improve the political and economic situation in Indonesia was to stage a full-scale revolution and throw out the colonialists. (At that time, the Dutch ruled Indonesia, and were ruthlessly exploiting the local population, as well as exporting many of the country's natural resources abroad.)

LIFE IN EXILE

While studying in Haarlem, Malaka contracted tuberculosis, and from that time on, suffered problems with his health, which often forced him to stop working. However, once he had completed his training, he went back to Indonesia and found a job in a tobacco plantation in Sumatra teaching the children of 'coolies', hired labourers from the Asian subcontinent. He experienced at first hand the appalling conditions and low pay of the workers and resolved to try to help them. He became involved with the East Indies Social Democratic Association (ISDV) and published articles in their newspaper. Later, the association became the Communist Party of Indonesia (PKI).

Malaka was now beginning to make a name for himself as an activist. He taught his students to think politically, wrote newspaper articles criticizing the Dutch administration and began to organize labour unions. In 1920, he helped to organize a strike by railway workers. In 1920, he left Sumatra and moved to Semarang, Java, to work for Saraket Islam, a nationalist political group. As well as teaching, he continued to organize labour unions, and in 1921 he was elected as chair of the PKI. Under his leadership, there were continual strikes, and Dutch colonial officials became more and more unhappy with the situation, until they finally banned his activities. Malaka was arrested and forced to flee the country as an exile in 1922.

FAILED REVOLUTION

Returning to the Netherlands, Malaka promptly ran in the elections as a candidate for the Communist Party of Holland (CPH). He did not expect to win, but wanted to draw attention to his country's plight, and as the first person from the colony to put himself up as a candidate in the Netherlands, he succeeded in making his voice heard. He then visited Berlin and Moscow, trying to persuade the communist governments there to support the nationalist struggles of the Asian peoples to free themselves from the yoke of Dutch colonialism. He was made an agent for the Comintern (the international wing of the Communist party) with responsibility for southeast Asia, and he also wrote a book about the situation in the Dutch East Indies, which was published in the USSR.

Next, Malaka went to China to set up a newspaper, and then moved on to Manila in the Philippines. The PKI was planning a revolution there, but Malaka found it was badly organized and felt that it had little chance of succeeding. However, he did not manage to persuade the party leaders that this was the case, and accordingly, the uprising went ahead. As he had predicted, the revolution failed and the PKI found itself in a worse position than before, with several leaders executed and political activism banned.

ON THE RUN

Undeterred, Malaka visited Bangkok, where he founded the Partai Republik Indonesia (PARI), criticizing the PKI for the debacle in the Philippines. By now, Malaka had become persona non grata in the Philippines, so when he travelled back there, he was arrested and charged with illegal entry. This created an angry backlash from the country's student population, and there were a number of strikes at universities.

Eventually, Malaka was deported rather than sent to trial. He travelled to China, where he went into hiding from the Dutch authorities. This period of his life remains somewhat mysterious, but it is thought that his years spent on the run in China influenced his politics greatly.

Malaka strongly criticized Japan for its expansionist foreign policy, so when the Japanese invaded Shanghai in 1932, he was forced to go on the run once again, this time to Hong Kong. There he was arrested and imprisoned by the British authorities, but then he was told that he could leave Hong Kong without charges. He returned to China, but to escape the Japanese, who were making inroads into the south of the country, he went first to Burma, and then to Singapore, where he worked as a teacher.

FINAL EXECUTION

In 1942, the Japanese invaded Singapore and overthrew the Dutch colonial government in Indonesia. Three years later, the Japanese themselves surrendered, at the end of the World War II. This was the moment Malaka had waited for, and he returned to Indonesia, but he soon realized that the incoming nationalist government, headed by Sukarno, was not going to be as radical as he had hoped. Instead of supporting complete independence, the government were making various deals with the Dutch. Malaka responded by forming a party, the Persatuan Perjuangan (United Action), and calling for full independence, as well as the nationalization of all foreign-owned agricultural and industrial concerns.

Malaka's demands were popular with the Indonesian people, and for a while it looked as though he could join forces with Sukarno and form a coalition. However, their political differences were too great and Malaka's followers began to openly criticize the government. In 1946, Sukarno's government arrested Malaka, and he was imprisoned for two years. After his release, he tried to rebuild his political career, but with the return of the Dutch to Indonesia, he was forced to go on the run again. Eventually, he was captured by the nationalist forces and in 1949, he was executed.

FREEDOM FIGHTER

Malaka's life was remarkable for his refusal to compromise and allow his countrymen and women to be exploited, whether by a colonialist government or an Indonesian ruling class colluding with it. Unlike many political figures, he made alliances to further his beliefs and philosophy, rather than to further his career. He also had a radical vision of the future, envisaging a state in which communism, nationalism and Islam were all vital elements, binding the people of Southeast Asia together into one state. He believed that only in this way would Asia be able to act as a counterbalance to the interests of the USA, the Soviet Union and China. He drew on his own cultural experiences as a member of the Minangkabau to put forward the idea of a state in which different elements would come into play: he believed that Islam could bring different ethnic groups together, uniting them as nation, and that communism was compatible with religious belief.

In the event, Malaka's vision of the future was rejected, and Indonesia went on to adopt a fiercely capitalist system under the leadership of Sukarno. Malaka's independence of mind earned him many enemies, and he spent most of his life on the run or in prison, as his autobiography *Dari Penjara ke Pendjara* (*From Jail to Jail*) records. However, today he is remembered as a great freedom fighter, a man who devoted his life to the cause of the Indonesian people, and died, as he had lived, fighting for justice.

MAHATMA GANDHI

Mohandas Gandhi, or Mahatma ('great soul'), as he became known, was one of the greatest and most successful freedom fighters in history. Today, he has a permanent place in history as one of the most important freedom fighters of the 20th century. He studied law in the UK, and then spent 20 years in South Africa, defending the rights of immigrants to the country, before returning to India in 1914 and becoming the leader of the Indian National Congress. His aim was to seek independence for India and to free the country from its British colonial rulers, but to do so without violence. Over his long career, he developed a philosophy and strategy of nonviolence and civil disobedience, which became the template for many peaceful protests around the world and continues to be followed to this day.

Gandhi's ambition to achieve political change without violence ultimately failed: the British were ousted from India, and the country became self-governing, but religious and ethnic divisions led to extreme violence, in the form of killings, arson and rioting. Eventually the country was partitioned into India and Pakistan, but a great deal of blood was shed over these years. However, Gandhi never lost his faith in the principle of nonviolence and continued to set an example to his people. During his lifetime, he pursued a highly principled, moral way of life, dressing in the clothes of an Indian peasant and eschewing the trappings of luxury. As well as advocating non-violence, Gandhi also believed that people of all religious persuasions should have equal rights, and that Hindus were no more important than Muslims, which made him many enemies among radical Hindu political factions in India. On January 30, 1948, Gandhi was assassinated at the hands of a Hindu fanatic, Nathuram Godse, who shot and killed him as he walked through the streets to attend a prayer meeting in New Delhi. At his funeral, the Prime Minister of the newly independent India announced, 'the light has gone out of our lives'.

IMMIGRANTS' RIGHTS

Mohandas Karamchand Gandhi was born on October 2, 1869, in the small town of Porbandar on the Kathia Peninsula of Western India. His father, Karamchand Gandhi, was a 'dewan', the leader of the region around the town, and a well-to-do civil servant. However, despite the family's wealth, they were not seen as part of the élite, because of their position in the caste system. The Hindu religion has four main castes, or classes: the highest are the Brahmins, who are spiritual leaders, scholars and teachers; then come the Kshatriyas, or warriors, from whom the earthly leaders arise; next are the Vaisyas, who are merchants, clerks and land owners; and lowest are the Sudras, who work on the land as peasants and craftsmen. Gandhi's family were Vaisyas. However, although his father was involved in commerce, he was not interested in amassing riches, a trait that Gandhi inherited. In later years, even though he had access to immense wealth, he always preferred the simple life.

As a young man, Gandhi went to university to gain his degree, and then travelled to London, England, to train as a barrister. In London, he met English socialists and radical thinkers such as the playwright George Bernard Shaw, and he was inspired by their ideas. On his return to India he began a career as a lawyer in Bombay, but then moved to South Africa. There, he experienced extreme racism and began to fight back, joining support groups for Indian immigrant workers and helping to educate his countrymen and women. He also defended their rights in court and attracted a great deal of attention for his cause. During this time, Gandhi developed his philosophy of 'satyagraha' ('devotion to truth') and took part in nonviolent protests against the government, spending the next two decades committed to the struggle.

On his return to India in 1915, he became involved in politics and began to campaign on behalf of the Indian National Congress against the British government, encouraging Indians to buy Indian rather than British goods. He consistently advocated nonviolent protest, but even so, he was imprisoned several times for his activities. He became a thorn in the side of the British authorities, showing up their hypocritical attitudes and attracting attention wherever he went. In

1931, he famously attended a political conference in the UK dressed only in the simple clothes of an Indian peasant, once again reminding the world of the harsh poverty in which many of his countrymen lived.

PARTITION YEARS

After many years of political campaigning, Gandhi began to see his dream of a free, independent India become a reality, with the breakup of British colonial rule. However, there were other problems on the horizon that threatened to destroy the country's peaceful transition to independence, in particular the deep antagonism that existed between Indian Hindus and Muslims. Having cooperated with the British, Gandhi was accused of helping to partition the country, a step that by all accounts he fundamentally opposed. He was also criticized for weakening the Hindus' political power through his belief in the equality of all religious faiths.

Despite the criticisms, Gandhi continued to be regarded by the majority of the Indian people as the father of Indian independence, and as such he became one of the most famous, well-loved figures in the country by the end of his life.

ASSASSINATION ATTEMPTS

During the Partition years, Gandhi appealed for calm, but his cries fell on deaf ears. So, to try to stop the rioting between Muslims and Hindus, he began to fast.

Such was his influence that the rioters in Delhi and Calcutta stopped their battles. However, on January 20, 1948, there was an assassination attempt on Gandhi. It failed, but ten days later, an assassin struck again, and this time, was successful. Gandhi was on his way to a prayer meeting at Birla House, the home of a prominent industrialist where he often stayed during his visits to New Delhi. At about 5.00 p.m., people began to gather for the meeting. According to witnesses, Gandhi arrived for the meeting at about 5.12 p.m., dressed in his usual garb, though wearing a homespun shawl over his loin cloth, because it was a cold evening. As he walked across the grass, accompanied by various followers, including some young women, onlookers knelt down or bowed their heads before him. Then, suddenly, several shots rang out. Gandhi fell to the ground, mortally wounded, his loin cloth heavily stained with blood. A doctor rushed to the scene, but it was too late to save the victim. As Gandhi lay dying, the police took charge, dispersing the weeping crowds, carrying the body away.

At 6.00 p.m., on *All India Radio*, it was announced that a lone gunman had shot Gandhi on his way to Birla House. He had been killed by three pistol shots in his chest. The killer was Nathuram Godse, a Hindu activitist who was thought to be connected to the Hindu nationalist organization Mahasabha.

Godse was immediately taken into custody and was tried and convicted. He received a death sentence and was hanged on November 15, 1949. Four other conspirators, including Godse's brother Gopal, were given life sentences. The president of the Mahasabha, Vinayak Damodar Savarkar, was also thought to be behind the assassination, but there was not enough evidence to link him to it.

INSPIRED FREEDOM FIGHTERS

Not surprisingly, given the confusion of the assassination events, accounts differ as to what Gandhi actually said as he lay dying. Some attest that his last words were 'He Ram!' (Oh God!), which may have expressed his spiritual commitment to God, or – as some commentators have pointed out – could just be a horrified expression of surprise and shock on being attacked. Whatever the truth, these are the words that are inscribed on Gandhi's memorial tomb in New Delhi. Others believe that the Mahatma exclaimed 'Rama Rama' and that as he fell, he put his hands together in the gesture of 'namaste', a religious gesture symbolising love, respect and connection to others.

After his death, Gandhi was cremated on a funeral pyre as is the Hindu custom, and his ashes were collected in 20 urns. These were taken around India, and the ashes scattered among the waters of the country's great rivers, in accordance with Gandhi's wishes. Today, Gandhi is remembered in India as the architect of independence, and his philosophy of non-violence and civil disobedience is thought to have inspired freedom fighters around the world, including Martin Luther King Jr, the Dalai Lama, Nelson Mandela, Steve Biko and Aung San Suu Kyi. But according to Gandhi himself, his teachings were nothing new: as he often stated, 'Truth and non-violence are as old as the hills'.

Of all the freedom fighters, Gandhi is remembered as one of the greatest. Although he achieved tremendous political power, he remained steadfastly opposed to violence and committed to leading a simple, spiritual life. He had his critics, both those who opposed him politically and those who sought to discredit his personal morality; however, he still remains one of the towering figures of his generation.

HO CHI MINH

Ho Chi Minh is remembered in Vietnam as the freedom fighter and revolutionary who fought to liberate the country from the rule of French colonialism, and afterwards to maintain its independence by resisting the incursions of the Chinese and Japanese. In North Vietnam today, he is hero worshipped as 'Uncle Ho', and the capital city, formerly Saigon, has been named Ho Chi Minh City after him. However, there are also many today who regard him as an opportunist and authoritarian, whose communist policies have held back the country; moreover, they hold him responsible for the terrorist actions of the military force, the Viet Cong, during the invasion of South Vietnam, in which one million civilians were killed.

RESISTANCE FIGHTERS

Ho Chi Minh was born on May 19, 1890, in the village Hoang Tru. His name means 'he who enlightens'. His father, Nguyen Sinh Huy, was an educated man, a scholar who followed the philosophy of Confucius and worked as a teacher for the French colonial administration. As a fervent nationalist, Huy was extremely critical of the French and refused to learn the language, so he soon fell out with his employers and was forced to travel the country making a living as best he could.

Even though he had refused to learn French himself, Huy sent his son to a French *lycee* (or secondary school), hoping that this would help him in his struggle against the colonialists. And as it turned out, his hopes were justified: all three of his children grew up to be committed nationalists. Ho's sister, Bach Lien, obtained a post working for the French army and stole weapons from them for the resistance, until she was caught and sentenced to life imprisonment.

TRAVEL AND ADVENTURE

Ho began his career as a schoolteacher, but then changed direction and became a sailor. He travelled around the world, learning as much as he could about different ways of life, political systems and cultures. In Europe, he worked as a waiter, a cleaner and as a cook's assistant. A highly intelligent man, he used this time to absorb as much as he could about current affairs, and he was often seen studying in public libraries. He lived in London for a few years, where he was employed as a pastry chef in a big hotel, before settling in Paris in 1917. In Paris, he immersed himself in the writings of Karl Marx and others, and in 1920 he became a founder member of the French communist party.

During this period, Ho Chi Minh visited the Soviet Union, which inspired him to return to Vietnam to try to overthrow the colonial government there. A letter from that time reveals that he felt it the duty of all communists 'to make contact with the masses to awaken, organize, unite and train them, and lead them to fight for freedom and independence'. However, he was aware of the difficulties that lay ahead for him. As a communist, he would be arrested immediately once in Vietnam. So he decided instead to settle in China, on the border of Vietnam, and help to organize a group of exiled nationalists there.

BUILDING THE REVOLUTION

In 1923, Ho went to Guangzhou, China, to organize the Vietnam Revolutionary League and spent the next 20 years waiting for his chance to take control of his country. This was a difficult period for him. In 1931, he was arrested while in Hong Kong and spent six years in jail and contracted tuberculosis. He then travelled to the Soviet Union, where he made a slow recovery, before returning to China once more.

In September 1940, the Japanese invaded Vietnam. Because of the occupation of France by the Germans, the French were not in a position to fight back. They surrendered to the Japanese. Ho saw this as an opportunity to lead a nationalist resistance movement against the Japanese and began a military campaign against the new regime. He and his colleagues assembled a group of guerrilla fighters called the Viet Minh, which received support in the form of weapons and ammunition from the Soviet Union. In the wake of the bombing of Pearl Harbor, in which Japanese forces made a surprise attack on the US navy, the United States also began to support Ho's revolutionary army.

RULE OF TERROR

For the next five years, war raged in Indochina, until the horrific bombings of Hiroshima and Nagasaki put an end to Japanese resistance. In 1945, the Japanese surrendered to the Allies. Ho Chi Minh's moment had arrived. That same year, the Viet Minh proclaimed the Democratic Republic of Vietnam, although it was some time before this was recognized by foreign powers such as the USA. The Viet Minh went on to attempt to wipe out internal opposition by radical means, including executing rival nationalists and socialists, so that eventually they were the one party left in control. Hundreds of the Viet Minh's political opponents were brutally murdered, imprisoned or forced to flee the country. Thus, from the start, the new Democratic Republic was anything but democratic.

In 1949, the Chinese revolutionary leader Mao Zedong achieved victory over Chiang Kai Shek and established a communist regime in China. This gave vital support to Ho Chi Minh and his allies, who now had a solid base in China. From this point on, they were able to consolidate their gains in North Vietnam; however, the French remained in control of the south, where they installed the former Vietnamese emperor, Bo Dai, as head of state.

GUERRILLA WARFARE

The war between the Viet Minh and the French continued for seven years. It became increasingly unpopular in France, which was already beleaguered by massive economic and social problems in the aftermath of the World War II. Realizing that they needed to bring a swift end to the fighting, General Navarre of France and General Vo Nguyen Giap of the Viet Minh confronted each other in a huge battle at Dien Bien Phu. Navarre had thought the French easily capable of winning, but Giap assembled a mass of weapons and troops from China and Vietnam, and after a long fight, in which thousands of men were lost, the French surrendered.

After the French withdrawal in 1954, it was decided that Vietnam would be divided into North and South, the North to be ruled by Ho Chi Minh, and the South by the anticommunist Ngo Dinh Diem. The Vietnamese people were to be consulted about this arrangement through elections and would be free to live where they chose to. Ho saw the division of the country as a temporary measure; however, it soon became clear that Diem had other plans and had no intention of holding fair elections. Soon, the country was at war again, with the North Vietnamese guerrilla forces conducting terrorist raids in the South. Initially, Ho was against this strategy, arguing that the North Vietnamese should build support in the South; but later, he agreed to support it. In 1960, the National Front for the Liberation of South Vietnam, which became known as the Vietcong, was formed.

DEATH OF A HERO?

It was at this point that the US president, Lyndon B. Johnson, intervened. In 1964, he launched Operation Rolling Thunder. Its aim was to launch a direct attack on Vietnam, to destroy its economy and wipe out the communist regime there. Johnson envisaged that this would take a matter of weeks, but in fact he launched a three-year war, which turned out to be horrifically destructive. Millions of lives were lost, both Vietnamese civilians and American troops, and the issue bitterly divided American society, and world opinion, for many years to come.

In 1969, Ho Chi Minh died at his home in Hanoi. He was 79 years old and had witnessed some of the most turbulent events of the 20th century. He had given orders that his body should be cremated, but instead, after his death, his body was displayed in an open tomb. Since that time, he has become the centre of a personality cult that almost certainly would have appalled him. However, the current government of Vietnam has abandoned communism and no longer follows his economic and social policies.

Today, there is some controversy as to the legacy of Ho Chi Minh. Many believe him to be an international hero, a freedom fighter whose commitment and bravery helped him to liberate his country from tyranny. However, others point to the terrorist acts of the North Vietnamese forces under his command, and later, to some of the actions of his government, particularly the implementation of the Land Reform

Campaign, during which many supposedly anti-communist landlords were persecuted and murdered. Vietnamese exiles, who were forced to flee the country because of their opposition to the regime, also hold him responsible for ruining the country. Yet, there is no doubt that within Vietnam today, 'Uncle Ho', as he is called, is a heroic figure for the majority of the population, who continue to remember him with affection, respect and pride.

FRENCH RESISTANCE FIGHTERS

Some of the most courageous freedom fighters of all time fought for the French Reistance during World War II. These were individuals and groups who resisted the occupation of France, that began in 1940. Under the leadership of Marshal Petain, France had signed an armistice with Germany, dividing the country into occupied and unoccupied zones. Under this agreement, large parts of France were to be directly controlled by Germany, while the rest would be administered by the French government at Vichy. In addition, all Jewish people living in France would be delivered to the German concentration camps. While the French government collaborated with these plans, many found them morally unacceptable. They so began a campaign of resistance that lasted throughout the occupation.

A huge variety of resistance organizations and groups sprang up, and they did everything within their power to sabotage the Nazi regime: there were armed groups who attacked road and rail networks, helped prisoners to escape, printed underground newspapers and spied on the Germans to help the Allies' intelligence operations.

Penalty for resistance was high: anyone found involved in such activities could be tortured, shot or imprisoned for many years. However, despite these dangers, many brave men and women joined the French Resistance and fought to liberate France from its brutal Nazi oppressors.

ARREST AND EXECUTION

The most prominent leader of the French resistance was Charles de Gaulle, who escaped to Britain when the Nazis took over. Broadcasting from London, he made a memorable speech in which he pledged to continue fighting for the liberation of France, come what may. He said: 'Whatever happens, the flame of French Resistance must not and will not be extinguished.' However, in the early days of the occupation, resistance was disorganized and scattered. There were a few acts of sabotage, but the authorities acted quickly to arrest the culprits, and most people were too frightened of the Nazis to mount any organized resistance.

The first stirrings of organized rebellion came when secondary school students in Paris met to celebrate the Allied victory over the Germans in World War II. They held a small demonstration at the Arc de Triomphe on November 11, 1940. Next, a small group of lawyers and scientists began to publish an underground newspaper. The group, named 'Musée de l'Homme' and led by Boris Vilde, encouraged all French citizens to resist the occupation. However, it was not long before the group was infiltrated by a supporter of Petain's Vichy government. The members were rounded up, arrested and almost all of them executed.

ESCAPE TO THE FOREST

Not surprisingly, such a brutal response to the mildest expressions of dissent terrified most Frenchmen and women, and initially it was difficult to persuade anyone to resist. However, the Germans themselves began to make it almost impossible for any self-respecting person to live under the regime, and accordingly, more and more people joined the resistance. The notorious Gestapo began to hunt down communist and socialist sympathizers, most of whom escaped into the forests of the unoccupied zone, along with escaped soldiers from the French army. Here, they survived as best they could and began to plot their revenge.

BRAVERY AND MORAL COURAGE

The groups operating from the woods became known as the 'Maquis'. They started to organize attacks on the Nazis, especially its armed forces. In addition, they helped British air force pilots, who had been shot down in France, escape back to their country. In 1941, the Comité d'Action Socialiste was formed by Pierre Brossolette and Daniel Mayer, both radical members of the Socialist Party. Meanwhile, the Communist party, which for many years had been banned and had been working in secret, began to publish their newspaper

L'Humanité. The editor, Pierre Villon, published an editorial calling for a united national front to fight for French independence, and in 1942, the resistance group Front National was born.

Impressed by the bravery and moral courage of the resistance movement, several supporters of Petain's Vichy government now lent their support. These were the men who had hoped that a compromise could be found with the Nazis and had collaborated to avoid bloodshed and chaos in the land. However, realizing that the Nazis were committed to a full-scale extermination of the Jews and all individuals who resisted their regime in France, these early collaborators jumped ship. One of these was Henry Frenay, who formed the group Combat in 1941 and began to publish various newspapers, such as *Vérités* and *Les Petites Ailes*. At around the same time, Emmanuel d'Astier and Jean-Pierre Lévy became active, publishing clandestine newspapers and setting up the resistance groups Libération-sud and Francs-Tireur.

TORTURED BY THE GESTAPO

Another resistance fighter, Jean Moulin, travelled to London to meet with Charles de Gaulle, and returned with the aim of uniting all the different resistance groups working in France. He went on to meet all the leaders of the major resistance groups, including Pierre Brossolette of the Comité d'Action Socialist, Jean-Pierre Lévy of Francs-Tireur, Pierre Villon of the Front National, Emmanuel d'Astier of Libération, and

Charles Delestraint of the Armé Secrète. Moulin managed to persuade all these groups, with their different political viewpoints, to unite in the common cause of defeating the Nazi occupation in France, and on May 27, 1943, the first meeting of the Conseil National de la Résistance, as the umbrella group was called, met in Paris.

It was not long before the Nazis became aware of what was going on, and they began the task of hunting down, torturing and executing members of the resistance. On June 7, 1943, the Gestapo tracked down René Hardy, a leading resistance fighter. Hardy was tortured by the notorious Klaus Barbie of the Gestapo, whose brutality and sadism had earned him the nickname, 'the butcher of Lyon'. In the process, Barbie managed to extract information about the activities of Jean Moulin, Pierre Brossolette, and Charles Delestraint, three of the most important leaders of the resistance.

The Gestapo went on to arrest Moulin at Caluire-et-Cuire on June 21. Less than a month later, on July 8, Moulin died while being tortured. Pierre Brossolette was also tortured, and, afraid that he would give away the names of his comrades in the resistance, he threw himself out of the window of the prison where he was being held. He died on March 22, 1944. Finally, Delestraint was arrested, tortured and deported to Germany. There, he was held in Dachau before being shot dead on April 19, 1945.

ACTS OF SABOTAGE

The loss of these brave men was a severe blow to the resistance movement, but worse was to come. In December 1943, an officer named Joseph Darnard became chief of the secret police at Vichy. Darnard was a fanatical anticommunist, and the secret police, known as the Milice, was a hotbed of fascists who were more than willing to use torture and whatever other means necessary to root out resistance to the regime. Undeterred, in 1944 the Conseil National de la Résistance issued a charter demanding social and economic reforms after the defeat of the Germans and the liberation of France, which now seemed a distinct possibility.

As the Germans grew more afraid of losing the war, they mounted more and more vicious attacks on the local population, hoping to scare them into defending the Nazi regime and withdrawing their support for the resistance fighters. However, the citizens of France knew that Germany's time was up and that, with the help of the French Resistance, the Allies had a good chance of winning the war. Thus, the French responded to the Allies' calls for help and acts of sabotage increased: German garrisons were attacked, trains were derailed and ammunition depots were blown up.

BRUTAL REPRISALS

The German army began a campaign of reprisals in towns and villages where resistance attacks had taken place. For example, in the town of Tulle, resistance fighters had responded to a call for help by the Allies during the D-Day landings, so in revenge the Germans hanged 120 men there. In the Vercors plateau, a Maquis resistance group had fought 15,000 Waffen SS soldiers, suffering great losses in the process but slowing down the German forces. In retaliation, the German army, under the leadership of Major Otto Dickman, marched into the small mountain village of Oradour-sur-Glane and brutally murdered over 600 men, women and children before setting fire to the village.

After heavy fighting and many losses on both sides, the Germans finally surrendered and Charles de Gaulle gave the order for the French Resistance fighters to disband. In the aftermath of the war, in order to unite the country quickly and bury old resentments, de Gaulle did not glorify his comrades' role in the struggle. However, since that time, there have been many tributes paid to the French Resistance fighters, whether by politicians, writers or film makers, who remember their heroes' crucial role as freedom fighters in the dark days of France's occupation and collaboration during World War II.

CHARLES DE GAULLE

Charles de Gaulle is one of France's greatest heroes, as leader of the French Resistance during World War II. Operating from his base in Britain, de Gaulle was a tower of strength to the French people during the war years, and his courage, determination and skill was a major factor in helping the French Resistance forces and the Allies defeat the Germans at the end of the war.

After the war, de Gaulle oversaw the creation of the Fifth Republic and served as its president until 1969. Under his presidency, France rapidly regained strength and rebuilt its economy, becoming an important voice in Europe and an independent nuclear power. However, there were many who criticized de Gaulle's leadership, especially his handling of the war in Algeria, in which the Algerians were struggling to free themselves from French colonial rule. By the time he left office, France had become the scene of bitter social unrest, as a young generation of radicals sought to transform society from the bottom up. Yet despite his eventual unpopularity in many circles as a politician, few disputed the fact that in his early years de Gaulle was a courageous freedom fighter, who not only helped the French keep their self-respect and dignity during the dark years of the German occupation, but was instrumental in defeating the Nazis at the end of the war.

LEFT FOR DEAD

Charles André Joseph Marie de Gaulle was born in Lille to a wealthy Roman Catholic family. His father's family boasted aristocratic lineage, while his mother's were industrialists and entrepreneurs. Members of the family had also distinguished themselves as writers, historians and professors. Young Charles was raised in an atmosphere of patriotism, and his parents instilled in him conservative tastes, education and moral standards, but there was also a streak of liberalism running through the family, derived from their religious beliefs. Moreover, his parents were supportive and helpful to him throughout his life, which helped him develop the confidence and self-belief that so characterized his political life.

As a young man, de Gaulle chose to pursue a military career and attended the military academy at Saint-Cyr. He graduated in 1912 and went on to join an infantry regiment. Soon afterwards, World War I broke out, and de Gaulle joined the fighting. In 1916, he was badly injured at the Battle of Verdun, which has gone down in history as one of the bloodiest battles of the period. He lay abandoned and left for dead on the battlefield until German soldiers picked him up and took him prisoner. He recovered sufficiently to make five escape attempts, all of which were unsuccessful, and as a punishment, he was forced to endure solitary confinement for many months.

BRAVE SOLDIER

At the end of the war, de Gaulle decided to remain in military service, despite his horrifying experiences as a soldier and prisoner of war. In 1919, he volunteered to go to Poland to fight in the Polish-Soviet War, where he learned a great deal about the mechanics of modern warfare. In the process, he led several successful operations, and won the Virtuti Militari, the highest military decoration in the Polish army. He was also promoted and could have stayed in Poland, but chose instead to return to France, where he began to write articles and books about military strategy. His experience in Poland had convinced him that France needed to modernize its army into a highly mechanized, professional force; but there were few within the old guard who agreed with him, and accordingly, his career advancement suffered.

It was only de Gaulle's expertise and skill as a military strategist and leader during World War II that convinced his superiors that he should be promoted. After his success in forcing the German infantry to retreat at Caumont in May 1940, Prime Minister Paul Reynaud made him a Brigadier General, and he began to play an important role in the war. Before long, he was appointed Undersecretary of State for National Defence, and he worked with Britain to coordinate defence strategies against the Germans.

ENEMY FIRE

When Germany eventually occupied France, de Gaulle argued against surrendering. He was supported by the British government, under Winston Churchill. In an extraordinary bid to save his country from ruin, de Gaulle travelled to London and negotiated a political union between France and Britain, which effectively made them into one state until the war ended. He then went back to France with his plan, only to find that Marshal Petain had become leader of the government and was seeking an armistice with Germany.

Even though everything was balanced against him, de Gaulle refused to accept the situation and called for the war to continue. This meant rebelling against the government of Petain and would have landed him in jail. Thus, he was forced to flee the country. Taking a stash of secret funds with him, given to him by Paul Reynaud, de Gaulle left France by plane and managed to avoid enemy fire to land safely in London. From then on, he set about building a resistance to the Nazi regime from his base in Britain.

SENTENCED TO DEATH

De Gaulle's independent stance made him many enemies, not only among the Germans but among the Allies, but it also inspired the French to maintain a staunch resistance to the Nazis who had overrun their country. Churchill supported de Gaulle's initiative, and the BBC broadcast the famous speech in which he claimed, 'France has lost a battle; she has not lost the war'. For the many Frenchmen and women displaced by the war, with families fragmented and loved ones lost or killed, de Gaulle provided a much-needed focus for hope throughout the dark days that followed.

The French authorities, which then began to collaborate with the Germans, were quick to try to curb de Gaulle's influence. In 1940, he was sentenced to death, in his absence, for treason against the Vichy regime. It became clear that unless the Allies won the war against Germany, de Gaulle would never again be able to set foot in his native land.

FETED AS A HERO

In May 1943, de Gaulle moved out of London and set up his headquarters in Algiers. Here, he continued working for the liberation of France. The following year, as the Germans grew more desperate, the Allies were able to invade France and fight their way from Normandy to Paris. A few hours before the liberation of Paris, de Gaulle flew in from Algiers and joined the Allied forces to celebrate the end of the war. He addressed a cheering crowd and was feted as a hero.

However, de Gaulle was not one to rest on his laurels for long. Within a short time, he had moved back into his office at the War Ministry and had begun the long task of rebuilding France's ruined economy. In order to minimize conflicts between the many differing political factions, he downplayed the role of the French Resistance during the war, and it was not until many years later that the full details of what the freedom fighters had done emerged.

THE SIMPLE LIFE

After the war, de Gaulle served as the provisional government's president, and later went on to head the Fifth Republic. He became known as the architect of Gaullism, a political philosophy that emphasized the independence of France as a major power in Europe and the world. This stance left him with many detractors as well as supporters. However, he had little time for his opponents, or for the radical leftist politics that inspired the events of 1968 in France, and which led to massive social unrest and strikes throughout the country.

In 1969, de Gaulle left office and retired to his country house at Colombey-les-Deux-Eglises and began to write his memoirs, but only a year later he died suddenly of an aneurism. He was two weeks short of his 80th birthday and, surprisingly for a man of his importance, he left little in the way of money or property. According to his wishes, he was buried quietly at the local cemetery, rather than in a grand ceremony. He asked only that his friends from the liberation days should attend his funeral, rather than heads of state, who remembered him at a service at Notre Dame in Paris. He also ordered that his gravestone should only give his name and the dates of his life, rather than any fancy inscription.

Thus ended the life of one of France's greatest heroes: Charles de Gaulle, freedom fighter, who masterminded the French Resistance forces throughout the war, and refused to surrender to the evil regime of Nazi Germany, even when all was lost; and who later returned to rebuild his country after the ravages of war. The fact that his policies as president of the Fifth Republic later attracted controversy, and that by 1968 many regarded him as autocratic and illiberal – especially as a result of events in the Algerian war – has done little, over time, to detract from his central achievement: that he provided an important beacon of hope in France's time of despair and helped the Allies to win World War II.

JEAN MOULIN

Jean Moulin is a legendary hero of the French Resistance. During the German occupation of France, he showed extraordinary courage as a major figure in the French Resistance movement, and he survived torture at the hands of the Gestapo head, Klaus Barbie, only to meet a tragic death as a prisoner on his way to a concentration camp. Today, he is remembered as one of the greatest freedom fighters of all time and has become a symbol of patriotism and moral virtue in modern France.

PACIFIST AND RADICAL

Moulin was born the son of a history professor in Beziers, France, on June 20, 1899. His first experience as a soldier came in 1918 when, as a young man, he was conscripted into the French army. However, he was lucky enough to avoid the horrors of World War I, since it came to an end shortly before he saw active service.

Shortly after that, he began his civilian career in the French civil service. He was a brilliant young official and soon became the youngest 'prefect', or deputy mayor, in the country. However, it was during this time that he became politicized, influenced by a friend of his named Pierre Cot, who was a pacifist and a radical. When the Spanish Civil War broke out, Moulin joined the Republican cause, and his position in the 'prefecture' enabled him to help smuggle a French aeroplane to the Republicans to help in their war effort.

SUICIDE ATTEMPT

In 1940, the German army won their battle against the French in World War II and their troops invaded France. Moulin refused to surrender to the new regime, and accordingly was arrested and tortured by the Gestapo, the army's secret police force. During his stay in prison, he became so despairing that he tried to kill himself by cutting his throat, using a piece of glass. He was found before he bled to death, and was taken to the prison hospital, where he began the process of recovery. Later, he was released from prison.

By agreement with the Germans, an independent French government had been set up at Vichy, headed by Marshall Petain, a distinguished general from World War I. However, this government soon began to collaborate with the Nazis, helping to send French Jews to concentration camps and persecuting minority groups, as well as all kinds of political opponents. In November 1940, as a 'prefect', Moulin received instructions to dismiss all mayors in his region that had left-wing sympathies. He refused to do this, and so was given the sack from his own job.

SECRET RESISTANCE

At this point, Moulin was forced to go underground.
He began to organize different activist groups to
provide a united resistance against the German
invaders. His aim, like that of many others, was to
overthrow the Vichy government, which was well
known to have fascist sympathizers among its ranks,
and which had eagerly collaborated with the Nazis'
rule of terror. Moulin and his comrades ultimately
sought to drive the Germans out of France, with the
help of the Allies, especially Britain, and to liberate the
country from its oppressors.

In order to create an effective resistance movement,
Moulin began to make links with the leaders of groups
who had spoken out against the Nazis. He contacted
Henry Frenay, who had set up the group Combat, one
of the first and most significant resistance groups. In
addition, he met with Pierre Villon, who had been
active among the communist sections of the
opposition. Moulin himself was not a member of the
Communist Party, although he had close links with it.

COURAGE AND DANGER

In 1941, Moulin travelled to London to meet with
Charles de Gaulle, the figurehead of the French
Resistance movement, who had publicly stood out
against the surrender to the Nazi regime and had fled
to Britain to conduct the resistance from his base there.
Before the meeting, Moulin had prepared a report on

the situation in France, which he called *The Activities, Plans and Requirements of the Groups Formed in France*. De Gaulle was impressed by his knowledge and thought that Moulin was ideally placed to act as a unifying force for all the resistance groups operating in France. He asked Moulin to act in this capacity on his return, and to try to coordinate the efforts of all the groups to help oust the Germans. Moulin agreed to de Gaulle's request, despite the dangers that lay in wait for anyone trying to pull off such a task – and despite the difficulty of uniting groups that, in many cases, held very different political views.

On New Year's Day 1942, Moulin covertly entered France, dropped in by parachute from an aeroplane. With money contributed by the French Resistance movement in Britain, he set up an underground press. Working on the newspaper were figures such as the novelist Albert Camus. Over the next year, Moulin worked feverishly to bring the leaders of the resistance groups together, meeting with Pierre Brossolette of the Comité d'Action Socialiste, Emmanuel d'Astier of Libération, Charles Delestraint of the Armée Secrète, Pierre Villon of the Front National, Henry Frenay of Combat, and Jean-Pierre Levy of Francs-Tireur. After a great deal of hard work and persuasion on Moulin's part, these leaders formed the first united movement of the Free French in the country, named the Conseil National de la Résistance (CNR). The council secretly convened for their first meeting in Paris on May 27, 1943, and Jean Moulin took the chair.

THE BUTCHER OF LYONS

Obviously, this new initiative posed great dangers for everyone concerned. The Nazis had made it clear that they would tolerate absolutely no opposition of any kind to their regime, and those Frenchmen and women who had dared to speak out or act against it had been tortured, killed or sent to concentration camps. Thus, the meetings and discussions were conducted furtively, and each member was sworn to secrecy.

However, on June 7, 1943, one of the leading members of the resistance movement, René Hardy, was captured. He was personally tortured by none other than the notorious Klaus Barbie, head of the Gestapo in Lyon, and dubbed the 'Butcher of Lyons' because of his reputation for brutality. (Later, at his war crimes trial, Barbie was accused of having killed, or ordered the killing of, over 4,000 people, including women and children.)

BRUTAL TORTURE

The story goes that Barbie managed to extract information from Hardy that led to the arrest of Jean Moulin on June 21 at Caluire-et-Cuire in the Rhone region. Moulin had travelled to Caluire to meet with resistance leaders at the home of Dr Frederic Dugoujon. After being arrested, Moulin was taken to be tortured, once again by the 'Butcher of Lyon'. Legend has it that Moulin refused to give away any information at all concerning his comrades, and that as a result his torturers intensified their efforts, nearly killing him. The story goes that Moulin enraged Barbie during one session: for, instead of writing down the names of his comrades in the French Resistance movement, as Barbie had asked, Moulin merely sketched a caricature of his torturer and handed it back.

Moulin endured many days of torture at the hands of the sadistic Barbie, but never gave anything away about his colleagues in the French Resistance movement. After weeks of appalling torture in which his ribs were repeatedly broken, and he was scalded, burnt, kicked and punched, he was finally released and put on board a train to a concentration camp, where further horrors awaited him. However, by now, his body and spirit were broken, and he finally died on the train, near the town of Metz.

MOULIN'S LEGACY

After his death, Moulin was buried in the Pere Lachaise Cemetery in Paris. However, to honour his memory, in 1964 his ashes were moved to the Pantheon. Since that time, many universities, schools and other public institutions have been named after him, and today his story as one of the most courageous leaders of the resistance is part of French history, taught to successive generations of schoolchildren.

The role of René Hardy in the demise of Jean Moulin has recently been re-examined, generating a certain amount of controversy as to what actually happened at the time of the arrests. According to some sources, after being released by the Nazis, Hardy recklessly went to the meeting at the doctor's house in Caluire, thus leading the Gestapo to Moulin's door. Others believe that Hardy was collaborating with the Germans to avoid being tortured to death, and told the Gestapo where Moulin was. However, members of Hardy's family deny that this was the case, and maintain that Hardy never divulged any information to Barbie, despite horrific torture. Later, ex-German officer Erhard Dabringhaus confirmed this story, saying that Barbie had told him of Hardy's refusal to give away information leading to the arrest of Moulin.

Today, Jean Moulin's image has become an icon of French culture. Wearing his rakish hat and the scarf that covered the tell-tale scar on his neck (from when he had tried to commit suicide in prison), Moulin epitomizes the French Resistance fighter of the 1940s: independent, free and fearless in the face of the enemy.

THE CUBAN
REVOLUTION

The Cuban Revolution was one of the most important
political events of the 20th century. It took place from
1953 to 1959, during which time the regime of Fulgencio
Batista was overthrown, and a new government led by
Fidel Castro was formed. The fighting during this time
was intense, as Castro and his rebel leaders, including
Che Guevara, led their forces victory. During the
1960s, the newly established Marxist regime was the
subject of repeated attacks from the USA, all of which
the communist government managed to repel. Castro
himself was also the subject of many assassination
attempts by the CIA. Today, Cuba continues to
maintain its independence as a communist country,
despite massive social and economic problems, and
Castro – now an octogenarian – remains at its head as
an iron dictator.

GUERRILLA TACTICS

The revolution began on July 26, 1953, when a group
of around 160 guerrillas attacked the Moncada
Barracks in the town of Santiago de Cuba. The

Barracks was one of the headquarters of the Cuban army under the command of President Fulgencio Batista. Leading the attack were brothers Fidel and Raúl Castro, political activists who had denounced the Batista regime as corrupt and over-dependent on US corporate finance. The attack failed, and 61 rebels were killed in the fighting. Others were captured and tortured, while a mere handful survived, escaping into the countryside. Fidel and Raúl Castro were tracked down and arrested. They later received long prison sentences, but Batista eventually bowed to political pressure and exiled them instead. This turned out, in retrospect, to be a grave mistake.

The brothers went to Mexico, where they continued to plot the revolution, gathering a band of Cuban exiles around them – one of whom was Ernesto 'Che' Guevara – and training them in guerrilla tactics. Thus, the future leaders of the Cuban Revolution were not only political activists and intellectuals, but soldiers and fighters as well, which later gave them legendary status as heroic freedom fighters prepared to sacrifice their lives for the cause of liberating Cuba.

BLOODY EXECUTIONS

By November 1956, the group were ready to return to their homeland and free it from the tyranny of Batista. Sailing in a small ship called the *Granma*, they arrived later than they had hoped and were unable to co-ordinate their attack with riots and strikes in the country as planned. Instead, they made their way in secret into the mountains of the Sierra Maestra, but government troops caught wind of their arrival and attacked them, killing the majority of the rebels. Undeterred, the survivors tried to regroup, helped by local peasants who were sympathetic to their cause. Over time, this tiny band of men – which included Fidel and Raúl Castro, Che Guevara and Camilo Cienfuegos – also made links with political activists such as Frank Pais in Cuba's urban areas. Together, the rebels conducted raids on army garrisons throughout the Sierra Maestra until eventually they gained control of the mountain region. However, this was achieved with a great deal of bloodshed, including brutal executions of individuals loyal to Batista. Today, the fact that Che Guevara ordered many of these executions has caused some critics to cast doubt on his status as a hero. Those related to the victims see Guevara as a terrorist instead.

REBEL VICTORY

Goaded into action, Batista responded with an offensive called Operation Verano, deploying thousands of their soldiers against Castro's rebel army of only 200 or so. Incredibly, after a series of hard-won battles, Castro's guerrillas managed to defeat the army, much to the horror of the Batista government. Encouraged by their success, Castro and his men began their own offensive, fighting on several fronts with weapons taken from the government forces during the previous battles. Advancing from the mountains, one by one, the rebels captured villages and towns, ambushing and destroying Batista's forces as they went, and joining forces with other rebel groups along the way.

When the rebels finally managed to take the city of Santa Clara in the central region of the country, Batista realized it was all over. On New Year's Day 1959, he was smuggled out of Cuba bound for the Dominican Republic. His days as ruler of Cuba were over.

Once Batista had left, the army's morale crumbled, and Castro had no trouble in capturing the town of Santiago de Cuba, where his first attempt at revolution had failed six years before. When Guevara and Cienfuegos entered Havana, it was the same story: the army capitulated immediately. Shortly afterwards, Castro himself arrived in Havana, and a new president was instated: Manuel Urrutia Lleó, who had struggled against the Batista government along with the revolutionaries. However, it soon became clear that Urrutia was a mere figurehead, and the real leader of Cuba was Castro. In fact, only a few months later, Urrutia was removed from office for objecting to the injustices of the new regime.

A ROD OF IRON

The ensuing period of the revolution is one that many sympathizers would prefer to forget. The Castro brothers and Guevara set about rounding up as many officials of the Batista regime as they could, including officials, police and members of the armed forces. They were found guilty of war crimes in public trials, and executed by firing squads. Obviously, these actions had a pragmatic aim, to get rid of Batista sympathizers who might launch a counter-revolution: but the enthusiasm with which the revolutionaries pursued their course of summary justice appalled and revolted many who had hitherto been supporters of their cause.

It soon became clear that Castro was to rule the new Cuba with a rod of iron, and that no opposition to his regime would be tolerated. Many Cubans fled to the USA, where they planned a counter-revolution. They were helped by the US administration, which was highly alarmed at having a communist neighbour and whose interests had been damaged by the revolution. In 1961, these exiles mounted an invasion at the Bay of Pigs, but once again, Castro's forces prevailed, although losses on both sides were high. Not surprisingly, from this period on, relations between the USA and Cuba deteriorated, leading to the Cuban Missile Crisis in 1962, in which a nuclear standoff between the two countries, in the context of a tense Cold War climate, was narrowly averted.

VIGILANTE MILITIAS

In the years that followed, Castro and his government zealously carried out the reforms that had been promised by the revolutionaries. Lands and property held by the Roman Catholic Church were confiscated and many religious figures exiled, while foreign ownership of Cuban farmland was banned. Later on, this confiscated land was nationalized. In addition, a programme of land reform was put into action, forcing many agricultural workers into cooperatives, where they had to work hard for little reward. Many of those who disagreed with the new regime – including former rebel leaders – were executed or had to flee the country, remaining in exile for the rest of their lives.

Partly as a result of the US government's hostile attitude towards Cuba, as well as the exiled Cubans' attempts to re-invade the country, Castro remained fearful of counter-revolutionary activity. Accordingly, he set up vigilante militias to carry out surveillance in local communities, instructing his men to report on suspicious activity of any kind among the population. It was not long before people became afraid to speak out against the regime, and Castro effectively became a dictator, a position he has maintained until the present day.

THE LEGACY

Over the years, there has been a great deal of criticism of Castro's regime in Cuba, from those whose relatives were executed during the revolution, or from exiles whose property and businesses were taken away from them. Criticism has also come from commentators not personally involved in the upheaval, who point to the fact that Cuba is run in an entirely undemocratic way, and that human rights abuses are endemic there.

However, there is also another side to the story. Supporters of Castro's Cuba point to the reforms that have brought enormous benefits to the population, in terms of free health care, improved state education and a measure of social support for the poorest in Cuban society. These supporters also argue that the forces ranged against Castro have been enormous, forcing him to adopt a strong stance against counter-revolutionary activity. It is certainly the case that the CIA have repeatedly attempted to assassinate Castro and to effect a counter-revolution in Cuba. In addition the disenfranchised Cuban middle classes, exiled in the USA, have mounted a formidable opposition to the regime.

Whatever the pros and cons of the Cuban revolution, it is clear that Fidel Castro and his small band of revolutionary comrades showed remarkable courage and determination in their fight to lead their country to independence and that – at least in the early days – they were indeed freedom fighters with a vision of a better future for the people of their nation. The fact that they succeeded against all odds in overthrowing the old regime remains an extraordinary achievement, and one that will always be remembered, not only in Cuba, but around the world, even if subsequent events have tarnished their reputation.

FIDEL CASTRO

Since 1959, Fidel Castro has been the president of Cuba, making him the longest serving head of state in the world today. In his early days as a freedom fighter, he promised to liberate his country, but today he is a [virtual] dictator, overseeing all aspects of life there, and forbidding all political opposition. At the same time, during his regime he has instigated significant social and economic reforms, such as land redistribution, free health care and state education, that have brought great benefits to the people of the country. Thus, although Cuba is no longer a democracy in any meaningful sense of the word, progress has been made in tackling poverty and ill health among the poorest sections of the population. In recent years, as he becomes an octogenarian, Castro's health has been failing, and there has been much speculation as to how fit he is to run the country. His brother Raúl, who helped him seize power as a freedom fighter in the Cuban Revolution, has been named as Castro's successor.

REBEL SPIRIT

Castro began life in 1926 as the illegitimate son of a sugar plantation owner. He was known for his rebellious spirit from a young age, and by the time he entered his teens he had organized a strike of the workers on his father's plantation. Neither of his parents could read or write, but they recognized the value of education, and sent Fidel to a Jesuit boarding school. The strict discipline of the school was anathema to the young rebel, but he found an outlet for his energy in sport. He loved baseball, football and running, and won a prize as the best all-round athlete in the school. He was not so enamoured of school work, and only showed enthusiasm for history. However, he was intelligent, and despite his lack of application, he managed to leave school with enough qualifications to study law.

After qualifying as a lawyer, Castro set up a practice in Havana, where he worked on behalf of poor clients, which restricted his own income. His work during this period opened his eyes to the injustices of the social system in Cuba: the few had great wealth, while the majority lived in abject poverty. Moreover, the richest people in the country tended to be foreigners, especially Americans, who were there to make a profit for themselves and had no interest in helping the people of Cuba whatsoever. The president of the country, General Fulgencio Bastista, had allowed this situation to persist for many years, letting foreigners extract wealth from the country while the people starved. In addition, Batista presided over a corrupt administration where his family, friends and political followers lined their own pockets instead of considering the general good of the nation.

FAILED REVOLUTION

Working as a lawyer, Castro soon became involved in politics and joined the Cuban People's Party in 1947. He became a candidate for the congress of the party, and revealed himself to be an effective public speaker. The Cuban People's Party, which spoke out against government corruption and foreign domination of economic interests in the country, began to attract a large following, especially among young people. However, in the elections of 1952, Batista became afraid that Cuban People's Party would win, and instead of allowing free and fair elections, he conducted a military coup and banned all opposition to his regime.

From this point on, Castro became convinced that the only way a just regime in Cuba could come about was through revolution. He and his comrades set about sabotaging the army garrisons of the country, beginning with an attack at the Moncada barracks. This first attempt at insurgency was an abject failure: out of 123 men and women, most were captured and many of them killed. Castro too was caught, along with his brother Raúl, who had helped mount the attack. The pair were lucky to escape with their lives. They were both convicted of treason and received long prison sentences. However, the trial attracted a great deal of attention to their cause, both in Cuba and worldwide, especially as Castro made an impassioned speech about the problems of the nation, which was later published under the title *History will Absolve Me*.

GUERRILLA WARFARE

After Castro had served two years of his sentence, President Batista bowed to public opinion and released him from prison. Realizing that he would not be able to fight his opponent in a democratic election, Castro went to Mexico to plot a revolution, returning in 1956 to set up camp in the Sierra Maestra region of the country, along with comrades such as Juan Almeida and Ernesto 'Che' Guevara. The group were attacked by Batista's forces and reduced to only 16 men, but Castro was undeterred, and he began to build up support among the local peasant population, as well as a supply of weapons. By seizing and protected lands for the peasants, the guerrillas earned the people's loyalty; and, as Batista's forces tortured and murdered the peasants in retaliation, support for the revolutionaries grew. By 1958, professional people in towns and cities had joined the July 26 Movement, as it became known, so that now Castro had the support of the middle classes as well as the peasantry.

For the next few years, civil war raged in Cuba as Batista launched a major offensive to wipe out the revolutionary forces. He marshalled thousands of troops to track down the guerrillas, who numbered less than 400. However, despite the disparity in numbers, Batista's offensive failed. Many of his troops began to join the revolutionary cause and it soon became clear that he had lost the support of the majority of his people. With Batista's forces demoralized and in disarray, Castro and his men were able to march on towns and cities and capture them. Soon, there was nowhere left for Batista to hide, and he was forced to flee the country.

BRUTAL EXECUTIONS

Amid much jubilation, Castro took over control of Cuba. From 1959, his government began to institute major reforms, confiscating land from foreign land-owners and redistributing it among the peasants, nationalizing utilities, setting up schools to lower the high rate of illiteracy, and creating one of the best free health care services in the developing world. Castro also closed down Cuba's notorious night clubs and casinos, which were largely run by the Mafia, forcing the black marketers to leave the country. More contro-versially, Castro set up public courts to try members of the Batista regime for war crimes, and hundreds of former officials were executed in a manner that horrified world opinion.

The USA's interests in Cuba had been badly damaged by the revolution, and the US government was also afraid that Castro would join forces with the Soviet Union. Thus, the USA began a programme of sanctions against Cuba, and the CIA followed it up with a series of hare-brained attempts to assassinate Castro. These efforts were supported, and in some cases bankrolled, by the many middle-class Cuban exiles living in the USA, who had lost money as a result of the revolution. In 1961, convinced that Castro had become unpopular and could be easily overthrown, an attempt was made to invade Cuba at the Bay of Pigs, but the Americans were proved wrong, and the attack was an abject failure.

NUCLEAR CRISIS

Meanwhile, the Cold War was growing more intense, and the USA began to suspect that communist Cuba now had a nuclear arsenal and was receiving nuclear weapons from the Soviet Union. After much discussion, the USA decided to impose a naval blockade, to stop Soviet ships from reaching the country. This was the nearest the world had come to nuclear war, and all eyes were on the crisis. At the last minute, the Soviets ordered their ships to turn back and disaster was averted.

With the USA and the Cuban exiles now ranged against him, Castro became more and more intolerant of political dissent within the country, and he stopped holding free and fair elections. In addition, political opponents were silenced, and, in keeping with his moralistic outlook, libertarian writers, homosexuals and others were imprisoned. The regime that had achieved so much in terms of improving the lives of the poorest people in society seemed unable to sustain a real democracy, and instead became dictatorial, relying on the Soviet Union for support. The situation further deteriorated when, in 1989 the Soviet Union crumbled, and Cuba suffered a major economic crisis.

CASTRO'S LEGACY?

In 2006, after rumours that he was suffering from cancer, from Parkinson's disease or the effects of a series of small strokes, Castro underwent a serious health crisis that necessitated gastric sugery. During his illness, he ceded power to his brother Raúl, but many commentators believe that, on his recovery, he will take charge of running the country once more. However, it is clear that this situation cannot persist indefinitely, and that Castro's 47-year-old regime must soon come to a close. When that happens, there will be many waiting to see what the future holds for Cuba, and what the legacy of Fidel Castro will be.

JOMO KENYATTA

Jomo Kenyatta is one of the world's most famous freedom fighters and a hero of the African continent. After taking part in Kenya's struggle to gain independence in 1963, during which he was imprisoned by the British colonial administration as a suspected member of the rebel guerrilla group the Mau Mau, he became the country's first prime minister, and went on to serve as president for over a decade.

POLITICAL REBEL

Kenyatta was born Kamau wa Ngengi in the small village of Ichaweri, in the central province of what was then known as British East Africa. His parents died when he was young, and he became an assistant to his grandfather, a medicine man. He was educated by Scottish missionaries and became a Christian, taking the name of John Peter. Later, he changed his name to Johnstone Kamau, reflecting both the African and the British aspects of his background.

As a young man, he lived in Nairobi, and then moved to Narok, a provincial town in South West Kenya, just as the World War I was breaking out. Here, he lived with people of the Masai tribe, who were relatives of his, and found work first as a clerk and then as an official of the Nairobi City Council's water department. During this time, he met and married his first wife, Grace Wahu, and the couple had a child, Peter Muigai. He also became involved in politics, in particular the efforts of the Kikuyu tribe to resist the colonial rule of the country by the British, which had begun in 1952.

CONFLICT DEEPENS

The Kikuyu were at the centre of a bitter dispute with the British rulers, because a great deal of their land had been appropriated by the government. The Kikuyus' ancestral lands were some of the most fertile in the country, being in the central highland area where the weather had a cooler climate. After the takeover of the country by the British, the best land went to European settlers, while the most of the tribespeople were forced to farm small plots as tenant farmers and were largely unable to earn a proper living. As a result, many of them moved to towns and cities to find work, where they lived in abject poverty. There were a few Kikuyu, however, who managed to hold onto their lands and were protected by the British. This rift, between the poverty-stricken masses and the privileged few, led to tremendous conflict between the Kikuyu themselves, as well as intense hatred among the black tribesmen of the white Europeans who had taken over their lands.

Kenyatta became a leading member of the Kikuyu Central Association (KCA), which had been formed to redress the situation and restore rights to the Kikuyu. In 1929, he was sent to London in the UK, as a KCA representative to find out whether the group could gain support there. He began to write articles about the Kenyan situation for British newspapers, and for the next few years, he continued his education in Europe. For a short time, he studied at Woodbroke Quaker College in Birmingham, then spent a year in Moscow studying economics under a scheme funded by the Comintern to educate black workers. He was sponsored during this period by a Trinidadian communist, George Padmore, but Padmore then argued with the Soviet Communist Party and Kenyatta had to move back to London.

FORMATIVE PERIOD

In 1935, Kenyatta spent a formative period studying social anthropology at the London School of Economics, under the famous anthropologist Bronislaw Malinowski, all the while continuing his political work and meeting many influential activists and intellectuals, including the Caribbean writer C. L. R. James and the black American actor Paul Robeson. He even appeared as an extra in one of Robeson's films, *Sanders of the River*, directed by Alexander Korda.

With the outbreak of World War II, Kenyatta was faced with being conscripted into the British army, but instead found work labouring on a farm in Sussex. Once again, he was accumulating valuable experience for his future role as a freedom fighter, and he took the opportunity to give lectures on the subject of Africa to the local Workingmen's Association. He also met and married an Englishwoman, Edna Clarke, and had another son, Peter Magana. However, after the war, he returned to Kenya and married again, this time to an African woman, Grace Wanjiku. In 1950, his wife gave birth to a daughter, Jane Wambui, but sadly, she died of complications in childbirth. His next wife, whom he married in 1951, was Ngina Muhoho.

VIOLENT CLASHES

Kenyatta had returned to his country with a purpose: to rid Kenya of the British colonial administration, and to restore the tribespeople their lands, especially the Kikuyu whose whole way of life had been destroyed by the European settlers. As a well-educated, political figure, he took up a position at Kenya Teachers College and set up the Pan-African Federation, a multinational organization that worked to establish independence for Kenya. He also became President of the Kenya African Union (later the Kenya African National Union, KANU), whose aim was to work for the advancement of all the tribes in Kenya. Because of his close ties with the Kikuyu, Kenyatta had been accused of favouring this tribe at the expense of others, and he now wanted to make clear that his political activism was not biased towards any particular tribal group in Kenya.

This was an intensely troubled time in the country, with constant clashes between the guerilla arm of the

Kikuyu, known as the Mau Mau, and the white settlers, who felt entitled to protect the land they had worked so hard to farm. During this period, Kenyatta often received death threats from white farmers, and he was also accused by the government of involvement in the violent activities of the Mau Mau. In 1952, he was arrested by the government and the following year, he was tried, convicted and sentenced to seven years' hard labour in prison. After his imprisonment, he was exiled to Lodwar, a town in a remote part of North West Kenya.

STATE OF EMERGENCY

Meanwhile, because of the fighting between the Mau Mau and the white settlers, a state of emergency had been declared by the government, which was lifted in 1960.After this, leading political figures began to demand the release of Kenyatta, whom they claimed had not been an instigator of the violence. He was even elected President of the KANU while he was in exile. In 1961, as a result of this pressure, Kenyatta was released and became a leading black politician.

When Kenya finally became independent in 1963, Kenyatta emerged as one of the most popular candidates in the elections, and he went on to become the Prime Minister of the first national government. However, Kenya's problems were far from over. There was strong pressure to force out the white communities who had prospered under the colonial government. However, Kenyatta supported some of the claims of the white settlers and thought that they should continue to remain in the country. He also wanted to retain many of the administrative class, for example white civil servants. He realized that these people had settled and worked in Kenya for many years and had a right to remain there, but he was also conscious that a great deal of expertise resided in these communities, and that it would be difficult to run the country without them. However, there were many who disagreed, and fighting continued, so much so that Kenyatta had to ask the British for troops to put down several uprisings among ethnic groups and mutinies in the army.

POWER AND CORRUPTION

The process of land reform after the country's declaration of independence was complex and difficult, but Kenyatta managed to oversee it with a minimum of bloodshed and violence. He was also able to sign important trade agreements with other African nations, including Uganda and Tanzania, and to attract foreign investment from the West. However, his autocratic style of government came under severe criticism, and he was accused of allowing corrupt practises within his administration, especially in regard to land ownership. In particular, he was said to favour people from his own tribe, the Kikuyu.

As his regime continued, Kenyatta himself began to amass a great deal of personal wealth and became the nation's largest landowner; in addition, he began to expand his political power by making changes to the country's constitution. His security forces took to harassing his political opponents, and several deaths of prominent political figures occurred, which were alleged to have been murders committed by Kenyatta's men. Soon KANU, his party, was the only functioning political party in the country, and this situation persisted until 1978, when Kenyatta died and was succeeded by Daniel arap Moi.

NATIONAL HERO

Thus, by the end of his life, Kenyatta had become an illiberal, autocratic ruler with a corrupt government that brooked no opposition. However, the fact remains that in his early years he was a national hero, who had dedicated his life to the cause of independence for Kenya and had been successful in his aim. Kenyatta had undergone a long prison sentence for his beliefs, and he had been courageous in maintaining his opposition to the colonial regime over many years. For these reasons, today he is seen as Kenya's greatest freedom fighters, and a hero of African independence.

NELSON MANDELA

Nelson Mandela is one of the most respected statesmen in the world. His long, turbulent career has been one of great personal sacrifice and courage, as he and his fellow nationalists struggled to overthrow apartheid in South Africa, replacing it with a multiracial democracy. When South Africa finally achieved independence, he won a triumphant victory as head of the African National Congress (ANC) and became the country's president. Today, he has stepped down from this role, but continues to work as South Africa's most prominent ambassador. He has been criticized for some of his opinions, but in general, he is held in great affection by most South Africans. He also commands tremendous respect across the world as one of the great freedom fighters of the 20th century, who dared to challenge the evil of apartheid and won a resounding victory against it, at immense personal cost.

POLITICAL ACTIVISM

Nelson Mandela was born Rolihlahla Dalibhunga, a member of the Madiba tribal clan. The village where he grew up was called Mvezo, in the eastern Cape region of South Africa. His father, Gadla Henry

Mphakanyiswa, was a counsellor for the royal leaders of the Thembu people, a post that Mandela would have inherited had he remained at home. His mother was Nosekeni Fanny, who was his father's third wife. His name, Rolihlahla, meant 'one who brings trouble to himself', which was certainly apt, as it turned out.

Mphakanyiswa had a total of 13 children. When Mandela was seven, he was sent to a Methodist school where he was given the name 'Nelson', after Admiral Nelson of the British Navy. Two years later, when he was nine, Mandela's father died of tuberculosis, and he was adopted, along with the rest of his siblings, by the royal leader of the Thembu, Chief Jogintaba Dalindyebo.

Now under the wing of the chief, Mandela continued his education and eventually gained a place at Fort Hare University, where he met Oliver Tambo, who was to become a lifelong friend. Along with other students, they organized a strike against the apartheid policies of the university. Mandela was expelled, but instead of returning home, where his guardian had arranged a marriage for him, he went to live in Johannesburg, finding work there as a guard in the mines. Later, he worked in a lawyer's office, completed his degree and began to study law. During this time, he became involved in the African National Congress (ANC), mounting protests against apartheid laws, and he opened a practice where poor black people could seek legal representation at little or no cost.

LIFE IMPRISONMENT

In 1956, Mandela was arrested and charged with treason. Along with 150 others, he was tried and acquitted. When he was freed, he went back to his political activities, this time trying to broaden the base of the ANC by alliances with white, coloured and Indian groups. This led to splits in the party, and in response Mandela went on to form a guerrilla wing of the ANC, Umkhonto we Sizwe (Spear of the Nation), calling on all the groups to resist apartheid.

In 1960, the ANC was banned and Mandela could no longer stay in South Africa, so he went to other countries in Africa to try to attract further support for the anti-apartheid cause. The situation in South Africa was worsening as the government there introduced new pass laws to restrict the movement of black people around the country. That same year, 69 black people were killed by police in the Sharpeville massacre. Mandela, who up until that point had advocated nonviolent resistance, now returned to his homeland and launched a new offensive of sabotage against the country's economy, by force if necessary.

FREEDOM CAMPAIGN

It was not long before Mandela was arrested and charged with sabotage. At his trial, he defended himself and remarked that he was prepared to die for his ideals. However, despite attracting a great deal of respect around the world for his courageous stand, he was sentenced to life imprisonment in 1964. Thus began one of the most dispiriting periods of his career, during which he was imprisoned on Robben Island for 18 years, followed by a spell at Pollsmoor Prison on the mainland. During this time, he was not allowed to attend the funerals of his mother, or his eldest son, who was killed in a car crash. In addition, hundreds of schoolchildren died during an uprising to protest against apartheid. Yet all Mandela could do was to watch and wait.

There was light at the end of the tunnel, however, as Mandela's friend Oliver Tambo, who was living in exile abroad, began to organize a campaign to free him. The world community was also becoming more and more critical of the South African government, and in 1967 it imposed sanctions on the country to try to pressurize it into adopting more liberal laws. These were tightened over the years, and in 1980, the policy finally had an effect, when President F. W. de Klerk lifted the ban on the ANC and released Mandela from prison.

VIOLENCE AND TURMOIL

Realizing that the policy of apartheid was under extreme pressure from the rest of the world, the South African government now began talks with the ANC as to how to bring about a multiracial democracy in the country. However, fighting then broke out between the ANC and the Zulu political group, Inkatha Freedom Party, led by Chief Buthelezi. Tension mounted as Ikatha's raids on the ANC began to find support from white police forces, but Mandela and de

Klerk continued to try to find a solution to the problems besetting the movement towards unity.

Mandela's personal life was also in turmoil as he divorced his second wife Winnie. His first wife, Evelyn Mase, whom he had married in 1944, had borne him three children. However, the marriage had broken down, largely because of his long periods of absence from home. In 1958, Mandela had married again, this time to Winnie Madikizela, who had steadfastly campaigned for his release during his long years of imprisonment. However, during that time she had become part of a corrupt, lawless band of thugs, and she had been convicted of kidnapping and violence. Mandela decided to divorce her as a result, both to clear his own name and because the relationship had irretrievably broken down.

THE END OF APARTHEID

After his release, Mandela had decided to try to work in tandem with the South African government to negotiate a peaceful transition towards a multiracial democracy. His policy of sabotage had only been a last resort in response to the government's oppressive apartheid system, and when the government lifted the ban on political activism, he began to pursue a policy of nonviolence once more. This strategy proved successful, and great progress was made in the years that followed. In 1993, Mandela and President de Klerk of the National Party were jointly awarded the Nobel Peace Prize.

Eventually, the day that Mandela had been waiting for finally arrived as South Africa held its first multi-racial democratic elections in 1993. The ANC won a majority in the National Assembly, and Mandela became president of the country, amid great jubilation both at home and worldwide. However, it soon became clear that South Africa faced huge economic and social problems, which the incoming government were expected to resolve immediately. Once it became obvious that they could not do so overnight, disillusionment set in, and fighting in the poor townships and slum areas of the cities continued.

AMBASSADOR FOR PEACE

Mandela took it upon himself to act as an ambassador for his country, persuading foreign investors to remain in South Africa, and thus helping to stabilize the economy. Meanwhile, his deputy, Thabo Mbeki, struggled to deal with the pressing problems of poverty, ill health, illiteracy, violence and drug abuse in the country's urban areas, especially in Johannesburg, which continues to be one of the most violent cities in the world.

In 1997, Mandela stepped down from the presidency of the ANC, handing over power to his successor Thabo Mbeki. Two years later, as the ANC celebrated a landslide victory in the South African elections, Mandela retired from his role as president of the country. He had been diagnosed with prostate cancer, and although he had received treatment for this, his health was failing. He also expressed a wish to spend more time with his family and in 'quiet reflection'. On his 80th birthday, he married his third wife, Graca Machel, the widow of the former president of Mozambique.

Today, Mandela is respected across the world as a great elder statesman. He continues to travel as an ambassador for various causes, especially that of AIDS, which claimed one of his sons, Makgatho Mandela, and which he feels he did not take seriously enough as an issue in his former days as president. In his own country, he is known as 'Madiba', an honorary title derived from his tribe. Others call him 'Mkhulu', meaning 'Grandfather', to show their respect and affection for the man who kept the faith, helped to overthrow apartheid and brought freedom to the people of South Africa.

CHE GUEVARA

Ernesto Guevara de la Serna, nicknamed 'Che', is perhaps the most famous freedom fighter of the 20th century. An Argentian, he helped Fidel Castro to lead the Cuban Revolution in 1959, and then moved on to lead revolutions in the Congo and in Bolivia, where he met his death in 1967. Since that time, he has become a potent symbol of socialism and revolution throughout the world.

EASY RIDER

Guevara was born in Rosario, Argentina, in 1928, into an upper-class family of mixed Irish and Spanish descent. Accounts differ as to the exact date of his birth. He was the eldest of five children, and even as a boy he was known for his charismatic, rebellious personality. He was highly intelligent and excelled at chess, which he had learned from his father. He was also a keen poet and read widely. Not only this, he was a skilled athlete and rugby player, even though he suffered badly from asthma. He was also a talented amateur photographer.

In 1948, he enrolled as a medical student at the university in Buenos Aires. During this time, he decided to take a year-long motorcycle trip around South America with a student friend, Alberto Granado. Their aim was to offer volunteer help at a leper colony in Peru. During the trip, Guevara wrote a detailed diary of events, *The Motorcycle Diaries*, in which he outlined his idealistic vision of a united Latin America, free from the poverty and injustice that he witnessed all around him.

ARMED STRUGGLE

When Guevara returned to Argentina, he completed his medical studies and set off on his travels around Latin America once more. In 1953, his visit to Guatemala coincided with a period of great social change in the country, in which a populist government headed by Jacobo Arbenz Guzmán was attempting to make radical reforms. Because of this, he decided to stay and become part of the revolution. In Guatemala City, he met various leading socialists, including Hilda Gadea Acosta, a Peruvian economist, whom he later married. It was also during this time that he gained the nickname 'Che', because of his habit of using this expression (meaning 'mate' or 'pal') learned in his native country.

In 1954, a coup was mounted against the Guatemalan government by Carlos Castillo Armas, with help from the CIA. During the fighting that ensued, Hilda Gadea was arrested, and Guevara fled to the Argentinian consulate for safety. Then, instead of accepting an offer of repatriation from the embassy, he decided to move on to Mexico and continue his revolutionary activities there. His experience in Guatemala had convinced him that American imperialism was a reality, and that the USA would block any attempts by countries around the world to bring down capitalism and improve conditions for the poor. Accordingly, he resolved to fight American imperialism by armed struggle, and he turned his attention to military techniques in guerrilla warfare.

THE 'SUICIDE SQUAD'

When Guevara arrived in Mexico, he made contact with other revolutionaries, such as Raúl and Fidel Castro from Cuba. Guevara was extremely impressed by Fidel Castro, and joined the brothers' revolutionary group, The 26 July Movement, which had pledged itself to overthrow the regime of Fulgencio Batista. He began to train as a soldier and emerged as his instructor's most brilliant student. As Jean-Paul Sartre later said of him, Guevara was one of the most 'complete human beings' of the 20th century, who seemed to be able to excel at everything he engaged in, whether poetry or guerrilla warfare.

Guevara was joined in Mexico by Hilda Gadea, and when she became pregnant, the couple married. In 1956, Gadea gave birth to their daughter, Hilda Beatriz. The same year, Guevara left for Cuba on the ship *Granma*, with the intention of overthrowing the Batista regime there and installing Fidel Castro as the new president. It was an extraordinarily ambitious plan, and at first, it seemed highly unlikely to succeed. Immediately the small revolutionary band arrived in the country, they were attacked by Batista's men, and most of them were killed or captured. Of the original group, only about 20 survived, fleeing to the mountains of the Sierra Maestra. There, they worked hard to build a revolutionary movement with the support of the local peasants and covert political activists within the towns and cities. Now a soldier rather than a doctor, Guevara and his men showed tremendous bravery, and they became known as the 'suicide squad' for their daring raids. However, Guevara also revealed a ruthless streak that struck fear into his enemies and earned him the reputation, in some circles, as a cold-blooded killer.

THE EXECUTIONER

In 1959, the revolutionaries overthrew Batista, and Castro took over control in Cuba. Guevara was feted as a hero of the revolution and made a Cuban citizen. The next episode of his life is perhaps the most controversial. In his new role as head of the prison at La Cabana, Guevara presided over the trials of many former members of the Batista regime, and he had hundreds of the prisoners executed by firing squad. No political dissent was tolerated, and many of the trials were unjust. His name came to be feared, and many middle-class Cubans fled to the USA, terrified of meeting the same fate. During this time, Guevara also divorced his former wife and comrade Gadea and married a Cuban woman, Aleida March, with whom he went on to have four children. In 1964, he also had an illegitimate child, Omar Perez, with his mistress Lilia Rosa Lopez.

Not content with settling in Cuba, Guevara now began to plot revolutions in Panama and the Dominican Republic. Neither of these was successful. He wrote several articles and books, outlining his theory that revolution could be effected by small guerrilla groups led by a new kind of soldier/intellectual, and became a prominent figure in Cuba. However, Guevara's continued radical political stance, advocating armed struggle against world capitalism in all countries, caused a great deal of controversy, and eventually he quarrelled with Castro and disappeared from public life.

FAILED REVOLUTIONS

For the next two years, there was much speculation as to the whereabouts of Guevara, but in 1965 it was announced that Guevara was about to lead a revolutionary offensive in the Congo, in support of Patrice Lumumba. The expedition was a total failure in every way, as Guevara recorded in his Congo Diaries. Guevara felt that he could not go back to Cuba, having pledged himself to leading revolutions around the world in an open letter to Castro, and thus he spent the next few years living clandestinely, writing books and preparing to lead his next revolutionary initiative: in Bolivia.

As it turned out, the Bolivian offensive of 1967 was equally unsuccessful. Without the guiding hand of

Castro to calm his revolutionary fervour, Guevara made a number of mistakes. He found himself unable to work with local leaders in the area, or to attract support from the local population. In addition, he had not taken account of the CIA's involvement in training the Bolivian army and supplying it with weapons for the conflict. On 8 October, he was captured in his guerrilla encampment in the Quebrada del Yuro ravine, and he surrendered after being shot in the legs. The Bolivian soldiers took him to an abandoned schoolhouse in the village of La Higuera, where he was executed.

THE LEGACY

After his execution, his body was taken to the town of Vallegrande, where it was displayed to the press. Then, a military doctor cut off both the corpse's hands, and the corpse was taken to an undisclosed location and buried. On October 15, Castro announced the death of Che Guevara and ordered three days of public mourning for his former comrade.

After his death, Guevara became a potent symbol for a rising generation of young people who were critical of Cold War politics and who were forging a counter-culture of their own. Despite the fact that, according to many of his exiled compatriots, Guevara was a ruthless, cold-blooded killer who would not tolerate any form of political opposition to his views, he was admired by many liberals as a freedom fighter who had given up the comforts of a bourgeois family life and political power to continue his task as a revolutionary in other countries around the world. Eventually, his image, captured in the photograph taken by Korda at a memorial service, began to lose its political significance altogether, and he came to be seen as a romantic figure, much to the irritation of both his supporters and critics.

Today, the legacy of Guevara is a controversial one. Some see him as a hero of the 20th century, a guerrilla fighter who was also a brilliant intellectual: indeed, an all-round 'renaissance man'. Others see him as a cold-blooded killer, and point to his failures in managing the Cuban economy and leading the revolutions in the Congo and in Bolivia. Yet others know him only as an iconic figure, from the photograph of him taken by Alberto Korda, which has been called, 'the most famous photograph in the world'. But whatever the truth, Che Guevara deserves to be known today as one of the most significant political figures of the 20th century, not just a decorative image on a T-shirt, poster or coffee cup.

MARTIN LUTHER KING JR

Martin Luther King Jr is perhaps the greatest of all freedom fighters, whose name has gone down in history as one of the heroes of our time. His vision of a world in which all people, black and white, would be equal, inspired the civil rights movement of the 1960s, giving rise to radical changes in the USA's economic, social and political life. Tragically, his life was cut short when he was assassinated in 1968 by a lone gunman, an escaped prisoner named James Earl Ray. Some suspected the involvement of government security services, and various other theories were advanced, but whatever the reason for his assassination, it was a massive blow to the liberal cause and ushered in a period of disillusionment with the American Dream which has persisted to this day.

PERSONAL COURAGE

Martin Luther King Jr was born Michael King in Atlanta, Georgia. During his early years, his parents changed his name from Michael to Martin. His father was a Baptist minister and his mother a teacher. As a young man, he decided to follow his father into a career as a minister, and after studying for several years, he received a doctorate. His first job was as a minister in Montgomery, Alabama. In 1953, King married Coretta Scott, and the couple went on to have four children, all of whom eventually became civil rights activists.

King had a charismatic personality and a great deal of energy, commitment and enthusiasm for his task. He soon attracted a large congregation, and he became a leading figure among the black community of Montgomery. He was outspoken in his condemnation of the segregationist laws of the South, which required black people to take second place to whites, and he showed great personal courage in preaching against these laws, as reprisals by the white community – in the form of bombings, lynchings and other atrocities – were common.

'I HAVE A DREAM'

In 1955, Rosa Parks, a black woman, refused to give up her seat to a white man on the bus and was arrested. In response, King helped to organize a boycott of the buses in Montgomery. As a result of this protest, the bus company was ordered to allow black and white people to share the same seats on the buses. After this victory, King became a spokesman for the growing US civil rights movement and began to lead protests in

Birmingham, Alabama, where racial tensions ran high. Even though he advocated a policy of nonviolent civil disobedience, he was imprisoned for his activities. In addition, he and his congregation became the target of several bomb attacks. Undeterred, in 1963 King went on to help organize a huge civil rights march on Washington. It was here that King made his famous speech about his dream of a united America, in which black people could live side by side with whites in an atmosphere of peace, harmony and racial equality.

By this time, King was being perceived by white America as an important voice in the political world, and in 1964, he was awarded the Nobel Peace Prize. His attention now focussed on gaining equal voting rights for blacks, for an end to the Vietnam war, in which many black soldiers were losing their lives, and for an end to the extreme poverty in which many Americans, both black and white, were forced to live. Not surprisingly, his outspoken opinions made him many enemies, including within the Kennedy administration, and he was put under constant surveillance from the FBI.

BRUTAL ASSASSINATION

However, despite the fact that there were daily threats on his life, the US security services seemed powerless to protect him. This became clear when, at about 6.00 p.m., on the evening of April 4, 1968, King was shot at close range while standing on the balcony of the Lorraine Motel in Memphis, Tennessee. He received a wound in his jaw, and a few minutes later, fell unconscious. He was rushed to hospital, but it was too late to save him, and he died a few hours after arrival.

Not only had the security forces failed to protect King, they seemed unable to find his assassin after the event. It was not until two months later that an escaped prisoner named James Earl Ray was picked up by police in Britain. Ray had been travelling under a false passport and was arrested. After interrogation, he was sent to Tennessee, where he confessed to the murder of Martin Luther King Jr. He was eventually convicted of the assassination and sentenced to 99 years in prison.

VICTIM OF A CONSPIRACY?

But this was not the end of the story. Ray later retracted his confession, saying that he had pleaded guilty to escape the death penalty on the advice of his attorney. Ray made several accusations as to the perpetrators of the crime, including his brother Johnny and a man named Raoul, but his account was muddled and unconvincing. Meanwhile, King's son Dexter accused the FBI of the assassination, pointing to the way in which the security services had harassed, rather than protected, his father in the days when he was campaigning for civil rights.

It was not until 1997 that a House Select Committee gave their verdict on the matter. They concluded that King may have been the victim of a conspiracy, but that it was definitely Ray who had shot King. Ray, meanwhile, maintained his innocence, and met with members of King's family to gain their support for a campaign that would exonerate him. In addition, Coretta Scott King launched a civil trial against Memphis bar owner Lloyd Jowers and 'other unknown conspirators', accusing them of committing the crime. Jowers was found guilty, but the King family were only awarded a symbolic sum of $100 for their legal costs, and a later investigation found no evidence of Jowers' involvement in any plot.

A number of other theories arose in the wake of King's assassination. For example, it was alleged that Ray had acted as a hit man for the FBI. According to this theory, Ray had travelled to Memphis to take part in a bank robbery while King was in town. It was pure coincidence that Ray had just happened to be staying in a rooming house next door to King's hotel on the evening when King was shot by an FBI gunman who, it was alleged, had been hiding in the bushes near the balcony. The FBI were accused of having planted the murder weapon, a Remington rifle, in Ray's car and gone on to frame him for the murder. Ray himself backed up this story, and continued to maintain that he was not King's assassin until his death in prison on April 23, 1998.

SMEAR CAMPAIGN

To date, it seems that no hard evidence has been found to link the FBI services to the assassination of Martin Luther King Jr. Commentators also point out that Ray was an open racist and might well have been acting as a lone gunman. However, there remain important questions about the FBI's attitude towards King when he was alive. In particular its attempts to smear him as a communist, and its constant, intrusive surveillance of his daily activities has undoubtedly caused some to question their innocence in the case.

Whoever did the deed, and whatever the truth of the matter, there is little doubt that the assassination of Martin Luther King Jr saddened many Americans, both black and white. King's idealistic campaign, as well as his extraordinary personal courage, had brought a vision of peace, justice and equality to a divided nation; and for many, when he was assassinated, that dream of a united America also died.

LEGACY OF A FREEDOM FIGHTER

At the time of his assassination, King's civil rights campaign had achieved an extraordinary change of heart among the mass of Americans. The day before he met his death, he had made a rousing speech to an ecstatic, cheering crowd of thousands. During the speech, King had referred to the constant threats that were being made on his life, and had hinted that he himself might not live to see the time when America became a 'Promised Land' of black and white people united in peace, freedom and justice. Sadly, his prophecy was proved right when, the following evening, he was shot dead on the balcony of his Memphis hotel.

King's assassination spelled the end of an optimistic period in American society, in which people began to hope that the racial discrimination and economic inequality, which had for so long divided the country, would one day come to an end. Sadly, his vision never became a reality, although many would argue that the civil rights campaign bore fruit, especially as regards antiracist discrimination legislation in the USA. Today, many streets, avenues, parks and buildings in the USA are named after Martin Luther King Jr, and as one of the great freedom fighters of the 20th century, he has become an international symbol of hope for black peoples across the world.

DAW AUNG SAN SUU KYI

Daw Aung San Suu Kyi is the daughter of Burma's Independence Hero Aung San and one of the world's most famous freedom fighters. She is General Secretary of the National League for Democracy (NLD) in Burma and is Burma's hope for freedom. She is a non-violent pro-democracy activist who has struggled for Burma's democracy without any thought for her own safety, since 1988. One of her most famous speeches, *Freedom from Fear*, begins:

> *It is not power that corrupts but fear. Fear of losing power corrupts those who wield it and fear of the scourge of power corrupts those who are subject to it . . .*

Suu Kyi is a devout Buddhist who won the Rafto prize and the Sakharov prize for Freedom of Thought in 1990. In 1991 she was awarded the Noble Peace Prize for her determined, but non-violent struggle under a repressive military dictatorship.

EARLY LIFE

Daw Aung San Suu Kyi was born on June 19, 1945. Her father, General Aung San, who negotiated Burma's independence from the United Kingdom, was assassinated when she was just two years old. She lived in Rangoon with her mother, Khin Kyi, and her two brothers Aung Sin Lin and Aung San U. When Suu Kyi was only eight years old, one of her brothers, Aung Sin Lin, died in a tragic drowning accident.

For the majority of her childhood in Burma, Suu Kyi was educated in English Catholic schools. In 1960, Suu Kui accompanied her mother to Delhi, where Khin Kyi was appointed Burmese ambassador to India and Nepal. Suu Kyi studied politics at Delhi University and graduated in 1964. She continued her education at St Hugh's College, Oxford University, where she obtained a BA degree in Philosophy, Politics and Economics in 1967. After graduation, Suu Kyi continued her education in New York and worked as assistant secretary on the Advisory Committee on Administrative and Budgetary Questions for the United Nations Secretariat.

Suu Kyi married Michael Aris in 1972 and the following year gave birth to their first son, Alexander. Their second child, Kim, was born in 1977. Aris was fully aware of his wife's political fervour and told a newspaper reporter, 'Before we were married I promised my wife that I would never stand between her and her country'. Little did he know at this time just how many years they would have to stay apart.

POLITICAL BEGINNINGS

In 1988, Suu Kyi was forced to return to Myanmar (Burma), to nurse her dying mother. It coincided with the nationwide uprising that had just begun, due to the long-time leader of the socialist ruling party, General Ne Win, stepping down. This led to mass demonstrations and democratization in Rangoon, in a response to the worsening ethnic conflict and economic situation. On September 18, 1988, the military deposed Ne Win's party, abolished the constitution, and established a new ruling junta, the SLORC (State Law and Order Restoration Council). They reacted violently to the demonstrations and sent out an army to try and restore order to the streets. An estimated 3,000 students were killed and as many as 10,000 more fled to the hills and border areas.

In an effort to stamp their authority, the SLORC changed the name of the country from Burma to Myanmar, after the name of the ruling party.

Heavily influenced by the non-violent campaigns of the American civil rights leader Martin Luther King and India's Mahatma Gandhi, Suu Kyi entered politics and immediately started to organize rallies, travelling around the country spreading the word for democratic reforms. She gave numerous speeches calling for freedom and democracy and on August 26, 1988, addressed half a million people in a rally at the famous Schwedagon Pagoda in Rangoon. She preached fervently for a democratic government so that the people of Burma could experience freedom.

However, her own freedom was to be taken away from her when a military unit in the Irrawaddy Delta confronted her on April 5, 1989, while she was delivering one of her speeches. The military were under instructions to aim their weapons directly at her while she spoke, waiting for the order to fire. However, at the last minute a major finally ordered his troops to fall back and she was saved from being assassinated like her father. The new military junta, however, responded with brute force. In just a matter of months as many as 10,000 demonstrators were killed, including students, women and children. On September 17, 1988, Suu Kyi helped to form the Burmese political party, the National League for Democracy (NLD).

Unable to maintain power in Burma, the SLORC was forced to call a general election. It was an outright win for Suu Kyi's NLD and, under normal circumstances, she would have been given the office of prime minister. However, the military junta refused to hand over power to the NLD and the results of the election were nullified.

As Suu Kyi started to campaign for the NLD she, along with many of her associates, were placed under house arrest on September 18, 1988 in Rangoon. The martial law under which she was held, allowed for a person to be placed in detention without any charge or trial, for a period of three years. Shortly after her arrest, Suu Kyi went on hunger strike in an effort to protect the students taken from her house to the Military Intelligence Interrogation centre and Amnesty International officially recognized her as a prisoner of conscience. Suu Kyi was offered freedom if she agreed to leave the country, but she flatly refused to give up her fight for Burma's freedom.

Despite the fact that many of the NLD were being held under house arrest, the party still went on to win by a staggering 82 per cent votes on May 27, 1990. Despite this landslide victory, the military junta still refused to recognize their defeat and refused to hand over power to the NLD, which caused a public outcry.

On October 12, 1990, Suu Kyi received the Rafto Humans Rights Prize in her absence. On December 19, 1990, the United Nationals secretary, General Perez de Cuellar, pressed for her release, and the SLORC issued a statement saying,

> *. . . should she wish to stay together with her husband and children, she would be allowed to leave Burma on humanitarian grounds.*

Once again, however, Suu Kyi refused to give up the fight for her country and people and she remained under house arrest. In July 1991 she was awarded the 1990 Sakharov Prize, *in absentia*, which was a human rights prize from the European Parliament.

In 1991 Suu Kyi received the Nobel Peace Prize, in recognition of her non-violent struggle for democracy and human rights. With the prize money of US$1.3 million, she set up a health and education trust for the Burmese people. Also in this year, the SLORC amended the law under which they were holding Suu Kyi, which meant she could be held for a period of five years, instead of three, without having to face a trial.

During her time of house arrest, Suu Kyi did not remain inactive in her fight for the freedom of the Burmese people and in December 1991, she had her paper *Freedom from Fear* and other writings published in London.

In 1992 General Than Shwe became the new leader of the SLORC and, with this move many political prisoners were released. He lifted many of the restrictions of the martial law decrees and plans for a new constitution were announced. However, despite these announcements the military junta showed no signs of returning the government to civilian control, which met with condemnation from the United Nations Security Council.

In 1993, seven fellow Nobel prize winners flew into Thailand, having been denied entry into Burma, and from there they called for the release of Suu Kyi. While in Thailand they visited various refugee camps and offered support to the democratic and ethic opposition taking place in Burma. From there they travelled to Geneva, and pressed further for the release of Suu Kyi to the UN Commission for Human Rights.

In January 1994, the SLORC used another excuse to continue holding Suu Kyi under house arrest, and claimed that they were able to hold her for six years without being charged. They claimed although it was normal for a prisoner to be held for only five years, an extra year could be added at the discretion of a three-member committee which comprised of the ministers of Foreign Affairs, Home Affairs and Defence.

Suu Kyi received her first visitors, outside of her family, on February 14, 1994. A representative from UNDP, Jehan Raheem, US Congressman Bill Richardson and *New York Times* reporter Philip Shenon managed to convince the SLORC to allow them to interview Suu Kyi. Following this visit, Suu Kyi demanded a meeting with senior members of the SLORC.

It wasn't until September 20, 1994, however, that she actually had a meeting with General Than Shwe and General Khin Nyunt of the SLORC. She did not make much progress at the first meeting, but a second audience was granted on October 28 that year between the General Khin Nyunt and Suu Kyi at the State Guest House.

SUU KYI'S RELEASE

Suu Kyi was held in detention until July 1995, but even though she had been released, the military denied her permission to leave Burma to visit her family in the United Kingdom. They said if she were to leave the country she would not be allowed to re-enter. Even when her husband, Michael Aris, was diagnosed with prostate cancer in 1997, the Burmese government denied him an entry visa. Suu Kyi never saw her husband again before he died in March 1999 and even today she remains separated from her children who still live in the United Kingdom.

Following her release, Suu Kyi sent a message to her people at the Burman Seminar in September 1995:

. . . It is a time when it is crucial to make the international community aware of the situation in our country and of our endeavours to establish a democratic political system in keeping with the will of the people. We who have been striving for democracy in Burma believe that peace and genuine progress can be achieved only by creating a climate of trust and confidence in our nation . . .

In 2000, the SLORC agreed to have talks with the political opposition which was still being led by Suu Kyi. Following these talks many more political prisoners were released and Suu Kyi and the NLD were given increased political freedom. Despite these advances, Suu Kyi was placed under house arrest again in September 2000, when she tried to travel to the city of Mandalay, which was in defiance of the travel restrictions imposed on her by the SLORC.

She was released unconditionally on May 6, 2002, following negotiations led by the United Nations. Once again her freedom was to be short-lived, when her caravan was attacked on May 30, 2003, in the village of Depayin by a government-sponsored gang. Many of her loyal supporters were wounded or killed, but Suu Kyi managed to escape with the help of her driver, Ko Kyaw Soe Lin. She was arrested when they reached Ye-U and once again placed under house arrest at Insein Prison in Yangon.

Following an operation for a hysterectomy in September 2003, Suu Kyi was allowed to return home, but was still technically under house arrest.

In the early years of her confinement Suu Kyi was often held in solitary confinement and was not even allowed to see her husband and sons. Suu Kyi said that the detention has made her even more resolute to dedicate the remainder of her life to representing the Burmese citizens.

Although the terms of her house arrest were due to expire in May 2006, the Burmese government were still up to their old tricks and extended the period for a further year. She continues to be held under the 1975 State Protection Act which grants the government the power to hold people without trial for up to five years.

She is probably one of the most prominent freedom fighters of modern times and still calls on people today around the world to join in the struggle for freedom in Burma, saying,

Please use your liberty to promote ours.